Developing Expertise for Tea Higher Education

This book provides a contemporary view of the characteristics of expertise for teaching in higher education, based on the strong foundation of research into expertise, and empirical and practical knowledge of the development of teaching in higher education.

Taking key themes related to the characteristics of expertise, this edited collection delivers practical ideas for supporting and enabling professional learning and development in higher education as well as theoretical constructs for the basis of personal reflection on practice. Providing an accessible, evidence-informed theoretical framework designed to support individuals wishing to improve their teaching, *Developing Expertise for Teaching in Higher Education* considers teaching excellence from an expertise perspective and discusses how it might be supported and available to all. It invites a call to action to all policymakers and strategic leaders who make a claim for teaching excellence to consider how professional learning and the development of expertise can be embedded in the culture, environment and ways of working in higher education institutions.

Full of practical examples, based on scholarship and experience, to guide individual teachers, educational developers and policymakers in higher education, this book is a must-read text for those new to teaching in higher education and those looking to improve their practice.

Helen King is Deputy Director and Professor of Academic Practice at the University of the West of England, Bristol, UK.

The Staff and Educational Development Series

Written by experienced and well-known practitioners and published in association with the Staff and Educational Development Association (SEDA), each book in the series contributes to the development of learning, teaching and training and assists in the professional development of staff. The books present new ideas for learning development and facilitate the exchange of information and good practice.

Series Editor: James Wisdom

Titles in the series:

Developing Intercultural Practice
Academic Development in a Multicultural and Globalizing World
David Killick

Delivering Educational Change in Higher Education
A Transformative Approach for Leaders and Practitioners
Edited by Jackie Potter and Cristina Devecchi

A Handbook for Student Engagement in Higher Education
Theory into Practice
Edited by Tom Lowe and Yassein El Hakim

Supporting Course and Programme Leaders in Higher Education
Practical Wisdom for Leaders, Educational Developers and Programme Leaders
Edited by Jenny Lawrence, Sue Morón-García, Rowena Senior

Developing Expertise for Teaching in Higher Education
Practical Ideas for Professional Learning and Development
Edited by Helen King

For more information about this series, please visit: https://www.routledge.com/SEDA-Series/book-series/SE0747

Developing Expertise for Teaching in Higher Education

Practical Ideas for Professional Learning and Development

Edited by
Helen King

LONDON AND NEW YORK

Cover image: © Getty Images

First published 2022
by Routledge
2 Park Square, Milton Park, Abingdon, Oxon OX14 4RN

and by Routledge
605 Third Avenue, New York, NY 10158

Routledge is an imprint of the Taylor & Francis Group, an informa business

© 2022 selection and editorial matter, Helen King; individual chapters, the contributors

The right of Helen King to be identified as the author of the editorial material, and of the authors for their individual chapters, has been asserted in accordance with sections 77 and 78 of the Copyright, Designs and Patents Act 1988.

All rights reserved. No part of this book may be reprinted or reproduced or utilised in any form or by any electronic, mechanical, or other means, now known or hereafter invented, including photocopying and recording, or in any information storage or retrieval system, without permission in writing from the publishers.

Trademark notice: Product or corporate names may be trademarks or registered trademarks, and are used only for identification and explanation without intent to infringe.

British Library Cataloguing-in-Publication Data
A catalogue record for this book is available from the British Library

Library of Congress Cataloging-in-Publication Data
A catalog record has been requested for this book

ISBN: 978-1-032-05699-9 (hbk)
ISBN: 978-1-032-05700-2 (pbk)
ISBN: 978-1-003-19877-2 (ebk)

DOI: 10.4324/9781003198772

Typeset in Galliard
by Taylor & Francis Books

Contents

List of figures — viii
List of tables — ix
Notes on the editor and contributors — x
Foreword — xv
Acknowledgements — xvii

Introduction: Developing expertise for teaching in higher education — 1
HELEN KING

PART I
Perspectives on expertise for teaching in higher education — 13

1 The characteristics of expertise for teaching in higher education — 15
   HELEN KING

2 Critical reflection as a tool to develop expertise in teaching in higher education — 29
   LEONARDO MORANTES-AFRICANO

3 Zhuangzi and the phenomenology of expertise: Implications for educators — 44
   CHARLIE REIS

4 A whole-university approach to building expertise in higher education teaching — 57
   DEANNE GANNAWAY

5 The importance of collaboration: Valuing the expertise of disabled people through social confluence — 69
   BETH PICKARD

6 Supportive woman, engaging man: Gendered differences in student perceptions of teaching excellence 85
KATHRYNA KWOK AND JACKIE POTTER

PART II
Pedagogical content knowledge 99

7 Exploring and developing pedagogical content knowledge in higher education 101
JOHN BOSTOCK

8 Professional identity in clinical legal education: Re-enacting the disciplinary concept of 'thinking like a lawyer' 114
RACHEL WOOD

9 Reflective practice as a threshold concept in the development of pedagogical content knowledge 129
REBECCA TURNER AND LUCY SPOWART

10 Developing pedagogical content knowledge through the integration of education research and practice in higher education 142
ERIKA CORRADINI

PART III
Professional learning for higher education teaching 155

11 Professional learning for higher education teaching: An expertise perspective 157
HELEN KING

12 Educative case-making: A learner-centred approach to supporting the development of pedagogical expertise in higher education 175
ALEXANDRA MORGAN AND EMMAJANE MILTON

13 Collaboration and mentoring to enhance professional learning in higher education 188
WARREN CODE, ASHLEY WELSH, DAWN REILLY, LIZ WARREN, LAURA HEELS, LINDSAY MARSHALL, ISABELLE BARRETTE-NG, JOHN DAWSON AND ELIANA EL KHOURY

PART IV
The artistry of teaching 201

14 Developing adaptive expertise: What can we learn from improvisation and the performing arts? 203
RICHARD BALE

15 Developing the improvising teacher: Implications for professionalism and the development of expertise 218
NICK SORENSEN

16 Emotion work and the artistry of teaching 231
PETER FOSSEY

Index 245

Figures

1.1	A model of expertise for teaching in higher education	19
2.1	Critical reflection and experiential learning	35
2.2	Critical reflection model	37
4.1	Elements of the Professional Learning Roadmap	63
4.2	Development of expertise continuum	65
11.1	Overview of key themes from thematic analysis with selected quotes from participants	167
12.1	Example of a final poster	183
15.1	Theoretical framework showing the dimensions of teacher expertise	220
15.2	The authorised teacher	225
15.3	The dimensions of improvisational teaching (mindset and skills)	227

Tables

6.1	Most frequently mentioned themes by gender category	89
7.1	A conceptualisation of teacher professionalism	107
10.1	Key data analysed during the first stage of the study	147
13.1	Relationships between the development of teaching expertise within the CWSEI and the facets of teaching expertise	189
14.1	Common teaching anxieties of GTAs (adapted from Bale, 2020, p. 23)	209

Notes on the editor and contributors

Editor

Helen King, PhD NTF SFSEDA PFHEA is currently the Deputy Director and Professor of Academic Practice at the University of the West of England, Bristol, UK. Her career in educational development spans over two decades and has included leading roles in UK-wide learning and teaching enhancement projects and organisations (including Assistant Director of the Higher Education Academy Subject Centre for Geography, Earth & Environmental Sciences, Senior HE Policy Adviser for the Higher Education Funding Council for England, and currently co-Chair of the Staff & Educational Development Association: SEDA), as an independent consultant collaborating with colleagues in the UK, USA and Australia, and institutional roles (previously Head of Academic Staff Development at the University of Bath and currently at UWE Bristol). She has broad interests across a range of learning, teaching and assessment themes, but her particular passion is supporting colleagues' professional learning and development. Her current research is exploring the characteristics of expertise for teaching in higher education. She is proud to hold a Senior Fellowship of the Staff & Educational Development Association (SFSEDA) and is a UK National Teaching Fellow (NTF), Principal Fellow of the Higher Education Academy (PFHEA) and Honorary Associate Professor at the University of Queensland. In her non-work time, she thoroughly enjoys trail running and Bluegrass banjo playing (not necessarily at the same time), both of which feed into her research and educational development interests in various ways!

Contributors

Ashley B. Akenson, PhD is Director of Graduate Programs (College of Education) at Tennessee Tech University, USA. She infuses mindfulness along with multicultural and contextual awareness in program planning and evaluation (PPE) practices and everyday interactions. Her work seeks to enact critical examination without reinscribing deficit conceptions and harmful blame–shame cycles.

James E. Akenson, PhD is Professor of Curriculum and Instruction at Tennessee Tech University, USA. He teaches introduction to education, social studies methods, a PhD seminar on educational issues, and a graduate course on K–12 applications of country music. He is interested in the integration of culturally responsive strategies in the classroom.

Andrea Arce-Trigatti holds a PhD in Education with a learning environments and educational studies concentration from the University of Tennessee, Knoxville, USA. An interdisciplinary scholar and educational evaluator, her research centers on cultural studies and issues in multicultural education, educational policy, advancements in critical and creative thinking, and collaborative learning strategies.

Richard Bale, PhD MEd PGCE BSc SFHEA is a senior teaching fellow in educational development at Imperial College London, UK. He has interests in teaching as performance and intercultural feedback literacy. He is the author of *Teaching with Confidence in Higher Education: Applying Strategies from the Performing Arts* (Routledge) and co-author of *Introduction to University Teaching* (Sage).

Isabelle Barrette-Ng, PhD is Professor and the Head of the Department of Integrative Biology at the University of Windsor. As a 2018 3M National Teaching Fellow and founding director of Program SAGES, Isabelle's scholarship is dedicated to the design and implementation of authentic teaching and learning experiences and faculty teaching development programmes.

David Baume, PhD SFSEDA SFHEA is an international higher education consultant, researcher, developer, evaluator and writer, and fellow of the University of London Centre for Distance Education, UK. David was founding chair of the Staff and Educational Development Association (SEDA) and founding editor of the *International Journal for Academic Development*.

John Bostock, PhD NTF PFHEA SFSEDA is a senior learning and teaching fellow (reader) in the Centre for Learning and Teaching at Edge Hill University, UK. His research interests include the significance of social interaction in online learning, conceptualisations of teacher education in professional training and developing pedagogical content knowledge.

Warren Code, PhD is associate director of the Science Centre for Learning and Teaching (Skylight, skylight.science.ubc.ca) at the University of British Columbia in Vancouver, Canada. He was the acting director for the final phases of the Carl Wieman Science Education Initiative (cwsei.ubc.ca). His areas of interest are in STEM education reform, institutional change, and undergraduate mathematics education.

Erika Corradini, MA PhD SFHEA is Principal Teaching Fellow in the Centre for Higher Education Practice, University of Southampton, UK. Her interests are the development of the HE teaching profession and supporting academics' professional journeys. Her activity takes an integrated approach to education and learning development, focusing on innovating practices through the scholarship of teaching and learning.

John Dawson, PhD is Professor in the Department of Molecular and Cellular Biology at the University of Guelph, Canada, a protein biochemist, and the founding director of the College of Biological Science Office of Educational Scholarship and Practice where he supports evidence-based teaching practice and student learning. He has won several teaching awards, including the 2020 John Bell Award and the 2021 3M National Teaching Fellowship.

James Derounian, PhD NTF FHEA FILCM lectures on the community governance courses run by the Society of Local Council Clerks and validated by De Montfort University, UK. James researches, writes, teaches and practises community engagement, rural development and active and blended learning approaches to higher education teaching. James is an active contributor to the Association of National Teaching Fellows.

Eliana El Khoury, PhD is Assistant Professor at Athabasca University, Canada, and her scholarship focuses on alternative assessments and innovation in teaching and learning both at the K–12 levels and in higher education.

Suzanne Fergus, BSc PhD NTF is Associate Professor of Learning and Teaching at the University of Hertfordshire, UK. Her area of interest includes enhancing and supporting student engagement, student approaches to learning including evidence-based study strategies, chemistry research of cognitive enhancers and the use of technology in assessment to support student-centred learning.

Peter Fossey, PhD is a senior teaching fellow in the Academic Development Centre at the University of Warwick, UK. His area of research includes practical reasoning, philosophy of emotions and philosophy of higher education. As an academic developer he supports colleagues who teach, in all areas relating to learning and teaching.

Deanne Gannaway, PhD PFHEA ALTF is Senior Lecturer in Higher Education, Institute for Teaching and Learning Innovation, University of Queensland, Australia. She is a higher education curriculum thought leader and curriculum transformation expert with over 20 years of experience in Australian universities. Her teaching and scholarship focus on continuing professional learning for university teachers and professional education for students.

Laura Heels is a lecturer at Newcastle University, UK. She researches diversity issues in computer science and their solution, with a particular focus on gender. In her spare time she likes to practise photography.

Fabia Jeddere-Fisher, MEng (Hons) CEng MIMechE PGCert SFHEA is a chartered engineer and Deputy Head of Department for the Department of Architecture and Built Environment, UWE Bristol, UK. Her pedagogic interests are in technology-enhanced learning, vocal confidence for teaching and improving graduate outcomes for under-represented groups in STEM subjects.

Kathryna Kwok is an educational researcher at the Oxford Centre for Staff and Learning Development at Oxford Brookes University, UK. Her research interests include race and gender disparity in higher education, and the student experience.

Lindsay Marshall, PhD NTF SFHEA is Emeritus Professor of Educational Practice in Computer Science at Newcastle University, UK. His research interests lie in learning support systems and learning analytics, with an emphasis on the application of mobile technology. He likes mandolins, banjos and steel guitars.

Emmajane Milton, NTF SFHEA is a Reader in Cardiff University. She has worked in education for 20 years, enjoying a wide range of leadership roles within academia, policy and the statutory school sector. Her research interests are focused around professional learning, educational practice, educative mentoring and having a learner-centred orientation to practice.

Leonardo Morantes-Africano, MEd FHEA is originally from Colombia and has been living and working in the UK since 2006. He works as an initial teacher educator at Newcastle College University Centre and is completing his doctorate in education at the University of Glasgow. His research interests include social justice, technology in education and critical pedagogy.

Alexandra Morgan, PhD is a lecturer in education at Cardiff University, UK. Her research interests include educational practice, professional learning and mentoring for practitioner inquiry; she works with educators from HE settings and schools to develop new approaches to professional learning that support research engagement and collaborative critical enquiry.

Beth Pickard, PhD NTF SFHEA is a senior lecturer, music therapist and researcher at the University of South Wales, UK. Her research and practice, informed by critical disability studies, explore how disability is socially constructed, interpreted and represented across disciplines and pedagogy. Beth is a passionate ally, activist and advocate of social justice and anti-oppressive practice.

Jackie Potter is Professor of Learning and Development in Higher Education and head of the Oxford Centre for Staff and Learning Development at Oxford Brookes University, UK, leading educational and organisational development activities. She is Principal Fellow of the Higher Education Academy and holds a senior fellowship of the Staff and Educational Development Association.

Dawn Reilly, SFHEA CMBE PhD is Associate Professor of Accounting Education at the University of Greenwich, UK. She joined the University in 2010 as a lecturer in financial accounting and, since 2016, has led the Business School's undergraduate accounting degrees. Her interests include widening participation and the role of formative feedback in inclusive teaching and learning.

Charlie Reis is director of the Educational Development Unit at Xi'an Jiaotong–Liverpool University (XJTLU), China, founder of the China-based Association for Partnership in Educational Development, and on the senior management team of XJTLU's Academy of Future Education. His areas of interest include the role of classical Chinese knowledge in contemporary education.

Nick Sorensen, PhD is a visiting research fellow at Bath Spa University, UK. His interdisciplinary research is concerned with understanding improvisation as a mode of creativity and is grounded in his practice as a jazz saxophonist. Current interests are the improvisational nature of teaching and leadership and the salience of silences in music.

Lucy Spowart, PhD NTF PFHEA FAcadMEd is an Associate Professor in Clinical Education at the University of Plymouth's Penisular Medical School, UK. Her main research interests are in continual professional development, teaching accreditation and impact evaluation.

Rebecca Turner, PhD MSc PGcert BSc Hons is an educational developer at the University of Plymouth, UK, and Principal Fellow of the HEA. Rebecca's research explores themes relating to professional development, reward and recognition and student transitions.

Esther E. van Dijk, MSc is a PhD candidate. Her area of interest is expertise development of university teachers and how this can be supported through academic development. Her PhD project is a collaboration between the Centre for Academic Teaching Utrecht University, the Education Center of University Medical Center Utrecht and the Department of Education at Utrecht University, Netherlands.

Liz Warren, PFHEA CMBE PhD joined the University of Greenwich, UK, in 2000. She became the director of learning and teaching for the Business School in 2016, is Professor of Accounting and Business Education and is responsible for the school's undergraduate and postgraduate portfolio. She publishes in pedagogic research and in her subject discipline of management accounting.

Ashley J. Welsh, PhD is faculty liaison for the Science Centre for Learning and Teaching (Skylight; skylight.science.ubc.ca) and the Centre for Teaching, Learning and Technology (ctlt.ubc.ca) at the University of British Columbia, Vancouver, Canada. Her work provides strategic leadership for enriching curriculum, pedagogy, scholarship and inclusive practices in undergraduate science and maths education.

Jennie Winter, PhD PFHEA NTF is Professor of Academic Development at Plymouth Marjon University, UK. Jennie is interested in a range of academic development themes including student voice, education for sustainable development and evidencing the impact of educational development.

Rachel Wood, SFHEA is the business and law clinic director at the University of the West of England, UK. She started professional life as a solicitor before becoming a lecturer in law. She has a particular interest in experiential learning and the role of reflection in legal education.

Foreword

This much-needed book maps important territory for the world of higher education. Helen King's framing of excellence is refreshingly original, and she brings together perspectives from her many contributors to shape a contemporary view of what 'being expert' might mean. The book challenges the notion that excellence in teaching in higher education can be captured by standardised metrics. Instead, it takes, in King's words, "a holistic view of the teacher in the context of their role interacting with learners".

In her introduction, King summarises the book's aims, highlighting a need to reconsider widely held assumptions. She examines accepted notions of excellence with a critical eye, pointing out the challenges of tying down such an elusive concept and applying it to teaching. Central to this discussion is the issue of becoming expert, which King and her contributors frame as a dynamic journey that unfolds over the course of a professional career. For me, this resonates with my own experience, first as a clinician and later as a university teacher and academic.

As a medical student and then a surgical trainee, my focus was on memorising large amounts of factual material, passing exams and gaining procedural skills. After completing my training as a surgeon, I changed direction and became a family doctor. In the unruly world of general practice, I came up against new complexities and challenges, working in an environment shot through with uncertainty, where my medical knowledge could only take me so far. I realised that the essence of my work was to establish and sustain a relationship of care with each patient, drawing on my own knowledge where relevant, but recognising when to tap into the expertise of others. Much of my role was about performance, and every day I had to improvise.

Later, as a mature PhD student in the 1990s, I began to research the nature of surgical education. There I grappled with ideas which reached far beyond my own experience as a clinician. Initially, I focused on 'expertise', exploring the topic's extensive literature. Soon I became dissatisfied with abstracted, disembodied accounts which spoke as if expertise could be separated from people. I became fascinated by encounters with experts from many areas – watching them work, talking to them and exploring how insights from one domain might cast light upon others. Gradually, I became aware of similarities between the worlds of teaching and medicine which I had overlooked.

Later, through working with clinicians, teachers, scientists, craftspeople and those in the performing arts, I came to think of becoming expert as a path which we are all treading. It may be possible to trace that path's beginning, but it is a continuing process that has no end. It is possible, though, to map out stages. Experts have all been through a long and demanding process, with many ups and downs along the way. Years of mastering the basics of a craft or profession are followed by working in the real world and building experience (including making and recovering from errors) that eventually leads to wisdom – the ability to guide and shape the experience of others. This, as King points out in the context of higher education, is a profoundly human process that cannot be reduced to metrics of attainment. It acknowledges that encounters between people are always complex and uncertain, and it highlights humility, care and a generous-minded curiosity as essential counterparts to factual knowledge and technical skill.

All this resonates with King's emphasis on what she terms the artistry of teaching – a central tenet of this book and one of its most illuminating insights. King describes artistry in this context as "those aspects of practice which enable teachers to manage the complex, non-routine facets of their profession". Underpinning and intersecting with pedagogical content knowledge and intentional learning and development, artistry is hard to define but crucially important.

Teaching in higher education, as in other kinds of professional practice, is about relationships of care. These may be between teachers and learners, clinicians and patients, or performers and audiences. Whatever the field, excellence in teaching is always rooted in personal interaction based on trust and integrity. This dimension is often overlooked in disembodied accounts of expertise and its measurable characteristics. Yet that humanity lies at the heart of any educational experience. This book brings fresh and much-needed insights not only for those in higher education, but for anyone who cares deeply about what it means to teach and to learn.

Roger Kneebone PhD FRCS FRCSEd FRCGP HonRCM
Professor of Surgical Education and Engagement Science,
Imperial College London
Royal Academy of Arts Professor of Anatomy
Gresham College Visiting Professor of Medical Education
2011 National Teaching Fellow, 2012 Wellcome Trust Engagement Fellow
Author: *Expert: Understanding the Path to Mastery*
(Penguin, August 2020)

Acknowledgements

This book is the outcome of several years of pondering the nature of excellence and expertise in higher education in the context of my career as an educational developer working with institutions, national projects and international collaborations. I'd like to thank all of those colleagues who have conversed with me about my ideas through informal chats over coffee and formal conference presentations and workshops, including the contributors and attendees at the 2020 Expertise Symposium, which was the catalyst for this publication. In particular, I would like to acknowledge James Wisdom, the SEDA Series editor for his encouragement, SEDA for awarding me the grant which enabled my research with National Teaching Fellows, and Anders Ericsson, the key figure behind the concept of deliberate practice, for his generosity in discussing a potential collaboration before he sadly passed away in June 2020.

My family and friends continue to be my support and inspiration; in particular, huge thanks are owed to Lucien Campbell-Kemp for his patience, love and unending supplies of tea and cake which have enabled me to persist with writing and editing during these unusual years of the Covid-19 pandemic. Music and trail running are my 'serious leisure' pursuits and also my opportunity for understanding and applying concepts of expertise. The Town & Country Harriers in Bristol, UK, have been a fabulous source of friendship, community, mud and cider, and all of those I play music with fill my life with joy. My singing and banjo teachers, Pam Jolley and Leon Hunt, respectively, have both given me insights into practice, performance and expertise that have been invaluable in the development of my ideas.

Finally, I'd like to thank the whole Academic Practice Directorate team at the University of the West of England, Bristol who are wonderful to work with, each bringing their own expertise and commitment to the collaborative endeavour of our work.

Helen King
August 2021

Introduction: Developing expertise for teaching in higher education

Helen King

Excellence: from the Latin *excellere* (*ex* – 'out, beyond'; *celsus* – 'lofty')
Expertise: from the Latin *expertus* (past participle of *experiri* – 'to try'; also the etymological origin of 'experience' and 'experiment')

Overview

As in many sectors, the rhetoric in higher education is one of excellence. And yet excellence in teaching is poorly understood and, by definition, is a characteristic achievable by only a few. The notion of excellence, therefore, is not a strong motivator for individuals to improve their teaching nor a helpful guide for those supporting them in doing so. However, now more than ever, it is important that teaching in higher education is of high quality in order to enable the increased number and diversity of students to learn effectively and to receive value for their tuition fee. This book offers a new discourse and a practical framework to inform individuals wanting to improve their teaching and those supporting them.

To this end, this book provides a contemporary view of the characteristics of expertise for teaching in higher education, based on the strong foundation of research into expertise, and empirical and practical knowledge of the development of teaching in higher education. The extensive literature on expertise indicates that, in many (if not all) fields, almost anyone can develop expertise, and that the idea of the naturally gifted or talented practitioner is broadly defunct (current thinking suggests that there is an element of 'nature' as well as 'nurture' to particularly high-performing individuals but that, if the environment and motivation are strong enough, anyone can perform well and continue to improve throughout their career). This is a fresh approach to considering teaching and its improvement in higher education that takes a holistic view of the teacher in the context of their role interacting with learners. It is needed in order to help motivate and inform teachers to continue to improve and to recognise their emerging and developing expertise. It can help educational developers to consider the broad range of support that teachers require beyond understanding the theory and practice of curriculum design. And it is timely in that it offers a new perspective on teaching

DOI: 10.4324/9781003198772-1

quality in order to ensure that students have their higher education facilitated by teachers who are committed to continuing to develop and improve all the characteristics necessary for expertise in their profession.

Excellence in teaching in higher education

The notion of excellence is prevalent in many sectors, including higher education. Excellence is considered at all levels, from national policy to organisations to individuals, and means different things in different contexts and to different stakeholders (Brusoni et al., 2014; Su & Wood, 2019). For example, many higher education institutions cite striving for excellence in their mission statements and strategies, and, in England, the government introduced the Teaching Excellence and Student Outcomes Framework (TEF) in 2017 to recognise the quality of a higher education provider above a baseline standard. In the UK and internationally, there are individual and team excellence awards for teaching. With the majority of higher education systems requiring tuition fees paid by their students and in contexts of change, such as the 2020–21 COVID-19 pandemic and the mass move to online teaching, the importance of high-quality learning and teaching is a key issue for higher education and its stakeholders.

Excellence in teaching in higher education can be conceptualised at different levels: that of the institution and that of the individual teacher. In reality, these two cannot be entirely separated as the policies, processes and culture of the institution (including its orientation in relation to research) will inevitably impact on the individual teachers' capabilities and motivations and potentially leave them "fragmented with uneven resources to commit to excellence" (Skelton, 2007a, p. 5). There is a complex interrelationship between teachers, institutions, national policy and global trends (Skelton, 2007b) that necessarily impacts on the profile of and investment in high-quality teaching.

The nature of teaching excellence has been oft debated over the last two decades, particularly in the UK where there was considerable government investment in improving teaching in higher education in the late 1990s to mid-2000s, including the Institute for Learning and Teaching's UK-wide 'Subject Centres' that took a discipline-based approach to support enhancement, Centres for Excellence and national teaching awards. Funding for all of these was gradually withdrawn leaving their legacies to be self-funded, and government attention turned away from supporting excellence in teaching to measuring it at an institutional level through the use of output metrics such as student satisfaction and graduate outcomes. But, despite this focus on excellence in the UK and increasingly internationally, "there is no general agreement as to what it constitutes" (Gakhal, 2018, p. 6).

From an educational development perspective, that of promoting and enabling the enhancement of learning and teaching within higher education institutions and with higher education teachers, the concept of excellence is somewhat problematic. As noted above, there are policy and political connotations for the term but, perhaps more importantly, despite many years of consideration excellence continues to be poorly defined in terms of the characteristics of an individual teacher. Excellent teachers might be those who meet the criteria to win a competitive award for excellence, such as the National Teaching Fellowships in the UK or 3M awards in Canada. Excellent teachers might be those who are outstanding or "go the extra mile" (Gunn & Fisk, 2013) but, by these definitions (and the derivation of the word 'excellent'), this means that not all teachers can ever hope to be excellent or have their excellence recognised. An alternative term is required to "breathe new life into" the concept of excellence (Skelton, 2007a, p. 268) in a way that promotes discourse and supports all teachers to improve their practice.

Expertise: a new discourse

The concept of expertise, in a wide variety of professions, has a deep and broad theoretical and empirical foundation which offers an alternative approach to considering the characteristics of high-performing practitioners (e.g. Ericsson et al., 2006, 2018 and references therein). Expertise has been explored from many different perspectives and research paradigms such as science, neuroscience, sociology, psychology, management, education and professional learning (e.g. Hambrick et al., 2018; Bilalić, 2017; Boshuizen et al., 2004). As described in Chapter 1, the generic characteristics of expertise can be used as a framework for considering the specific characteristics in a given field. And, in the expertise and educational development literature, it has been suggested that identifying and supporting the development of these characteristics for a particular profession will necessarily then improve the performance of those who engage with such development (e.g. Saroyan & Trigwell, 2015; Ericsson, 2017).

It is a given that expertise is, in part, defined by high performance as measured by the appropriate outputs for the profession. Hence, the focus in the literature is more on the inputs – the characteristics of the expert practitioners themselves and how these are developed. Unlike excellence, expertise is not conceptualised as a static point to be reached but as a dynamic journey that is travelled from someone's first steps in a profession throughout their career. By derivation (in the English language at least), expertise is about a *process* of experiencing and experimenting rather than the state of being better than others. Hence, expertise is a process potentially accessible to all.

One difficulty with the term 'expert' or 'expertise' is that it may have connotations of elitism where special status is given (Turner, 2001), or that expertise has been degraded by the prevalence of information available on the internet (everyone's an expert). By the dictionary definition, an expert is simply someone with a high level of knowledge and skill; colloquially, they are the person brought in by the media to provide opinion on a topic in their field. For the purposes of this book, and any related literature, discussions, applications, research and development, the term is considered within the context of the study of expertise as an academic field in its own right. Of course, other terms, such as craftsmanship, might be used to describe the same concept. But it is the nature of the concept, as discussed here, and the breadth of discourse that this elicits that are more important than the specific term we choose to describe it. A further conceptual barrier arises when the term 'expert' is equated with 'experienced'. There is a literature which describes experts as inflexible to changing situations and stuck in their well-established ways of knowing and doing (Trinh, 2019). Conversely, literature on expertise, which identifies the difference between experts and experienced non-experts, has learning, adaptability and flexibility at its heart through ongoing processes of intentional learning and development described variously as deliberate practice (Ericsson et al., 1993), reflective practice (Schön, 1982), progressive problem-solving (Bereiter & Scardamalia, 1993), professional learning (Eraut, 1994), evidence-informed evolution of practice (King, 2019; Chapter 11, this volume), proactive competence (Perkins, 2008) and so on. It is this dynamic conceptualisation of expertise that is embodied within this book.

Expertise in teaching has been explored in a number of contexts including primary and secondary education, but much less so in higher education. Where it has been considered in higher education, it generally refers to the professional learning and development aspect of expertise (e.g. Tiberius et al., 1998; Kreber et al., 2005) and institutional frameworks to support this (Kenny et al., 2017; Gannaway, Chapter 4, this volume). So far, however, less has been researched or written in relation to the characteristics of expertise that these processes and frameworks are intending to develop (van Dijk et al., 2020).

The concept of expertise, therefore, has the potential to offer a new approach to thinking about high-quality teaching in higher education, and a new discourse founded on an academic field of study with strong empirical foundations that provides a springboard for further research and educational development.

Structure of the book

The contributions in this book arose from presentations at a symposium on Expertise in Teaching in Higher Education convened by the editor and expertly organised by colleagues at the University of the West of England in October 2019. Originally planned as a small, local event with 30 participants on campus, the Covid-19 pandemic forced it online and opened it up to bookings from over 500 colleagues nationally and internationally. Although many of the contributions are from the UK, others from Australia, Canada, China, the Netherlands and the USA provide a rich and diverse perspective.

Part I: perspectives on expertise for teaching in higher education

The first section of the book explores more broadly how the concept of expertise might be applied to teaching in higher education. In Chapter 1, the editor, Helen King, briefly describes the generic characteristics of expertise and considers what these might look like for teaching in higher education. Her model for teacher expertise, comprising pedagogical content knowledge, artistry of teaching and professional learning, is then used as the structure for the parts of the book that follow. This model is in no way intended to constrain the definition of expertise for teaching but, rather, to provide a fresh starting point for conversation, research and thinking about high-quality teaching and how to support and develop it. Within this chapter, a short contribution from Esther van Dijk sets out the importance of exploring expertise for higher education teaching as a profession distinct from teaching in other contexts. In Chapter 2, Leonardo Morantes-Africano picks up these three elements and views them through the lens of critical reflection and in the context of the complexity of education in order to present the case for "characterisation of expertise in teaching in higher education [that] conceptualise[s] educators as ethical decision-makers". Given that these discussions on expertise don't specify a particular pedagogy, the model may be more open to different cultural interpretations, or it may be that the model itself might look very different to a non-Western view of teaching and learning. Charlie Reis begins to explore this in Chapter 3, where he unpacks some of the concepts of expertise through a close reading of a passage from the Zhuangzi and considers how these might apply to teaching. Through this analysis he builds a cross-cultural connection between the Western-focused underpinnings of expertise and traditional Chinese philosophy. Having established an understanding of the nature of expertise through these first three chapters, an application of the concept to whole-university strategy is narrated in Chapter 4, through Deanne Gannaway's story of the University of Queensland's Development of Expertise in Teaching approach to professional learning.

Chapter 5 introduces the idea that, as expertise is domain-specific, then it should bring with it an element of humility. Beth Pickard calls for a model in which the expert practitioner doesn't (indeed, can't) hold all the knowledge and skills themselves but acknowledges and engages with expertise outwith. Beth discusses this in relation to the expertise of people with disabilities and challenges the assumption that expertise is currently *accessible* to all given the existing inequalities in higher education. In another, shorter example, Becky Turner offers a reminder of the need to engage with the expertise of students and to give them the expertise and agency to engage with their teachers. This first part is rounded off in Chapter 6 with a reminder to be cautious in interpretations and evaluations of excellence and expertise, in that they are liable to a range of biases including, as described by Kathryna Kwok and Jackie Potter, gender. Given that the quality of teaching is usually measured by outputs, including student satisfaction and students' perceptions of excellence, if there is a bias determined by the students' and/or teacher's gender, the teacher has no agency to change this (compared with pedagogical aspects of their practice). While Kathryna and Jackie acknowledge that the concept of expertise may not be unsusceptible to bias, they suggest that "moving away from a model of teaching excellence to one of expertise would help shift evaluative foci onto practices and competencies that are within an individual's control".

Part II: pedagogical content knowledge

The second section of the book explores aspects related to the development of pedagogical content knowledge (PCK). Chapters 7 and 8 explore the higher education teacher's dual identity as subject matter expert and pedagogue. John Bostock explores the notion of dual professionalism and emphasises that professional development programmes for staff new to teaching in higher education need to include opportunities for contextualising generic pedagogical ideas within different subject areas. Rachel Wood picks this up and explores it in the context of legal education with her concept of the 'identity wobble board' on which law professionals are balancing as they work as both teachers and lawyers in their interactions with students and clients in law clinic settings, not to mention the managerial, quality assurance and legal compliance aspects of running a 'live brief' experiential learning activity. The importance of reflection and dialogue is emphasised in both chapters to enable students and teachers to make meaning of their experiences, and this is also picked up in Chapter 9 where Lucy Spowart and Becky Turner explore the role of reflective practice and engagement with the pedagogic literature in developing experienced teachers' PCK. In Chapter 10, Erika Corradini describes a study to research higher education teachers' experience of researching their practice as a process for developing their PCK. She discusses how curiosity is a feature that connects teaching and research, and that those who are supported to engage with educational research find that it has the potential to improve their students' learning and begin "to think about teaching design inquisitively rather than as a routine activity".

Part III: professional learning for higher education teaching

Taking a scholarly and evidence-informed approach to improving one's practice is also a common theme in the third part, on professional learning. In Chapter 11, Helen King explores professional learning and development for teaching in higher education and how to support and motivate teachers to conceptualise it as integrated into their everyday rather than being an add-on. Empirical research with nine UK National Teaching Fellows provides the foundation for a progressive problem-solving model in which professional learning is conceived as an "evidence-informed evolution of teaching practice". A short contribution from David Baume reminds us of the role of scholarship of teaching in enabling the proactive competence that leads to the development of expertise. This aligns with a number of other perspectives on higher education teaching which suggest that the specific pedagogy does not matter so much as the teacher's commitment to student learning and continual evaluation, analysis and revision of practice. A short diversion within the chapter, by Suzanne Fergus, offers the student perspective on teacher expertise, which endorses this and emphasises the importance of the "quality of the interactions among students and between students and the teacher". To conclude, King argues that, as learning organisations with teaching excellence in their mission, higher education institutions should engender and enable a culture of learning and development for teaching rather than supporting its continuing existence only as an expert subculture.

Although the focus of the first chapter in this section is on the individual teacher's conceptualisation of and approach to professional learning and development, the remaining chapters explore different collaborative tools and approaches to supporting this in ways that provide the insights and feedback that are important features of the professional learning required to develop and maintain expertise. In Chapter 12, Alexandra Morgan and Emmajane Milton discuss the use of narrative case studies of teachers' and students' experiences that are unpacked in the 'educative case-making' process of collaborative, critical reflection, thus enabling "participants to become active researchers of their own experiences of education". Chapter 13 presents four short examples of approaches to coaching and mentoring that can support those newer to teaching in higher education and those with more experience. First, Warren Code and Ashley Welsh describe the well-established science initiative of disciplined-based education specialists which employs pedagogic specialists to partner with faculty members to develop and enhance their teaching practice. In the second example, Dawn Reilly and Liz Warren share two approaches to support and share practice through cross-departmental peer observation and peer mentoring. This concept is taken a step further in the third example, where Laura Heels and Lindsay Marshall discuss the benefits of paired teaching in which collaboration is at the heart of the curriculum design and delivery of a module. To close the chapter, Isabelle Barrette-Ng, John Dawson and Eliana El Khoury outline their SAGES programme of development for graduate teaching assistants, which includes peer support and mentoring from faculty members. As well as setting the graduate students off on the road to expertise in teaching, the programme had an unexpected benefit for faculty members' own development as they learnt about scholarship and new teaching strategies and became more reflective practitioners.

Part IV: the artistry of teaching

The fourth and final section of the book begins to explore the idea of artistry in teaching. Here, we begin to diverge from traditional educational development views and approaches and start to explore those aspects of practice which enable teachers to manage the complex, non-routine facets of their profession: those "artistic, intuitive processes which some practitioners do bring to situations of uncertainty, instability, uniqueness and value conflict" (Schön, 1982, p. 49). In Chapter 14, Richard Bale discusses the concept of 'adaptive expertise', which moves beyond the routine to apply experience, skills and intuition to novel situations. Richard echoes the ideas developed through earlier chapters in the book regarding the importance of a reflective and curiosity-driven approach to teaching. He argues that this approach is one also taken in the performing arts' field of improvisation where the "ability to improvise is underpinned by a depth of expertise which enables the improviser to shift their attention from themselves to the other 'actors'" – something that is not dissimilar to the pedagogical concept of student-centred learning. He describes a number of improvisation exercises he uses in a training course for graduate teaching assistants with clear connections back to learning and teaching. Within this chapter, Fabia Jeddere-Fisher provides some helpful advice on the use of voice for developing teacher–learner relationships, particularly in the context of online learning. Discussions on performance and improvisation often lead to concerns about the role of the teacher in providing 'entertainment': also offered within this chapter, James Derounian provides a short and compelling argument that entertainment does indeed have a place in providing effective learning experiences.

Chapter 15 develops further the idea of teacher as improviser. Nick Sorensen highlights that, like improvisation, expertise is a journey on which there "is no mature or final state but just the perpetual engagement with identity and difference, continuity and transformation that happens in real time", providing a connection back to the idea of proactive competence developed in Part III. Nick's framework for describing expertise in teaching leads to the concept of the 'improvising teacher', which is predicated on improvisation being at the heart of teaching and not an add-on, thereby giving the teacher agency to develop their expertise rather than pursuing an ill-defined notion of excellent practice. He then explores this as a basis for considering what professionalism and professional identity mean in the context of teaching in higher education, concluding with the concept of 'the authorised teacher'. To conclude, Nick argues that professional development should, therefore, include both skills and the development of an 'improvisational mindset' in order to support teachers to develop and inhabit their own professional identity and expertise.

Throughout the chapters in this book, themes emerge that relate to teaching and learning as a collaborative endeavour that requires an element of 'care' from the teacher: caring about students' learning enough to want to continue to improve one's teaching, and caring for each other through respectful and supportive relationships. In Chapter 16, Peter Fossey brings this to the fore through a discussion of teaching and learning through the lens of the 'emotion work' framework. This framework acknowledges the role of emotions in both teaching and learning and explains the state of 'burnout' that can occur when one is continually having to act in a way that belies one's underlying emotional response. Peter illustrates how the emotional response of learners might be better managed in order to enhance their learning experience from, for example, negative feedback or curriculum content such as environmental sustainability that causes them to question their behaviours. To conclude the chapter, a short contribution from Ashley B. Akenson, Andrea Arce-Trigatti and James E. Akenson introduces 'wide open knowledge environments': "educational spaces conducive to curiosity-driven, equity-focused, critical conversations" which through "cultivating curiosity, compassion, and respect when encountering discomfort and challenging content [offer] the possibility for awareness, examination, and transformation".

Conclusion

The model of expertise for teaching in higher education presented in Chapter 1 offers a Venn-diagram schematic to depict three elements of expertise. Throughout the book we see the importance of this particular mode of illustration with blurred boundaries and intersections between the elements. In higher education, pedagogical knowledge and skills are those most usually addressed within professional development programmes, and here the authors advocate for more opportunities to explore the contextual intersection of these with the existing subject knowledge and skills that researchers and professional practitioners bring to their academic practice. Reflective practice and an evidence-informed approach ('scholarship') are emphasised by multiple authors as key tools for professional learning that supports pedagogical content knowledge. While these might not be new arguments, they are critical for a model of expertise that is founded itself on scholarship.

The third dimension of this model of expertise for teaching in higher education, artistry, was originally inspired by a peer observation in which a colleague noted the editor's intuition and improvisation in responding to participants' activities when facilitating an online interactive webinar. Exploring this further led her to Schön's (1982) and Eisner's (2002) ideas on artistry and provided the link to the other dimensions of the model through the idea of reflection-in-action. However, the contributions to the symposium, which are further expanded through the chapters in this book, developed this initial narrow conception of artistry into a substantial and critical element of teaching practice that is rarely explicitly addressed in higher education. The artistry of teaching, as a named dimension of the model, is a powerful reminder of the need for a conception of expertise that is dynamic and socially constructed (Tennant et al., 2010) and recognises the complexities of a profession that engages with humans – teachers and students – rather than with objects such as chess pieces. Artistry includes acknowledging our own limitations and the expertise of others (and in this way expertise has more humility than 'excellence'), the importance of care and empathy (McCune, 2019) and the importance of community and collaboration, both with our students and with other teachers (Shulman, 1993; Collins & Evans, 2018). The concept of expertise necessarily shifts the focus from teacher as didact to the teacher and learners as communal players where everyone has a valid perspective to share. It also recognises that expertise in teaching is not simply about practised routines but requires creativity, improvisation and curiosity for what is going on in the learning space. Expertise is characterised theoretically and illustrated empirically as an ongoing journey motivated by our curiosity as teacher-evaluators (Hattie, 2015) and our care for effective student learning. While this model of expertise does not prescribe any specific pedagogy, the ideas developed through the book might be aligned to the western pedagogical notion of student-centred learning. It would be interesting to explore further how expertise might be characterised in other cultures and what pedagogies might emerge from these.

As in many fields and professions, excellence in higher education is commonly assessed through outputs – in this case, measures such as student satisfaction or graduate outcomes (e.g. the TEF in England). This effectively ignores a critical feature that distinguishes those with expertise from those with experience: a commitment to professional learning. If higher education institutions are to achieve their missions of excellence in education, then they must also foster and enable a culture of professional learning for teaching that is integrated into everyday practice rather than being seen as an add-on. Without this active institutional-level commitment, expertise in teaching will only ever be a subculture of the few.

As illustrated in the examples throughout the book, this model of expertise connects a wide variety of concepts about teaching in higher education and brings them together into a coherent whole, which might be used as a starting point for designing development programmes, exploring one's own personal and professional learning and development, enhancing learning and teaching, research and development projects, and wider strategic and policy initiatives related to enhancement and recognition. As a starting point for conversation, this model has already been powerful and evocative, and, of course, it is likely that it will evolve over time as it is used, discussed and researched in different ways. For the editor, the specific model itself isn't as important as the discourse it provokes and the challenge to our ways of thinking and practising as teachers in higher education.

References

Bereiter, C. & Scardamalia, M. (1993) *Surpassing Ourselves: An Inquiry into the Nature and Implications of Expertise*. Open Court, Chicago, IL.

Bilalić, M. (2017) *The Neuroscience of Expertise*. Cambridge University Press, Cambridge.

Boshuizen, H.P.A., Bromme, R. & Gruber, H. (2004) *Professional Learning: Gaps and Transitions on the Way from Novice to Expert*. Kluwer Academic, Amsterdam. doi:10.1007/1-4020-2094-5

Brusoni, M., Damian, R., Sauri, J.G., Jackson, S., Kömürcügil, F., Malmedy, M., Matveeva, O., Motova, G., Pisarz, S., Pol, P., Rostlund, A., Soboleva, E., Tavares, O. & Zobel, L. (2014) The Concept of Excellence in Higher Education. European Association for Quality Assurance in Higher Education, Occasional Papers 20.

Collins, H. & Evans, R. (2018) A sociological/philosophical perspective on expertise: the acquisition of expertise through socialization. In: Ericsson, K.A., Hoffmann, R.R., Kozbelt, A. & Williams, A.M. (Eds.) *The Cambridge Handbook of Expertise and Expert Performance* (2nd edn). Cambridge University Press, Cambridge, 21–32. doi:10.1017/9781316480748.002

Eisner, E.W. (2002) From episteme to phronesis to artistry in the study and improvement of teaching. *Teaching and Teacher Education*, 18, 375–385. doi:10.1016/s0742-051x(02)00004-5

Eraut, M. (1994) *Developing Professional Knowledge and Competence*. RoutledgeFalmer, Abingdon. doi:10.4324/9780203486016

Ericsson, K.A. (2017) Expertise and individual differences: the search for the structure and acquisition of experts' superior performance. *WIREs Cogn Sci*, 8(1–2). doi:10.1002/wcs.1382

Ericsson, K.A., Krampe, R.Th. & Tesch-Romer, C. (1993) The role of deliberate practice in the acquisition of expert performance. *Psychological Review*, 100(3), 363–406. doi:10.1037/0033-295x.100.3.363

Ericsson, K.A., Charness, N., Feltovich, P.J. & Hoffman, R.R. (Eds.) (2006) *The Cambridge Handbook of Expertise and Expert Performance*. Cambridge University Press, Cambridge. doi:10.1017/cbo9780511816796

Ericsson, K.A., Hoffmann, R.R., Kozbelt, A. & Williams, A.M. (Eds.) (2018) *The Cambridge Handbook of Expertise and Expert Performance* (2nd edn). Cambridge University Press, Cambridge. doi:10.1017/9781316480748

Gakhal, S. (2018) What is teaching excellence? In Broughan, C., Steventon, G. and Clouder. L. (Eds.) *Global Perspectives on Teaching Excellence: A New Era for Higher Education*. Routledge, Abingdon, 6–20. doi:10.4324/9781315211251-1

Gunn, V. & Fisk, A. (2013) Considering Teaching Excellence in Higher Education: 2007–2013: A Literature Review since the CHERI Report 2007. Project Report. Higher Education Academy, York.

Hambrick, D.Z., Campitelli, G. & Macnamara, B.N. (Eds) (2018) *The Science of Expertise: Behavioral, Neural, and Genetic Approaches to Complex Skill*. Routledge, Abingdon. doi:10.4324/9781315113371

Hattie, J. (2015). The applicability of visible learning to higher education. *Scholarship of Teaching and Learning in Psychology*, 1(1), 79–91. doi:10.1037/stl0000021

Kenny, N., Berenson, C., Chick, N., Johnson, C., Keegan, D., Read, E. & Reid, L. (2017) *A Developmental Framework for Teaching Expertise in Postsecondary Education*. International Society for the Scholarship of Teaching and Learning (ISSOTL) Conference, October 11–14, Calgary, Canada.

King, H. (2019) Continuing professional development: what do award-winning lecturers do? *Educational Developments*, 20(2), 1–4.

Kreber, C., Castlden, H., Erfani, N., & Wright, T. (2005) Self-regulated learning about university teaching: an exploratory study, *Teaching in Higher Education*, 10(1), 75–97. doi:10.1080/1356251052000305543

McCune, V. (2019) Academic identities in contemporary higher education: sustaining identities that value teaching, *Teaching in Higher Education*, 26, 1–17. doi:13562517.2019.1632826

Perkins, D. (2008) Beyond understanding. In: Land, R., Meyer, J.H.F. & Smith, J. (Eds.) *Threshold Concepts within the Disciplines*. Sense, Rotterdam.

Saroyan, A. & Trigwell, K. (2015) Higher education teachers' professional learning: process and outcome. *Studies in Educational Evaluation*, 46, 92–101. doi:10.1016/j.stueduc.2015.03.008

Schön, D. (1982) *The Reflective Practitioner: How Professionals Think in Action*. Routledge, Abingdon.

Shulman, L.S. (1993) Forum: teaching as community property. *Change: The Magazine of Higher Learning*, 25(6), 6–7. doi:10.1080/00091383.1993.9938465

Skelton, A. (Ed.) (2007a) *International Perspectives on Teaching Excellence in Higher Education: Improving Knowledge and Practice*. Routledge, Abingdon.

Skelton, A., (2007b) Understanding teacher excellence in higher education. *British Journal of Educational Technology*, 38(1), 171–183. doi:10.1111/j.1467-8535.2007.00682_8.x

Su, F. & Wood, M. (2019) Reinterpreting teaching excellence. *International Journal of Comparative Education and Development*, 21(2), 78–82. doi:10.1108/ijced-05-2019-052

Tennant, M., McMullen, C. & Kaczynski, D. (2010) Reconceptualising the development of university teaching expertise. In: Tennant, M., McMullen, C. & Kaczynski, D. (Eds.) *Teaching, Learning and Research in Higher Education: a critical approach*. Routledge, Abingdon. doi:10.4324/9780203875919-3

Tiberius, R.G., Smith, R.A. & Waisman, Z. (1998). Implications of the nature of "expertise" for teaching and faculty development. *To Improve the Academy*, 17, 123–138. doi:10.3998/tia.17063888.0017.011

Trinh, M.P. (2019) Overcoming the shadow of expertise: how humility and learning goal orientation help knowledge leaders become more flexible. *Frontiers in Psychology*, 10. doi:10.3389/fpsyg.2019.02505

Turner, S. (2001) What is the problem with experts? *Social Studies of Science*. 31(1), 123–149. doi:10.1177/030631201031001007

van Dijk, E.E., van Tartwijk, J., van der Schaaf, M.F. & Kluijtmans, M. (2020) What makes an expert university teacher? A systematic review and synthesis of frameworks for teacher expertise in higher education. *Educational Research Review*, 31. doi:10.1016/j.edurev.2020.100365

Part I

Perspectives on expertise for teaching in higher education

Chapter 1

The characteristics of expertise for teaching in higher education

Helen King

An introduction to expertise

The introduction to this book noted that the word 'expert' comes from the Latin *experiri*, which translates literally as 'experienced in' or 'having experience of'. One of the first known examples of the word expert being used in written form comes from Book I of Geoffrey Chaucer's *Troilus and Criseyde*, completed in the mid-1380s. Here, Chaucer uses the term to mean "wise through experience" (Middle English Dictionary, n.d.) in describing the soothsayer Calkus's proficiency in his science (Chaucer, 1380, line 67) and also Troilus's knowledge of love (line 1367). However, although the term has been in use in the English language for well over 600 years, it wasn't until the mid-1960s that what it means to be an expert began to be explored in depth. Since then, an extensive literature has developed exploring expertise in a wide range of fields and professions. Although the specific details of what expertise looks like will vary from domain to domain, there are a number of common features that can be identified which offer a framework for exploring how expertise might be characterised for teaching in higher education. These features can be categorised into three main elements: high performance based on knowledge and skills, ways of thinking and practising, and intentional learning and development.

High performance based on knowledge and skills

It almost goes without saying that, whether considering expertise or excellence, a key characteristic of both is high performance as measured by particular outputs. Colloquially, the term 'expert' is most often used to describe someone with superior knowledge and/or skills in a particular field. Experts in academic fields other than our own are usually encountered in the media where they are sought for commentary on specific topics. Of course, expertise is not limited to academia or the professions but exists across the breadth of activities within modern human life, including games and sports, the service industries, performing arts and so on. Indeed, it is these latter type of activities that have most often been explored through research on expertise.

DOI: 10.4324/9781003198772-3

Ways of thinking and practising

Expert ways of thinking and practising were first considered through research on the memory and recall of chess masters (de Groot, 1966). De Groot (a chess master himself) discovered that, after being presented with a configuration of chess pieces for 5 seconds, chess masters could recall the layout of the board almost perfectly, whereas novices struggled to remember more than a few pieces. Later, Chase and Simon (1973) reproduced and extended de Groot's work and found that the chess masters only excelled when the configuration was one that could actually occur within a game. When the configuration of pieces was not meaningful, their performance was little better than that of novices. Chase and Simon also examined expertise in a number of other fields, including sport, music and physics, and concluded that expert performance is based on extensive knowledge stored through a pattern-based memory system that has been acquired through many years of experience.

Differences between novices and experts are also seen in their approach to problem-solving. Novices will tend to conceptualise a problem based on fairly superficial features, whereas the expert will have a deeper conceptual understanding based on principles. In addition, experts tend to take much more time in qualitatively analysing a problem and considering it from a variety of viewpoints before attempting a solution (e.g. Larkin et al., 1980). This is something the author experienced for herself first hand when attempting problems posed in a final year general physics undergraduate exam. Her approach was to identify the topic of the problem and then try to remember the right equation to use. A more expert approach would be to step back and consider the overall picture and develop a qualitative understanding of the problem and a sense of what the solution might look like. Similarly, research with geoscientists in the field demonstrated that experts visually surveyed the whole field area and carefully planned which locations they would visit based on the overall features they could see and their knowledge of geological processes. Their movements through the field area were thus more effective than the novices', who systematically worked their way through the space covering more distance less efficiently (Baker et al., 2012).

An expertise approach to problem-solving also draws on a well-organised knowledge system (Chi et al., 1981). Years of experience enable the development of a large amount of knowledge, which the practitioner can quickly, even automatically, sift through and make connections in order to draw down what might be required to tackle the current situation. There is an automation of practice which can exhibit as a grace or flow (Csikszentmihalyi, 1990). This automation is commonly experienced by people who drive cars: when learning to drive, we have to carefully think through every gear change and manoeuvre; however, after hours of practice behind the wheel, we can easily drive safely while listening to the radio or holding a conversation. The automation frees up our cognitive load, enabling us to tackle other problems and, for some practitioners, this also provides space for continuous improvement.

To summarise, experience can lead to developing particular patterns and ways of thinking, information is better organised, and routine problems can be quickly, even automatically, addressed. However, in many professions, the reality is rarely routine (e.g. van Tartwijk et al., 2017). An element of adaptability is required to respond to unexpected or unique situations. This adaptive expertise (Holyoak, 1991) is a critical distinction between experts and those who have merely acquired a lot of experience: "the expert addresses problems whereas the experienced non-expert carries out practiced routines" (Bereiter & Scardamalia, 1993, p. 11).

As noted above, the colloquial expectation of an expert is that they hold all the knowledge required to perform highly in their field. However, expertise is domain-specific: the knowledge, skills and ways of thinking and practising are confined to their particular specialism. In many professions, high performance also requires support from fields outside one's own domain. For example, however skilled or expert a surgeon might be, they cannot operate at their highest level without the assistance of an anaesthetist, nurse, technician and so on. True expertise, therefore, requires an element of humility, of realising that one doesn't and can't know everything, and that the expertise of others might need to be drawn upon in order to solve a problem (Pickard, Chapter 5, this volume). This also means that experts are more likely to know the limits of their knowledge and, hence, better appreciate the difficulty of the problem they are attempting to solve.

Intentional learning and development

The generic characteristics discussed above illustrate what is seen of the expert by an external audience: they are highly knowledgeable and skilled with a honed problem-solving approach relevant to their profession. In this respect, those who reach high levels of performance in any field are popularly considered to be in some way superhuman or extraordinarily talented. However, this notion of natural talent was bought into question with Bloom's pioneering research with 'gifted' young people in the 1980s (Bloom, 1985) which indicated that it was dedication to practice and improvement, and an environment conducive to this, which led to high achievements. This idea was more recently popularised through publications such as *Bounce: The Myth of Talent and the Power of Practice* (Syed, 2010) and Dweck's influential work on growth mindset (Dweck, 2006). Expertise research has been highly influenced by Ericsson et al.'s work on deliberate practice (1993), which emphasises a focused and dedicated approach to improvement in one's field above other factors:

> expertise derives not from basic cognitive ability, nor from the sheer amount of experience. Rather, it develops – particular forms of training and practice induce cognitive, perceptual, physiological, neurological, and anatomical changes necessary for the acquisition of complex domain-specific skills.
>
> (Ericsson, 2017, p. 1)

"Deliberate practice is a highly structured activity, the explicit goal of which is to improve performance" (Ericsson et al., 1993, p. 368). A useful example is in music: an experienced pianist might have a number of favourite pieces they play regularly for their own enjoyment. They may play competently, but in some pieces there may be some notes or passages which are a bit tricky, and so errors are made or they're just skipped entirely. This approach will never lead to improvement. In order for them to play these pieces better, there needs to be a focus specifically on those difficult parts: they need to be repeated many times, listened to carefully and continued until they are honed. This approach is hard work, it can be boring and, therefore, requires considerable intrinsic motivation, but it is highly effective for improving performance

A review of literature on deliberate practice indicates that it "is one important predictor of expertise" (Macnamara et al., 2018, p. 164). Other factors are also relevant, as noted above: there must be an environment conducive to this practice, and genetic physical or cognitive factors will be important depending on the field (it is rare to see a very short basketball player, for example). However, the factor we can personally control is that of 'practice', and this suggests that, in the context of teaching in higher education, expertise is potentially achievable by everybody. Unfortunately, this intentional learning and development are rarely seen by the people watching the sport, listening to the music or being taught by their teachers. Expertise (and excellence) tends to be judged by the outputs, which can mean that insufficient consideration and support are given to the inputs. This can lead to an 'expert subculture' (see Chapter 11) in which only a few people in the profession are dedicated to intentional learning, development and improvement.

Another model of intentional learning and development in the expertise literature is that of progressive problem-solving (Bereiter & Scardamalia, 1993). It is suggested that the automation of skills brought about by extensive experience frees up cognitive capacity. Practitioners who use this spare capacity to explore their practice through identifying and working on areas for improvement will continue to enhance their effectiveness and develop their expertise.

Reflective practice (Schön, 1982) might also be considered as an activity that enables the development of expertise by exploring one's performance, identifying areas for improvement and modifying one's approach accordingly. Whatever practice or development model we choose, it is the intentionality and purposefulness of the activity which enable the practitioner to continue to develop and improve throughout their career.

> The world's foremost cellist, Pablo Casals, is 83. He was asked one day why he continued to practice four and five hours a day. Casals answered, "Because I think I am making progress."
>
> (Lyons, 1959, p. 30)

Summary of generic characteristics of expertise

To summarise, the generic characteristics of expertise might be categorised into three key elements:

- High performance based on knowledge and skills developed through study and experience;
- Ways of thinking and practising;
- Intentional learning and development.

Characteristics of expertise for teaching in higher education

Categorising the generic characteristics of expertise into three key areas provides an opportunity to draw parallels and analogies for the profession of teaching. Drawing on relevant literature, personal experience and research interviews with nine UK National Teaching Fellows (King, 2019, 2020), a broad model of teacher expertise is proposed that transcends subject boundaries and discipline pedagogies. While being relevant and adaptable for teaching at other educational levels, this model is specifically thought out in the context of higher education, with good reason, as discussed by van Dijk below.

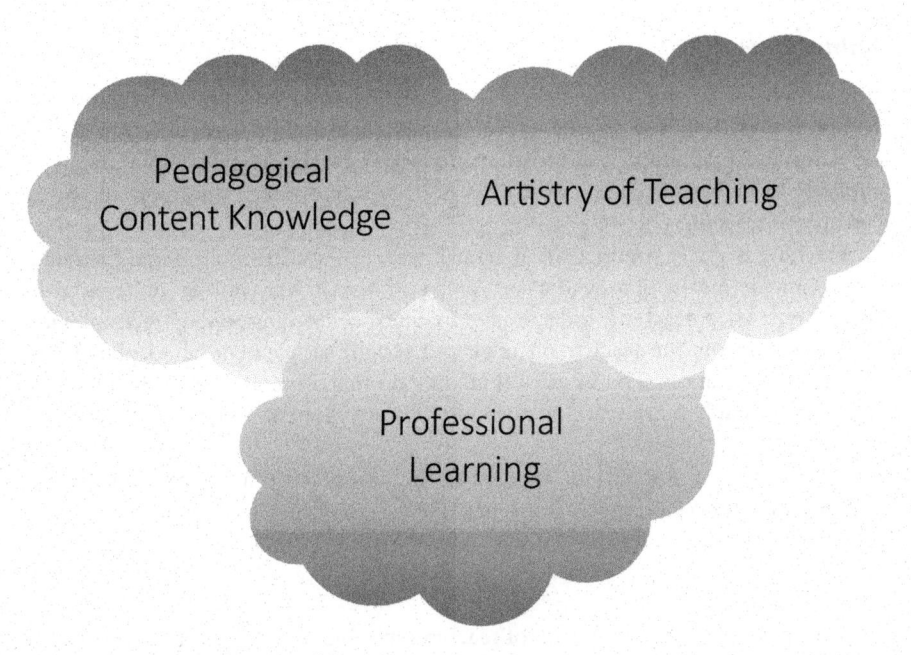

Figure 1.1 A model of expertise for teaching in higher education

Pedagogical content knowledge

A teacher in any context must weave together skills and knowledge from two domains, that of their subject matter and that of teaching itself (pedagogy). This integration is described by Shulman (1986) as pedagogical content knowledge (PCK).

> [PCK] represents the blending of content and pedagogy into an understanding of how particular topics, problems, or issues are organized, represented, and adapted to diverse interests and abilities of learners, and presented for instruction. Pedagogical content knowledge is the category most likely to distinguish the understanding of the content specialist from that of the pedagogue
>
> (Shulman, 1987, p. 8)

Shulman's description of PCK provides a strong argument for the need to provide teachers in higher education with the time and space required to develop their teaching skills to complement their subject knowledge. This challenges the traditional rhetoric in higher education that knowledge (usually in the form of a PhD) is sufficient in order to teach effectively. Furthermore, research has suggested that teachers without PCK may be more fixed in their approaches, with little facility for critical reflection or innovation (Fraser, 2016; Vereijken & van der Rijst, 2021).

Artistry of teaching

The simplicity of the Venn-style diagram in Figure 1.1 belies the extent and complexity of the interactions of each of its constituent categories. 'Ways of thinking and practising' is a broad and considerably under-researched aspect of teaching in higher education which has been captured under the single theme of 'artistry of teaching'.

Teaching is rarely routine; the dynamic nature of student cohorts and learning environments means that even a well-prepared session may not go quite as planned. Even when teaching didactically, an unexpected question or technological failure may throw the teacher off track and require an element of adaptability to retrieve the situation. The ways of thinking and practising as a teacher, therefore, cannot necessarily be reduced to a simple formula. As Schön says:

> Let us search, instead, for an epistemology of practice implicit in the artistic, intuitive processes which some practitioners do bring to situations of uncertainty, instability, uniqueness and value conflict
>
> (1982, p. 49)

This is, perhaps, particularly true of teaching in a higher education context where the knowledge being taught is often as changing as the learning environment. Van Dijk describes this further in Box 1.1, arguing for the need for expertise in teaching in higher education to be considered distinctly from that in other levels of education.

> **Box 1.1 Context matters: the distinct characteristics of higher education**
>
> In light of extensive research that has shown expertise is domain-specific (Ericsson et al., 2018), it is appropriate that expertise in teaching in higher education be explored as distinct from primary or secondary education. There are three distinct characteristics of higher education that are particularly relevant to this discussion:
>
> First, higher education teachers are academics who are often expected to combine research and teaching, and sometimes other professional tasks (e.g. clinical work). This implies that development of teacher expertise should be studied and supported in relation to development in other tasks. Attention should be paid to how different academic tasks relate to each other (Boyer et al., 2015; Tight, 2016) and consequences of combining different tasks for academics, for example on their motivation (Visser-Wijnveen et al., 2014).
>
> Second, knowledge taught in higher education is often dynamic and highly specialized. As a result, HE teachers have more autonomy to define the curriculum and may need to constantly adapt it to new insights. This draws attention to educational design, educational leadership and management, and educational scholarship and research as core tasks of higher education teachers (van Dijk et al., 2020). It also implies that insight is needed into how to translate knowledge into a course or curriculum and how to facilitate student learning within a certain discipline. Powerful knowledge (Young & Muller, 2010) and pedagogical content knowledge (Shulman, 1986) are important theoretical concepts for exploring these issues.
>
> Third, contrary to many other education contexts, professional development for teaching is not always (extensively) available and/or mandatory in higher education, particularly beyond the early career period. Additionally, research into how higher education teachers (continue to) develop their expertise is sparse. Further exploration is thus necessary and would benefit from the consideration of different perspectives: individual teachers (e.g. Töytäri et al., 2017), social contexts for learning (e.g. Van Waes et al., 2018) and institutional and organizational structures (e.g. Skelton, 2005).
>
> Of course, other characteristics may also influence teacher expertise in higher education – for example, student population and opportunities for career development. Nevertheless, it is clear that, for any discussions about teacher expertise, the higher education context matters. Although the literature on teacher expertise at other levels can still offer important insights (e.g. Postholm, 2012), being cognisant of the peculiarities of higher education better enables us to translate this literature into the HE context and justifies additional research that focuses on the higher education domain.
>
> (Esther van Dijk)

The ways of thinking and practising, the pattern recognition, problem-solving and adaptive expertise of teaching, therefore, "require[s] sensibility, imagination, technique, and the ability to make judgements about the feel and significance of the particular". "Teaching profits from – no, requires at its best – artistry" (Eisner, 2002, p. 382).

Artistry, in this model of teacher expertise, encapsulates those more intangible characteristics that makes expertise recognisable. It emphasises the relational nature of teaching, that it is fundamentally about human interactions. Artistry relates to aspects of performance such as being authentic to oneself, engaging an audience and improvisation as Bale and Sorensen explore further in Chapters 14 and 15. It also links to the importance of relational pedagogy and the need to make meaningful connections with students (Gravett & Winstone, 2020). A teacher with expertise will have care: they will care enough for their students' learning to better understand them as individuals and to develop effective relationships, and also to spend time on continuing to improve their own teaching.

Professional learning

Intentional learning and development are the key differentiators between experience and expertise. This dimension of the expertise model interacts with the other two to maintain the dynamic nature of expertise and to characterise it as a journey that can be embarked upon from the first day of one's teaching career. As discussed in the introduction, expertise is an ongoing process, not a fixed point to be attained.

The concept of deliberate practice may, at first, seem irrelevant in a profession where one rarely has the opportunity to rehearse (the music analogy only works so far). In their study of secondary school teachers, Dunn and Shriner (1999) suggest that "teachers do not 'practice' teaching in order to improve but instead engage in patterns of planning, evaluation and revision so that students improve" (p. 647). This notion of 'teacher as evaluator' is considered by Hattie (2015) as one of the defining features of high-quality teaching in higher education, independent of any particular pedagogy. And similar to models of reflection and experiential learning (e.g. Kolb, 1984), the concept of progressive problem-solving might also be characterised as the scholarship of teaching (Smith, 2001; Kreber et al., 2005; Corradini, Chapter 10, this volume) leading to expertise as "proactive competence" (Perkins, 2008).

Whether we call this activity reflective practice, deliberate practice, progressive problem-solving or scholarship of teaching, the key point from the expertise literature is that there is intentional and purposeful learning that leads to improvement. As discussed more fully in Chapter 11, where deliberate practice and progressive problem-solving are unpacked and described in the higher education context, the commonly used umbrella term 'professional development' can convey a sense of something being done 'to' the passive practitioner. It is suggested that the term 'professional learning' might be preferable for the active and self-directed nature of intentional learning and development. And, in the context of teaching in higher education, this professional learning might be considered as an evidence-informed evolution of teaching.

Summary of the characteristics of expertise for teaching in higher education

To summarise, the characteristics of expertise for teaching in higher education are categorised into three key areas:

- Pedagogical content knowledge;
- Artistry of teaching;
- Professional learning.

This model presents a future-facing view of a professional educator: someone who has the underpinning knowledge and skills and also the flexibility to respond to immediate and longer terms changes in their teaching environment. It also acknowledges and recognises the complexity of the dialogic, human-interaction nature of teaching. The specific nature of expertise, what it looks and feels like, will differ from teacher to teacher, and it is part of the journey of one's teaching from a novice starting point to develop, understand and define, and continue to develop one's own teaching philosophy and expertise (Tennant et al., 2010).

For someone considering their own teaching, this model, in its current form, only provides a snapshot of expertise at a moment in time. If expertise is an ongoing process that is initiated from the moment one starts one's foray into the domain, how might it develop over time in relation to career development and progression? In their review of frameworks for expertise in higher education, van Dijk et al. (2020) identify three key features of performance that develop over time: "better task performance", "ability to carry out a greater number of tasks" and an "increased sphere of influence". This latter feature also reflects the collaborative nature of expertise: as we develop our teaching we begin to share practice with colleagues or help support their learning as teachers; we expand our repertoire from teaching single sessions to leading entire programmes; and we influence others' teaching more widely across our institution, country or even internationally. Expertise in teaching, thus, cannot be an entirely individual pursuit: it requires engagement with a broader community of practitioners from whom we can learn and with whom we can share our practice (Collins & Evans, 2018).

Implications for institutions and educational development

As in many fields and professions, excellence in higher education is commonly assessed through outputs, in this case measures such as student satisfaction or graduate outcomes (e.g. the Teaching Excellence and Student Outcomes Framework in England). This effectively ignores a critical feature that distinguishes those with expertise from those with experience: a commitment to professional learning.

If higher education institutions are to achieve their missions of excellence in education, then they must also foster and enable a culture of professional learning for teaching that is integrated into everyday practice, rather than being seen as an add-on. Without this active institutional-level commitment, expertise in teaching will only ever be a subculture of the few.

Within educational development, strategies to support the development of teachers and the improvement of teaching and learning in higher education have traditionally focused on introducing staff to appropriate pedagogies and supporting them to implement these. More recently, the interest in topics such as threshold concepts (Meyer & Land, 2003) and signature pedagogies (Shulman, 2005) has provided a vehicle to engage staff in developing a more integrated pedagogical content knowledge. But, according to the model presented here, a focus on pedagogical development may not be enough; we also need to facilitate and enable intentional learning and development, and the growth of artistry.

Educational development programmes and courses tend to emphasise reflective practice as an approach to continuous improvement. Expertise offers a number of other ways of conceptualising professional learning that provides an alternative, though complementary, perspective to reflective practice. When supporting staff who are new to teaching in higher education, the expertise model can help them find a way to express and explore professional learning that is meaningful to them. For some, this is reflective practice; for others, deliberate practice, progressive problem-solving, scholarship or an evidence-informed evolution of teaching might feel more relevant.

Most important for educational development, however, is that using an expertise model highlights components of teaching that are often neglected in formal development programmes. The artistry of teaching maybe something that emerges through experience but it can also be nurtured and supported through educational development. Offering workshops and courses in voice, performance and improvisation can provide an added dimension of support that is enthusiastically welcomed, particularly by staff who wish to feel more confident in their interactions with students.

The concept of expertise is also important for pedagogy and the development of students from novice to emerging expert. If the teacher has acquired expertise in that subject area, then their ways of thinking and practising will be different from those of their relatively novice students. For example, experts are aware of particular patterns that may not be immediately obvious to novices; this might result in our students noticing different features than we do in our slides, videos or other learning materials. Additionally, if pattern recognition is a key aspect of expertise, then this ought to be brought more intentionally into our pedagogies in whatever way is meaningful to our particular subject area (Bransford et al., 2000; Kinchin et al., 2000). This book is concerned with the nature of expertise of the HE teacher, but the interested reader (or expert teacher!) might also want to explore how their pedagogy could support the development of expertise in their students (Wieman, 2019).

The traditional didactic teacher is often described derogatorily as a 'sage on the stage', with the term 'guide on the side' being preferred for more student-centred learning (King, 1993). However, as Reis suggests in Chapter 2 of this volume, on closer inspection, the notion of a sage may be nearer to teacher expertise than meets the eye. In classical philosophy, experts known for their extensive knowledge *and* who had attained wisdom were referred to as sages. Wisdom itself, being beyond the acquisition of knowledge and skills, refers to sound and ethical judgement and compassion and requires the intentional development of oneself. As in Chaucer's use of the term, an expert is, therefore, truly 'wise through experience' rather than simply having accumulated extensive knowledge. Given our consideration of the artistry of teaching, maybe the expert teacher is Reis's 'sage on the side', utilising their wisdom and working together *with* their students to support and enable learning.

References

Baker, K.M., Petcovic, H., Wisniewska, M. & Libarkin, J. (2012) Spatial signatures of mapping expertise among field geologists. *Cartography and Geographic Information Science*, 39(3), 119–132. doi:10.1559/15230406393119

Bereiter, C. & M. Scardamalia (1993) *Surpassing Ourselves: An Enquiry into the Nature and Implications of Expertise*. Open Court, Chicago, IL.

Bloom, B.S. (1985) *Developing Talent in Young People*. Ballantine Books, New York.

Boyer, E.L., Moser, D., Ream, T.C. & Braxton, J.M. (2015) *Scholarship Reconsidered: Priorities of the Professoriate*. John Wiley, Oxford.

Bransford, J.D., Brown, A.L. & Cocking, R. (Eds) (2000) *How People Learn: Brain, Mind, Experience, and School*. National Academy Press, Washington, DC. doi:10.17226/9853

Chase, W.G., & Simon, H.A. (1973) The mind's eye in chess. In: Chase, W.G. (Ed.), *Visual Information Processing*. Academic Press, New York, 215–281. doi:10.1016/b978-0-12-170150-5.50011-1

Chaucer, G. (~1380) *Troilus and Criseyde*. www.gutenberg.org/files/257/257-h/257-h.htm [accessed 08/04/2021]

Chi, M.T.H., Feltovich, P.J. & Glaser, R. (1981) Categorization and representation of physics problems by experts and novices. *Cognitive Science*, 5(2), 121–125. doi:10.1207/s15516709cog0502_2

Collins, H. & Evans, R. (2018) A sociological/philosophical perspective on expertise: the acquisition of expertise through socialization. In: Ericsson, K.A., Hoffmann, R.R., Kozbelt, A. & Williams, A.M. (Eds.) *The Cambridge Handbook of Expertise and Expert Performance* (2nd edn). Cambridge University Press, Cambridge, 21–32. doi:10.1017/9781316480748.002

Csikszentmihalyi, M. (1990) *Flow: The Psychology of Optimal Experience*. Harper & Row, New York.

de Groot, A.D. (1966) Perception and memory versus thought. In: Kleinmuntz, B. (Ed.) *Problem Solving Research, Methods and Theory*. Wiley, New York, 19–50.

Dunn, T.G. & Shriner, C. (1999) Deliberate practice in teaching: what teachers do for self-improvement. *Teaching and Teacher Education* 15, 631–651. doi:10.1016/s0742-051x(98)00068-7

Dweck, C.S. (2006) *Mindset: Changing the Way You Think to Fulfil Your Potential.* Robinson, London.

Eisner, E.W. (2002) From episteme to phronesis to artistry in the study and improvement of teaching. *Teaching and Teacher Education,* 18, 375–385. doi:10.1016/s0742-051x(02)00004-5

Ericsson, K.A. (2017) Expertise and individual differences: the search for the structure and acquisition of experts' superior performance. *WIREs Cogn Sci,* 8(1–2). doi:10.1002/wcs.1382

Ericsson, K.A., Hoffman, R.R., Kozbelt, A. & Williams, A.M. (Eds.) (2018) *The Cambridge Handbook of Expertise and Expert Performance* (2nd edn). Cambridge University Press, Cambridge. doi:10.1017/9781316480748

Ericsson, K.A., Krampe, R.T. & Tesch-Römer, C. (1993) The role of deliberate practice in the acquisition of expert performance. *Psychological Review,* 100(3), 363–406. doi:10.1037/0033-295x.100.3.363

Fraser, S.P. (2016) Pedagogical content knowledge (PCK): exploring its usefulness for science lectures in higher education. *Research in Science Education,* 46, 141–161. doi:10.1007/s11165-014-9459-1

Gravett, K. & Winstone, N.E. (2020) Making connections: authenticity and alienation within students' relationships in higher education, *Higher Education Research & Development.* doi:10.1080/07294360.2020.1842335.

Hattie, J. (2015) The applicability of Visible Learning to higher education. *Scholarship of Teaching and Learning in Psychology,* 1 (1), 79–91. doi:10.1037/stl0000021.

Holyoak, K. J. (1991) Symbolic connectionism: towards third-generation theories of expertise. In: K.A. Ericsson & J. Smith (Eds.), *Toward a General Theory of Expertise: Prospects and Limits.* Cambridge University Press, Cambridge, 301–335.

Kinchin, I.M., Hay, D.B. & Adams, A. (2000) How a qualitative approach to concept map analysis can be used to aid learning by illustrating patterns of conceptual development, *Educational Research,* 42 (1), 43–57. doi:10.1080/001318800363908

King, A. (1993) Sage on the stage to guide on the side. *College Teaching,* 41(1), 30–35. doi:10.1080/87567555.1993.9926781

King, H. (2019) Continuing professional development: what do award-winning lecturers do? *Educational Developments,* 20(2), 1–4.

King, H. (2020) *Future-ready Faculty: Developing the characteristics of expertise in teaching in higher education.* Proceedings of the International Consortium for Educational Development Conference, ICED2020.

Kolb, D.A. (1984) *Experiential Learning: Experience as the Source of Learning and Development.* Prentice-Hall, New Jersey.

Kreber, C., Castleden, H., Erfani, N. & Wright, T. (2005) Self-regulated learning about university teaching: an exploratory study. *Teaching in Higher Education,* 10(1), 75–97. doi:10.1080/1356251052000305543

Larkin, J.H., McDermott J., Simon, D.P. & Simon, H. A. (1980) Expert and novice performance in solving physics problem. *Science,* 208, 1335–1342.

Lyons, L. (1959, May) Personal glimpses. *Reader's Digest,* 74, 29–30. The Reader's Digest Association, Pleasantville, NY.

Macnamara, B.N., Hambrick, D.Z., Frank, D.J.King, M.J., Burgoyne, A.P. & Meinz, E.J. (2018) The deliberate practice view: an evaluation of definitions, claims and empirical evidence. In: Hambrick, D.Z., Campitelli, G. & Macnamara, B.N. (Eds) *The Science of*

Expertise: Behavioral, Neural, and Genetic Approaches to Complex Skill. Routledge, Abingdon, 151–168.

Meyer, J.H.F. & Land, R. (2003) Threshold concepts and troublesome knowledge 1 – linkages to ways of thinking and practising. In: Rust, C. (Ed.) *Improving Student Learning – Ten Years On*. OCSLD, Oxford, 412–424.

Middle English Dictionary. (n.d.) expert (adj. and n.). https://quod.lib.umich.edu/m/middle-english-dictionary/dictionary/MED14950/ [accessed 08/04/2021].

Perkins, D. (2008) Beyond understanding. In: Land, R., Meyer, J.H.F. & Smith, J. (Eds.) *Threshold Concepts within the Disciplines*. Sense, Rotterdam, 1–19.

Postholm, M.B. (2012) Teachers' professional development: a theoretical review. *Educational Research*, 54(4), 405–429. doi:10.1080/00131881.2012.734725

Schön, D. (1982) *The Reflective Practitioner: How Professionals Think in Action*. Routledge, Abingdon.

Shulman, L.S. (1986) Those who understand: knowledge growth in teaching. *Educational Researcher*, 15(2), 4–14. doi:10.3102/0013189x015002004

Shulman, L.S. (1987) Knowledge and teaching: foundations of the new reform. *Harvard Educational Review*, 57, 1–22.

Shulman, L.S. (2005) Signature pedagogies in the professions. *Daedalus*, 134, 52–59. doi:10.1162/0011526054622015

Skelton, A. (2005) *Understanding Teaching Excellence in Higher Education: Towards a Critical Approach*. Routledge, Abingdon. doi:10.4324/9780203412947

Smith, R. (2001) Expertise and the scholarship of teaching. *New Directions for Teaching and Learning*, 86, 69–78. doi:10.1002/tl.17

Syed, M. (2010) *Bounce: The Myth of Talent and the Power of Practice*. Fourth Estate, London.

Tennant, M., McMullen, C. & Kaczynski, D. (2010) Reconceptualising the development of university teaching expertise. In: Tennant, M., McMullen, C. & Kaczynski, D. (Eds.) *Teaching, Learning and Research in Higher Education*. Routledge, Abingdon, 35–53. doi:10.4324/9780203875919-3

Tight, M. (2016) Examining the research/teaching nexus. *European Journal of Higher Education*, 6(4), 293–311. doi:10.1080/21568235.2016.1224674

Töytäri, A., Tynjälä, P., Piirainen, A. and Ilves, V. (2017) Higher education teachers' descriptions of their own learning: a quantitative perspective. *Higher Education Research & Development*, 36(6), 1295–1304. doi:10.1080/07294360.2017.1303455

van Dijk, E.E., van Tartwijk, J., & van der Schaaf, M.F. (2020) What makes an expert university teacher? A systematic review and synthesis of frameworks for teacher expertise in higher education. *Educational Research Review*, 31. doi:10.1016/j.edurev.2020.100365

van Tartwijk, J., Zwart, R. & Wubbels, T. (2017) Developing teachers' competences with the focus on adaptive expertise in teaching. In: Husu, J. & Clandinin, D.J. (Eds.) *The SAGE Handbook of Research on Teacher Education*. Sage, California, 820–835. doi:10.4135/9781526402042.n47

Van Waes, S., De Maeyer, S., Moolenaar, N.M., Van Petegem, P. and Van den Bossche, P. (2018) Strengthening networks: a social network intervention among higher education teachers. *Learning and Instruction*, 53, 34–49. doi:10.1016/j.learninstruc.2017.07.005

Vereijken, M.W.C. & van der Rijst, R.M. (2021). Subject matter pedagogy in university teaching: how lecturer use relations between theory and practice. *Teaching in Higher Education*, 1–14. doi:10.1080/13562517.2020.1863352

Visser-Wijnveen, G.J., Stes, A. and Van Petegem, P. (2014) Clustering teachers' motivations for teaching. *Teaching in Higher Education*, 19 (6), 644–656. doi:10.1080/13562517.2014.901953

Wieman, C.E. (2019). Expertise in university teaching & the implications for teaching effectiveness, evaluation & training. *Daedalus*, 148, 47–78. doi:10.1162/daed_a_01760

Young, M. & Muller, J. (2010) Three Educational Scenarios for the Future: Lessons from the sociology of knowledge. *European Journal of Education*, 45(1), 11–27. doi:10.1111/j.1465-3435.2009.01413.x

Chapter 2

Critical reflection as a tool to develop expertise in teaching in higher education

Leonardo Morantes-Africano

Introduction

Models of professional learning and professional practice in education highlight the need to be critical as a means of dealing with the complexity inherent in late-modern educational practice and the multiple roles and responsibilities of educators. For a characterisation of expertise in teaching in higher education, this chapter explores critical reflection as a key strategy used in initial teacher education to support the professional formation of educators. Drawing on my experience as a teacher educator for the post-compulsory education sector in England, I conceptualise critical reflection as having a twofold purpose: (1) as a practical tool, it helps educators analyse and evaluate their practice to inform their future; and (2) as a normative guide, it urges educators to interrogate their practice from a moral and ethical perspective, which is necessary to unveil hegemonic assumptions, biases and systemic issues that hinder the advancement of social justice.

Expertise development is a complex and fluid, rather than a fixed and straightforward, endeavoured process. I argue that criticality is an underpinning skill needed for professional learning, extends to professional practice and continuous professional development, and has a place in a conceptualisation of expertise in teaching. Criticality is particularly relevant in our current climate where the neoliberal agendas of performativity and accountability are undermining educators' professionalism, "in the hunt for measures, targets, benchmarks, tests, tables, audits to feed the system in the name of improvement" (Ball, 2016, p. 1046). Drawing on the distinction between *teaching* and *education* made by Kemmis (2005) – that is, of teaching as *instrumental promotion of learning* versus "the wider and deeper activity characterised by commitment to developing, through teaching or upbringing, the good for each individual and the good for humankind" (Kemmis & Smith, 2008, p. 27) – the term *educator* will be used henceforth.

Complexity largely defines the professional practice of educators working in post-compulsory education, a field also characterised by "uncertainty, instability, uniqueness, and value conflict" (Schön, 1983, p. 18), where practitioners are required to have a strong set of knowledges, skills and values. Thus, I argue that

DOI: 10.4324/9781003198772-4

expertise is inherently multidimensional and does not follow a linear "novice-to-expert trajectory" (Hager et al., 2012). Over the years, various national regulatory frameworks (Furlong & Whitty, 2017) have been devised to guide professional expectations in education. Although higher education is widely associated with universities, college-based provision is also part of the higher education landscape; hence, for the UK, two sets of standards are relevant here: the UK Professional Standards Framework for teaching and supporting learning in higher education (UKPSF, 2011), which encompasses areas of activity, core knowledge and professional values; and the Education & Training Foundation (ETF, 2014) Standards for Teachers and Trainers in Education and Training, which are also divided into the categories of professional knowledge and understanding, skills, and values and attributes. Although these standards do not represent a prescribed set of competences, they do provide a useful guide to strive towards, especially when trying to characterise areas of expertise required in higher education. The ETF (2014, p. 1) standards explicitly conceptualise educators as "dual professionals" – that is, as specialists in their subject and/or vocational areas, as well as *experts* in teaching and learning (emphasis added). Moreover, they are considered "reflective and enquiring practitioners who think critically about their own educational assumptions, values and practice in the context of a changing contemporary and educational world" (ETF, 2014, p. 1).

Many teacher education programmes claim to form reflective practitioners (Belvis et al., 2013; Hatton & Smith, 1995; McLaughlin, 1999; Rodgers, 2002). However, reflection is perhaps a notion that is taken for granted but worthy of re-examination. For example, McLaughlin (1999, p. 10) questions whether reflective practice diminishes the "importance, scope and sophistication of professional thoughtfulness, judgement and autonomy". Hatton and Smith (1995, p. 34) also question whether reflection is limited to thought processes about action, or inextricably bound up in action; whether the time frames for reflection are immediate and short-term or extended and systematic; whether reflection is by its very nature problem-centred or not; and finally, how conscious is the person doing the reflection of "wider contextual historic, cultural and political values and beliefs". It is, however, widely used in accreditation schemes for both academic and practical work through reflective journals, evaluations of own practice, portfolios and accounts of critical incidents. I argue that exploring reflection and what makes it critical adds a valuable perspective to the various conceptualisations of expertise explored in this book.

Rodgers (2002, p. 863) defines reflection as "the transformation of raw experience into meaning-filled theory that is grounded in experience, informed by existing theory, and serves the larger purpose of the moral growth of the individual and society". The notion of meaning-making is core to the value that we assign to an experience (Rodgers, 2002, p. 848) and requires what Dewey (1933) called intellectualisation as the process of locating or naming the problem. Schön (1983, p. 40) also supports the idea of problems as constructions "from the materials of problematic situations which are puzzling, troubling, and uncertain".

Perhaps *problem-setting* precedes *problem-solving*, because "a question well put is half answered" (Dewey, 1933, p. 201). This, I would argue, should be a key consideration for a conceptualisation of expertise in teaching in higher education, especially when dealing with dilemmatic and complex situations, which are ever-present in educational practice (Fransson & Grannäs, 2013).

The above provides the foundations to illustrate the practical and normative dimensions of critical reflection in expertise development. Aspects of knowledge and skills will be discussed first through an exploration of how at the intersection of content knowledge and pedagogical knowledge lies the "pedagogical content knowledge" (Shulman, 1987) that we can use as one of the characteristics of expertise in teaching. Second, I will focus on the values and contextual factors that invite a moral and ethical perspective to the role of critical reflection in expertise development. As individuals and as a community of practice, we must go beyond revision and contemplation of our experience to ask, "in whose interests are we acting?" (Kemmis & Smith, 2008). Thus, expertise in teaching in higher education will be associated with the notion of *praxis*, or ethical decision-making.

The practical dimension of critical reflection: developing pedagogical content knowledge

According to Shulman (1987, p. 7), teaching begins with the teacher understanding "what it is to be learnt and how it is to be taught". The former statement relates to subject knowledge, the latter to pedagogy; I consider both essential components for a categorisation of expertise in teaching in higher education. Based on the knowledge, skills and practices outlined in the professional standards (UKPSF, 2011; ETF, 2014), this section explores Shulman's (1987) content knowledge, pedagogical knowledge and how the amalgamation of these two concepts can develop 'pedagogical content knowledge'. Shulman (1987, p. 8) defined it as "the blending of content and pedagogy into an understanding of how particular topics, problems, or issues are organized, represented, and adapted to the diverse interests and abilities of learners, and presented for instruction".

I suggest here that critical reflection can be an effective tool to develop pedagogic content knowledge and will illustrate this through two examples used in teacher education: experiential learning (loop input approach; Woodward, 2003) as a pedagogy used in professional learning, and the dialogic process of feedback (Carless et al., 2011) established between teacher educators and student teachers to make sense of lived practice. Both examples extend to approaches that can be used for continuous professional development.

Content knowledge

Furlong and Whitty's (2017) work on international perspectives on the study of education and teacher education identified 12 major knowledge traditions, grouped into three major categories: academic knowledge traditions, practical knowledge traditions and integrated knowledge traditions. This categorisation highlights that there is more than one type of knowledge, and more than one way in which it can be acquired. Any attempt to define foundational knowledge that claims to be the truth of what constitutes expert knowledge is challenged by the postmodern plural, fluid and contingent nature of knowledge. As previously outlined, we are dealing with a multidimensional and complex set of competences and professional expectations that cannot be simplified in one framework, or that such framework would apply to all educational contexts. Therefore, knowledges (in the plural) are perhaps a more apt and nuanced construct to conceptualise expertise in teaching. For Dall'alba and Barnacle (2007, p. 680), knowledges are to be understood as "socially constructed in relation to specific knowledge interests".

In the case of teacher education, participants are welcomed to accreditation programmes on the assumption that they already possess a strong subject knowledge. Such knowledge is usually acquired through scholarly, practical or combined experiences. For example, the 'academic knowledge' normally comes from qualifications and engagement in research, whereas 'practical knowledge' involves experience in a field of practice. Academic credentials are important; however, divisions of academic versus non-academic knowledge are unhelpful for a conceptualisation of what constitutes expert knowledge. As Grundmann (2017, p. 25) explains, one crucial element of all expertise is its role in "guiding action". This is particularly relevant for practitioners from non-academic backgrounds entering the profession, as they may bring the equally important 'know-how' that comes from practical experience.

This has significant implications for a conceptualisation of expertise that recognises that content knowledge is necessarily diverse in the ways in which it is acquired. Most programmes in higher education rarely deal with pure forms of knowledge, distant from practical use in real-life environments. A strong knowledge syntax for educational practice must consider both: knowledge *of* education and knowledge *for* education.

Pedagogical knowledge

Apart from content knowledge, educators need to demonstrate expertise "in teaching and learning" (ETF, 2014, p. 1), extended to aspects of planning, teaching/supporting learning, assessment and feedback, developing effective learning environments, and engagement with continuous professional development in subject/disciplines, pedagogy, research, scholarship and the evaluation of professional practices (UKPSF, 2011, p. 6). For a simplified conceptualisation of pedagogical knowledge, Shulman (1987, p. 8) referred to it as the "tools of the trade". This requires a combination of theoretical understandings as well as practical skills that constitute the foundational "practice architecture" of teacher education (Kemmis & Smith, 2008, p. 10). Theory is explored, for example, through the study of theories of learning and assessment, models of curriculum, research methodology, policy analysis and so on. Teaching practice is a key component for accreditation in teaching education programmes, where pre-service candidates engage in practicums (teaching placements) while in-service practitioners use their lecturing (or otherwise) roles to develop their pedagogical knowledge.

Many teacher education programmes form a triad between a tutor, a mentor and a student teacher for the development of pedagogical knowledge. Tutors support aspects of pedagogical theory, while mentors act as the *in situ* more-knowledgeable-other that supports their protégé (Barnett, 1995) in their practicums. Kemmis and Smith (2008, p. 31) argue that practicums are crucial as "a vehicle for a student teacher to move from inexperience to experience, under the supervision of practising teachers (who may or may not be good models either as teachers or as educators)", whereas Furlong and Whitty (2017, p. 41) conceptualise them as pivotal spaces for 'on-the-job' training. The roles of classroom experience and exposure to a range of pedagogical approaches when engaging in work-based learning are significant factors for educators' pedagogical knowledge development. Importantly, although teacher educators and mentors may model pedagogy as part of professional learning for a student teacher, central to their development of pedagogical knowledge is personal engagement and commitment to reflect on their experiences. The classroom, in its many forms, could be conceptualised as a research space for pedagogical knowledge development.

In terms of the curriculum, owing to the vast array of disciplines that make up higher education, the use of generic teacher education programmes is common. In line with Furlong and Whitty's (2017) categorisation of 'practical knowledge', the use of generic standards and competences focussing on practical skills implies an operative and instrumentalist function of teacher education. Although generic aspects of pedagogy are necessary and useful, the effectiveness of transmission models of knowledge and skills can be questionable (Dall'alba & Barnacle, 2007). It is perhaps ambitious to claim that having strong content knowledge and awareness of generic pedagogical knowledge and skills is enough to develop expertise, as generics are "produced by a functional analysis of what is taken to be the underlying features necessary to the performance of a skill, task, practice or even area of work" (Hordern, 2017, p. 197).

A main concern here is that 'generic modes' of pedagogical knowledge facilitate the shift "from professional education to professional training" (Hordern, 2017, p. 48). This instrumentalist view of teacher education threatens the development of a strong syntax of disciplinary knowledge, which, according to Hordern (2018), allows governments and policymakers to manipulate such knowledge for their own economic or political purposes. The use of the word training to describe the professional formation of educators brings a reductionist view of what it is otherwise a complex and sophisticated practice, and, thus, the use of the term teacher education, rather than teacher training, has been deliberate here. A critical approach is needed to recognise that knowledge and skills that are considered "attributes that can be decontextualised from the practices to which they relate" (Dall'alba & Barnacle, 2007, p. 680) do not guarantee the development of pedagogical content knowledge. Thus, critical reflection takes a favourable place as an essential skill for educators to effectively translate their subject expertise into "forms that are pedagogically powerful" (Shulman, 1987, p. 15) for learners.

Pedagogical content knowledge

We return here to the practical function of reflection to make sense of educational experiences, articulate our understanding of situations and inform our future from the learning of such experiences. The role of pedagogical experience is an essential condition for the development of expertise in teaching. The onus is on learning from the experience, on metacognition, also defined as learning to learn, "from one's own experience as much as, if not more than, from relevant books, ideas, colleagues and others" (Kemmis & Smith, 2008, p. 33). This supports the notion of expertise where practitioners can demonstrate *knowing-in-action* (Schön, 1983) by using their experience to make decisions while considering the circumstances and potential effects at play. Knowing-in-action departs from generic modes of understanding and moves towards internalised processes where the knowledge, tacit or otherwise, is "measured rather than impulsive" (Rodgers, 2002, p. 864) and aims to benefit the students ultimately. Shulman (1987) explains that at the intersection between content and pedagogy lies an act of interpretation and translation. A knowledgeable subject specialist is not enough for effective teaching and learning. Hence, these two notions can help us to illustrate the nuances that are necessary for the effective communication of content (teaching) and the impact that such information has on the audience (learning). Carter (2018) characterised teaching excellence as the balance of inputs and outputs – that is, teachers' expertise and their methods to communicate it (input), as well as the impact that these have on students' learning (outputs).

Central to teaching are processes of "communication and interaction" (Biesta, 2018, p. 19). However, Eisner (2002, p. 382) brings a more elegant notion of pedagogical content knowledge as *artistry*, a term apt to describe the nuanced thinking and doing of an expert educator who uses "sensibility, imagination, technique, and the ability to make judgements about the feel and significance of the particular" to make learning an *"aesthetic experience"* (emphasis added). According to Eisner (2002, p. 383), when a lesson goes well "we call it aesthetic. There is a sense of pride in craft". Learning is an aesthetic experience for learners when their senses are fully alive, when the topics excite them, and the manner of the teacher, their passion for the subject matter and the pedagogies employed result in productive learning (in the widest sense; we must be careful with instrumentalist outcomes-based metrics of learning).

If we consider learning, and not just teaching, as central to the role of an educator, any display of artistry must consider the complex mesh of factors at play. Artistry does not mean that all lessons are melodic; some require improvisation very much like playing in a jazz band, while some others require difficult compromises when competing ends leave educators in dilemmatic situations. Educators truly are the glue that bonds individual learners' needs and curricular, organisational and wider stakeholders' expectations. The conditions in which educators practice their profession can be defined as "a swampy lowland where situations are confusing 'messes' incapable of technical solution" (Schön, 1983, p. 42). To deal with such complexity, educators become lifelong learners – for example, by keeping up to date with developments in their subject area and innovations in pedagogy, technology, educational research, policy and theories of learning, which must also be considered a professional expectation of expert teachers. I argue that reflection is critical when it engages with more than one perspective, in that our thoughts and feelings are a fundamental place to start with, but they can be limited: engaging with additional perspectives is fundamental to make sense of our experience. Two examples are explored below to illustrate.

Two examples of critical reflection for professional learning

The first example of a pedagogically powerful teaching and learning strategy that supports expertise development in teacher education programmes is the use of the "loop input" (Woodward, 2003). The loop input is a form of experiential learning that uses the interplay of *content* (what it is to be learnt) and *process* (how it is to be learnt) to develop pedagogical content knowledge through analyses and critical reflections about the experience of learning. The process is akin to Kolb's (1984) experiential learning cycle; the following illustrates its key stages (Figure 2.1):

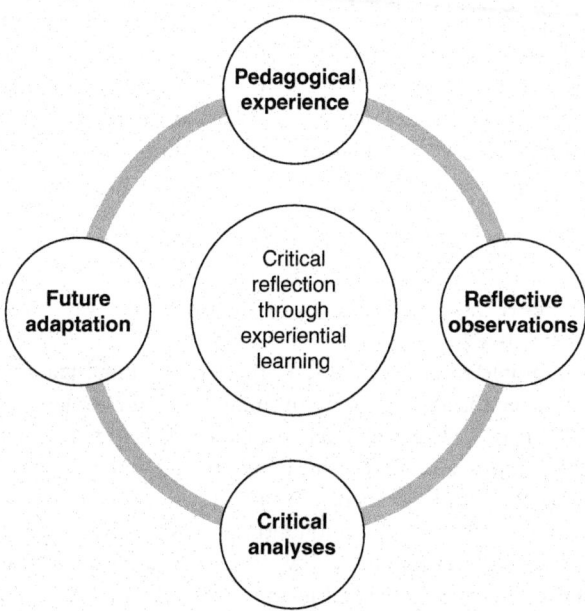

Figure 2.1 Critical reflection and experiential learning

1   Pedagogical experience: teacher educators plan activities and resources for student teachers to experience as learners (initial engagement through their student identity).
2   Reflective observation: student teachers take part in activities, observe the pedagogical process – for example, on the task set-up – and reflect on the steps followed (individual reflection of the contents and process of the activity).
3   Critical analyses: student teachers analyse and evaluate their experience, individually and collectively, to make sense of the pedagogical process (sense-making processes through perspectives: own, peers/colleagues, theory/research).
4   Future application: student teachers switch their student persona to the teacher one. They reflect on ways to adapt or adopt the pedagogies experienced in their own classroom, subject areas or groups of students (new insights of pedagogical content knowledge have been formed; the next stage would be to test such in their own classrooms).

A worked example: rather than telling student teachers that some research found that the use of recorded audio feedback is received favourably by students as they find it "clear, detailed and personal" (Voelkel & Mello, 2014, p. 16), a teacher educator can plan a series of steps to implement a loop input approach. They record and share personalised audio feedback files with student teachers – for example, about their last assignment. As part of the task instruction, students are asked to reflect on the content of the feedback received, as well as the process followed to obtain it (practical considerations, such as devices needed to record audio files, ways to share them and specific task instructions to engage with it). Students are also given a copy of the paper to be read in preparation for a session during which the personal experiences of receiving audio feedback can be discussed and analysed against the research. Once the contextualisation of theory and practice happens, they can explore ways to implement it with their own groups of students. The loop input approach prompts educators to make sense of their experience by using perspectives in their analyses (own, peers, research) to develop new insights of pedagogical content knowledge from a lived experience. The process iterates between student and teacher identity; in a way, an expert teacher needs to be an effective learner too.

The second example of applied critical reflection in initial teacher education is the use of dialogic feedback to facilitate meaning-making after lesson observations. Carless et al. (2011, p. 397) defined dialogic feedback as the "interactive exchange in which interpretations are shared, meanings negotiated and expectations clarified". In this scenario, student teachers plan and deliver sessions and are observed by tutors and mentors as part of accreditation processes, and feedback sessions are factored in to discuss the experience. However, peer-based models of observations that involve reflection for professional learning extend to educators at all levels of their career (Cosh, 1998; O'Leary, 2020). Based on Rodgers's (2002) characterisation of reflection, I have devised the following model of critical reflection as a dialogic process (Figure 2.2):

Critical reflection as a tool 37

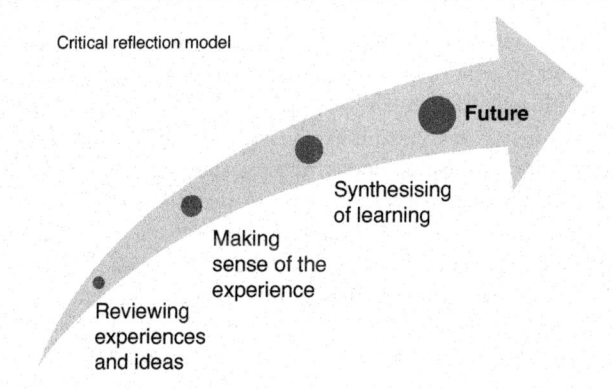

Figure 2.2 Critical reflection model

1   Review of experience and ideas: after a lesson observation, student teachers are prompted to explain how the lesson went regarding the plan, how effective their strategies were, and whether they would do anything differently and why. Here, students' reflection shows levels of self-awareness and emerging criticality – for example, when they can articulate how their plan had to be changed to meet unexpected circumstances (reflection-in-action: Schön, 1983). A critically reflective practitioner can demonstrate here strong levels of agency, understanding of pedagogical content knowledge and confidence in their decisions.
2   Sense-making: here the observer can debrief and explain what they observed and what they identified as strengths and areas for development. Through an engagement with dialogue, the process departs from looking at the past (feeding back) to a deeper engagement with what, why and how the events observed occurred. Observations are a valuable phenomenological approach to research and record lived experience (Bold & Chambers, 2009). There are opportunities here to contextualise theory and research, which makes the process critical, in that various perspectives are considered to make sense of the experience (teacher, observer and literature, in this case). At the intersection of these perspectives, we can find valuable new insights into pedagogical content knowledge; once students identify them, and nurture them, they are on a journey towards expertise. However, as Gibbs (2015) reminds us, students do not always learn from experience. We need others to help us elucidate learning from our experience. The process of critical reflection is very much a collective endeavour.
3   Synthesis of learning: a useful conclusion of a dialogic process is the articulation of the new realisations from the perspectives explored and how these will inform future work. This stage of the process invites synthesis, although, as multiple perspectives have been explored, aspects of problem-setting are

salient here, for which there might not be easy and straightforward solutions (we might end up with more questions than answers, and that is an invaluable position to critically interrogate our practice). As Edwards and Usher (1994, p. 180) remind us, "the meanings through which experience is interpreted, being so dependent on signifying structures and processes, thus have a fluidity which leaves experience constantly open to reassessment".

4   Future practice: the process is futures-oriented. Students are expected to further reflect on, articulate and record key learning points from the experience. Action planning is prompted here to invite an active engagement with areas of practice that could be further improved, which is a key characteristic of a reflective practitioner (Brookfield, 2017; Rodgers, 2002).

These two examples illustrate how critical reflection has a place to develop metacognition and construct meanings with others through dialogue. An expert educator engages in critical reflection, individually and collectively, to understand and improve their practice. This extends to equipping their students with the analytical and critical tools for decision-making; thus, learning about contents (subject matter), as well as ways and processes of learning (pedagogies), can result in core skills for learning as a lifelong process. Reflection here is critical in that it uses various perspectives to make sense of experience. However, a second notion of criticality brings a moral dimension of decision-making, which will be explored in the next section.

The normative dimension of critical reflection: values and contextual factors for expertise in teaching

In the same way that I have argued that critical reflection supports the development of pedagogical content knowledge, we must also look to engage with the personal and collective values (ethics and morals), as well as the contextual factors, that enable and/or hinder expertise development. Education as a field of practice is characterised by "uniqueness, uncertainty and value-conflict, which cannot be dealt with by the application of routinisable and pre-specifiable procedures and strategies" (Schön, 1983, in McLaughlin, 1999, p. 14). As Edwards and Usher (1994, p. 3) argue, education is "the site of conflict and part of the stakes in that conflict", and such conflict is shared by both dilemmas and problems. In the previous section, we explored problems and problem-setting; however, dilemmas are "far messier, less structured, and often intractable to routine solutions" (Cuban, 1992, p. 6). Dilemmas involve choices, often moral ones that result in "good enough compromises, not best solutions" (Cuban, 1992, p. 7). I propose that *ethical decision-making* should be considered a key professional expectation for a characterisation of teaching expertise.

I also suggest that teacher education has an important role to play here to extend critical reflection beyond its practical application for pedagogic content knowledge. A normative dimension is needed to develop agency and be prepared to navigate conflict and complexity, as educators normally find themselves "between a hard place and a hard place" (Davies & Heyward, 2019, p. 372) when confronted with ethical dilemmas. Teacher education is not about indoctrination or training to behave in prescribed ways but training to use critical pedagogy to educate the educator (Biesta, 2005). A normative perspective of critical reflection invites a "sustained and intentional process of identifying and checking the accuracy and validity of our teaching assumptions" (Brookfield, 2017, p. 3). Experience is very important for conceptualisations of expertise; however, "experience that's not subject to critical analysis" can be "unreliable and sometimes dangerous" (Brookfield, 2017, p. 25).

Kemmis and Smith (2008, p. 3) state that "education and being an educator are inextricably linked to social and moral responsibility". However, it is important to acknowledge that the tensions caused by stakeholders' expectations in higher education are not just rare and unique circumstances of conflict; the "ever-presence" of dilemmas clearly makes education a "dilemmatic space" (Fransson & Grannäs, 2013). An expert educator must be empowered and supported to deal with "messy but crucially important problems" (Schön, 1983, p. 43). Ethical decision-making must be guided through critical thinking, critical reflection and critical action. However, for this to happen, educators need to start by finding a voice to formulate the issues in their practice (problem-setting and problem-posing), with a view to making sense of the issues (critical reflection) and taking the appropriate, though sometimes compromised, ethical action.

The role of language is important here to articulate issues, although, as Schön (1983, p. 55) explains, those working in the "swampy lowlands" involve themselves in "messy but crucially important problems and, when asked to describe their methods of inquiry, they speak of experience, trial and error, intuition, and muddling through". This reminds us that problem-solving does not follow the application of formulaic solutions; instead, an expert approach to problem-solving is to step back and consider the nature of the problem first (King, Chapter 1, this volume). An expert educator must develop a disposition to work collaboratively with others in the working out of ways to deal with dilemmas. Ehrich et al.'s (2011, p. 2) research on ethical dilemmas offers additional strategies to support educators, which include "sharing dilemmas with trusted others", "having institutional structures in schools that lessen the emergence of harmful actions occurring" and "the necessity for individual teachers to articulate their own personal and professional ethics". The key message here is that language plays an important part in developing human agency, even when our thinking is "tacit and unexamined" (McLaughlin, 1999, p. 12). This is especially important for educators working in higher education, a field full of competing forces, which makes criticality an essential skill for expert educators to "live with, live by, interpret, extend and sometimes creatively trouble or avoid the rules of organisations" (Kemmis & Smith, 2008, p. 5).

Neoliberal agendas compromise educators' professional values. Kinsella and Pitman (2012, p. 8) express a concern: "as the mechanisms of professionalisation have been put in place, so too have the levels of prescription increased, thereby circumscribing the capacity of members to act autonomously in situations that demand the exercise of judgement". We need to consider the increasingly instrumentalised function of education, aided by the fragmentation of the university, its hyper-specialisation and a focus on knowledge rather than learning (Dall'alba & Barnacle, 2007, p. 679). Teacher education is perceived by many policymakers as an exercise of 'training', which brings a reductionist view of educators as actors who disseminate materials and reproduce received training through top–down systems (Hibbert, 2012, in Kinsella & Pitman, 2012, p. 5).

This is where the Aristotelian notions of *phronesis* and *praxis* bring ethical and moral dimensions to the professional values and attributes expected of educators in higher education. Kinsella and Pitman (2012, p. 9) explain that, "in the context of professional practice, phronesis might be oriented slightly more toward morally committed thought, whereas praxis might be oriented slightly more toward morally committed action, but the lines between the two appear uncertain". Kemmis and Smith (2008, p. 4) consider praxis as "a kind of enlightened and 'elevated' action", also asserting that "praxis is the doing" whereas "phronesis is the disposition towards acting rightly" (p. 9). This resonates with Carr's (1995, p. 71) notion of phronesis as a "comprehensive moral capacity which combines practical knowledge of the good with sound judgement about what, in a particular situation, would constitute an appropriate expression of this". I argue that a conceptualisation of expertise in teaching must include both the internal disposition to act ethically and an ability to critically evaluate the impact of our actions by questioning "in whose interests are we acting?" (Kemmis and Smith 2008, p. 3) when trying to decide what is the right thing to do in complex situations. This means that, beyond having ethical awareness, we must also act ethically.

To summarise, we must consider the moral dimension of critical reflection as a core expectation for a characterisation of expertise in teaching. Education as a field of practice is complex and inextricably linked to ever-present dilemmas that require sound reasoning and that cannot be solved through prescribed solutions. Thus, I argue that a characterisation of expertise in teaching in higher education must conceptualise educators as *ethical decision-makers.*

Conclusion

Central to my argument in this chapter is the conceptualisation of expertise as a multidimensional, complex and sophisticated process that requires a careful balance of knowledges, skills and practices. Reflection, as a futures-oriented process that aims to improve our educational practice, encourages a critical examination of our experiences and ideas. Given that educators operate in "the domain of the variable, not the domain of the eternal" (Biesta, 2018, p. 19), a characterisation of educators' expertise must consider critical reflection as a core skill and a commitment to constantly engage with the evaluation and analysis of our experiences. Making sense of our experience requires a disposition to welcome alternative perspectives, engage with theory and involve others to allow the generation of new insights. An expert educator should be able to articulate the learning from their experiences and inform their future from such learning.

By exploring Shulman's (1987) knowledges typology – (a) content, (b) pedagogical and (c) pedagogical content knowledge – I placed critical reflection as a useful tool to make sense of how experiencing processes of learning (pedagogy) can help us to develop our repertoire of teaching strategies to *translate* our content knowledge (subject expertise) into forms that are pedagogically powerful. The examples given on experiential learning and dialogic feedback illustrate the need to engage with others and their perspectives. Critical reflection is a collective endeavour.

Finally, the normative dimension of critical reflection reminds us that our educational practice is 'messy' and dilemmatic by nature. Thus, an expert educator must adopt a critical stance to engage with ethical decision-making at all times. This also includes questioning "what works" type of research (Hayes & Doherty, 2017, p. 128) that claims to have answers for a practice that is inherently 'messy'. Expertise goes beyond the "technical rationality" that Schön (1983, p. 21) defined as "instrumental problem solving made rigorous by the application of scientific theory and technique", inherited from a "positivist epistemology of practice" (Schön, 1983, p. 31). A critical educator would question notions of professional practice aligned to the relationship of means to ends, because, as Cuban (1992, p. 6) remind us, when technical rationality is "laid over a messy social or educational problem, it seldom fits". The notion of *phronesis*, as our disposition to think ethically, and *praxis*, as our moral decision-making, places critical reflection as an essential quality for a characterisation of expertise in teaching in higher education.

References

Ball, S.J. (2016) Neoliberal education? Confronting the slouching beast. *Policy Futures in Education*, 14(8), 1046–1059 doi:10.1177/1478210316664259

Barnett, B.G. (1995) Developing reflection and expertise: can mentors make the difference? *Journal of Educational Administration*, 33(5), 45–59. doi:10.1108/09578239510098527

Belvis, E., Pineda, P., Armengol, C. & Moreno, V. (2013) Evaluation of reflective practice in teacher education. *European Journal of Teacher Education*, 36(3), 279–292.

Biesta, G.J.J. (2005) What can critical pedagogy learn from postmodernism? Further reflections on the impossible future of critical pedagogy. In: Gur-Ze'ev, I. (Ed.) *Critical Theory and Critical Pedagogy Today: Toward a New Critical Language in Education*. University of Haifa, Haifa, 143–159.

Biesta, G.J.J. (2018) Teaching's about communication and interaction, so it can't be a science. *InTuition*, 33, 18.

Bold, C. & Chambers, P. (2009) Reflecting meaningfully, reflecting differently. *Reflective Practice*, 10(1), 13–26. doi:10.1080/14623940802652680

Brookfield, S. (2017) *Becoming a Critically Reflective Teacher*. Jossey-Bass, San Francisco, CA.

Carless, D., Salter, D., Yang, M. & Lam, J. (2011) Developing sustainable feedback practices. *Studies in Higher Education*, 36(4), 395–407. doi:10.1080/03075071003642449

Carr, W. (1995) *For Education: Towards Critical Educational Inquiry*. Open University Press, Buckingham.

Carter, D. (2018) Teaching Excellence in Its Global Context. Higher Education Academy. www.heacademy.ac.uk/blog/teaching-excellence-its-global-context [accessed 01/03/2021].

Cosh, J. (1998) Peer observation in higher education – a reflective approach. *Innovations in Education and Training International*, 35(2), 171–176. doi:10.1080/1355800980350211

Cuban, L. (1992) Managing dilemmas while building professional communities. *Educational Researcher*, 21(1), 4–11. doi:10.2307/1176344

Dall'Alba, G. & Barnacle, R. (2007) An ontological turn for higher education. *Studies in Higher Education*, 32(6), 679–691. doi:10.1080/03075070701685130

Davies, M. & Heyward, P. (2019) Between a hard place and a hard place: a study of ethical dilemmas experienced by student teachers while on practicum. *British Educational Research Journal*, 45(2), 372–387. doi:10.1002/berj.3505

Dewey, J. (1933) Analysis of reflective thinking. In: *How We Think: A Restatement of the Relation of Reflective Thinking to the Educative Process*. Houghton Mifflin, Boston, 102–118.

Education & Training Foundation (ETF). (2014) Professional Standards for Teachers and Trainers in Education and Training. Education and Training Foundation. www.et-foundation.co.uk/wp-content/uploads/2014/05/ETF_Professional_Standards_Digital_FINAL.pdf [accessed 01/03/2021]

Edwards, R. & Usher, R. (1994) *Postmodernism and Education Different Voices, Different Worlds*. Routledge, Abingdon.

Ehrich, L.C., Kimber, M., Millwater, J. & Cranston, N. (2011) Ethical dilemmas: a model to understand teacher practice. *Teachers and Teaching*, 17(2), 173–185. doi:10.1080/13540602.2011.539794

Eisner, E.W. (2002) From episteme to phronesis to artistry in the study and improvement of teaching. *Teaching and Teacher Education*, 18(4), 375–385. doi:10.1016/s0742-051x(02)00004-5

Fransson, G. & Grannäs, J. (2013) Dilemmatic spaces in educational contexts – towards a conceptual framework for dilemmas in teachers work. *Teachers and Teaching*, 19(1), 4–17. doi:10.1080/13540602.2013.744195

Furlong, J. & Whitty, G. (2017) Knowledge traditions in the study of education. In: Furlong, J. & Whitty, G. (Eds.), *Knowledge and the Study of Education: An International Exploration*. Symposium Books, Oxford, 13–57.

Gibbs, G. (2015) 53 Powerful ideas all teachers should know about. Students don't always learn from experience. www.seda.ac.uk/resources/files/publications_182_32%20Students%20don [accessed 01/03/2021]

Grundmann, R. (2017) The problem of expertise in knowledge societies. *Minerva*, 55(1), 25–48. doi:10.1007/s11024-016-9308-7

Hager, P., Lee, A. & Reich, A. (2012) Problematising practice, reconceptualising learning and imagining change. In: Hager, P., Lee, A. & Reich, A. (Eds.) *Practice, Learning and Change: Practice-Theory Perspectives on Professional Learning*. Springer, Dordrecht, 1–14. doi:10.1007/978-94-007-4774-6_1.

Hatton, N. & Smith, D. (1995) Reflection in teacher education: towards definition and implementation. *Teaching and Teacher Education*, 11(1), 33–49. doi:10.1016/0742-051x(94)00012-u

Hayes, D. & Doherty, C. (2017) Valuing epistemic diversity in educational research: an agenda for improving research impact and initial teacher education. *The Australian Educational Researcher*, 44(2), 123–139. doi:10.1007/s13384-016-0224-5

Hordern, J. (2017) Bernstein's sociology of knowledge and education(al) studies. In: Furlong, J. & Whitty, G. (Eds.) *Knowledge and the Study of Education: An International Exploration*. Symposium Books, Oxford, 13–57.

Hordern, J. (2018) Is powerful educational knowledge possible? *Cambridge Journal of Education*, 48(6), 787–802. doi:10.1080/0305764x.2018.1427218

Kemmis, S. (2005) Knowing practice: searching for saliences. *Pedagogy, Culture & Society*, 13(3), 391–426. doi:10.1080/14681360500200235

Kemmis, S. & Smith, T. (Eds.) (2008) *Enabling Praxis: Challenges for Education*. Sense, Rotterdam.

Kinsella, E. & Pitman, A. (2012) Engaging phronesis in professional practice and education. In: Kinsella, E. & Pitman, A. (Eds.) *Phronesis as Professional Knowledge*. Sense, Rotterdam, 1–11. doi:10.1007/978-94-6091-731-8_1

Kolb, D.A. (1984) *Experiential Learning: Experience as the Source of Learning and Development*. Prentice-Hall, London.

McLaughlin, T.H. (1999) Beyond the reflective teacher. *Educational Philosophy and Theory*, 31(1), 9–25. doi:10.1111/j.1469-5812.1999.tb00371.x

O'Leary, M. (2020) *Classroom Observation: A Guide to the Effective Observation of Teaching and Learning*. Routledge, New York. doi:10.4324/9781315630243

Rodgers, C. (2002) Defining reflection: another look at John Dewey and reflective thinking. *Teachers College Record*, 104(4), 842–866. doi:10.1111/1467-9620.00181

Schön, D.A. (1983) *The Reflective Practitioner: How Professionals Think in Action*. Arena, Ashgate, UK.

Shulman, L. (1987) Knowledge and teaching: foundations of the new reform. *Harvard Educational Review*, 57(1), 1–23.

UKPSF. (2011) UK Professional Standards Framework for Teaching & Support Learning in Higher Education. www.advance-he.ac.uk/knowledge-hub/uk-professional-standards-framework-ukpsf [accessed 01/03/2021].

Voelkel, S. & Mello, L.V. (2014) Audio feedback – better feedback? *Bioscience Education*, 22(1), 16–30. doi:10.11120/beej.2014.00022

Woodward, T. (2003) Loop input. *ELT Journal*, 57(3), 301–304. doi:10.1093/elt/57.3.301

Chapter 3

Zhuangzi and the phenomenology of expertise

Implications for educators

Charlie Reis

This chapter will give a close reading of a short passage from Zhuangzi in order to explore how a text from the Warring States period of Chinese history can inform the contemporary discussion about expertise, specifically as embodied in teaching in higher education. In this case, the activity is revisiting an ancient text from an intellectual tradition not usually considered in Western thinking about learning and teaching to see how we might increase the depth and breadth of our toolkit in approaching staff development as curators of pedagogical environments, in short, what expertise looks like and feels like.

King (Chapter 1, this volume) offers a model of expertise for teaching in higher education, aligned to generic characteristics of expertise, as the interaction of pedagogic content knowledge (Shulman, 1986), artistry of teaching and intentional learning and development, with this latter being defined as, "A self-determined and purposeful process of evolution of teaching and learning approaches informed by evidence gathered from a range of activities" (King, 2019b). This determined and purposeful evolution takes shape from the topoi of practice, any practice, within which expertise is developed, informed by overlapping themes: deliberate practice (Ericsson et al., 1993), progressive problem solving (Bereiter & Scardamalia, 1993), the reflective practitioner (Schön, 1982) and a process of self-determined and purposeful proactive competence (Perkins, 2008; King, 2019a).

Zhuangzi is a Daoist philosopher who lived in the 4th century BCE, wrote much about expert practice and is known for his 'knack passages' in which people display or describe incredible levels of skill in different areas of activity (Needham, 1956, p. 121; Moeller & D'Ambrosio, 2017, p. 151). These knack passages are clearly models of expertise in one way or another, but, unlike some contemporary models, they take the form of a reflective account of the changes in practice and the phenomenology of doing.

Butcher Ding is a famous allegory and the best known of the knack passages in Chapter 3 of *The Zhuangzi*, entitled "Primacy of Nourishing Life", which Hansen (2014, p. 22) calls the "most beautifully and elaborately expressed" example of skilful practice in Zhuangzi. Moeller (2020) calls the Butcher Ding passage "The Mother of all Knack Passages".

DOI: 10.4324/9781003198772-5

Note that the title of the chapter and the translation used are from Ziporyn's 2009 translation, which will be presented sequentially with the development of the argument within this chapter.

Wu wei, skill and expertise

Wu wei could be the Daoist philosophical articulation of 'knack' as it encapsulates spontaneity or effortlessness. It is a fundamental concept of Daoism and early Chinese thinking that underlies skilled practice. It is translated in various ways, all of which are useful for thinking about learning and teaching:

- Doing nothing (Graham, 1989);
- Non-action (Chan, 1963);
- Non-doing, inaction (Everest-Philips, 2015);
- Purposeful inaction (Moon, 2015);
- Non-interference (Kirkland, 2001);
- Non-purposive action (Schwartz, 1985);
- 'Non-doing', the absence of deliberate activity (Ziporyn, 2009, note 15);
- Effortless action, perfected action, acting without acting, acting without purpose, no doing/effort/exertion, no-self (Slingerland, 2000);
- Non-deliberative doing (Chai, 2014b);
- Working to align with the will of the way (Tadd, 2019);
- Action that is in tune with the spontaneous tendencies of things, minimizes interference and artifice, remains sensitive to the unfolding of circumstances, and thereby enables us to live harmoniously and to our fullest natural potential (Coutinho, 2015).

> "*Wu wei*" refers not to what is or is not being done but to the phenomenological state of the doer. As Pang Pu notes in his discussion of *wu wei*, the term denotes "not a basic form of action, but the mental state of the actor – the spiritual state (*jingshen zhuangtai*) that obtains at the very moment of action" (1994: 15).
> (Slingerland, 2000, p. 7)

For the purposes of examining 'the new science of expertise' through the lens of an ancient Daoist text, *wu wei* can be thought of as the embodiment of expertise or the ability to act unconsciously in its most heightened form, the embodiment of expertise. This is different from uses of *wu wei* in other contexts, and this chapter in no way intends to suggest that this is the definitive word on the term. Here is the opening of Ziporyn's (2009, p. 22) translation of the Butcher Ding passage:

> The cook was carving up an ox for King Hui of Liang. Whenever his hand smacked it, whenever his shoulder leaned into it, whenever his foot braced it, the thwacking tones of flesh falling from bone would echo, the knife would whiz through with its resonant thwing, each stroke ringing out the perfect

> note, attuned to the "Dance of the Mulberry Grove" or the "Jingshou Chorus" of the ancient sage-kings.
> The king said, "Ah! It is wonderful that skill can reach such heights."

This is an incredibly odd passage to find in a philosophy text because it is cartoonish, complete with sound effects, and very physical. Also, it immediately gives a sense of the dismemberment of an animal that is the practice of butchery. Watson notes, "the Mulberry Grove is identified as a rain dance from the time of King Tang of the Shang dynasty, and the Jingshou music as part of a longer composition from the time of Yao," (Slingerland, 2000, note 60, p. 319), and so the context of this activity is both sacred and public. Focus on skill here happens in a very Zhuangzian way, through one of the most disgusting jobs imaginable, for he typically uses the grotesque to illustrate his ideas.

A phenomenology of acquiring expertise

> The cook put down his knife and said, "What I love is the Course [Dao], something that advances beyond mere skill. When I first started cutting up oxen, all I looked at for three years was oxen, and yet still I was unable to see all there was to see in an ox."
> (Ziporyn, 2009, p. 22)

After the exposition of butchery, we get a discussion of how expertise is embodied. This is not just skilled practice as a result of repeated practice, but "something that advances beyond mere skill". In a sentence, we move from the novice encountering the physical things to deeper seeing, with a sense of hidden depths or more to come. This is an illustration of Schön's (1982) artistry of the reflective practitioner, using supple professional wisdom to navigate practice. This is not only a new sort of intelligence about the field of practice, but as a mental representation and full of potentialities for action, which as we shall see is a hallmark of those with expertise. Sterckx, (2005, p. 12) remarks that "Ding's unhindered gestures of cutting and slicing the ox are guided by a new sort of intelligence that is no longer inspired by the outer shape of the animal". There is progressive engagement at more sophisticated levels as practice continues.

According to Bereiter and Scardamalia's (1993) theory of the development of expertise, experts are those who continually work at the edge of their competence by progressively problem solving, seeing more of the ox in this case. We know from Schön (1982, p. 60) that professional practitioners encounter similar situations again and again, which can become sites for deliberate practice (Stigler & Miller, 2018, pp. 447–448). Ding's articulation of skill continues:

> But now I encounter it with the spirit rather than scrutinising it with the eyes. My understanding consciousness, beholden to its specific purposes, comes to a halt, and thus the promptings of the spirit begin to flow.
> (Ziporyn, 2009, p. 22)

The area of activity is engaged with via something other than physical – in Ziporyn's translation, the spirit rather than the eyes. There is a qualitative shift in the experience of seeing after years of repeated practice. Understanding consciousness, translated by Watson as perception and understanding, have come to a halt as the promptings of the spirit flow. This fits with Bereiter and Scardamalia, who suggest that the ground for progressive problem solving rests on an automation of basic skills and knowledges, thus freeing the mind for deeper exploration.

This view implies that reflection on practice is essential. Ericsson and Smith (1991) point out that "one should be particularly careful about accepting one's number of years of experience as an accurate measure of one's level of expertise" (p. 27), because learning from doing is as important as repeatedly doing. Encountering with the spirit rather than the eyes halts the normal consciousness and sense of purpose of the Butcher Ding, who now flows according to the spirit. In Ding's story, there is a progression of engagement as embodied in new ways of seeing (new ways of thinking and practising) that parallel the progression of time, although we are getting the reflection on practice all at once in Zhuangzi's vignette.

Huberman says "recurring episodes in which the demands of the situation are slightly beyond one's existing repertoire" are crucial for professional development (1993, p. 112). He observed that career satisfaction was high "when teachers felt 'pushed' or 'stretched' beyond their customary activity formats or materials and met this challenge through systematic revisions of their instruction repertoire" (ibid., p. 113). Although there is no indication in Zhuangzi about Ding's career satisfaction, he does remark on satisfaction after the successful dismemberment at the conclusion of the passage, suggesting an impetus towards engagement not only in butchery, but in deliberate practice towards expertise. We can, additionally, see Butcher Ding reflecting on challenging episodes in his practice:

> I depend on heaven's unwrought perforations and strike the larger gaps, following along with the broader hollows. I go by how they already are, playing them as they lay. So my knife has never had to cut through the knotted nodes where the warp hits the weave, much less the gnarled joints of bone.
> (Ziporyn, 2009, p. 22)

The language of heaven's unwrought perforations, larger gaps, following broader hollows, being played as they lay is central to understanding much of Zhuangzi, as it is central to understanding his illustration of expertise. Zhuangzi's is a philosophy of emptiness in that finding and following what is empty, such as 'free and easy wandering' in how to live, but here it is how to do (in butchery). Free and easy wandering is a theme of Zhuangzi's thinking, the traditional title of the first chapter of his work, and held up as the ideal for human activity. Watson, who makes this theme central to his introduction to his translation, translates this passage as "going along with the natural makeup of things" (2003).

There is a rhythm of the practice of Ding, and navigating the innards of an ox with the spirit, being able to foresee knotted nodes and gnarled joints, all signify the use of mental representations and models to engage intuitively in deliberate practice, to use the language of Ericsson and Pool (2016). They write:

> So everyone has and uses mental representations. What sets expert performers apart from everyone else is the quality and quantity of their mental representations. Through years of practice, they develop highly complex and sophisticated representations of the various situations they are likely to encounter in their fields – such as the vast number of arrangements of chess pieces that can appear during games. These representations allow them to make faster, more accurate decisions and respond more quickly and effectively in a given situation. This, more than anything else, explains the difference in performance between novices and experts.
>
> (p. 47)

Although Zhuangzi uses different language to describe the use of mental representations here, there are other passages, notably in Chapter 19, "Fathoming Life", which give several accounts of making accurate decisions under pressures of time that might not be immediately evident through the metaphor of butchery. We shall see later that time is in a sense irrelevant to the adept user of mental models, as they account for a more complete picture of possibility that has assumed change.

Progressing in skill

Butcher Ding gives us a picture of the tools used in practice through a description of the blades of those with various levels of skill in butchery:

> A good cook changes his blade once a year: he slices. An ordinary cook changes his blade once a month: he hacks. I have been using this same blade for nineteen years, cutting up thousands of oxen with it, and yet it is still as sharp as the day it came off the whetstone.
>
> (Ziporyn, 2009, p. 22)

Moving from hacking to slicing shows progressive levels of skill that align imperfectly but sufficiently with Berliner's (1998) writing on the development of expertise in pedagogy, which can perhaps show us where Berliner's categories are too neat or well defined while giving indications for staff development about how the growth of expertise is experienced:

1   The novice who applies ideas without experience where the commonplaces must be discerned – or someone who hacks at a carcass;

2   The advanced beginner who has experience modifying understanding or action, but is not yet responsible for decision-making as they are still getting the lay of the land – or a butcher still seeing more and more in an ox;
3   The competent practitioner who is more fluid and flexible as they can make reliable decisions – a butcher who slices;
4   The proficient practitioner with professional intuition, such as where to change course or speed as things will become difficult;
5   The expert who acts fluidly with tacit knowledge.

It is noteworthy that Zhuangzi's depiction of proficiency leads directly into unconscious expert, as we shall see below; however, as Berliner himself mentions, a person at one stage of development may exhibit characteristics of another stage at times or in specific contexts. Clarke and Hollingsworth (2002, p. 965) explain this, commenting that the personal, non-linear and somewhat idiosyncratic nature (problems faced and progressively solved) of professional development is due to the practice, meaning and context of professional growth. Ding, for example, would not be developing expertise in teaching, by doing so in butchery. According to Benner et al. (1996), "being situated" means neither total determination or constraint according to specific context, nor total freedom to act according to whim or personal desire. Rather, there are "situated possibilities" that allow for progressive problem solving and deliberate practice.

Progressive problem solving and the spaces between

Continuing on why he does not need to sharpen his blade, Butcher Ding comments:

> For the joints all have spaces within them, and the very edge of the blade has no thickness at all. When what has no thickness enters into an empty space, it is vast and open, with more than enough room for the play of the blade. That is why my knife is still as sharp as if it had just come off the whetstone, even after nineteen years.
>
> (Ziporyn, 2009, p. 22)

The centrality of emptiness, of the non-being in being, predicates the play of the blade, the free and easy wandering, here located in the act of butchering an ox, in the ox itself as physical spaces through which the blade can pass, as well as the conditions for the possibility of this. This is a particular area where looking at Zhuangzi can enhance contemporary thinking about expertise. Emptiness is situated possibility if one sees it (mental modelling 'nurtured' through repeated practice to have this level of detail and familiarity with the landscape of practice), which seems to be the result of reflection (Butcher Ding sees with the "Course", not with his eyes, after 19 years of practice).

Chai's (2014a, p. 668) explanation of Butcher Ding's exposition highlights the Daoist nature of seeing the non-being in being, the situated possibilities in the language of expertise. "Indeed, Ding's skill relies on nonbeing in that it uses that which is without (i.e., the edge of the knife's blade) to enter into the nothingness connecting the ox's flesh, joints, and bones." Chai goes on to claim that these spaces are "pillars of nonbeing that prop-up the being of the ox", which is true insofar as bodies need emptiness in order for things like blood to flow. Expertise in ox butchery allows Ding to follow the perforations of heaven in the ox. His butchery is thus far a description of free and easy wandering of experience.

Being able to move through emptiness, having no thickness so that spaces are vast and open, may be true of expert butchers, yet these are also metaphors for skills in a variety of professional practices. Situated possibilities include alternatives for practice. This is quite literally seeing options where before there was a default version of practice. In the context of learning and teaching, this means looking for emptiness, for spaces as not necessarily defined, to create and recreate new ways of thinking and practising: for example, shifting from asking 'Do you understand?' – a rather ineffective way of checking comprehension – to an array of strategies based on student articulation of comprehension. A more sophisticated version might be moving from a standard delivery of content in a lecture to having students negotiate their sense-making of content with peers, such as Mazur's (2014) story of the origins of his peer learning pedagogies.

In terms of the narrative as an exemplar of expertise, never having had to sharpen his knife is problematic. It means Ding started as more than a mediocre or even a good cook, as he has never hacked or sliced and hasn't needed to return to the grindstone, and it does not align well with "not being able to see all there was to see in an ox" when Ding was a novice. However, this could be a feature of a textual corruption, as there is some debate about what is the authentic or original text and what was added later. While growing insight about the innards of an ox points towards the development of expertise, the claims about his blade also represent Ding as already possessing expertise.

The significance of the distinction between developing and possessing expertise is critical, as talent is often portrayed as natural (Kneebone, 2020) or even mystical (Chiu, 2018). Kneebone demonstrates that expertise is the result of years of work, and that the naturalness of practice is an indication of development, a point not necessarily highlighted in classical Chinese knowledge.

I restrain myself as if terrified

Rejoining the narrative, we come to a clustered tangle of Berliner's stages of proficient practitioner and expert:

> Nonetheless, whenever I come to a clustered tangle, realising that it is difficult to do anything about it, I instead restrain myself as if terrified, until my seeing comes to a complete halt. My activity slows, and the blade moves ever so slightly. Then all at once, I find the ox already dismembered at my feet like clumps of soil scattered on the ground. I retract the blade and stand there

gazing at my work all around me, dawdling over it with satisfaction. Then I wipe off the blade and put it away.

(Ziporyn, 2009, p. 23)

We see the slowing of activity and careful attention of the proficient practitioner here, using judgements and models to foresee problem areas, which is common to many studies of expertise (Kneebone, 2020; Ericsson & Pool, 2016). In the Ziporyn translation, the blade does not stop, but slows to a crawl. Restraining oneself as if terrified also may cause us to rethink some of the definitions of *wu wei*, or acting without acting. There is definitely mental activity here, and possibly significant conscious activity. Slingerland reports that the verb used here is the same as used for a congealing liquid, such as freezing water (2000, note 72, p. 319), but he also writes that Ding remains completely relaxed and open to the situation confronting him (Slingerland, 2014), neither of which seem to be the case. What stops is seeing. The enrapturement of the practitioner with practising cuts off at least attention to normal sensory data, and there seems to be a gap in time of reported experience. This is an early description of going into the zone or entering a flow state.

Stopping seeing, with the eyes, and stopping knowing form a description of action where a state of flow is achieved or 'the zone' has been entered. In other parts of *The Zhuangzi*, there is "the fasting of the heart-mind", notably in the other knack passages (e.g. "Woodcarver Qing", Chapter 19), which might be a necessary precondition for effortless action (entering into the cognitive state of *wu wei*). Moreover, in Chapter 4 of *The Zhuangzi*, the character of Confucius comments to Yan Hui, "But the vital energy is an emptiness, a waiting for the presence of beings. The Course [Dao] alone is what gathers in this emptiness. And it is this emptiness that is the fasting of the mind" (Ziporyn, 2009, p. 27) The opposite of the fasting of the heart-mind, and therefore a useful comparison for understanding it, is the understanding consciousness which comes to a halt when Ding's seeing stops. This chapter argues that perceiving without seeing is not so much perceiving without seeing as it is the absence of the perception of seeing. The *wu wei* state of flow that we also call 'being in the zone' comes not from effortless action in this case, but from compete engagement, albeit an engagement complete to the extent that seeing stops. It also does not arise from a meditative state, sitting and forgetting, but from a site of repeated practice.

In the context of Csíkszentmihályi's (1996) notion of flow, Zhuangzi seems to describe a state of flow, which is also Berliner's (1998) description of an expert, someone who acts fluidly, on autopilot or intuitively, and can also move in and out of this state. Additionally, there is no need to elevate a state of flow, of unconscious action, to a transcendent spiritual plane. The description offered by Ding offers no promise of spiritual fulfilment or religious transcendence, as discussed by Barrett (2011). Indeed, Moeller (2020) makes the point that, in a chapter titled "Nourishing Life", Zhuangzi has provided the example of butchery, extinguishing life, to be the medium through which to describe expertise. When the understanding consciousness comes to a halt, when 'seeing' stops, something else is happening – likely a shuffle of mental models for problem solving, following Ericsson and Pool's (2016, p. 45) description of a person with expertise examining strings of mental representations in order to act. However, defining this as such or calling it transcendent is an interpretive step away from the text.

Numerous thinkers have ascribed a transcendent spirituality to this section of the Ding passage. Kwek (2019) call this a clairvoyance, and Chiu (2016) calls Ding a daemonic person as he can "fully release the potential of ... inner spirit". The description in the text definitely describes a retreat of the conscious mind, but not in the face of something with a label. Looking at Zhuangzi's description of the precedents to flow, it seems to align with the very banal activities of repeated practice and progressive problem solving.

The Watson (1968, p. 20) translation is quite different:

> I size up the difficulties, tell myself to watch out and be careful, keep my eyes on what I'm doing, work very slowly, and move the knife with the greatest subtlety, until – flop! the whole thing comes apart like a clod of earth crumbling to the ground. I stand there holding the knife and look all around me, completely satisfied and reluctant to move on, and then I wipe off the knife and put it away.

There is no 'stopping seeing' as in the Ziporyn translation, but a focused looking. Also, the sound effects are back in this version.

Conclusions

The Ding passage concludes:

> The king said, "Wonderful! From hearing the cook's words I have learned how to nourish life!"
>
> (Ziporyn, 2009, p. 23)

This is ridiculous, because a gore- and gall-splattered butcher surrounded by a dismembered ox scattered on the ground is hardly the first image that comes to mind when we think of spiritual edification or how to nourish life. Sterckx (2005), in *Food and Philosophy in Early China*, points out that the business of killing animals and preparing food was quite different from performing official duties, even those involving symbolic feast preparation, so that such a conversation is completely implausible. There is a literary reason Zhuangzi places a king in an abattoir. Moeller (2020, p. 168) points out that the chapter entitled "Nourishing Life" has as a feature its extinguishing:

> The Pao Ding story is certainly informed by the medicinal values of "nourishing life". ... Instead of counterintuitively using the figure of a butcher to

illustrate the art of protecting life, though, it points to the life-threatening and life-extinguishing aspects of the political practice and the ideological frameworks of its time. The narrative is not primarily about a cure, but about diagnosing a pathology and making it evident.

Moeller's position is that the Ding passage is a critique of similar stories about nourishing life and of rulership during the Warring States period, and indeed a critique of the practice of ruling as well.

The *Dao de Jing*, the Laozi text, opens with the remark that the only true Dao is the Dao that cannot be spoken; obviously, Butcher Ding is only too happy to discourse at length about how he sees with the Dao to manifest expertise in butchery. Moeller (2020, p. 170) points out that it "is very rare, if not unique [in *The Zhuangzi*] to see a character confessing at once his being attuned to the Dao". So what are we to make of his claims? Does this mean that all of Ding's words are empty for all purposes? For one thing, Zhuangzi often uses grotesque imagery to make a point, so this could be why the butcher is speaking and not the king. Also, given what hopefully has been shown in this chapter, that Ding's story aligns with the science of expertise shows that there is something to be learned from looking to Zhuangzi to enrich our understanding of expert practice.

We can learn from Zhuangzi's story of Butcher Ding how expertise might be experienced. Additionally, this lends both philosophical validity and cross-cultural resonance to the empirical work currently being done on expertise.

Expertise in teaching contra Ding

Expertise in teaching can be reflected upon by the amount of time spent unconsciously or by the effortlessness of the act of teaching, but this is a canard in terms of the development of practice. For a teacher to embody *wu wei*, they would need to:

- Hyper-focus: from the reading of the Ding passage, it is clear that *wu wei* as expert practice evidenced by unconscious action or effortlessness comes from incredible attention to practice; a total commitment to the specific problem being solved in the process of progressive solving; loss of self as foci is an indicator – "transcendence through total immersion"; in terms of teaching, this could mean being focused not on the teacher or teacher's delivery of content, but on the process of students' learning; while not a new idea, using a Daoist exemplar in which the stakeholder should be the focus of planning and 'execution' for pedagogy reflects the combination of skill and content knowledge in doing so; if King (1993) suggested that educators move from being the sage on the stage to the guide on the side, Zhuangzi can be read as an exemplar of a sage on the side;
- Move freely and easily in spaces of non-being found by seeing more closely: in thinking about progressive problem solving and focus, it is clear that the level

of detail about practice on reflection in and on practice done by one with expertise makes the small vast or sees more emptiness within which to move around; examples of questioning strategies were provided above, but other approaches include seeing possibilities where there was previously only a standard approach, such as incorporating students as partners or allowing them choices in how learning will take place in order to engage with learning as it is happening, rather than from the dictates of the teacher, such as giving a choice between small or large group activity for a task with the same pedagogical goal;

- Use tools that have no thickness; much has been made of Ding's blade, but it is clear that the direction of fit of the tool is towards the problem or area of practice; in the context of teaching, this means both literal teaching tools and technologies as well as concepts that allow us to take different approaches to our work in order to achieve, rather than become enmeshed in process or policy; if a problem with learning is lack of factual knowledge in the learner, the solution might be a different type of knowledge – that is, how to *understand, exemplify, articulate* or *justify* – rather than simply more knowledge of the same type;
- Use mental models to recognise patterns and respond unconsciously-in-action; this is significant as it is a deeper description than reflection-in-action, but otherwise similar to Schön (1982); the practical manifestation of unconscious response to patterns might take the shape of being able to 'read the room' in order to shift channels of learning and teaching when one pathway seems to be about to dry up or lose efficacy, such as switching from technical explanations to examples in order to re-engage students and deepen learning.

The development of expertise is specific to a practitioner's domain of practice and is self-determined and purposeful through an individual's practice (King, 2019a); this chapter is part of a larger project to make professional development more sensible and relevant to academics in a Chinese context, and so it is hoped that local models of engagement and expertise can be found across cultures and contexts.

References

Barrett, N. (2011) Wu wei and flow: comparative reflections on spirituality, transcendence, and skill in the Zhuangzi. *Philosophy East and West*, 61(4), 679–706. doi:10.1353/pew.2011.0051

Benner, P., Tanner, C.A., & Chesla, C.A. (1996). *Expertise in Nursing Practice – Caring, Clinical Judgment and Ethics*. Springer, New York.

Bereiter, C. & Scardamalia, M. (1993) *Surpassing Ourselves: An Enquiry into the Nature and Implications of Expertise*. Open Court, Chicago, IL.

Berliner, D. (1998) *The Development of Expertise in Pedagogy*. ACCAT, Washington, DC.

Chai, D. (2014a) Daoism and Wu 無. *Philosophy Compass*, 9(10), 663–671.

Chai, D. (2014b) *Zhuangzi and the Becoming of Nothingness.* SUNY Press, Albany.
Chan, W.T. (1963) *A Source Book in Chinese Philosophy.* Princeton University Press, Princeton.
Chiu, W.W. (2016) Zhuangzi's idea of "spirit": acting and "thinging things" without self-assertion. *Asian Philosophy*, 26(1), 38–51. doi:10.1080/09552367.2015.1136201
Chiu, W. (2018) Zhuangzi's knowing-how and skepticism. *Philosophy East & West*, 68(4), 1062–1084. doi:10.1353/pew.2018.0097
Clarke, D., & Hollingsworth, H. (2002) Elaborating a model of teacher professional growth. *Teaching & Teacher Education*, 18, 947–967. doi:10.1016/s0742-051x(02)00053-7
Coutinho, S. (2015) Conceptual analysis of the Zhuangzi. In: Liu, X. (Ed.) *Dao Companion to Daoist Philosophy.* Springer, New York, 159–191. doi:10.1007/978-90-481-2927-0_7
Csíkszentmihályi, M. (1996) *Flow: The Psychology of Optimal Experience.* Harper & Row, New York.
Ericsson, A., & Pool, R. (2016) *Peak: Secrets from the New Science of Expertise.* Penguin Random House, New York.
Ericsson, K.A., Krampe, R.Th. & Tesch-Romer, C. (1993) The role of deliberate practice in the acquisition of expert performance. *Psychological Review*, 100(3), 363–406. doi:10.1037/0033-295x.100.3.363
Ericsson, K.A., & Smith, J. (1991) Prospects and limits of the empirical study of expertise: an introduction. In: Ericsson, K.A. & Smith, J. (Eds.) *Towards a General Theory of Expertise: Prospects and Limits.* Cambridge University Press, Cambridge, 1–38.
Everest-Philips, M. (2015) Wu-wei as professional ethos of public service: non-action for the 21st century. *International Journal of Civil Service Reform and Practice*, 5, 11–27.
Graham, A.C. (1989) *Disputers of the Tao.* Open Court, La Salle, IL.
Hansen, C. (2014) Zhuangzi. In: Zalta, E.N. (Ed.) *The Stanford Encyclopedia of Philosophy.* https://plato.stanford.edu/archives/spr2017/entries/zhuangzi/ (accessed 08/10/2020).
Huberman, M. (1993) Steps towards a developmental model of the teaching career. In Kremer-Hayon, L., Vonk, H. & Fessler, R. (Eds.) *Teacher Professional Development: A Multiple Perspective Approach.* Swets & Zeitlinger, Amsterdam, 93–118.
King, A. (1993) Sage on the stage to guide on the side. *College Teaching*, 41(1), 30–35. doi:10.1080/87567555.1993.9926781
King, H. (2019a) Continuing professional development: what do award-winning academics do? *Educational Developments*, 20(2), 1–5.
King, H. (2019b) *Professional Development: Reframing the Paradigm.* SEDA Winter 2019 Conference presentation.
Kirkland, R. (2001) Responsible non-action in a natural world: perspectives from the Neiye, Zhuahgzi, and Dao de jing. In: Girardot, N.J., Miller, J. & Xiaogan, L. (Eds.) *Daoism and Ecology.* Harvard University Press, Cambridge, MA, 238–304.
Kneebone, R. (2020) *Expert: Understanding the Path to Mastery.* Penguin, London.
Kwek, D. (2019) Critique of imperial reason: lessons from the Zhuangzi. *Dao*, 18(3), 411–433. doi:10.1007/s11712-019-09673-4
Mazur, E. (2014) Peer instruction for active learning. *Serious Science.* www.youtube.com/watch?v=Z9orbxoRofI [accessed 05/06/2020]
Moeller, H. (2020) The king's slaughter – or the royal way of nourishing life. *Philosophy East and West*, 70(1), 155–173. doi:10.1353/pew.0.0167

Moeller, H.-G. & D'Ambrosio, P.J. (2017) *Genuine Pretending: On the Philosophy of Zhuangzi*. Columbia University Press, New York.

Moon, S. (2015). Wu Wei (non-action) philosophy and actions: rethinking "actions" in school reform. *Educational Philosophy and Theory*, 47(5), 455–473. doi:10.1080/00131857.2013.879692

Needham, J. (1956) *Science and Civilization in China*, vol. 2. Cambridge University Press, Cambridge.

Perkins, D. (2008) Beyond understanding. In: Land, R., Meyer, J.H.F. & Smith, J. (Eds.) *Threshold Concepts within the Disciplines*. Sense, Rotterdam.

Schön, D. (1982) *The Reflective Practitioner: How Professionals Think in Action*. Routledge, Abingdon.

Schwartz, B.I. (1985) *The World of Thought in Ancient China*. Belknap, Harvard University Press, Cambridge, MA. doi:10.2307/j.ctv1smjt32

Shulman, L. (1986) Those who understand: knowledge growth in teaching. *Educational Researcher*, 15(2), 4–14. doi:10.3102/0013189x015002004

Slingerland, E. (2014) *Trying Not to Try: The Art and Science of Spontaneity*. Crown, New York.

Slingerland, E. (2000) *Effortless Action: Wu-Wei as Conceptual Metaphor and Spiritual Ideal in Early China*. Oxford University Press, New York.

Sterckx, R. (2005) Food and philosophy in early China. In: Sterckx, R. (Ed.) *Of Tripod and Palate: Of Food, Politics, and Religion in Early China*. Palgrave Macmillan, London, 34–61. doi:10.1057/9781403979278_3

Stigler, J.W. & Miller, K.F. (2018) Expertise and expert performance in teaching. In: Ericsson, K.A., Hoffman, R.R., Kozbelt, A. & Williams, A.M. (Eds.) *The Cambridge Handbook of Expertise and Expert Performance* (2nd edn). Cambridge University Press, Cambridge.

Tadd, M. (2019) Ziran: authenticity or authority? *Religions*, 10(3), 207. doi:10.3390/rel10030207

Watson, B. (Trans.) (1968) *The Complete Works of Chaung Tsu*. Columbia University Press, New York.

Watson, B. (Trans.) (2003) *Zhuangzi: Basic Writings*. Columbia University Press, New York.

Ziporyn, B. (Trans.) (2009) *Zhuangzi: The Essential Writings with Selections from Traditional Commentaries*. Hackett, Indianapolis.

Chapter 4

A whole-university approach to building expertise in higher education teaching

Deanne Gannaway

Are you sitting comfortably? Then I'll begin

I've shamelessly appropriated this storytelling trope as a way of starting, because I've adopted a narrative style for this chapter. Rather than a more traditional academic paper, I have adopted "storying" (after Phillips & Bunda, 2018) as a means to share how we have come to support teachers at the University of Queensland in Brisbane, Australia, in writing their own stories about how they have developed, and continue to develop, expertise in teaching and learning. This narrative captures how we worked to cultivate a deeper understanding of teaching expertise, a process co-created in partnership with embellishments and enhancements to develop expertise in university teaching across time and in a guided manner that is individualised and adaptable to individual experiences and needs.

Of course, to anyone who didn't grow up in an anglophone country within the earshot of BBC radio at some point between the 1950s and 1980s, the opening title is probably somewhat unintelligible. These words are meaningless if you aren't aware that they were used to begin a daily storytelling radio show, called *Listen with Mother*, designed for children and mothers. Perhaps, if you aren't familiar with this trope, these words could even be alienating. Or perhaps, if you are familiar, you might find the fact that the show was predicated on the idea that mothers and small children were expected to be in the home and able to listen to a radio confronting, even insulting. I have begun this story in this way as a reminder that all stories are context-specific: situated or located in place and time. Contextualised stories draw on a common language and build on well-travelled ground that is recognisable to all who might wish to tell or receive these stories.

Context is imbued with the culture of the place in which a story is situated, a culture that adapts and morphs as the people within the space evolve and change. Understanding, or not understanding, the culture and the values that underpin a story is central to a sense of connection or identity (Fisher, 1987). Stories, therefore, can be inclusive or exclusive. They can enculturate or alienate. So, it's important that I introduce you to the context in which this story operates: the place, the values and the culture that make up the University of Queensland (or UQ, as it's more colloquially known).

DOI: 10.4324/9781003198772-6

The UQ context

UQ is one of the top universities in Australia, consistently highly ranked in international league tables. A comprehensive research-intensive university that first opened doors to students in 1911, UQ now has over 55,000 undergraduate and postgraduate students. These students select from over 300 award or degree programmes in 50 of the 52 discipline areas open for possible study in Australia. UQ has three main campuses, with the majority of classes held on the St Lucia campus, just outside the Brisbane Central Business District. These students are taught by just over 3000 full-time equivalent academic teaching staff, most of whom have also managed to maintain high research standards.

UQ has a strong and proud history of rewarding teaching excellence. We have one of the longest-running institutional teaching awards schemes that annually celebrates teaching excellence at a very lavish event. Since the national award schemes began in the late 1990s, UQ has won more national teaching awards than any other Australian university. In addition, UQ has a long history of teaching innovation. UQ was one of the first universities in Australia to adopt teaching-focused positions as a tenure track and now boasts a number of teaching-focused academics promoted to full professor on the basis of their scholarship of teaching and teaching expertise. UQ has also contributed teaching innovations on a large scale, having led many of the national competitive teaching and learning innovation grants funded by the federal government through agencies such as the Australian Learning and Teaching Council and the Office for Learning and Teaching. By 2011, UQ had either led or contributed to a substantial portion of the teaching innovation projects funded through these government agencies (Gannaway et al., 2011).

While UQ could be considered, on a world scale, to be a relatively new university, UQ's campuses are built on ancient Country traditionally owned by the Jagera people south of the Brisbane River and the Turrbal people north of the Brisbane River. In the traditions of this Country, I acknowledge this ownership and pay my respects to the past and present and emerging Elders of this Country. In acknowledging the importance of Country and the Traditional Owners of this Country and of Lands elsewhere, I am continuing an ancient protocol that has been practised in this Country for thousands of years. As this chapter is one of many in a book about building expertise in teaching and learning, I'm also using this protocol as a reminder that the story I'm telling is not within a *terra nullius*[1] paradigm. Building expertise doesn't happen in a void or a place where no expertise exists. Expertise is not built from scratch, but is part of a continuum, an evolution across time and experience.

This evolution is well captured in a visual representation of UQ's story[2] in *A Guidance Through Time*, created by Quandamooka artists Casey Coolwell and Kyra Mancktelow. This artwork maps the locations of the three main campuses that form UQ. It graphically represents the core values of UQ, linking the values to traditional stories and symbols. In so doing, the artists forge ongoing connections with Country, knowledges, culture and kin, capturing the sense of belonging and truth-telling about local Aboriginal histories. The artwork reminds us that the land on which UQ is built has been a space of evolving and changing teaching, learning, research and collaboration for tens of thousands of years. Here, people have worked together, guided by tradition, story and teachings, to build knowledge and expertise.

I'm taking my definition of expertise as a characteristic distinct from excellence, agreeing with the definition developed by Helen King, who has observed that:

> Excellence is a position to be reached and not available to everyone, whereas expertise has its etymological roots in the Latin verb 'to try' and is thus related to words such as experience and experiment. In this sense, expertise is a process that is accessible to all.
>
> (King, 2019)

I have interpreted this to mean that expertise is something that can be built and developed by everyone. This means that, for us, the team with responsibility to support professional learning in the central teaching and learning centre at UQ, every teaching academic has the capacity to build teaching expertise, but not everyone will or needs to be an excellent teacher. Distinguishing between excellence and expertise is important because, by 2016, we realised that traditional understandings of teaching excellence were no longer sufficient for UQ. By definition, excellence is limited to the few, the exceptional. Since the early 2000s, UQ has been consistently lauded in league table rankings and peer review for research expertise. Now, as the teaching environment changes, UQ also needs to be a university filled with teachers building their expertise.

This need is prompted by the increase in student numbers. Since 2008, when I first started teaching at UQ, the student cohort had increased from approximately 33,000 students to 55,000 in 2019. This increase is by no means unique to UQ, but rather illustrates an increased engagement with higher education across the Australian sector. There are a number of reasons for this increase, but the impact of the increase is that the intimacy of small class teaching is a thing of the past. The present, and the future, of higher education is massive class teaching. For many UQ first year students, "massive" means being in a cohort of over 1000 students, where repeated lectures are conducted by academics in a tiered lecture theatre across two 13-week semesters.

In recent times, it was becoming painfully obvious that the student experience at UQ was varied. We had pockets of teaching excellence and innovation, but, for many students, their experience was limited to the litany of lecture, tutorial and practical (or wet lab experience). These learning activities were often offered by academic staff with little or no industry experience, staff employed and rewarded for research excellence rather than teaching expertise. UQ simply wasn't taking advantage of new and emerging technologies and integrative systems capable of generating a nuanced, personalised student experience.

In contrast, our local competitors were embracing the technology shifts transforming both our daily life and work and the higher education sector. The marketing arms of our local competitors highlighted employment outcomes, work experience and industry-based networks, publicised state-of-the-art collaborative learning spaces, flexible timetables and online learning opportunities.

By 2016, we noticed that high-achieving students from local feeder schools were starting to shift away from UQ towards our competitors – one a mere 6 km away from our main campus. Suddenly, the sandstone cloisters, the jacaranda blooms and the solid research reputation weren't acting as the draw card they always had been. UQ had been the university of choice for the high-achieving school leaver in Queensland,[3] but now it was being left behind. Students were voting with their feet, filing on to competing campuses – virtual and physical. This shift had not occurred in a huge way – yet. But the slow drip of students away from UQ was starting to become a trickle.

Changing the context

To address this situation, after a monumental consultation process with students, industry, parents, government, alumni and schools, the UQ Student Strategy[4] was born – a new, wide-ranging approach towards learning that put the student experience front and centre. The UQ Student Strategy included a large number of promises to students. Sweeping changes were made to curriculum and pedagogy to ensure we could meet those promises, including a degree programme architecture project that heralded a transition away from atomistic, discipline-focused study (where the academic had total control over what was taught and how teaching occurred) towards a whole-of-programme view of curriculum with a focus on learning outcomes. Suddenly, curriculum design, feasibility studies, financial viability and market research entered the teaching conversation.

Addressing such seismic shifts requires an academic workforce that is adaptable, adaptive and future-focused, sufficiently trained, experienced and motivated (Coates & Goedegeburre, 2012). This is not the workforce typically recruited into a research-intensive university, which tends to privilege research over teaching. The UQ Student Strategy recognised that there was a need to support and enable existing staff in adapting to the shift in teaching style and focus. This was articulated within the strategy as "Goal 3: Dynamic People and Partnerships", aiming to "Develop contemporary and comprehensive ongoing professional development provisions that support and reward teaching and learning performance and facilitate career progression".

However, similar to most Australian universities, UQ's existing teaching and learning-related professional development offerings tended to focus on induction programmes, largely ignoring the needs of mid- and later-career teaching staff. Traditional professional development has been critiqued as failing to support the needs of individuals across long-term career paths (Webster-Wright, 2010) and failing to address the kinds of long-term, systemic change required to meet a changing context (Gibbs, 2013). It's almost as if, once teachers had been 'bloo-ded' by being thrown into teaching a large first year class on Day One of their teaching, they are considered 'teacher-ready'.

Educational development activities, often framed as 'staff development' (as evident in the wording of Goal 3 above), tend to be facilitated by centralised service units in Australian universities. The practices and approaches advocated by these units are often seen to be at odds with the attitudes, values and practices in departments (Trowler & Bamber, 2005) and in conflict with the disciplinary culture of which early career academics are seeking membership (Roxå & Mårtensson, 2009). The disconnect from local discipline-based contexts is particularly noticeable in centralised induction programmes. Equally, informal support structures such as school- or discipline-based 'buddy' programmes or charging heads of schools with coaching new staff (Staniforth & Harland, 2008) can appear to be divorced from the formal centralised offerings and at odds with institutional strategic directions.

Further, for many research-focused academics, the need to be on top of cutting-edge knowledge, skills and practices that apply to research or professional accreditation does not seem to apply to teaching. This is partly owing to institutional recognition and promotion processes that privilege research-orientated measures and metrics, rewarding success in research. 'Buy-out' of teaching by paying casual teachers to do one's teaching to allow a focus on research is standard and often recommended practice.

The end result is that, while we know educational development in teaching can impact student learning and change teacher-practitioner thinking and behaviour (Cilliers & Herman, 2010), provision of continuous professional learning is frequently uncoordinated, under-resourced and disconnected from departmental or school activities and processes (Boud & Brew, 2013). It is often viewed as punitive, addressing deficiencies rather than empowering teaching (Trowler & Bamber, 2005). Additionally, it's often out of reach of the aforementioned casual teaching staff, most of whom are only paid for hours spent on actual teaching (usually defined as face-to-face transmission-mode activities), with no allocation for time spent in professional learning about how to teach. Obviously, there was a clear need for further change in the way that professional learning was conceptualised – a change that could enable, encourage and engage staff in a transformation in teaching and learning.

However, for many academic colleagues, change was becoming a dirty, painful word. This university-wide focus on curriculum rationalised taught modules, reviewed course and programme offerings, and brought a knife to units of study that were often intrinsically connected to personal research interests and academic identity. The process operated under an altered view of the role of 'teacher' and introduced different and new systems, policies, pedagogies and learning environments. All of this meant that, for many, teaching at UQ today bears little resemblance to teaching 10 years or even 5 years previously – when the majority of the current workforce first began teaching.

Enabling the change

Between 2018 and 2019, I led a working party to develop a roadmap as to how we would support this fundamental shift. The working party represented the diversity of the university, including people from different faculties and disciplines, with different levels of experience: academic and professional staff and students; some with teaching awards, some with senior executive responsibilities, some just new teachers who really wanted to do a good job. This motley crew brought their personal stories and experiences together to develop a way forward for professional learning across the university.

A core unifying concept that we determined early into the work was that self-motivation was central to ensuring engagement from colleagues. The negative attitude towards change meant that another top–down directive would just build resentment. The long socialisation of the pressure for success in research as a means to ensure academic success, rather than teaching expertise, meant that this change was a cultural shift – a cultural shift that required personal commitment. So, rather than depending on existing interest, altruism or compulsion, we recognised that personal motivation was central to ensuring colleagues' engagement with professional learning. Consequently, we adopted as core principles those motivational elements identified by Pink (2009):

- *Autonomy* – people's desire to be self-directed, to have ownership of their own skill development, increasing creativity, engagement and trust.
- *Mastery* – the urge to improve, get better skills and confidence; provision of tools that people require to improve their skills.
- *Purpose* – the desire to do something that has meaning and is important, something that people can be passionate about.

All our activities, outcomes and recommended strategies addressed these elements.

The first step for the working party was to engage with UQ senior executive and gain support embracing the notion: the role of an educator in higher education is a profession and should be developed in the same manner as other professions. Once this notion was accepted, it was possible to begin the process of transforming 'staff development' into a notion of 'professional learning' – a transformation with an aim to develop, reward and recognise educators across a whole career.

In approaching this process of transformation, we decided to return to basics and follow the types of curriculum design protocols we typically recommend to colleagues designing a degree programme, drawing on seminal curriculum work (Barnett & Coate, 2005; Laurillard, 2010; Fung, 2017). We identified who needed to learn, what was necessary to learn, what we needed to provide to facilitate learning, and how we would recognise when that learning had occurred. These elements, illustrated in the Professional Learning Roadmap (Figure 4.1), were held together by Pink's motivational elements to stimulate engagement.

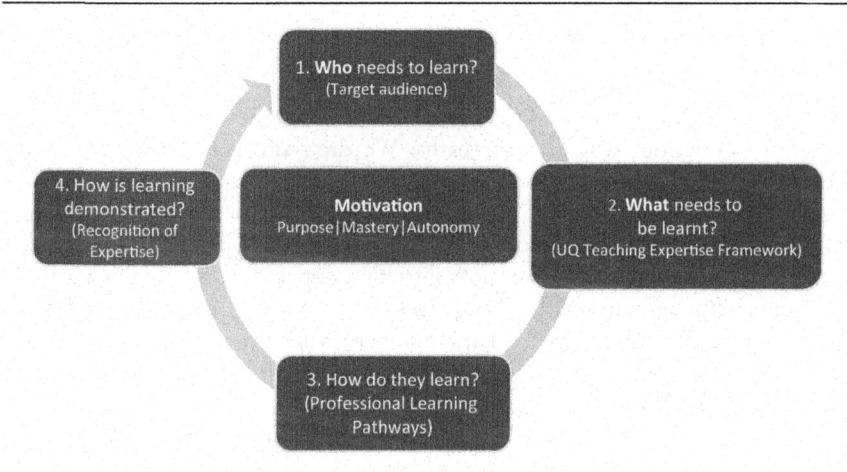

```
        1. Who needs to learn?
           (Target audience)

4. How is learning                            2. What needs to
   demonstrated?      Motivation                 be learnt?
   (Recognition of   Purpose | Mastery | Autonomy   (UQ Teaching Expertise Framework)
    Expertise)

        3. How do they learn?
         (Professional Learning
              Pathways)
```

Figure 4.1 Elements of the Professional Learning Roadmap

Who needs to learn? Describing the target audience

The Professional Learning Roadmap aims to acknowledge the diversity of staff and the range of expertise required to fulfil academic work in the contemporary academy, and to address the need to build expertise in different areas across a whole career path.

To begin forming the elements of the roadmap, we needed to describe our target audience – who would benefit from a university-wide shift from staff development to professional learning? Acknowledging the career diversity of the people who would benefit from this work, we began to capture people's personal career stories, which we reconstructed as 'career journey maps'.

Personal career journeys and learning experiences were captured through a series of workshops that integrated journey/experience mapping and analysis through a design-based thinking paradigm. A range of staff at various levels were invited to participate in the project. Over 60 unique staff with a wide range of experience volunteered to participate in ten storyboarding workshops held between July and September 2019. The workshops explored experiences of career milestones, teaching identities and key messages or elements of the teaching and learning journey. Called the Teaching Pathways project, this process of story capture, distillation and confirmation helped us categorise our target audience, which we confirmed with key institutional stakeholders. Initially, this categorisation was in terms of types of teaching roles, regardless of the name of the role, such as novice/inexperienced, experienced, tutors, curriculum leaders and so on. These terms, however, did not sit well with participants within the Pathways project, who often did not recognise themselves in the descriptors, even though the descriptors emerged from their own stories. What did resonate with the participants was the continuum of expertise: regardless of role, participants saw themselves along a continuum, as part of a trajectory of developing expertise.

What needs to be learnt? The developing expertise in teaching framework

We then moved on to building a framework to guide development of teaching expertise throughout whole career paths. We drew on work conducted at the University of Calgary – a developmental framework for teaching expertise (Kenny et al., 2017). These colleagues recognised similar needs to those at UQ, underwent a similar consultation process and produced a framework that seemed to address most of our needs. The most intriguing aspect for us was this idea of a developmental continuum that seemed to resonate with what our UQ colleagues were telling us. It also covered a large number of the knowledge, skills and capabilities that were identified as necessary to developing teaching success that were emerging from the Pathways project.

The Calgary Developmental Framework provided the structure and the three-level developmental continuum, along with some of the categories of expertise. To make it our own, we supplemented the Calgary Framework with additional aspects emerging from scholarly literature and findings from the Pathways project. We also adjusted the language to that which UQ colleagues would find familiar. We ensured alignment with the UK Professional Standards Framework (UKPSF)[5] so that the Higher Education Academy (HEA) Fellowship Scheme could provide a mechanism to recognise when the expertise had been already been developed. This adaptation resulted in a set of learning outcomes that UQ staff could be expected to achieve in order to build expertise to the expected levels in the phases of development across a career journey.

It's important to note here that these phases are not linear. It is just as easy for a seasoned professor with many years of experience to be suddenly a novice in a new way of teaching and finding themselves exploring a new pedagogy. Similarly, a relatively new tutor might be leading the way with innovative teaching and influencing the teaching practices of others. This mechanism of categorising interchangeable expertise is crucial, as it helps us recognise that expertise is constantly evolving, and that professional learning needs to be flexible and personalised in order to accommodate this dynamic.

COVID-enforced adaptations to teaching were a painful case in point! Suddenly, excellent, award-winning teachers who had been recognised for sustained excellent practice had to substantively adjust all that they knew – on the fly. Suddenly, seasoned teachers became novices, and some people who considered themselves novice teachers were leading the way. Our framework needed to ensure that there was a continuum of development, allowing people to identify as novice in one domain, but expert in another – and allow for the changes to take place as situations and experience evolved. The continuum also needed to adhere to Pink's notions of autonomy, purpose and mastery that we understood were fundamental to ensuring our colleagues' motivation to engage with the phases of development we had identified. Through consultation with our Pathways participants, we finally settled on the terms described in Figure 4.2.

EXPLORE
Growth of self in a local context
e.g. recognises, reflects on, identifies, articulates, explores, becomes aware of, knows and understands

ENGAGE
Actively participates in, implements new strategies, seeks out opportunities, works with peers
e.g. develops, implements, collects, seeks out, applies, tries, aligns, participates

ENHANCE
Contributes to the growth of others and of the field, creates resources for broader teaching and learning community, expands upon knowledge, creates community
e.g. contributes, creates, shares, leads, advances, supports, drives

◄──────────────── Development Continuum ────────────────►

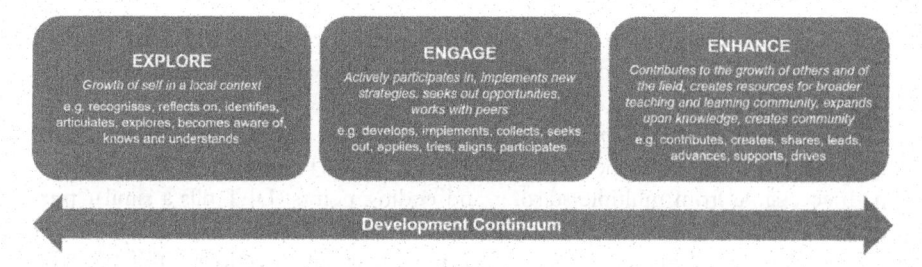

Figure 4.2 Development of expertise continuum

Finally, all these elements were brought together in a framework document called Developing Expertise in Teaching (DET).[6] DET provides a scholarly approach to recognising the breadth of characteristics involved in the development of teaching expertise in higher education across all career stages.

The framework aims to address the challenge of acknowledging the diversity of staff and the range of expertise required to fulfil academic work in the contemporary academy and aims to address the need to build different expertise across a whole career path. Presented as a continuum, DET supports staff to build expertise from exploration through to engagement and then enhancement. Educators will move across the domains and dimensions, back and forth, along this continuum throughout their careers. It is important to note here that it is not the intention that all teachers would be expected to demonstrate attainment of every aspect covered by the DET Framework, but rather that this can be used as a guide to purposeful career path mapping, developing professional learning opportunities and supporting teachers as they reflect on and articulate their expertise. Career paths are varied and have multiple starting and end points, and there's always a possibility of switching directions at any station! Our Professional Learning Roadmap needs to be as flexible, allowing individuals to purposefully change career direction, rather than expecting all to conform to a standard path.

Equally, the roadmap needs to be adaptable; new elements need to be mastered to achieve new purposes. The roadmap must address the needs of our highly varied academic workforce, but also must be compatible with the university's shift in strategic directions, now and in the future. DET, as a core element of the roadmap, is a living document, one that can be adapted in response to shifting contexts.

Contextualising the change

I began this chapter drawing on the genre of story. As I outlined early on, a story has to be understood by the story receiver in order to be meaningful. Stories with longevity and relevance draw on a common language and are built on well-travelled ground, recognisable to all who might wish to engage in telling or receiving these stories. But good stories are not fixed – they are adaptable and customisable.

DET helps people develop a common language that can be understood. And, in true storying fashion, this story is offered to you, the reader, to appropriate, adapt and make your own.

Let's return to the art piece *A Guidance Through Time* – a visual story. This work leads in exploring the values and history of UQ along the path of time, a path accessible from multiple starting and ending points. DET fills a similar purpose: it is a mechanism of connecting personal stories that trace the development of expertise across time and along institutional strategic directions. DET provides a consistent language and development continuum and is being used to:

- Guide UQ teachers in ways to understand and tell their own personal story by:

    a   identifying and communicating their existing expertise
    b   recognising aspects of their teaching that need further development
    c   reflecting on the learning that emerges from everyday activities that ultimately develops their teaching expertise
    d   developing a new common language that describes their teaching.

- Guide academic developers in ways to help UQ teachers change their stories by:

    a   designing flexible learning and recognition pathways that are personalised to the needs of the individual
    b   helping UQ teachers navigate and recognise professional learning options that are relevant.

- Support school and department heads and other campus leaders to nurture individual teachers and contribute to teaching and learning cultures across UQ.

UQ teachers can have their expertise recognised through our HEA@UQ programme, a peer review process accredited by Advance HE. Through the programme, UQ teachers capture their stories and evidence their expertise against the standards outlined by the UKPSF. HEA Fellowship status is captured in institutional annual appraisal documentation and is counted as evidence in teaching awards and in promotion and tenure applications.

In addition, as HEA Fellows, they become part of a larger community – the HEA Commons – a UQ-wide professional learning community (Eaker & Sells, 2016) where members can share and build practice through regular networking events. As members use a common language in their applications for HEA fellowship, this common language allows them to exchange teaching and learning innovations, practices and knowledge across disciplinary boundaries. Further, members of the HEA Commons who are recognised as experts in particular areas of teaching practice can be invited to become Principal Practitioners, working with our central teaching and learning centre at UQ and leading institution-wide initiatives that highlight their teaching expertise as they support the transformation of teaching and learning across UQ.

The HEA@UQ programme recognises, through a formal written portfolio, the attainment of expertise across the DET domains. For those who are not interested in drafting an application or perhaps have not yet built expertise in the areas outlined in DET, it is possible for them to do this through formal and informal learning. This learning is tracked and captured as microcredentials via the Pathways to Expertise in Teaching and Learning (PETL) professional learning scheme – a highly personalised and personalisable, flexible and contextualised set of modules, activities and communities.

But the PETL story is a story for another time.

Notes

1 In 1835, Governor Bourke proclaimed that, prior to British rule, Australian lands were owned by no one, effectively disenfranchising any Aboriginal and Torres Strait Islander claims to the Land. The reclamation and recognition of traditional ownership of the Lands remain an ongoing struggle and underpin contemporary reconciliation processes.
2 See www.uq.edu.au/news/article/2019/05/uq-rap-artwork-reveal
3 It's important to note that, in an Australian context, most students study within 50 km of their parental homes, with few students (only 17% of the entire HE cohort in 2017) living in halls of residence or travelling interstate to study (Grattan Institute, 2018).
4 https://student-strategy.uq.edu.au/
5 UKPSF is a framework for benchmarking success within higher education teaching and learning support: www.advance-he.ac.uk/guidance/teaching-and-learning/ukpsf
6 DET is available from https://student-strategy.uq.edu.au/initiatives/professional-learning

References

Barnett, R., & Coate, K. (2005) *Engaging the Curriculum in Higher Education*. Open University Press, Maidenhead.

Boud, D., & Brew, A. (2013) Reconceptualising academic work as professional practice: implications for academic development. *International Journal for Academic Development*, 18(3), 1–14. doi:10.1080/1360144x.2012.671771

Cilliers, F.J., & Herman, N. (2010) Impact of an educational development programme on teaching practice of academics at a research-intensive university. *International Journal for Academic Development*, 15(3), 253–267. doi:10.1080/1360144x.2010.497698

Coates, H., & Goedegeburre, L. (2012) Recasting the academic workforce: why the attractiveness of the academic profession needs to be increased and eight possible strategies for how to go about this from an Australian perspective. *Higher Education*, 64(6), 875–889. doi:10.1007/s10734-012-9534-3

Eaker, R.E., & Sells, D. (2016) *A New Way: Introducing Higher Education to Professional Learning Communities at Work*. Solution Tree Press, Bloomington, IN.

Fisher, W.R. (1987) *Human Communication as Narration: Toward a Philosophy of Reason, Value, and Action*. University of South Carolina Press, Columbia, SC.

Fung, D. (2017) *Connected Curriculum for Higher Education*. UCL Press, London. doi:10.2307/j.ctt1qnw8nf

Gannaway, D., Hinton, T., Berry, B., & Moore, K. (2011) A review of the dissemination strategies used by projects funded by the ALTC grants scheme. www.uq.edu.au/evaluationstedi/Dissemination/ALTC_Final_Report.pdf [accessed 25/08/2021]

Gibbs, G. (2013) Reflections on the changing nature of educational development. *International Journal for Academic Development*, 18(1), 4–14. doi:10.1080/1360144X.2013.751691

Grattan Institute (2018) Mapping Australian higher education 2018. https://grattan.edu.au/wp-content/uploads/2018/09/907-Mapping-Australian-higher-education-2018.pdf

Kenny, N., Berenson, C., Chick, N., Johnson, C., Keegan, D., Read, E., & Reid, L. (2017) *A developmental framework for teaching expertise in postsecondary education*. International Society for the Scholarship of Teaching and Learning (ISSOTL) Conference, Calgary, Canada. http://connections.ucalgaryblogs.ca/files/2017/11/CC4_Teaching-Expertise-Framework-Fall-2017.pdf [accessed 25/08/2021].

King, H. (2019) Developing the Characteristics of Expertise in Teaching in Higher Education. https://thesedablog.wordpress.com/2019/10/10/helen-king/ [accessed 25/08/2021].

Laurillard, D. (2010) *An Approach to Curriculum Design*. Institute of Education, London.

Phillips, L.G., & Bunda, T. (2018) *Research through, with and as Storying*. Routledge, New York.

Pink, D.H. (2009) *Drive: The Surprising Truth about What Motivates Us*. Riverhead Books, New York.

Roxå, T., & Mårtensson, K. (2009) Significant conversations and significant networks – exploring the backstage of the teaching arena. *Studies in Higher Education*, 34(5), 547–559. doi:10.1080/03075070802597200

Staniforth, D., & Harland, T. (2008) A family of strangers: the fragmented nature of academic development. *Teaching in Higher Education*, 13(6), 669–678. doi:10.1080/13562510802452392

Trowler, P., & Bamber, R. (2005) Compulsory higher education teacher training: joined-up policies, institutional architectures and enhancement cultures. *International Journal for Academic Development*, 10(2), 79–93. doi:10.1080/13601440500281708

Webster-Wright, A. (2010) Authentic professional learning. In *Authentic Professional Learning*. Springer Netherlands, Dordrecht, 107–142.

Chapter 5

The importance of collaboration

Valuing the expertise of disabled people through social confluence

Beth Pickard

Introduction

This chapter explores the potential for expertise in higher education pedagogy to be identified through collaboration with disabled stakeholders within and beyond the academy. This values the expertise inherent in the social identity of disabled people and the lived experience of disablement. This is a different perspective from either subject-specific expertise or pedagogical expertise and reframes the role of the educator from necessarily being an expert themselves to a facilitator of learning through wider engagements and interactions with expertise, according to a wider definition. Following a brief comment on my personal positioning in this work, I will discuss the constructs of subject expertise and pedagogical expertise and introduce a critical disability studies (Goodley, 2017) perspective to the debate. This is intended to challenge existing definitions of expertise accepted in higher education. The discipline of critical disability studies will be defined and explored, from its roots in disability studies and the disability rights movement (Watson & Vehmas, 2020) to its application in higher education (Liasidou, 2014; Pickard, 2020). The construct of academic ableism (Dolmage, 2017; Brown & Leigh, 2020; Brown, 2021) is discussed, at the intersection between critical disability studies and higher education pedagogy, to give context to this debate. Themes of epistemic ignorance and testimonial injustice (Fricker, 2007) are explored as potential lenses for understanding the lack of acceptance of standpoint epistemology in higher education (Kapp, 2019; Toole, 2020). Further, a brief case study will illustrate how the hierarchical notion of academic expertise can be challenged through an inclusive arts project which demonstrates how an educator can promote the expertise of partners in a pedagogical project through collaboration by inviting students to learn from experts with lived experience of disablement in their communities. Lubet's (2014) notion of social confluence contextualises this reframing of disabled participants' roles in different interactions to value their expertise. To conclude, a challenge is posed to the "ivory tower of academia" (Dolmage, 2017, p. 44). The value of standpoint epistemology (Kapp, 2019; Toole, 2020) is celebrated and advocated to enable a more holistic understanding of expertise in higher education pedagogy, potentially providing a more

DOI: 10.4324/9781003198772-7

meaningful and inclusive education for students and wider opportunities for engagement in higher education for disabled people.

Personal positioning

In the spirit of acknowledging both my expertise and lack of expertise in the context in which I plan to discuss this topic, it feels important to reflect on my personal positioning as an author, researcher and educator. I acknowledge my multifaceted, intersectional identity as a music therapist, sibling, researcher, educator, female, activist and ally. I acknowledge that many of the markers of my identity afford significant privilege, such as being white, cisgender, allistic, neurotypical, non-disabled and holding an academic post. As an ally and activist, my intention is to utilise my position of privilege to highlight the opportunities less frequently afforded colleagues, peers, students and other stakeholders with marginalised or oppressed identities and experiences of disablement, and to challenge this injustice (Baglieri & Lalvani, 2019). I intend to deeply consider and reflect upon the critical questions Barton (1994, p. 10) implores non-disabled researchers to consider:

- What right do I have to undertake this work?
- What responsibilities arise from the privileges I have as a result of my social position?
- How can I use my knowledge and skills to challenge the forms of oppression disabled people experience and thereby help to empower them?
- Does my writing and speaking reproduce a system of domination or challenge that system?
- Have I shown respect for the disabled people I have worked with?

This chapter is informed by the depth of learning I have experienced by engaging with the expertise of those with lived experience of disablement. As a non-disabled person, I acknowledge my lack of expertise, when defined according to standpoint epistemology (Kapp, 2019), and humbly draw from my insights as a researcher, ally and sibling of a sister who has a learning disability.

The model of expertise proposed in Chapter 1 only includes those elements of skill, knowledge, artistry, learning and development that practitioners possess themselves. In acknowledging my own lack of experience in this area, I propose an addition to this model that, in contrast, acknowledges skills, knowledge and experiences which are *lacking* and for which the expert practitioner must turn to others.

My identity, qualifications and experiences do *not* give me the expertise which I am discussing and advocating for in this chapter, and I want to recognise this in a transparent way. I believe this reflexivity and self-disclosure around *lack of* expertise is central to developing a valid, ethical stance. I do hope that discussing these ideas may in turn enable more disabled and neurodivergent people to participate in this discussion, whether verbally or through action and other modalities. I seek to remain respectful in my approach and receptive to developing my own knowledge and understanding through learning from and advocating for a platform for the expertise of others.

Critical disability studies

While I mentioned my identity as a music therapist and educator, my own research interest and passion is that of critical disability studies (Goodley, 2017; Watson & Vehmas, 2020). During my studies in this field, I found the experience of engaging with activists, scholars and practitioners with a shared worldview and belief in the social construction of disability to be transformative. I also recognised the value of learning from the expertise of disabled people. This discipline has subsequently underpinned my experiences as a therapist, educator and researcher and continues to shape my approach to pedagogical practice.

While an expanded history of disability studies and critical disability studies is beyond the scope of this chapter, a brief overview will be offered here for context.[1] Disability studies emerged as an academic discipline in the latter half of the twentieth century in tandem with the advent of the disability rights movement in the UK (Watson & Vehmas, 2020). A central tenet of disability studies is the reframing of the 'problem' of disability from a medicalised, individual issue to a systemic, societal issue, through the framework of the social model of disability (Oliver, 1983; Goodley, 2017). This reframing is highly relevant to this discussion of expertise as a medical model interpretation of disability would perceive disabled people as deficient and unlikely to be agents of expertise. Conversely, the social model of disability values individual differences and recognises that systems and societies disable people. Within this paradigm, there is much more scope for valuing the expertise of disabled people as much as any other group of people. Further, the notion of standpoint epistemology (Kapp, 2019; Toole, 2020) specifically values disabled people's social identity and lived experiences as explicit sources of expertise.

Disabling barriers to participation and access have relevance to the discussion on subject expertise and pedagogical expertise too, considering the under-representation of disabled people who access higher education as students (Liasidou, 2014) and the further lack of disabled researchers and academics (Hannam-Swain, 2018; Brown & Leigh, 2020; Saltes, 2020). The social model of disability offers a framework for understanding that disabling attitudes, systems and practices result in the exclusion of disabled people from academia and, subsequently, from this discourse of expertise. This is echoed in recent publications which outline additional and disproportionate burdens and barriers disabled students and academics face (Martin et al., 2019; Hector, 2020; Brown, 2021), also impacting progression and retention rates (Osborne, 2019; Martin et al., 2019).

While some argue that the evolution of the social model of disability informed lexicons across subject areas (Goodley et al., 2019), others pose that the fundamental paradigm shift of the social model was met with avoidance and resistance, particularly within the academy (Bolt & Penketh, 2017; Dolmage, 2017). This chapter acknowledges the presence of social model thinking in policy and practice (Martin et al., 2019) but concurs with Bolt and Penketh (2017) that a deeper acceptance and embodiment of such approaches are not forthcoming in academia. Mitchell (2016) describes the academy as a training ground for the professions of normalcy, maintaining a normative divide between academics and non-academics and, potentially between disabled and non-disabled people, too (Gillberg, 2020) as a primary agenda.

The evolution of disability studies into critical disability studies in the twenty-first century is defined by Goodley (2017, p. 190) as a discipline "populated by people who advocate building upon the foundational perspectives of disability studies whilst integrating new and transformative agendas". These agendas include increasingly interdisciplinary, transdisciplinary and intersectional considerations. It is these evolving disciplines of critical disability studies and cultural disability studies in education (Bolt, 2019), at the intersections of education, higher education, pedagogy, disability studies, philosophy and other subject areas, which inform the position of this chapter and the pedagogical case study within it.

Inclusive, participatory and emancipatory research involving and valuing disabled people has gradually increased (Nind, 2014, 2016), with recognition of the expertise disabled people can bring to the research process:

> Inclusive research's shift away from the privileged voice of the professional towards those labelled with learning difficulties acknowledges them as experts on what life is like for them.
>
> (Ollerton & Horsfall, 2012, p. 620)

However, valuing of expertise in lived experience in a pedagogical context, through partnership, collaboration, co-production and co-teaching, is much less widely discussed (Greenstein et al., 2015; Lillywhite & Wolbring, 2019). As co-authors in Greenstein et al. (2015, n.p.) express:

> We [disabled people] know more about our lives than academics ... You need to know our [disabled people's] experiences and what we have been through in our past ... Because you are not disabled you don't know the ins and outs of it.

This emphasis on valuing lived experience of disablement in pedagogical practice is the focus and intention of this chapter and of my own learning and teaching practice.

Expertise, subject expertise and pedagogical expertise

In researching the topic of expertise in higher education, my attention was particularly drawn by the way constructs were explained and positioned, and how this differed from my own, subject-specific reading of some of these definitions in relation to critical disability studies. I was interested in the suggestion that "expertise", unlike excellence, is "a process potentially accessible to all" (King, Introduction, this volume). This term "accessible" is one widely discussed in critical disability studies, and so I interpret this notion of accessibility from a slightly different vantage point than intended in the introduction to this book. In my experience and research, there are many facets of academia that remain highly *inaccessible*, and so I was interested to look further into this in relation to the concept of expertise in higher education.

When researching further definitions of expertise, I reviewed Skovholt et al.'s (2016) and Ericsson's (2018) definitions, which both chime with and are challenged by my own understanding from a critical disability studies perspective. For example, the suggestion that "Expertise ... refers to the characteristics, skills and knowledge that distinguish experts from novices and less experienced people" (Ericsson, 2018, pp. 3–4) rings true with the notion of expertise in critical disability studies, which is typically attributed to expertise in the lived experience of disabled people. In this context, their expertise does indeed stem from "characteristics, knowledge and experiences" that I, as a non-disabled person, do not possess. This is also reflected in Skovholt et al.'s (2016, p. 1) definition, which states that "an expert, as conceived in its original sense, is someone whose fluency of skill in a given domain is grounded in an accumulated set of experiences in that domain".

However, in moving forward through Ericsson's (2018) definition, other statements were problematic as there is a suggestion that through time, Western civilisation has taken a particular interest in the "superior knowledge" of such experts (Ericsson, 2018, p. 5). Sadly, this is untrue of the expertise of disabled people, which is too often unnoticed, unrecognised and undervalued (Greenstein et al., 2015; Goodley, 2017).

Ericsson (2018, p. 5) continues to suggest that "much of this knowledge can be verbally described and shared with others" and can "help educate students and facilitate their progress towards expertise". Both concepts are problematic from a critical disability studies perspective, as I believe there to be a wealth of expertise to be gleaned from colleagues and individuals who do not articulate their ideas or expertise in a verbal domain (Penketh, 2016; Pickard, 2020). This is perhaps beyond the scope of this chapter, but is a discussion of critical importance in advocating for a holistic education in many subject areas. Equally, I have found that, often, these perspectives are excluded from higher education students' educational experiences and, thus, do not contribute to students' subject knowledge or mastery of their own learning experiences or "facilitate their progress towards expertise", although they have infinite potential to do so. Having said this, it is important to note that the interpretation of expertise Ericsson (2018) describes and that which I am proposing are potentially not synonymous, and students may be developing subject expertise but through engaging with expertise in lived experience.

In considering the relevance of Skovholt et al.'s (2016) and Ericsson's (2018) discussion of expertise to higher education, the separate constructs of subject expertise and pedagogical expertise are considered. Murtonen et al. (2019, p. 8) suggest that many academics in higher education may have little if any pedagogical training or expertise initially, following the Humboldtian tradition of universities in many countries that "relies on the high-quality content knowledge and collaboration in research groups that is assumed to ensure the high-quality teaching". Cotton et al. (2018) further propose that pedagogic research is both undervalued and ill-defined, which could compound the emphasis on subject expertise over pedagogical expertise in many sources. In discussing expertise in the context of teaching more broadly, Stigler and Miller (2018) propose that expertise in teaching is not an individual endeavour and cannot happen in isolation, but rather relies on cooperation with students. While this broadens the discussion slightly, in acknowledging teachers' "pseudo-expertise" gleaned from their own experiences as students, Stigler and Miller (2018) are potentially still reporting on a relatively normative definition of expertise in learning and teaching. This chapter goes beyond Lampert's (2003) definition of teaching as working in relationships between the teacher, the students and the content being taught, and challenges Stigler and Miller's (2018, p. 432) proposition that this definition of teaching need occur in a classroom.

While other sources recognise that the relationship between the learner, the academy and the wider context is important, this is usually framed from the perspective of work-based learning (Wallin et al., 2019) and focuses on the concrete subject expertise to be gained from moving the learning beyond the boundaries of the university, rather than the pedagogical gains possible from engaging with different experts and conceptions of expertise in such a vital pedagogy (Penketh, 2020, p. 17):

> Curricular cripistemologies[2] are essential in advancing a position where pedagogic practice becomes open to the generative capacities of difference and the transformative dimension of crip ontology is therefore highly significant.

I was interested in both the synergy and tension between the literature on expertise, pedagogical expertise and how I have interpreted and understood this construct from a critical disability studies perspective. As a researcher, practitioner and educator in the subject area of critical disability studies, I can gain expertise in theories of disablement, paradigms of disability, the history and current work of the disability rights movement, and application of critical disability studies perspectives across disciplines. In this sense, I have some subject expertise to share with students and other stakeholders. Having also studied and researched in higher education pedagogy, I hope to have some pedagogical expertise in the way I design curricula and learning opportunities and engage with diverse stakeholders.

However, the potentially most critical expertise, of insight into the lived experience of disablement and facing oppression in an ableist society, is not something I have, as a non-disabled person. No amount of "deliberate practice" (Ericsson, 2018, p. 17) will afford me this expertise. To access this invaluable expertise, I will need to continually collaborate with disabled people in my learning and teaching practice as well as my research, to learn from those who know more than I do and ever will. This is the premise of this chapter – to advocate for this humble recognition of the potential limitations of our own expertise and the necessity to collaborate and engage in both allyship and activism for standpoint epistemology to emerge (Kapp, 2019; Penketh, 2020; Toole, 2020) and benefit learners and those who facilitate learning in this model (Greenstein et al., 2015).

From a philosophical perspective, Toole (2020) defines standpoint epistemology as recognition that social identity is relevant to knowledge acquisition. From a neurodiversity perspective, Kapp (2019, p. v) defines standpoint epistemology as claiming authority over knowledge "through direct experience of a condition or situation", with strong connections to the notion of 'lay expertise' widely discussed in sociological literature:

> Standpoint theory suggests inequalities foster particular standpoints, and that the perspectives of marginalized and oppressed groups can generate a fairer account of the world. Individuals from such groups are in a distinctive position to call out forms of behavior and practices of the dominant group, hopefully leading to social change.
>
> (Kapp, 2019, p. vi)

Further, Penketh (2020, p. 24) promotes the potential for pedagogic gains when normative assumptions and practices are problematised through the development of "counter narratives that can challenge typical expectations regarding the ways in which learning takes place". Penketh (2020) goes on to discuss the importance and potential impact of overtly anti-ableist pedagogies which promote expansive definitions of pedagogic practice.

It is this aspiration for the generation of more accurate accounts of ableist society and for opportunity to acknowledge and challenge oppressive practices in knowledge construction that a wider conception of expertise seeks to enable. This poses a challenge to the dominant discourse of academic ableism and of most conceptions of intellectualism, subject expertise and pedagogical expertise, which are so highly valued in academia.

Ableism in academia

An important concept which epitomises the disconnect between the literature on expertise in general and on expertise in critical disability studies is that of ableism. Campbell (2001, p. 44) defines ableism as: "A network of beliefs, processes and practices that produces a particular kind of self and body that is projected as perfect, species-typical and therefore essentially fully human […] Disability then is cast as a diminished state of being human". Baglieri and Lalvani (2019, p. 2) continue:

> Ableism occurs because of the persistent devaluing of disability and the dominance of viewpoints in which disability is cast as an inherently flawed and undesirable state of being. Ableism operates in overt and subtle ways at individual, cultural and institutional levels.

These definitions of ableism are powerfully relevant to the ways in which disability is portrayed, responded to and understood in higher education, with a continuing assumption of disabled people as Other impacting knowledge production and institutional injustices (Penketh, 2016, 2020). Through my own research and practice (Pickard, 2019, 2020, 2021) as well as through engagement with the work of other critical disability studies-informed scholars (Dolmage, 2017; Brown & Leigh, 2020; Penketh, 2020; Brown, 2021), ample examples have emerged of the prevalence of ableist attitudes, practices and systems in higher education. In a recent lecture, West (2020) coined the term "the neurotypical university" where she described in detail, with the insight and expertise of a neurodivergent academic, the ways in which the higher education system is not designed for, built for or arguably intended for neurodivergent learners or academics. Gillberg (2020, p. 18) concurs that: "The normative framework of the ever-available able-bodied academic driven by ambition, and in a climate of university rankings, leaves little room for those who do not conform with this ableist framework".

Literature on the topic of ableism in higher education (Mitchell, 2016; Bolt, 2019; Brown & Leigh, 2020; Brown, 2021) reminds us that it could be argued that the very intention of higher education is to normalise and homogenise, rather than to embrace and celebrate diversity. Dolmage (2017) suggests that disability has long been conceptualised as the inverse of higher education. Certain forms, sources and methods of knowledge generation are, therefore, privileged, and others are oppressed or marginalised (Bolt, 2019). The lack of disabled students and academics further inflates this challenge and emphasises the potentially inhospitable nature of academia for disabled people (Hannam-Swain, 2018; Brown & Leigh, 2020; Burke & Byrne, 2020; Gillberg, 2020; Saltes, 2020; Brown, 2021).

Two final theoretical constructs which offer opportunity for understanding this situation are epistemic invalidation (Kuokkanen, 2008) and testimonial injustice (Fricker, 2007). Epistemic invalidation can be defined as the ways in which dominant groups define the valid mode of knowledge production, undermining or excluding oppressed groups who don't have access or opportunity to contribute to this discourse. Further, the wilful erasure or ignorance of marginalised perspectives in the knowledge construction process could be understood as epistemic ignorance. Testimonial injustice is when an individual's or group's contribution is given less credibility based on their status as a knower (Fricker, 2007). This is where significant conflict between conceptions of expertise arises, with Stone and Priestley (1996, p. 19) suggesting that disabled people are the "true knowers", or experts, of the experience of disablement, whereas Mitchell (2016) and Dolmage (2017), among others, document the myriad ways that the ableist, systemic injustices of academia devalue the expertise of disabled people, resulting in epistemic invalidation.

Case study example from an inclusive arts project

This project sought to embody standpoint epistemology in its critical disability studies-informed pedagogical approach, challenging ableist systems of expertise. The inclusive arts project, which formed part of the first-year curriculum of an undergraduate degree in creative and therapeutic arts, was heavily informed by the following ethos:

> Through teaching *with*, and *by*, rather than *about* [disability], we [...] may move beyond normalizing understandings and practices of inclusion, towards an expanded notion of professionalism.
> (Laes & Westerlund, 2018, p. 34)

While both Laes and Westerlund (2018) and Greenstein et al. (2015), whose work was also influential, invited disabled people into the classroom to share their insight and expertise, this project developed this idea further by taking students outside the classroom to meet collaborators in relevant and authentic contexts. This project enabled students to collaborate beyond the academy with disabled and non-disabled stakeholders in order to access relevant expertise, enriching their knowledge acquisition and knowledge production processes and challenging ableist pedagogic practices (Penketh, 2020). It is hoped that this chapter may encourage other practitioners to widen their understanding of expertise through similar collaborative ventures.

A cohort of creative and therapeutic arts students engaged in a series of pedagogical activities to embody and learn about the discipline of inclusive arts practice. This included engagement in taught lectures and workshops on campus, informed by literature and research about inclusive arts and disability studies. Students also engaged in a work-based placement where they visited four local special schools to facilitate art workshops and consulted and collaborated with a local inclusive theatre company. At the conclusion of the project, students had designed and facilitated inclusive arts workshops with local school children, informed by consultation with the inclusive theatre company, to develop accessible puppets and an art exhibition of collaborative outputs which was shared in a public performance series at a prestigious national arts venue. Students documented, reflected upon, evaluated and wrote about their learning in a range of submissions, in a continued challenge to ableist forms of knowledge production, logocentrism and lexism (Bolt, 2019) by welcoming a range of assessment types and modes.

The learning community contributing to this project involved a range of stakeholders and many forms of expertise. Myself and my non-disabled, neurotypical colleague at the university taught the lectures and workshops, introducing theoretical concepts and the relevant evidence base and skills for the project. The literature and artistic sources explored prioritised the voices and contributions of disabled people wherever possible, in the spirit of Kumashiro's (2000) anti-oppressive education. In addition, the students engaged with our professional partner, a neurotypical, non-disabled outreach co-ordinator at the inclusive theatre company, to understand the context of the organisation and some of the logistical and systemic working of the project.

Finally, but critically, students were taught by twenty-one disabled and neurodivergent school pupils and thirty-one disabled and non-disabled members of a local, inclusive theatre company. This teaching and learning experience involved sharing lived experiences, engaging in consultation, facilitating and participating in creative workshops, sharing insights and ideas and offering authentic truths and knowledge. This engagement occurred both verbally and non-verbally and often through creative, visual means. This expertise could not have been accessed or engaged with within the parameters of the "neurotypical university" (West, 2020), as these participants are likely to face multiple barriers to accessing the role of 'teacher' or 'expert', as defined by the university.

These experiences of accessing expertise beyond the academy and beyond the normative divide (Mitchell, 2016) were central to students' authentic understanding of the lived experience of disability and disablement and pose an alternative to a traditional conception of academic, subject or pedagogical expertise. Through the project, students' understanding of inclusive arts, diversity, difference and disability was challenged and transformed in a way only possible by accessing these authentic sources of expertise. My learning and teaching practice was also enriched through expertise not accessible when the module was taught solely by myself.

Lubet (2014) describes the process whereby individuals' social roles are transformed through the context of their interactions as social confluence. Through this lens, disabled actors and disabled school pupils shifted their identity from service users and pupils to artists and teachers. The recognition of expertise and repositioning of social roles offer reciprocal opportunities for all stakeholders, valuing the critical insights disabled people can offer to education and to wider society (Greenstein et al., 2015; Nind, 2016; Lillywhite & Wolbring, 2019).

Discussion

The outcomes of the case study were that students' perceptions of diversity and difference were transformed, as was evidenced through a concurrent research study (Pickard, 2021). Students articulated heavily deficit-based understandings of disability at the outset of the project but were able to offer increasingly social model and interactional definitions having worked alongside and learned from disabled people.

Students, pupils and actors were all credited as artists in the collaborative, creative process, resulting in a well-received public performance and celebration.

Disabled actors and school pupils authentically and meaningfully contributed to the education of university students, potentially shifting their own self-concept and self-identity to raise their aspirations and enable recognition of their potential as educators (Nind, 2016). Their expertise was recognised and valued and provided learning that would not traditionally have been possible within the parameters of the university. This challenges historical engagements with disabled people in higher education, which typically saw disabled people as patients and research subjects (Dolmage, 2017). A further critical consideration, beyond the scope of this chapter, is the contribution that disabled university students within the cohort made to this project, sharing their perspectives as stakeholders with multiple and intersectional identities.

An important consideration in the context of this book is how we enable the wider higher education community to recognise and access a wider conception of expertise in teaching practices. I propose that this is part of a wider movement of consciousness raising that is necessary in higher education to reconceptualise how disablement is understood (Pickard, 2020). I believe anti-oppressive pedagogy is a vital component of the continuing professional development (CPD) of higher education practitioners, and that this can be effectively delivered through engagement with critical disability studies discourse in PGCert programmes as well as CPD programmes for qualified and experienced educators. In the spirit of this chapter, disabled people should be central to this experience, whether disabled students, disabled staff or members of the wider community who can collaborate to share their expertise in lived experience. This expertise should be suitably valued and recognised as such, and not imposed as a burden upon disabled people to contribute without suitable reimbursement.

While it is hoped that establishing a culture of standpoint epistemology will nurture these values in future generations as today's students become tomorrow's educators, it is also imperative to nurture a shift in existing educators' understanding of expertise and pedagogical practices too. This case study offers one example of how standpoint epistemology could be manifested in a pedagogical project. It would be exciting to consider how this might transpire in other disciplines across the academy. The importance of understanding another perspective on pedagogy, that of students, is given in Box 5.1.

Box 5.1 Engaging with the expertise of students: enhancement opportunities for student academic representation

Another expertise that may lie outwith that of the academic is that of being a student. Systems of student academic representation (SAR) play an integral role in both student voice and quality assurance processes (Quality Assurance Agency, 2012; TSEP, 2015). They involve elected students (often referred to as course reps) drawn from a programme cohort whose role is to advocate on behalf of their peers (Carey, 2013). Course reps capture the student experiences, attend meetings and communicate issues to the programme team and solutions back to their peers

(Carey, 2013). Course reps occupy an interesting space. They represent their peers, engage with the programme team, but are trained and supported by a students' union (TSEP, 2015). Course reps can potentially promote innovation and enhance the student experience, but only if/when supported and trained to do so.

Course reps are positioned to influence change through conversations with both programme teams and the students' union and can potentially be part of a course rep community, working alongside peers performing the same role for different year groups. This potentially provides privileged access, in relation to a programme team, the networks and the students they access.

However, the role of the course rep could be enhanced. They can access institutional data (e.g., through the National Student Survey, NSS, in the UK) but are rarely trained to engage with this. Training course reps to engage with data could provide a valuable evidence base to support the claims they present for consideration. Likewise, engagement with course rep peers can depend on a significant individual (i.e., an academic responsible for student voice) facilitating and supporting networking. These are not standard features of systems of SAR but could potentially increase the efficacy of course rep practice.

Strengthening collaboration between programme teams and the students' union could promote shared understandings of the course rep role. These groups could work together to train and network course reps. They could foster dialogue around course rep practice between the students' union and programme teams. This may also embed an ethos of problem solving across all course reps, and, therefore, rather than course rep practice being bounded by level of study, it could extend institutionally. Fostering the expertise of course reps would ensure the role maintains relevance, and the potential for enhancement through course rep activities is better articulated.

(Jennie Winter, Rebecca Turner & University of Plymouth Students Union)

Conclusion

In returning to the original distinction between 'excellence' and 'expertise', Gillberg (2020, p. 25) confirms:

> The organisational framework of academia is not conducive to knowledge production in the spirit of solidarity and collaboration. The excellence framework is devoid of incentives for knowledge based in social realities for the simple reason that it is not produced fast enough to be published in the highest-ranking journals and for a university to maintain its position on prestigious ranking lists, which is exactly what the upholding of knowledge systems means.

Although 'expertise' may be broadly more accessible than 'excellence' in its definition, as noted in Chapter 1, the extent and impact of academic ableism mean that subject-specific expertise is still not necessarily 'accessible to all' and certainly not equitably accessible to all. Further, there are other conceptions of expertise that exist beyond the academy. There is scope for an alternative conception of expertise, such as standpoint epistemology (Kapp, 2019; Toole, 2020) and other transformational knowledge production methods, to hold a valid and important place in higher education to ensure holistic and meaningful education of a future generation of practitioners and citizens (Penketh, 2020).

In this sense, this focus on expertise could be more accessible and constructive than the focus on excellence, which Mitchell (2016) notes may be intended to protect normative divides and binaries in higher education. Other ways of being and expressing expertise also exist and could be more highly explored and valued in higher education (Penketh, 2020; Pickard, 2020).

Finally, this discussion bears relevance to all subject areas and disciplines, whether the explicit focus includes disability or not, as disabled people could be students, tutors, clients, service users, customers, friends or family of any student on any course (Pickard, 2020). As such, there is a moral responsibility for the higher education sector to consider in more depth the conception of expertise it provides access to, and whether this is providing students with the most holistic and valid education for their futures (Liasidou, 2014).

Notes

1 Goodley (2017) is recommended as an excellent introductory text.
2 See Johnson and McRuer (2014) for a thorough introduction to and history of their term 'Cripistemology' ('crip' and 'epistemology'), which refers to ways of knowing and navigating the world through the experience of disability and disablement.

References

Baglieri, S. & Lalvani, P. (2019) *Undoing Ableism: Teaching About Disability in K–12 Classrooms.* Routledge, Abingdon.
Barton, L. (1994) Disability, difference and the politics of definition, *Australian Disability Review*, 3(94), 8–22.
Bolt, D. (2019) *Cultural Disability Studies in Education: Interdisciplinary Navigations of the Normative Divide.* Routledge, Abingdon. doi:10.4324/9781315102894.
Bolt, D. & Penketh, C. (Eds.) (2017) *Disability, Avoidance and the Academy: Challenging Resistance.* Routledge, Abingdon. doi:10.4324/9781315717807
Brown, N. (Ed.) (2021) *Lived Experiences of Ableism in Academia: Strategies for Inclusion in Higher Education.* Policy Press, Bristol. doi:10.2307/j.ctv1nh3m5m
Brown, N. & Leigh, J. (Eds.) (2020) *Ableism in Academia: Theorising Experiences of Disabilities and Chronic Illness in Higher Education.* UCL Press, London. doi:10.2307/j.ctv13xprjr
Burke, C. & Byrne, B. (Eds.) (2020) *Social Research and Disability: Developing Inclusive Research Spaces for Disabled Researchers.* Routledge, Abingdon. doi:10.4324/9780429426124

Campbell, F.K. (2001) Inciting legal fictions: "disability's" date with ontology and the ableist body of the law, *Griffith Law Review*, 10(1), 42–62.

Carey, C. (2013) Representation and student engagement in higher education: a reflection on the views and experiences of course representatives. *Journal of Further and Higher Education*, 37(1), 71–88. doi:10.1080/0309877x.2011.644775

Cotton, D.R.E., Miller, W. & Kneale, P. (2018) The Cinderella of academia: is higher education pedagogic research undervalued in UK research assessment? *Studies in Higher Education*, 43(9), 1625–1636. doi:10.1080/03075079.2016.1276549

Dolmage, J.T. (2017) *Academic Ableism*. University of Michigan Press, Ann Arbour. doi:10.3998/mpub.9708722

Ericsson, K.A. (2018) An Introduction to the Second Edition of *The Cambridge Handbook of Expertise and Expert Performance*: Its Development, Organization and Content. In: Ericsson, K.A., Hoffman, R.R., Kozbelt, A. & Williams, A.M. (Eds.) *The Cambridge Handbook of Expertise and Expert Performance*. Cambridge University Press, Cambridge, 3–20. doi:10.1017/9781316480748.001

Fricker, M. (2007) *Epistemic Injustice: Power and the Ethics of Knowing*. Oxford University Press, Oxford.

Gillberg, C. (2020) The Significance of Crashing Past Gatekeepers of Knowledge: Towards Full Participation of Disabled Scholars in Ableist Academic Structures. In: Brown, N. & Leigh, J. (Eds.) *Ableism in Academia: Theorising Experiences of Disabilities and Chronic Illness in Higher Education*. UCL Press, London, 11–30. doi:10.2307/j.ctv13xprjr.7

Goodley, D. (2017) *Disability Studies: An Interdisciplinary Introduction* (2nd edn). Sage, London.

Goodley, D., Lawthom, R., Liddiard, K. & Runswick-Cole, K. (2019) Provocations for critical disability studies, *Disability & Society*, 34(6), 972–997. doi:10.1080/09687599.2019.1566889

Greenstein, A., Blyth, C., Blunt, C., Eardley, C., Frost, L., Hughes, R., Perry, B. & Townson, L. (2015) Exploring partnership work as a form of transformative education: "you do your yapping and I just add in my stuff", *Disability Studies Quarterly*, 35(2). doi:10.18061/dsq.v35i2.4653

Hannam-Swain, S. (2018) The additional labour of a disabled PhD student, *Disability & Society*, 33(1), 138–142. doi:10.1080/09687599.2017.1375698

Hector, M. (2020) *Arriving at Thriving: Learning from Disabled Students to Ensure Access for All*. Policy Connect, London.

Johnson, M.L. & McRuer, R. (2014) Cripistemologies: introduction, *Journal of Literary & Cultural Disability Studies*, 8(2), 127–148. doi:10.3828/jlcds.2014.12

Kapp, S. (Ed.) (2019) *Autistic Community and the Neurodiversity Movement: Stories from the Front Line*. Palgrave Macmillan, London.

Kumashiro, K.K. (2000) Toward a theory of anti-oppressive education. *Review of Educational Research*, 70(1), 25–53. doi:10.3102/00346543070001025

Kuokkanen, R. (2008) What is hospitality in the academy? Epistemic ignorance and the (im)possible gift. *Review of Education, Pedagogy and Cultural Studies*, 30(1), 60–82. doi:10.1080/10714410701821297

Laes, T. & Westerlund, H. (2018) Performing disability in music teacher education: moving beyond inclusion through expanded professionalism. *International Journal of Music Education*. 36(1), 34–46. doi:10.1177/0255761417703782

Lampert, M. (2003) *Teaching Problems and the Problems of Teaching*. Yale University Press, New Haven, CT.

Liasidou, A. (2014) Critical disability studies and socially just change in higher education. *British Journal of Special Education*, 41(2), 120–135. doi:10.1111/1467-8578.12063

Lillywhite, A. & Wolbring, G. (2019) Undergraduate disabled students as knowledge producers including researchers: a missed topic in academic literature. *Education Sciences*, 9 (4), 259. doi:10.3390/educsci9040259

Lubet, A. (2014) Social Confluence and Citizenship: A View from the Intersection of Music and Disability. In: Hirschmann, N. & Linker, B. (Eds.) *Civil Disabilities: Citizenship, Membership, and Belonging*. University of Pennsylvania Press, Philadelphia, 123–142. doi:10.9783/9780812290530.123

Martin, N., Wray, M., James, A., Draffan, E.A., Krupa, J. & Turner, P. (2019) Implementing Inclusive Teaching and Learning in UK Higher education – Utilising Universal Design for Learning (UDL) as a Route to Excellence. Society for Research into Higher Education.

Mitchell, D. (2016) Disability, Diversity and Diversion: Normalization and Avoidance in Higher Education. In: D. Bolt & C. Penketh (Eds). *Disability, Avoidance and the Academy: Challenging Resistance*. Routledge, Abingdon, 9–20. doi:10.4324/9781315717807-2

Murtonen, M., Laato, S., Lipponen, E., et al. (2019) Creating a national digital learning environment for enhancing university teachers' pedagogical expertise – the case UNIPS. *International Journal of Learning, Teaching and Educational Research*, 18(13), 7–29. doi:10.26803/ijlter.18.13.2

Nind, M. (2014) *What Is Inclusive Research?* Bloomsbury, London.

Nind, M. (2016) Inclusive research as a site for lifelong learning: participation in learning communities. *Studies in the Education of Adults*, 48(1), 23–37. doi:10.1080/02660830.2016.1155847

Oliver, M. (1983) *Social Work with Disabled People*. Macmillan, Basingstoke. doi:10.1007/978-1-349-86058-6

Ollerton, J. & Horsfall, D. (2012) Rights to research: utilising the Convention on the Rights of Persons with Disabilities as an inclusive participatory action research tool. *Disability & Society*, 28(5), 616–630. doi:10.1080/09687599.2012.717881

Osborne, T. (2019) Not lazy, not faking it: teaching and learning experiences of university students with disabilities. *Disability & Society*, 34(2), 228–252. doi:10.1080/09687599.2018.1515724

Penketh, C. (2016) Special educational needs and art and design education: plural perspectives on exclusion. *Journal of Education Policy*, 31(4), 432–442. doi:10.1080/02680939.2015.1113570

Penketh, C. (2020) Towards a vital pedagogy: learning from anti-ableist practice in art education. *International Journal of Education Through Art*, 16(1), 13–27. doi:10.1386/eta_00014_1

Pickard, B. (2019) Demystifying the process of engaging with the disability and dyslexia service in higher education. *Journal of Inclusive Practice in Further and Higher Education*, 10(1), 40–58.

Pickard, B. (2020) Challenging Deficit-Based Discourse in Higher Education through a Social Connection Model of Responsibility: A Critical Disability Studies Perspective. Unpublished PhD Thesis, University of South Wales.

Pickard, B. (2021) How is disability portrayed through Welsh universities' disability service web pages: a critical disability studies perspective. *Learning and Teaching: International*

Journal of Higher Education in the Social Sciences, 14(1), 1–34. doi:10.3167/latiss.2021.140102

Pickard, B. (2021) Undergraduate creative arts students' perceptions and attitudes toward disability: advancing a critical disability studies informed curriculum. *Art, Design and Communication in Higher Education*, 20(2), 141–161. doi:10.1386/adch_00036_1

Quality Assurance Agency (2012) Chapter B5: Student Engagement. In: *UK Quality Code for Higher Education. Part B Ensuring and Enhancing Academic Quality*. Quality Assurance Agency.

Saltes, N. (2020) "It's all about student accessibility. no one ever talks about teacher accessibility": examining ableist expectations in academia. *International Journal of Inclusive Education*. doi:10.1080/13603116.2020.1712483

Skovholt, T.M., Hanson, M., Jennings, L. & Grier, T. (2016) A Brief History of Expertise. In: Skovholt, T.M. & Jennings, L. (Eds.) *Master Therapists: Exploring Expertise in Therapy and Counselling* (10th Anniversary edn). Oxford University Press, Oxford, 1–16. doi:10.1093/med:psych/9780190496586.003.0001

Stigler, J.W. & Miller, K.F. (2018) Expertise and Expert Performance in Teaching. In: Ericsson, K.A., Hoffman, R.R., Kozbelt, A. & Williams, A.M. (Eds), *The Cambridge Handbook of Expertise and Expert Performance*. Cambridge University Press, Cambridge, 431–452. doi:10.1017/9781316480748.024

Stone, E. & Priestley, M. (1996), Parasites, pawns and partners: disability research and the role of non-disabled researchers. *British Journal of Sociology*, 47(4), 699–716.

TSEP (2015) Ten Principles of Student Engagement. http://tsep.org.uk/wp-content/uploads/2017/08/TSEP-principles-of-Student-Engagement.pdf [accessed 25/08/2021].

Toole, B. (2020) Demarginalizing standpoint epistemology. *Episteme*, 1–19. doi:10.1017/epi.2020.8

Wallin, A., Nokelainen, P. & Mikkonen, S. (2019) How experienced professionals develop their expertise in work-based higher education: a literature review. *Higher Education*, 77(2), 359–378. doi:10.1007/s10734-018-0279-5

Watson, N. & Vehmas, S. (2020) Disability Studies: Into the Multidisciplinary Future. In: Watson, N. & Vehmas, S. (Eds.) *Routledge Handbook of Disability Studies* (2nd edn), Routledge, Abingdon, 3–13.

West, K. (2020) #WhyDisabledPeopleDropOut: A Neurodivergent Student-Turned-Academic on the Neurotypical University. Oxford Disability Lecture 2020. http://podcasts.ox.ac.uk/whydisabledpeopledropout-university-oxford-2020-annual-disability-lecture [accessed 12/06/2020].

Chapter 6

Supportive woman, engaging man
Gendered differences in student perceptions of teaching excellence

Kathryna Kwok and Jackie Potter

The pursuit of expertise in teaching in the guise of teaching excellence has become a sector-wide concern in the UK in recent years, in part owing to the introduction of the Teaching Excellence Framework (O'Leary & Wood, 2019). Critics of teaching excellence as a concept have pointed out that, as excellence is contextually dependent, commitments simply to teaching excellence are meaningless (Saunders & Ramírez, 2017; Skelton, 2005). At the same time, there has been much research attempting to describe and characterise teaching excellence in practice (Lubicz-Nawrocka & Bunting, 2019). The increasing trend of metrication in UK higher education (Bamber, 2020) makes it necessary to take a critical view of teaching excellence and how it actually relates to what students perceive as high–quality teaching. The study described in this chapter questions implicit assumptions present in recent research into teaching excellence that students perceive excellent teaching in an objective, gender-neutral way.

The myth of objectivity in teaching excellence: why gender matters

Practical research into teaching excellence has focused on identifying the characteristics and behaviours of 'excellent' higher education teachers, with more recent studies shifting attention from what teachers themselves think to the student perspective (Lubicz-Nawrocka & Bunting, 2019). The characteristics of teaching excellence as identified by students have largely been similar across these studies, with common characteristics including the ability to teach engagingly, being passionate and knowledgeable about one's discipline area, being friendly, having a sense of humour, and being organised (Bradley et al., 2015; Lubicz-Nawrocka & Bunting, 2019; Moore & Kuol, 2007; Revell & Wainwright, 2009; Su & Wood, 2012). One limitation of these studies, however, is that they do not take into account the subjectivity of student judgements. As evaluative processes are relational, they are subject to sociocultural biases and prejudice (O'Connor et al., 2017). The criteria that students use to judge teaching excellence thus can vary between and within individuals in a way that systematically adheres to and perpetuates stereotypes, such as those relating to gender (Biernat, 2003).

DOI: 10.4324/9781003198772-8

Certainly, evidence from research into gender and student evaluations of teaching has shown that gender can influence what students notice and value in their higher education teachers. For instance, women are often viewed in terms of female-type emotional competencies, such as being caring or nurturing (Basow et al., 2006; Nesdoly et al., 2020; Sprague & Massoni, 2005), and tend to be rated lower than men for male-type cognitive traits, such as instructional and scholarly competence (Boring, 2017; MacNell et al., 2015; Mitchell & Martin, 2018). A recent study by Babin et al. (2020) found that greater perceived attractiveness was associated with higher teaching evaluation ratings—but only for female teachers. This finding suggests that a female teacher's perceived level of competence is partly determined by how attractive she is seen to be. This is consistent with the observation that women in the workplace can be evaluated more harshly if they do not meet social expectations of what and how women should be (Eagly & Karau, 2002). It is perhaps worth noting that the discussion in Babin et al. (2020) somewhat downplays this problematic implication. For instance, a number of explanations are offered which frame their finding as an advantage for women rather than a disadvantage. As one explanation goes, women, aware that others are likely to judge them by their appearance, put more effort into their self-presentation. This leads to them feeling and behaving in a more confident manner, which students, in turn, respond to positively. Similarly, another explanation considers that students may simply be more motivated to engage in their studies for female teachers they find attractive (Babin et al., 2020, p. 12). The authors additionally suggest that gender inequalities in the professional outcomes of academics have largely disappeared (p. 12). The framing of this so-called beauty premium as an advantage enjoyed by women, rather than being indicative of harmful expectations around the role of women in society, highlights that, beyond the boundaries of (mostly female) gender and feminist scholars, there is relatively little recognition of how gender can influence student perceptions of teaching. As the study described in this chapter will hopefully illustrate, it is important that gender is recognised in any consideration of how students perceive and respond to teaching.

The study

The study's context was a mid-sized research-focused university in England. Nominations for teaching staff submitted by students for an annual institution-wide excellence award were thematically analysed to determine if there were gendered differences in what students most often mentioned about their excellent teachers. Nominations were taken from the 2015–16 and 2016–17 rounds of the excellence award. A number of inclusion criteria were applied to the initial data set (n = 586) in preparation for analysis. First, nominations had to be submitted by a student and be for a single teacher. Second, nominations had to be from a student not already represented in the data set. Where an individual made repeated submissions, only the first valid nomination (i.e. which met all the other inclusion criteria) was accepted into the data set. Where the same individual made submissions over multiple years, only the first valid nomination from the more recent year (2016–17) was accepted. Third, nominations had to be able to be coded for student and teacher gender. Gender was inferred from various sources of information provided with the submissions. Most often, gender was able to be determined by the names provided with the nominations (noting that ambiguous names for which no certain judgements on gender could be made were excluded from analysis). Gender could also be inferred from the use of personal pronouns in the nominations themselves. In all, 168 nominations were excluded after these criteria were applied, leaving a final data set of 418 nominations.

A thematic analysis of the content of the nominations was then conducted. Themes were identified and coded on NVivo software. A grounded line-by-line approach was employed, which enabled a thorough identification of the themes in the nominations. Student and teacher gender were hidden from view during the coding process in order to minimise potential researcher bias, of course noting that the presence of personal pronouns nevertheless meant that teacher gender was able to be identified for some nominations. Once the identification of themes was complete, frequency tables were generated which showed, for all the themes identified in the data, the frequency at which each theme was mentioned in each of the four student-by-teacher gender categories—that is, female student nominations for female teachers (FF), female student nominations for male teachers (FM), male student nominations for female teachers (MF), and male student nominations for male teachers (MM). The proportion of mentions (i.e. the number of nominations of a particular gender category which mentioned a theme over the total number of nominations in that gender category, expressed as a percentage) was then calculated for all the themes in all the gender categories and subsequently arranged in descending order. The ten most frequently mentioned themes for each gender category (in terms of proportions of mentions) were then identified for analysis. As there were multiple instances of tied ranks, it should be noted that the selection process prioritised the number of themes, rather than the number of filled ranks, such that, as far as possible, only ten themes were analysed for each gender category. This meant that additional themes were not added to make up for tied ranks; two tied themes would be treated as occupying two rank positions. This enabled a fair comparison with the same number of themes examined per gender category. One exception to this was for the MF category, which had multiple themes tied for the final rank spot. Thus, 13 themes had to be included in the analysis for this category.

Who was excellent and why?

The gender distribution of the overall sample will first be described to provide some context for the thematic findings. In total, there were 418 nominations in the data set, of which 132 (31.6%) were in the FF category, 128 (30.6%) in the FM category, 39 (9.3%) in the MF category, and 119 (28.5%) in the MM category. The gender distribution of the data set was found to be significantly uneven in a separate analysis (Kwok & Potter, 2021). It was noted that same-gender nominations (FF and MM) were over-represented and opposite-gender nominations (FM and MF) were under-represented. Although the same-gender nominations were over-represented to similar extents, nominations by male students were only about a third as likely to be for a female teacher as nominations by female students were to be for a male teacher. These differences could not be explained by the gender distribution of the university's teaching staff, which was roughly evenly distributed between male and female staff, even within individual faculties. The uneven gender distribution of the nominations suggests that gender can influence the extent to which students recognise teaching excellence, where teaching excellence may be more readily recognised in teachers of the same gender as the student. The disproportionately low frequency of MF nominations additionally suggests that male students may be disproportionately unlikely to recognise teaching excellence in female teachers (ibid.).

Table 6.1 lists the ten most frequently mentioned themes for each gender category (note: 13 themes are listed for MF owing to a tie in the final rank). In the interest of space, these themes will not be detailed in full, though it is worth noting that they are largely self-explanatory. For instance, *supportive* teachers were willing to offer help and guidance ("Provides incredible amounts of support"), while *available* teachers "always" made time for students, often beyond what students perceived to be their professional or personal obligations ("always finding time in his busy schedule to help students"; "She has offered to help outside of her hours of work"). A few themes worth clarifying include *encouragement (emotional)*, which pertained to descriptions of emotionally encouraging teachers who boosted their students' confidence and helped them overcome self-doubt ("without her encouragement I would have given up"). This was in contrast to descriptions of academic encouragement (e.g. encouraging students to participate in conferences or to "think critically"). The theme *exceptional* pertained to the use of high-intensity (see Stewart, 2015) descriptors, such as "exceptional", "brilliant", and "amazing" ("down right AMAZING, [Name] is an exemplary lecturer"), while *teaching techniques (generic)* pertained to generic mentions of high-quality teaching ("excellent teaching strategies and methods"; "very good teaching style").

Overall, the topmost themes were very similar across the gender categories: *supportive, available, engaging*, and *passionate* all appear within the top five themes of each category. Additionally, *approachable* was notable as it generally featured highly across the gender categories (with perhaps the exception of MM). These themes, as well as those in the relatively lower ranks, are consistent with student characterisations of teaching excellence as reported in other studies (e.g. Bradley et al., 2015; Lubicz-Nawrocka & Bunting, 2019). However, a closer examination of the themes and their relative proportions of mentions within and across the gender categories reveals a number of interesting differences in how students described their male and female teachers.

To start, although female student nominations for teachers of both genders (FF and FM) were similar in terms of the themes mentioned and their ranks, gendered

Table 6.1 Most frequently mentioned themes by gender category

| Female students ||||| Male students ||||
| Female teacher (FF) n = 132 || Male teacher (FM) n = 128 || Female teacher (MF) n = 39 || Male teacher (MM) n = 119 ||
Theme	%	Theme	%	Theme	%	Theme	%
Supportive	49.2	Supportive	53.0	Supportive	41.0	Engaging	33.6
Available	32.6	Engaging	33.6	Available	30.8	Supportive	27.7
=Engaging	29.5	Available	28.1	Engaging	28.2	Passionate	20.2
=Passionate	29.5	Passionate	19.5	=Approachable	20.5	Available	19.3
Inspiring	28.0	Inspiring	17.2	=Passionate	20.5	Teaching techniques (generic)	16.8
Approachable	20.5	Clear teaching	16.4	Knowledgeable	17.9	Inspiring	15.1
Exceptional	16.7	=Approachable	14.8	=Good feedback	15.4	Exceptional	13.4
TT(G)[1]	15.2	= Teaching techniques (generic)	14.8	=Caring	15.4	Approachable	12.6
Encouragement (emotional)	12.1	Good explanations	14.1	==Friendly	12.8	=Good feedback	10.9
Knowledgeable	11.4	Humorous	12.5	==Humorous	12.8	=Clear teaching	10.9
				==Patient	12.8		
				==TT(G)[1]	12.8		
				==Values students	12.8		

differences can be seen in the male student nominations for female and male teachers (MF and MM). For the female student nominations, many of the same themes appear in both the FF and FM categories in a very similar order, particularly for the topmost themes. By contrast, a number of gendered distinctions can be seen between the male student categories. Male students most often mentioned that their male teachers were *engaging*, whereas they most often mentioned that their female teachers were *supportive*. It should be noted that, while *engaging* was mentioned in somewhat similar proportions in the MM and MF nominations (at 33.6% for MM and 28.2% for MF), *engaging* nevertheless ranked only third in the MF category and, further, at some distance away from the topmost theme, *supportive*, which was mentioned by 41.0% of MF nominations. Gendered patterns in the male student nominations can be also seen for the themes *available* and *approachable*, which both relate to communal, self-sacrificing behaviours often expected in women in a way they are not in men (Eagly & Karau, 2002). *Available* was ranked second for MF nominations and was mentioned 30.8% of the time, whereas it ranked fourth for MM nominations where it was mentioned only 19.3% of the time. Similarly, *approachable* was ranked (tied) fourth for MF nominations and mentioned 20.5% of the time, whereas it ranked eighth for MM nominations, being mentioned 12.6% of the time. On the whole, there was a greater emphasis on pastoral traits (e.g. *supportive, friendly, caring, values students*) in the MF nominations compared with MM nominations, which tended to prioritise traits reflecting a high quality of instruction. This suggests that male students perceive teaching excellence in gendered ways, preferring male-type cognitive competencies in their male teachers and female-type emotional competencies in their female teachers.

Although the MM nominations were generally less concerned with emotional aspects of teaching relative to the other gender categories, emotion nevertheless appeared to be an important part of how students experienced excellent teaching. Examining the themes across the four gender categories, it is clear that the emotional and pastoral aspects of teaching constitute a crucial part of the student experience, regardless of student and teacher gender. *Supportive* was the most frequently mentioned theme for FF, FM, and MF nominations and the second most frequently mentioned theme for MM nominations. This suggests that, above all, what many students value most about excellent teaching is the sense of emotional security that a teacher is able to provide. Two other emotional themes that ranked highly across the four gender categories were *passionate* and *inspiring*. This suggests that excellent teaching goes beyond the efficient imparting of content or skills—more than that, excellent teaching involves strong, positive emotional responses towards one's subject. The prominence of emotional themes in the nominations across the four gender categories highlights the crucial role of emotion in how students experience teaching excellence.

Moving on, there are two findings pertaining to specific themes worth mentioning here. First, it was notable that the masculine *knowledgeable* appeared only in the female teacher categories, ranking sixth for MF and tenth for FF, while not appearing in either of the male teacher categories (i.e. it was not one of the ten most mentioned themes). The appearance of *knowledgeable* in the MF category was an interesting exception to the general trend of MF nominations prioritising stereotypically feminine characteristics. Perhaps counter-intuitively, this may be explained by lowered expectations of the scholarly capacities of female teachers (Biernat, 2003). This will be discussed further in the next section. Second, another notable theme was *values students*, which appeared only in the MF category, where it was ranked (tied) last. As will be discussed in the next section, this was consistent with previous evidence that one consideration that male students make when evaluating teaching is the preservation of their status relative to their teacher (Basow et al., 2006).

Different but not equal: the implications of a gendered teaching excellence

This study thematically analysed the content of student nominations for a university excellence award to investigate whether there were gendered differences in how students described their excellent teachers. While the themes mentioned were consistent with what previous research has identified as characteristics of teaching excellence (e.g. Bradley et al., 2015; Lubicz-Nawrocka & Bunting, 2019), comparing the themes' relative ranks and frequency of mentions across the four student-by-teacher gender categories revealed gendered differences in how students described their teachers. Female students described male and female teachers in similar ways; however, male student descriptions of female teachers tended to emphasise stereotypically feminine (pastoral) competencies relative to their descriptions of male teachers.

It should be noted that male and female teachers being valued for different reasons is not problematic in and of itself; however, female-type competencies are usually ascribed lower values in academia compared with male-type competencies—for instance emotional labour versus cognitive labour (Crabtree & Shiel, 2019; Heijstra et al., 2017; Moore & Kuol, 2007; Ogbonna & Harris, 2004) and, indeed, teaching versus research (Crabtree & Shiel, 2019; O'Connor et al., 2017). The lower values ascribed to feminine competencies and 'responsibilities' can result in tangible disadvantages faced by women in formal recognition processes (O'Connor et al., 2017; O'Connor & O'Hagan, 2016). For example, student evaluations of teaching on modules and programmes gathered by universities tend to focus on cognitive aspects of teaching and less on interpersonal or emotional aspects. An example of this at the national level in the UK can be seen in the 2020 National Student Survey (NSS),[1] where the first 7 core items (of 28 total) directly concern cognitive aspects of teaching (e.g. "The course is intellectually stimulating" and "My course has provided me with opportunities to explore ideas or concepts in depth"). By contrast, only two items pertain to emotional dimensions of teaching ("I feel part of a community of staff and students" and "Staff value students' views and opinions about the course"). The remaining items concern assessment guidance and various administrative and organisational aspects of the course (Office for Students, n.d.). As the NSS and similar evaluative metrics are commonly used in recognition schemes at the institutional and national level (Bamber, 2020; O'Connor & O'Hagan, 2016), structural inequalities which particularly disadvantage women are reinforced in higher education. Crucially, it is not that women are necessarily more adept (and men more inept) at female-type competencies; rather, the issue is that women are associated with and perceived to be naturally skilful in areas regarded as relatively unimportant in higher education (Heijstra et al., 2017). Indeed, although it was not the focus of this discussion, the disproportionate infrequency of MF nominations in the overall sample—a finding that cannot be explained by the gender distribution of teaching staff—offers a striking illustration of the devaluing of women's labour in higher education.

A related effect of the devaluing of female labour is that students' emotional responses to teaching are overlooked. A number of commentators have observed that emotion is not afforded the same legitimacy as cognitive and other non-emotional aspects of higher education teaching (Moore & Kuol, 2007; Ogbonna & Harris, 2004; Quinlan, 2016). This is also reflected in the foci of teaching evaluations such as the NSS, as described above. The findings here suggest that, in fact, students' emotional responses are a key part of how students experience high-quality teaching. Recall that, for instance, *supportive* was the most frequently mentioned theme for all but one of the gender categories, where it nevertheless ranked second. There is, thus, an apparent mismatch between what formal recognition structures prioritise and what students actually value about teaching. The findings here suggest that, at least when it comes to recognising excellence in teaching, emotional competencies are relatively valued over cognitive ones.

One notable finding was the appearance of *knowledgeable* in the female teacher categories (FF and MF) but not the male teacher categories (FM and MM). This was particularly unusual for the MF nominations, considering an otherwise clear preference for female-type traits. It is possible that owing to lower expectations of women's scholarly capacities relative to men (Basow et al., 2006; Miller & Chamberlin, 2000), any evidence that students had of this would have been particularly salient. This interpretation would be consistent with the shifting standards theory, which posits that subjective evaluations (such as the open-ended descriptions of teachers examined here) can contradict stereotyped expectations (Biernat, 2003). This is because subjective measures allow standards to be shifted such that judgements are made with reference to group stereotypes. For instance, a woman described as knowledgeable may nevertheless be estimated to have a lower IQ score than a man also considered to be knowledgeable. Hence, the finding that *knowledgeable* only appeared in the female teacher categories may, rather counter-intuitively, be indicative of lower student expectations of female scholarly competence.

Next, recall that the theme *values students* was ranked (tied) tenth in the MF category, while not appearing (i.e. not being one of the most frequently mentioned themes) in any other gender category. This finding is similar to an observation made in Basow et al's (2006) examination of students' descriptions of their best and worst professors. They noted that, when evaluating professors of either gender, male students were at least partly influenced by whether or not a professor infringed upon their sense of status. For example, male students tended to describe their best female professors as accommodating and their worst male professors as condescending. As Basow et al (2006, p. 32) note:

> Perhaps because male students challenge female professors more than male professors (Statham et al., 1991), male students may be especially appreciative when they are allowed to do so.

The finding here that MF nominations frequently mentioned *values students* could thus also be indicative that the preservation of personal status is a consideration for male students when it comes to evaluating teaching. In this case, perhaps owing to expectations that women in positions of relative power nevertheless behave in an agreeable way (Eagly & Karau, 2002), male students were particularly positive when female teachers made the effort to make them feel valued.

A number of limitations should be noted about the study. The first concerns the descriptive analytical approach employed here. Although it enabled the thematic makeup of nominations across the four gender categories to be directly compared, it was unclear whether the differences between themes' frequencies of mentions were statistically meaningful. Inferential testing was done in a separate analysis (Kwok & Potter, 2021), though this came with a different set of limitations on what it could reveal about the data (for instance, as only a relatively small number of themes qualified for statistical testing). What the analytical approach described in this chapter offers is an overall perspective of what nominations across the gender categories most often mentioned, even if it is unclear at what point differences become statistically meaningful.

A related limitation is that, as the analysis concerned the proportions of mentions across gender categories, nominations in smaller gender categories carried relatively more weight. Particularly, as there were only 39 MF nominations in the sample, each MF nomination had substantially more influence in determining a theme's proportion of mention—consider, for example, that 65 FF nominations mentioned *supportive*, whereas only 16 MF nominations did (noting that *supportive* was the most frequently mentioned theme for both these categories). Less uneven gender category sizes would have allowed more balanced comparisons to be made.

A third limitation was that the analysis could only represent individual characteristics with a single binary variable representing gender. The analysis was thus unable to investigate other characteristics that could have influenced students' judgements of teaching, such as race (Fan et al., 2019) and attitudes towards gender (Nesdoly et al., 2020). Additionally, gender itself was represented simplistically, even though it is a complex construct able to be expressed and performed in different socioculturally meaningful ways (Burke et al., 2013; Garvey et al., 2019). This said, the gendered patterns in what students mentioned most about their excellent teachers were largely consistent with findings from previous research (e.g. Basow et al., 2006), as well as the gendered biases and expectations present in higher education and wider society (Eagly & Karau, 2002; Laube et al., 2007; Rosa et al., 2021).

Concluding notes and the way forward

Gender bias can shape how HE teachers are perceived, whether in the classroom (as illustrated here) or in professional contexts (O'Connor & O'Hagan, 2016). It is important to be aware that evaluations of teaching quality, as with any sort of evaluative behaviour, are subject to sociocultural biases and expectations (O'Connor et al., 2017). At the individual level, an awareness of one's own assumptions or preconceptions, as well as the preparedness to accept evidence contrary to these expectations, is critical. By being comfortable with—and even expectant of—contrary evidence, it becomes easier to consider individuals on their own terms, rather than by their most superficially apparent traits.

With regards to the implications for educational development, moving away from a model of teaching excellence to one of expertise would help shift evaluative foci on to practices and competencies that are within an individual's control. For instance, the three aspects of expertise proposed in King's (2020) model—pedagogical content knowledge, artistry of teaching, and self-determined and purposeful approaches to learning and development—emphasise individual practices and applications of experience, in contrast to broad notions of excellence that leave judgements of teaching quality much more susceptible to subjective biases. For educational developers and the staff they work with, a model of teaching expertise which locates 'good' teaching practice within the agency of individuals would enable clear and attainable goals of development. This said, the risk of sociocultural bias would still be present, even under a model of expertise. To illustrate using King's model, the male bias found for the theme *engaging* suggests that teaching artistry would be more easily recognisable in male teachers than in female teachers. More generally, as scholarly competence tends to be seen as a masculine rather than a feminine trait (e.g. Basow et al., 2006), women may be evaluated more harshly on pedagogical content knowledge. Similarly, women's efforts towards purposeful learning and development risk being undervalued or seen as trivial relative to men's. Certainly, van den Brink & Benschop's (2012) observation that academic excellence is a male-type quality can also be applied to the notion of expertise. In all, this study illustrated that gender bias can shape perceptions of teaching. It is important that HE practitioners and educational developers cultivate an awareness of gender and other biases, starting at the individual level, so that the normalisation of these attitudes can be more effectively challenged. A model of expertise which locates high-quality teaching practice within the control of individual academics (e.g. King, 2020) would help to mitigate against sociocultural biases in teaching evaluations.

Note

1 The NSS is an annual survey of student satisfaction open to all final year HE students in the UK, and its results contribute towards the calculation of an HE provider's TEF rating (Office for Students, 2020). The NSS comprises a core set of questions which all HE providers must include in their survey, though providers can additionally draw from a bank of optional questions.

References

Babin, J.J., Hussey, A., Nikolsko-Rzhevskyy, A. & Taylor, D.A. (2020) Beauty premiums among academics. *Economics of Education Review*, 78. doi:10.1016/j.econedurev.2020.102019

Bamber, R. (2020) Our days are numbered: Metrics, managerialism, and academic development. SEDA Paper 125, SEDA, London.

Basow, S.A., Phelan, J.E. & Capotosto, L. (2006) Gender patterns in college students' choices of their best and worst professors. *Psychology of Women Quarterly*, 30, 25–35. doi:10.1111/j.1471-6402.2006.00259.x

Biernat, M. (2003) Toward a broader view of social stereotyping. *American Psychologist*, 58 (12), 1019–1027. doi:10.1037/0003-066x.58.12.1019

Boring, A. (2017) Gender biases in student evaluations of teaching. *Journal of Public Economics*, 145, 27–41. doi:10.1016/j.jpubeco.2016.11.006

Bradley, S., Kirby, E. & Madriaga, M. (2015) What students value as inspirational and transformational teaching. *Innovations in Education and Teaching International*, 52(3), 231–242. doi:10.1080/14703297.2014.880363

Burke, P.J., Crozier, G., Read, B., Hall, J., Peat, J. & Francis, B. (2013) Formations of gender and higher education pedagogies (GaP). Final report. Higher Education Academy, York.

Crabtree, S.A. & Shiel, C. (2019) "Playing mother": channeled careers and the construction of gender in academia. *SAGE Open*, 9(3). doi:10.1177/2158244019876285

Eagly, A.H. & Karau, S.J. (2002) Role congruity theory of prejudice toward female leaders. *Psychological Review*, 109(3), 573–598. doi:10.1037/0033-295x.109.3.573

Fan, Y., Shepherd, L.J., Slavich, E., Water, D., Stone, M., Abel, R. & Johnson, E.L. (2019) Gender and cultural bias in student evaluations: why representation matters. *PLoS One*, 14(2). doi:10.1371/journal.pone.0209749

Garvey, J.C., Hart, J., Metcalfe, A.S. & Fellabaum-Toston, J. (2019) Methodological troubles with gender and sex in higher education survey research. *The Review of Higher Education*, 43(1), 1–24. doi:10.1353/rhe.2019.0088

Heijstra, T.M., Einarsdóttir, Þ., Pétursdóttir, G.M. & Steinþórsdóttir, F.S. (2017) Testing the concept of academic housework in a European setting: part of academic career-making or gendered barrier to the top? *European Educational Research Journal*, 16(2–3), 200–214. doi:10.1177/1474904116668884

King, H. (2020) Future-ready faculty: developing the characteristics of expertise in teaching in higher education. Special Issue: ICED 2020 Proceedings, *ETH Learning and Teaching Journal*, 2(2), 333–337.

Kwok, K. & Potter, J. (2021) Gender stereotyping in student perceptions of teaching excellence: applying the shifting standards theory. *Higher Education Research & Development*. doi: 10.1080/07294360.2021.2014411

Laube, H., Massoni, K., Sprague, J. & Ferber, A.L. (2007) The impact of gender on the evaluation of teaching: what we know and what we can do. *NWSA Journal*, 19(3), 87–104.

Lubicz-Nawrocka, T. & Bunting, K. (2019) Student perceptions of teaching excellence: an analysis of student-led teaching award nomination data. *Teaching in Higher Education*, 24(1), 63–80. doi:10.1080/13562517.2018.1461620

MacNell, L., Driscoll, A. & Hunt, A.N. (2015) What's in a name: exposing gender bias in student ratings of teaching. *Innovative Higher Education*, 40(4), 291–303. doi:10.1007/s10755-014-9313-4

Miller, J. & Chamberlin, M. (2000) Women are teachers, men are professors: a study of student perceptions. *Teaching Sociology*, 28(4), 283–298. doi:10.2307/1318580

Mitchell, K.M.W. & Martin, J. (2018) Gender bias in student evaluations. *PS: Political Science & Politics*, 51(3), 648–652. doi:10.1017/s1049096520000566

Moore, S. & Kuol, N. (2007) Matters of the heart: exploring the emotional dimensions of educational experience in recollected accounts of teaching excellence. *International Journal of Educational Development*, 12(2), 87–98. doi:10.1080/13601440701604872

Nesdoly, N., Tulk, C. & Mantler, J. (2020) The effects of perceived professor competence, warmth and gender on students' likelihood to register for a course. *Assessment & Evaluation in Higher Education*, 45(5), 666–679. doi:10.1080/02602938.2019.1689381

O'Connor, P., López, E.M., O'Hagan, C., Wolffram, A., Aye, M., Chizzola, V., Mich, O., Apostolov, G., Topuzova, I., Sağlamer, G, Tan, M.G. & Çağlayan, H. (2017) Micro-political practices in higher education: a challenge to excellence as a rationalising myth?. *Critical Studies in Education*, 61(2), 195–211. doi:10.1080/17508487.2017.1381629

O'Connor, P. & O'Hagan, C. (2016) Excellence in university academic staff evaluation: a problematic reality?. *Studies in Higher Education*, 41(11), 1943–1957. doi:10.1080/03075079.2014.1000292

Office for Students (2020) TEF data. www.officeforstudents.org.uk/advice-and-guidance/teaching/tef-data/ [accessed 31/01/2021].

Office for Students (n.d.) NSS 2020 core questionnaire [Online] Available at: www.officeforstudents.org.uk/media/d462a46b-0eba-42fd-84a1-c8b6dc883c99/nss-2020-core-questionnaire-and-optional-banks.pdf [accessed 31/01/2021].

Ogbonna, E. & Harris, L.C. (2004) Work intensification and emotional labour among UK university lecturers: an exploratory study. *Organization Studies*, 25(7), 1185–1203. doi:10.1177/0170840604046315

O'Leary, M. & Wood, P. (2019) Reimagining teaching excellence: why collaboration, rather than competition, holds the key to improving teaching and learning in higher education. *Educational Review*, 71(1), 122–139. doi:10.1080/00131911.2019.1524203

Quinlan, K.M. (2016) How emotion matters in four key relationships in teaching and learning in higher education. *College Teaching*, 64(3), 101–111. doi:10.1080/87567555.2015.1088818

Revell, A. & Wainwright, E. (2009) What makes lectures "unmissable"? Insights into teaching excellence and active learning. *Journal of Geography in Higher Education*, 33(2), 209–223. doi:10.1080/03098260802276771

Rosa, R., Drew, E. & Canavan, S. (2021) An overview of gender inequality in EU universities. In: Drew, E. & Canavan, S. (Eds.) *The Gender-Sensitive University: A Contradiction in Terms?* Routledge, Abingdon. 1–15. doi:10.4324/9781003001348-1

Saunders, D.B. & Ramírez, G.B. (2017) Against "teaching excellence": ideology, commodification, and enabling the neoliberalization of postsecondary education. *Teaching in Higher Education*, 22(4), 396–407. doi:10.1080/13562517.2017.1301913

Skelton, A. (2005) *Understanding Teaching Excellence in Higher Education: Towards a Critical Approach*. Routledge, Abingdon. doi:10.4324/9780203412947

Sprague, J. & Massoni, K. (2005) Student evaluations and gendered expectations: what we can't count can hurt us. *Sex Roles*, 53(11/12), 779–793. doi:10.1007/s11199-005-8292-4

Statham, A., Richardson, L. & Cook, J.A. (1991) *Gender and University Teaching: A Negotiated Difference*. SUNY Press, Albany, NY.

Stewart, M. (2015) The language of praise and criticism in a student evaluation survey. *Studies in Educational Evaluation*, 45, 1–9. doi:10.1016/j.stueduc.2015.01.004

Su, F. & Wood, M. (2012) What makes a good university lecturer? Students' perceptions of teaching excellence. *Journal of Applied Research in Higher Education*, 4(2), 142–155. doi:10.1108/17581181211273110

van den Brink, M. & Benschop, Y. (2012) Gender practices in the construction of academic excellence: sheep with five legs. *Organization*, 19(4), 507–524. doi:10.1177/1350508411414293

Part II

Pedagogical content knowledge

Chapter 7

Exploring and developing pedagogical content knowledge in higher education

John Bostock

Introduction

This chapter examines the conceptions of pedagogical content knowledge (PCK) arising from experiences of professional development in teaching by participants who have vocational or professional backgrounds outside higher education. These experiences include provision accredited by Advance HE to award a Higher Education Academy (HEA) fellowship to experienced staff with more than 3 years' experience of teaching, and taught courses such as postgraduate certificates in teaching that might be offered to staff newer to teaching in HE. The observations on which it is based involved exploring the diversity of these conceptions across subject or professionally related disciplines. Disciplines/subjects are seats of highly specialised knowledge in which professionals, as communities of practice, engage in developmental dialogues which preserve and enhance that knowledge (Becher & Trowler, 2001). A perspective of teacher professionalism referred to as 'dual professionalism' requires that participants become expert teachers as well as expert subject specialists. However, the research presented here suggests that the predominantly generic focus of professional development and the subject diversity of participants can create confusion as the staff struggle to apply pedagogical approaches to their professionally related disciplines. It appears that teacher professionalism, as understood by the participants, is predicated on a perceived need to promote much stronger links between subject matter and pedagogy. Many participants note, for instance, a desire for increased opportunities to develop their subject or professional pedagogies. It is proposed that various approaches to dialogue may provide such opportunities, including critical reflection on how 'subject' matter becomes taught matter. Indeed, certain professional standards for lecturers, such as the UK Professional Standards Framework for teaching and supporting learning (UKPSF; HEA, 2011), do encourage dialogue that produces and reproduces useful concepts around teaching in the disciplines through the specification of knowledge of "teaching, learning and assessing in the subject" and "how students learn both generically and within their subjects/disciplinary area (s)". Dialogue is premised here on using academic knowledge to interpret and translate 'subject' knowledge into discipline-focused pedagogical practice. In other

DOI: 10.4324/9781003198772-10

words, content knowledge (CK) becomes PCK (Bostock, 2019). Thinking in the disciplines and a desire to further explore subject pedagogies is considered in HE through lenses such as threshold concepts (Meyer & Land, 2003), ways of thinking and practising (McCune & Hounsell, 2005) and signature pedagogies (Gurung et al., 2008), and King (2013) offers some educational development resources to support these, which provide an insightful backdrop to this research.

Professionalism and teacher professionalism

At this point, a brief review of historical perspectives of professionalism around specialised knowledge and autonomy specifically is useful. Professions are usually understood as occupations with special statuses as experts or disciplinary authorities, as with lawyers and doctors, often as a result of extensive training and licence to practise. Such professions are often analysed at length in non-contemporary literature and remain pertinent. For example, Hodkinson and Issit (1995), Hargreaves and Goodson (1996), Goodson (2007), and Goodson and Lindblad (2010) have provided relevant, substantive, traditional and contemporary perspectives on professionalism, knowledge and competence which are of particular relevance. Two prevailing views emerge on what constitutes professional knowledge in a teaching context building on the earlier work of Fullar and Brown (1973; in Hargreaves & Goodson, 1996, p. 187): first, as "something that teachers learn from researchers or something they construct with the assistance of researchers". On the one hand this may be true when engaging in university-based continuing professional development (CPD) but, on the other hand, may also come from their own professional experiences and backgrounds. Second, they accentuate the relevance of "stages through which teachers pass to enable a better understanding of the types of knowledge that would be beneficial at a certain period in a teacher's development" (p. 188). They define professionalism in terms of shared attributes and theoretical and practical knowledge acquired through the attainment of qualifications and statuses (Hargreaves & Goodson, 1996). The characteristics of this traditional discourse include having specialised knowledge and self-regulation; therefore, according to them, professions, including teaching, consist of adherents who are trained, expert and subject to peer appraisal and approval which enhances the status of the professional group. Crucially, Goodson (2007) identifies the development of teachers' professional knowledge as theoretically informed practice among professionals engaged in critical discussion. This has been identified as a vital element of conceptual understanding and development (Bostock, 2019), and it is these professionals who, upon entry as teachers into higher education, undertake professional development in terms of teaching and learning.

Hodkinson (1998) also identified professionalism in teaching as being prescribed by detailed standards of performance, determined by lead bodies, arguing that teachers are to be competent and above all flexible, and contentiously describing them as technicians to be controlled. Juxtaposing two dimensions of teacher professionalism, he highlighted as pivotal a process of staff development wherein contracted staff who are full- or part-time are empowered with a responsibility for their own development. He pointed conclusively to a form of professionalism which can lift staff to higher levels of expertise, arguing for a "different level of professionalism to reflect the varying complexities of teaching" (1998, p. 206). In all, this is indicative of professionalism as a dually codified expectation which attempts to replicate established professions on two fronts: professional standards or codes and specialised knowledge. This dual professionalism is defined in the first instance by Kennedy (2007) and, second, by Graal (2012):

> While there is no overall agreement as to exactly what constitutes a profession, there are certain key aspects which are commonly cited as being likely to pertain to an occupational group seeking claim to professional status. These generally include reference to specialist knowledge, autonomy and responsibility. Professionalism, therefore, implies that such characteristics are evident in an individual's work.
>
> (Kennedy, 2007, p. 4)

And

> This dual professionalism is one focus which offers good working definitions of what professionalism might mean in the Lifelong Learning Sector (and beyond) and how continuing professional development (CPD) is central to professional formation for all teachers.
>
> (Graal, 2012, p. 154)

In more specific terms, Taubman (2013), writing from a University and College Union (UCU) perspective, elaborates on this interpretation: "This puts forward the view that a lecturer possesses two forms of professional expertise: around their subject and around the practice of teaching" (p. 18).

Dual professionalism (DP), therefore, focuses on a variety of discourses of professional practice that lead to conceptualisations which stress the salience of disciplinary knowledge over pedagogic practice or, at the very least, the need to bring parity of importance to each. However, this can be seen as an artificial distinction associated with an unsound assumption that it implies a simplistic view of the role of the professional teacher and, indeed, the concept of DP. Clearly, DP stresses the importance of expertise and experience around subject matter, but it is important to acknowledge how this plays only a small part in helping students to learn. Many assumptions centre on the autonomy of professional staff who can, with guidance, CPD and mentoring, readily marry or apply the art of teaching with their subject specialism, but what precisely might be the processes of this application? DP perhaps obscures and diminishes a wider understanding and appreciation of the contextual diversity inherent within professional development processes. Thus, a debate that has emerged most strongly with this in mind has been the concept of discipline-specific or subject-specific pedagogy. This recognises that teaching may be different in different disciplinary, subject or industry areas, implying that pedagogical approaches may need to be quite different when teaching, for example, law students or physics and mathematics students (Shulman, 2005). Although the principles of teaching remain constant, the methods used may change. In essence, generic pedagogy aims to ensure every member of staff has a range of methods at his or her disposal, and there may be some methods that apply more readily to some disciplines than others. Shulman (1987), for instance, actually opposed any emphasis on the mutual exclusivity of subject knowledge and pedagogy, arguing for a construct of teacher knowledge, labelled pedagogical content knowledge, as a critical and sophisticated amelioration and amalgamation of traditional teacher education models. Speaking about education in general, he maintained that all teachers need to have both general pedagogical knowledge and discipline-specific pedagogical knowledge. Current staff development processes tend to focus on generic pedagogy and as such are created for use across the HE sector. The subject specialist elements are not usually taught explicitly; rather, they are mentored in the workplace and/or researched by staff. Prominent among the findings, in particular regarding the mentoring aspects of CPD, is a perception of it offering too little focus on subject or professionally focused pedagogy. The consistency and quality of mentoring are considered sporadic, and so a movement to improve them perhaps remains an issue of mentoring rather than of embedded subject specialist input.

Subject pedagogies

What are subject pedagogies and how do these relate to PCK? PCK refers to the overlap of information about subject knowledge and pedagogic knowledge. To quote Shulman (1986, p. 9) it concerns:

> the most regularly taught topics in one's subject area, the most useful forms of representation of those ideas, the most powerful analogies, illustrations, examples, explanations, and demonstrations – in a word, the ways of representing the subject that make it comprehensible to others.

Shulman's view of PCK readily acknowledges the intersection of two interdependent aspects of teacher knowledge representing an effective and necessary component of professional development, but no reference is made specifically and practically as to how this can be effectively developed. In his favour, Shulman certainly could not have envisaged the growth and range of diverse professionals engaged in teaching during the last decade. According to him, discipline-specific pedagogical knowledge can be explained as ways of representing and formulating the subject that makes it comprehensible for others (1986, pp. 9–10), and this view remains relevant in current contexts. Therefore, Shulman's focus on the significance of language in context and professionally based pedagogical practices has not dissipated; rather, it has enabled a stronger understanding of how PCK processes can bring useful affirmations and insights for professional development in teaching. The interdependency of generic and subject-focused pedagogy affords staff the opportunity to see PCK as an explorative, problem-solving activity designed to influence and enhance their potential teaching styles and approaches. In turn, these effectively support their deepened appreciation of PCK – that is, the practical and reflective explorations of their teaching preparation to consider three important aspects, namely interaction, context and professional situation. As staff encounter new contexts and situations, their practices evolve to take account of these supported by generic and subject input plus mentor support. Indeed, this discipline-focused approach was also an endeavour proposed by Jenkins (1996) – for instance, recognising particular curricular and pedagogic concerns of the disciplines and helping staff to develop the teaching of their discipline, acknowledging where staff's primary allegiances tend to lie (Robson, 1998; Bostock, 2019). In other words, the discipline is not a barrier to promoting best practice in teaching and learning.

Methodology

The research discussed in this chapter sought to explore how professionals from certain disciplines developed and learned as teachers in higher education and, thereby, how they came to develop their understanding of PCK. The professional development programmes depicted are predominantly generic, groups are mixed-subject – that is, heterogenic rather than homogenous or subject-specific – and subject-specific input is largely absent, provided, somewhat sporadically, through mentoring. The cohorts examined have typically participated in programmes on a part-time basis over a 2-year period, either in the evening or in the daytime, and have covered, through lectures, seminars and assignments, specifics such as planning, learning and teaching, assessment and professional values. The programme of study typically involved exploring teaching practice in higher education, curriculum design and pedagogical research opportunities. Integrated into these activities is the UKPSF (HEA, 2011) and, of particular note, the dimensions of practice Core Knowledge (K) 1–3 and Area of Activity (A) 5, which specifically refer to 'subject/discipline', as follows, with A5 specifically of paramount importance in this research:

K1: The *subject* material;
K2: Appropriate methods for teaching and learning in the *subject* area and at the level of the academic programme;
K3: How students learn, both generally and within their *subject/disciplinary* area(s);
A5: Engagement in continuing professional development in *subjects/disciplines* and their pedagogy, incorporating research, scholarship and the evaluation of professional practices.

To achieve specific and pertinent data, certain criteria as to who could be involved were employed. Participants needed to be undertaking a programme of professional development in teaching on a part-time basis and be contracted staff within their departments. This would ensure that each participant, despite their varying professional roles and backgrounds, was undertaking the same programme type.

Data were gathered through professional discussions with programme participants, using reflective diaries, transcripts, field notes and observation data to give a direct, authentic voice to each professional. One of the defining characteristics of this research was an inductive approach to the analysis using a constant comparative method (Lincoln & Guba, 1985). Interrogation of such discursive practice, particularly for identifying patterns, regularities, recurring words and phrases, involved a particularly multidirectional methodology with well-constructed, finely tuned methods in particular professional discussions. The primary aim of these was to generate data which gave an authentic insight into people's experiences and views of professionalism.

Data from professional discussions provided greater insight, for example, where they produced threads which suggested that all staff had very similar things to say in terms of dissatisfaction with the staff development programme – that is, totally generic activity and a lack of subject-specialist input. These were codified as such according to the aforementioned constant comparative method, using NVivo software, as a reasonable reconstruction of the raw, recorded data (see Findings below). However, the methodological approach was not intended to be a form of triangulation to arrive at a single conclusive viewpoint or solution as to how PCK is conceptualised. Rather, the intention was to provide a depth of understanding which could still allow a variety of perspectives. It was necessary to describe how, when and in what context the voices of the staff were to be heard, who actually heard them and the impact of this. Kvale (1996), for instance, has discussed how reality is multilayered, so that reliability in professional discussions is, therefore, open to many interpretations which simultaneously exist and are produced according to the contexts and situations encountered, including, for instance, how professionals use texts, dialogue and practice to create their professional identities as teachers. Thus, the methodology adopted assisted in making sense of the meanings inherent within speech particularly to understand the phenomena which led to and emerged from the dialogue.

Findings and discussion

The aim of the research was to engage with participants through dialogue and discussion and reveal their concepts of teacher professionalism. As outlined above, the discursive framework and the methodological approaches involved critical reflective practice that enabled a construct of teacher professionalism derived through professional discussions – that is, dialogue. Coding involved adapting an *in vivo* method (Saldaña, 2015) – a form of qualitative data analysis that places emphasis on the actual spoken words of participants. In this instance, a label was assigned to a section of data – that is, the professional discussion transcript – using a word or short phrase taken from that section of the data. Although in vivo coding is probably the most common name for this form of coding, it can also be referred to as verbatim coding, literal coding and natural coding (Saldaña, 2015). The primary aim was to find out the participants' concepts of teacher professionalism and whether they felt that this was appropriately addressed in the professional development programme. Such professionalism is deeply premised on the distinctions between content knowledge and pedagogical content knowledge viewed, respectively, as the teacher's understanding of the subject matter taught and the knowledge needed to make the subject matter accessible to students, and that this knowledge is at the heart of their professional competence as dual professionals. Thus, participants could develop and appreciate PCK as a useful, deep and complex process in theorising ideas on subject-related teaching and instruction. Just as it recognises distinct subject, or indeed professionally relevant, practices in teaching, PCK development also acknowledges the significance of dialogue as the medium of such practice. Commitment to professional practice in teaching is not only personal but an obligation to the profession itself. Staff need to develop communities of professional practice (Wenger et al., 2002) where they can engage in developmental dialogues about teaching. The words and phrases from the professional discussions captured in this research are correlated and tabulated in Table 7.1.

Discussion

The existence of the requirement to become dually professional – that is, expert teacher and expert subject specialist – in a setting where the first occupational identity is prioritised over the second can result in tension. Table 7.1 clearly

Table 7.1 A conceptualisation of teacher professionalism

Teacher professionalism foci derived from the literature review	HE staff's concepts of teacher professionalism mentioned in the professional discussions
Social construct with assistance from researchers (Hargreaves & Goodson, 1996)	Not directly mentioned
Qualifications/trained/expert/status/professional codes (Turner, 1990)	Yes
Professional standards (Hodkinson, 1998; Institute for Learning, 2009)	Inferred but not directly mentioned
Specialised knowledge and self-regulation (Hoyle & John, 1995; Freidson, 2001)	Yes
Subject discipline (Shulman, 1987; Lenze, 1995; Jenkins, 1996)	Yes
Reflexive practice in action and on action (Boud & Walker, 1998)	Yes

indicates how staff recognise the importance of qualifications, reflexivity and specialised knowledge as essential in their respective professional identities. Despite this, the situation renders the latter component in a state of flux: shared professional knowledge about what constitutes specialised pedagogical knowledge and skills is understood by each respective profession in their specific contexts, but the relationship and application of teacher education pedagogy and professional practice remain divided. Consequently, the concept of teacher is as diverse as the professions themselves. Robson (1998), for instance, found that staff prioritised their former professional identity over that of being a teacher, because, as she later argued, that previous experience provides the credibility required for their new teaching role (Robson, 2005). This emphasis on their former vocation or dual professionalism affects their perception of their role as a teacher and how they relate to the staff development they will have to undertake:

> My tutor really tried to make all this theory make sense for me, but I would still prefer more direct instruction on how to teach my subject or at least how the theory is applied specifically to my subject area.
>
> I can already "teach" my subject so why do I need to do it differently? Indeed, how do I do it differently? This never really gets explained.

Focus on the development of PCK of contractually employed HE staff continues to remain largely unresearched. Their backgrounds, qualifications and experiences are manifestly diverse and have clear implications for engagement with staff development processes. As Clow (2001) historically argued, "There is no guarantee that they have any theoretical knowledge about teaching, although they may have theoretical knowledge about their original profession/vocation/subject" (p. 409). She further pointed out that, "there remain features of teaching that are not comfortably described by any one theory" (p. 416). Staff on professional development programmes conceded on this long-standing issue:

> I wish that we could have formalised the process somehow to include subject pedagogy including associated theories and engage more closely with other staff from my professional background.

The research suggests through the data that the various professional settings already have established discourse and protocol and these practices are particularly strong:

> I find it challenging to reflect on my practice. Not because it is complex but more so because I have to ensure that what I am saying fits in with the terminology used by the tutors on the programme. What I find, however, is that we do the things required by the programme. We just call it something else.

The concept of teacher identity relates directly to the experiences and the internalised concepts gained professionally and through CPD. The participants regarded themselves as professionals and recognised and valued the significance of applied pedagogical subject knowledge as key to this identity. However, the process necessary to implement this in a manner which reflected their perceived needs – that is, PCK development – remained absent:

> We all try to understand the generic pedagogy and apply it to our subject. This is challenging but could we be a subject-specific group where we can all gain a common understanding of its application relatively quickly.

Pivotal to this is the realisation that context refers to environments and dialogic spaces in which new meanings and concepts around teacher professionalism – that is, contextual values associated with CPD – were discursively being produced:

> There are so many instances where I ask for clarification on what something means, and I get no helpful response. It's not my tutor's fault that he doesn't know my subject area, but it is really confusing and has meant that I am spending more time seeking explanations and clarifications than getting on with the work.

To clarify again, at the beginning and end of the periods of this research, staff were asked for their views on professional development programmes. They made qualitative statements based on their experiences over a period of 2 years. They reported a significant leaning away from generic pedagogy, distancing themselves from the view that pedagogical theories can be systematically and effectively applied to professional practice without issue. They had developed a subject-focused orientation which recognised the significance of discussion and practice and more subject-related pedagogical skills. In other words, an interconnected subject-related body of ideas created through discussion where misunderstandings are explicitly worked on and resolved. This was a positive move and conclusively opened up a direct correlation between CK and PCK, regarding CK as the necessary prerequisite for the development of PCK.

Yet it is worthwhile noting that most 'subjects' are in fact increasingly interdisciplinary, indicating an approach to curriculum integration that generates an understanding of themes and ideas that cut across disciplines – that is, the connections between different disciplines and their relationship to the real world. Professionals from various backgrounds, perhaps unwittingly and unconsciously, played a significant role in the co-creation of concepts around 'teacher' as they formed heterogeneous groups studying and practising alongside each other. This emphasised process and collaboration among two or more academic disciplines, building a theoretical framework that surpasses the constraints of individual disciplinary interpretations. This echoes what Lenze (1995) also found: that much of the discipline-specific knowledge of teaching was implicit rather than explicit. In order to understand university teaching, it is, therefore, necessary to establish what staff hold as the core concepts of teaching in their field, as the core concepts are the basis to understanding the reasons for the teaching processes adopted. Again, this can be achieved through critical reflection and dialogue. In summary, the findings can be thematically arranged as follows:

- Dual professional identities among higher education staff are problematic as each professional brings with them considerable but diverse experiential, professional knowledge of practices and a professionally related and specific concept of 'higher education teacher'.
- One of the main challenges concerns opportunities to explore and discuss professional subject knowledge and its distinct pedagogical application. The reasoning behind subject-specific pedagogy relies on the argument that different models of learning may be employed for different subjects. The findings in this research presented a powerful theoretical argument for a re-emphasis on promoting exploration and discussion of application of subject knowledge to pedagogical practice.
- An implicit assumption is that subject expertise rather than knowledge and skills is the chief determinant of the quality of teaching and learning. Clearly, it is more about how that subject expertise becomes teaching expertise.
- This helps further the research on teacher professionalism and CPD in higher education, specifically with regard to supporting subject pedagogy. The affinity of staff with their former professional subject matter is strong, yet the quality of their teaching is affected adversely by their limited knowledge of how to teach their subject. A re-emphasis on developing PCK which is based on strong subject knowledge is desired.
- Even in the absence of a return to face-to-face subject-focused CPD, there is scope at least for the re-emergence of opportunities to promote PCK multimodally for diverse professionals.

Therefore, this research can enable further, significant debate around the development of the scholarship of teaching in higher education, arguing that it needs to be developed within the context of the culture of the disciplines in which it is applied, providing a challenging agenda for the development of subject-based teaching in higher education.

Conclusion

This chapter has provided insights into and perceptions of how professionals see their role as a teacher in light of the way in which teacher professional development in higher education is delivered, arguing that professional identity is determined by an adherence on the part of staff to the concept of dual professionalism. Their subject/discipline or content knowledge is clearly significant, but equally so is the development of that knowledge as PCK. The chapter has also revealed several areas in which individuals struggle with the concept and many instinctively look back to their own established practices and pedagogies. It is clear that

Exploring and developing pedagogical content knowledge 111

participants bring with them their own individually constructed histories, perceptions and beliefs, and yet these can be significant in developing a fuller appreciation of what constitutes PCK in higher education.

The chapter has also explored the significance of dialogue in real professional situations. As such, professionals, as carriers of discourse, are an important conceptual move. Dialogue can enable a deeper exploration and understanding of the relevance of subject matter and taught matter, thereby helping staff to understand and be understood as higher education practitioners. Higher education practitioner constructions of 'teacher' subvert and refract dominant academic discourses – that is, higher education teachers as subject experts, or the assumption that subject expertise alone is more important than teaching – and, in so doing, open up space for new practices and alignments, while at the same time constraining other possibilities. The main theme was the struggle staff felt during their engagement with professional development programmes, and yet the very struggle redefined the space and was in itself educative. Emerging from this space are six ideas to support staff to develop their understanding of PCK and the relevance of their subject pedagogy:

1. Watching others teach their subject (e.g. real-time, on video/DVD/digital recordings);
2. Finding out about pedagogy for their subject (e.g., session planning, research, textbooks, subject publications/websites/associations);
3. Talking/working with other subject staff (e.g., face-to-face, online fora, conferences, staff development);
4. Getting guidance/support from an experienced colleague (e.g., through formal or informal mentoring);
5. Developing or accessing learning resources specific to their subject (e.g., creating resources, accessing resource collections/libraries, publishing resources/articles);
6. Engaging with professional communities related to their subject (e.g., course teams, staff development, conferences, online discussion groups/fora).

These approaches focus on improving teaching and not only consider the social and cultural factors which influence the design and delivery of teaching and learning, but also take a transformative view of teacher professionalism, one which seeks to develop staff who are creative designers of curriculum and who are innovative pedagogues in their subject. Yet the opportunities for developing teachers' practice and improving professional development programmes become limited if staff are seen purely as implementers of subject knowledge. There remains a number of aspects of teaching that are common across disciplines, which justifies an equal emphasis on professional development as an intervention to improve staff's generic as well as subject-specific classroom practice.

Finally, the notion of intersectionality recognises that professional identities do not exist independently of each other, and so dialogue on professional development programmes should focus on a more dynamic style of debate and discussion about the differences in experience among staff with different overlapping identities. When staff share their experiences, they should take the opportunity to listen to how they construct their identity through participation in their discipline and its environment, which then shapes a particular view of teaching through discipline-related experiences, values and beliefs. These are (or should be) captured, nurtured, encouraged and opened up to further scrutiny, reformulation, understanding and dissemination, which, as proposed throughout this chapter, involves deep and critical reflection on how content in all its variation and diversity becomes PCK. Even subjects or disciplines themselves encompass great diversity and variation and, perhaps, are better termed cognate clusters. This would, in turn, permit a more flexible approach to discipline-related pedagogies which transcends the limiting term 'subject-specific'. I shall reiterate what has been said previously when participants query the relevance of staff development in their disciplines: "When they ask to be taught how to teach their 'subject', they must appreciate the necessity of dialogue and language as processes of meaning making to achieve an understanding of what this actually means" (Bostock, 2019, n.p.).

References

Becher, T. & Trowler, P.R. (2001) *Academic Tribes and Territories: Intellectual Enquiry and the Cultures of Disciplines* (2nd edn). Open University Press/SRHE, Buckingham.

Bostock, J. (2019) Exploring in-service trainee teacher expertise and practice: developing pedagogical content knowledge, *Innovations in Education and teaching International*, 56 (5), 605–616. doi:10.1080/14703297.2018.1562358

Boud, D. &Walker, D. (1998) Promoting reflection in professional courses: the challenge of context. *Studies in Higher Education*, 23 (2), 191–206. doi:10.1080/03075079812331380384

Clow, R. (2001) Further education teachers' constructions of professionalism. *Journal of Vocational Education & Training*, 53 (3), 407–420. doi:10.1080/13636820100200166

Freidson, E. (2001) *Professionalism: The Third Logic*. Polity Press, London.

Goodson, I.F. (2007) *Professional Knowledge, Professional Lives: Studies in Education and Change*. Open University Press, Maidenhead.

Goodson, I.F. & Lindblad, S. (Eds.) (2010) *Professional Knowledge and Educational Restructuring in Europe*. Sense, Rotterdam. doi:10.1007/978-94-6091-379-2

Graal, N. (2012) Continuing professional development in the lifelong learning sector. *Professional Development in Education*, 38 (1), 154–155. doi:10.1080/19415257.2011.574510

Gurung, R.A.R., Chick, N.L. & Haynie, A. (2008) *Exploring Signature Pedagogies: Approaches to Teaching Disciplinary Habits of Mind*. Stylus, Sterling, VA.

Hargreaves, A. & Goodson, I. (1996) *Teachers Professional Lives: Aspirations and actualities*. Falmer Press, London.

HEA (2011) *The UK Professional Standards Framework for Teaching and Supporting Learning in Higher Education*. HEA, York.

Hodkinson, P. (1998) Technicism, teachers and teaching quality in vocational education and training. *Journal of Vocational Education and Training*, 50 (2), 193–208. doi:10.1080/13636829800200045

Hodkinson, P. & Issit, M. (Eds.) (1995) *The Challenge of Competence: Professionalism through Vocational Education and Training.* Cassell, London.

Hoyle, E. & John, P.D. (1995) *Professional Knowledge and Professional Practice.* Cassell, London.

Institute for Learning (2009) Professionalism and the Role of Professional Bodies: A Stimulus Paper. Institute for Learning.

Jenkins, A. (1996) Discipline-based educational development, *International Journal for Academic Development*, 1 (1), 50–62. doi:10.1080/1360144960010106

Kennedy, A. (2007) Continuing professional development (CPD) policy and the discourse of teacher professionalism in Scotland. *Research Papers in Education*, 22 (1), 95–111. doi:10.1080/02671520601152128

King, H. (2013) OERs for discipline-orientated academic development. *Educational Developments*, 14 (2), 10–12.

Kvale, S. (1996) *Interviews: An Introduction to Qualitative Research Interviewing.* Sage, London.

Lenze, L.F. (1995) Discipline-specific pedagogical knowledge in linguistics and Spanish. In: Hativa, N. & Marincovich, M. (Eds.) *Disciplinary Differences in Teaching and Learning: Implications for Practice.* Jossey-Bass, San Francisco, 65–70.

Lincoln, Y. & Guba, E. (1985) *Naturalistic Inquiry*, Sage, Beverly Hills, CA.

McCune, V. & Hounsell, D. (2005) The development of students' ways of thinking and practising in three final-year biology courses. *Higher Education*, 49 (3), 255–228. doi:10.1007/s10734-004-6666-0

Meyer, J.H.F. & Land, R. (2003) Threshold concepts and troublesome knowledge 1 – linkages to ways of thinking and practising. In Rust, C. (Ed.) *Improving Student Learning – Ten Years On.* OCSLD, Oxford, 7–22.

Robson, J. (1998) A profession in crisis: status, culture and identity in the further education college, *Journal of Vocational Education and Training*, 50 (4), 585–607. doi:10.1080/13636829800200067

Robson, J. (2005) *Teacher Professionalism in Further and Higher Education: Challenges to Culture and Practice.* Routledge, Abingdon. doi:10.4324/9780203397299

Saldaña, J. (2015) *The Coding Manual for Qualitative Researchers* (3rd edn). Sage, London.

Shulman, L.S. (1986) Those who understand: knowledge growth in teaching. *Educational Researcher*, 15 (2), 4–14. doi:10.3102/0013189x015002004

Shulman, L.S. (1987) Knowledge and teaching: foundations of the new reform. *Harvard Educational Review*, 57 (1), 1–22.

Shulman, L.S. (2005) Signature pedagogies in the professions. *Daedalus*, 134 (3), 52–59. doi:10.1162/0011526054622015

Taubman, D. (2013) Towards a UCU Policy on Professionalism. Universities & Colleges Union.

Turner, R. (1990) Role change. *Annual Review of Sociology*, 16, 87–110.

Wenger, E., McDermott, R. & Snyder, W.M. (2002) *Cultivating Communities of Practice.* Harvard Business School Press, Boston, MA.

Chapter 8

Professional identity in clinical legal education

Re-enacting the disciplinary concept of 'thinking like a lawyer'

Rachel Wood

Introduction

In this chapter, I examine the theme of professional identity in the context of the development of a pedagogical approach for clinical legal education. I write reflexively from the perspective of my work as a clinic teacher, creating and piloting the pedagogic design and ethos for a new law clinic module, Lawyering in Practice, for third-year law undergraduates at a university in England. I explore how my understanding of teaching expertise has been challenged by a shift between academic teaching and clinical legal education. I identify how this shift has been connected to development of a deepened understanding of the epistemological and ontological possibilities of clinical education, considering ways in which clinical pedagogy might support students to explore what they can know as law students, but also who they can become as future lawyers. I discuss how the context of clinical education has required my colleagues and me to inhabit complex, professional identities as both lawyers and teachers. Finally, I outline an approach embedded within the new module, which draws on wider pedagogical expertise from an entrepreneurship business degree, where traditional pedagogy is replaced by coaching, adopting an approach which aims to support both students and teachers to navigate Schön's "swampy lowlands" (1987) of professional legal practice and develop as reflective practitioners.

A shift from 'knowing' to 'being'

Barnett (2009) suggests that a policy shift has taken place during recent decades towards a student being "constructed as an acting being rather than a cognitive being" and proposes that the emergence of the "performative student" (Lyotard, 1984) requires us to transform the way in which we look at students and their ability to adapt to cope with unpredictability and the possibility of multiple careers. Students are not immune from the wider pressures of "liquid modernity" (Bauman, 2000) which influence how individuals navigate development of a reflexive sense of identity (Giddens, 1991; Archer, 2007) to survive the constantly evolving demands of society. In UK higher education, including law schools, this

DOI: 10.4324/9781003198772-11

shift is reflected in the growing importance of 'employability', and more recently entrepreneurship, as dominant themes in the discourse surrounding legal education (Susskind, 2017; Alexander & Boothby, 2018; Bleasdale & Francis, 2020).

In England and Wales, the long-established structure of legal education (the core degree subjects were determined by the Ormrod Report in 1971; Lord Chancellor's Advisory Committee on Legal Education and Conduct, 1971) was set to be disrupted by the introduction in 2021 of the Solicitors Qualifying Examination (SQE; Solicitors Regulation Authority, 2020). The SQE is a centrally set suite of assessments based on the testing of 'functioning' legal knowledge, using 'best answer' multiple choice questions, and professional legal skills, through a set of discrete skills assessments. The SQE has been critiqued for its focus on specific (narrow) ways of legal thinking (Davies, 2018; Guth & Dutton, 2018; Mason, 2018). It is having significant impact not only on professional legal education, but also on undergraduate law degrees, requiring law schools to rethink and re-articulate the epistemological aims and values within their programmes in response to the opportunities and threats the SQE presents.

My own teaching career has taken me from teaching professional skills and knowledge in postgraduate professional legal education (following a change in direction from an initial career in legal practice as a litigation solicitor) to a more academic focus teaching employment law within an undergraduate law degree programme. I have had the opportunity to explore more experiential approaches to pedagogy, in particular co-creating a dispute resolution skills module. Most recently, I have been given the opportunity to embed clinical education into an undergraduate programme, drawing on and extending the impact of previously co-curricular pro bono work within the law school.

My previous experiences of teaching and developing modules for both professional and academic law programmes have led me to an interest in developing the expertise to support students in developing a sense of who they are, and not just what they know. A law clinic setting has the potential to deliver what Dall'Alba and Barnacle (2007) describe as an "ontological turn" where:

> the focus is no longer knowledge transfer or acquisition. Instead, knowing is understood as created, embodied and enacted. In other words, the question for students would be not only what they know, but also who they are becoming.
>
> (2007, p. 683)

Within a law clinic setting, students can be given the opportunity to explore what it might mean to become a lawyer, beyond development of specific professional skills. This is a process which involves what Shulman categorises as a "pedagogy of *formation*" which "can build identity and character, dispositions and values". He suggests that, in law and other professional signature pedagogies, this aspect teaches:

habits of mind because of the power associated with the routinization of analysis. But I think in a very deep sense [it] also teaches *habits of the heart*, as well, because of the marriage of reason, interdependence and emotion.

(2005, p. 13; original italics)

This is a holistic characterisation of pedagogy that views cognition as a sense-making activity that "is also simultaneously *affective*" (Colombetti, 2014, p. 18; original italics). It contextualises knowledge and professional skills development within a more expansive idea of what it can mean to become a lawyer. It creates epistemological space for values, approaches to ethical practice and the role of emotion as an aspect of practice. Lawyers do not often speak of 'habits of the heart'. There is something uncomfortable in even writing about this idea here. It could, in one sense, be seen as a romantic ideal, out of touch with the hard-nosed realities of preparing students for a competitive, neoliberal and rapidly changing legal services market (Thornton, 2012; Susskind, 2017). However, I suggest that the tough nature of today's professional legal environment makes this holistic concept of professional formation more important, as students need considerable self-awareness and strength of character to draw on if they are to succeed in a legal career (Thornton, 2012; Somerlad, 2016; Bleasdale & Francis, 2020).

The impact of 'thinking like a lawyer' as a way of knowing in legal education

'Habits of the heart' are a long way from the traditional pedagogy adopted in undergraduate, academic legal education, which "tends to draw substantially upon a traditional objectivist epistemology" (Webb, 2011, p. 218). The jurist William Twining summarises the "standard dichotomies" in discourse about legal education as including:

> liberal/vocational; theory/practice; book-learning/experience; academic/practical; education/training; clinical/intellectual; skills/understanding.
>
> (1988, p. 5)

However, the doctrinal approach to academic law teaching is recognised as holding a dominant place in this discourse (Burridge & Webb, 2007). It can be described as a 'black letter' approach. which focuses on the "synthesis of various rules, principles, norms, interpretive guidelines and values. It explains, makes coherent or justifies a segment of the law as part of a larger system of law" (Kelly, 1992, p. 89). It is often linked to the process of teaching students to 'think like a lawyer', developing a "way of knowing" (Belenky et al., 1986) which foregrounds intellectual analysis and legal reasoning skills (Baron & Corbin, 2012). 'Thinking like a lawyer' can be seen as what Schön (1987) categorised as a "technical rational" way of thinking, where intellectual skills are exercised in a specifically created and contained academic learning environment. This contrasts with Schön's metaphor of the "swampy lowlands" of professional practice, where lawyers have to work with the complexity and messiness of problems served up by real people. As one of my undergraduate students succinctly put it, "In law school we 'Advise Henry, 25 marks'. In real life it's like 'Advise Henry'".

The ability to use intellectual skills to analyse, synthesise and reason in this way is a powerful cognitive approach for law students to learn and work with. It is one which they will certainly need to master if they wish to move forward into legal practice; however, when it is the dominant approach adopted within legal education it can have negative consequences. The US and Australian legal education literature of the last 20 years highlights the potentially damaging impact of this way of thinking on the psychological wellbeing of law students (Krieger, 2002; Mertz, 2007; Sheldon & Krieger, 2007; O'Brien et al., 2011; Baron & Corbin, 2012). The literature suggests that this approach can lead to a narrow conceptualisation of legal understanding, isolated from critical consideration of the role of law within society (Burridge & Webb, 2007). It becomes particularly problematic when it:

> teaches that tough-minded analysis, hard facts, and cold logic are the tools of a good lawyer and it has little room for emotion, imagination, and morality.
>
> (Hess, 2002, p. 78)

When disconnected from practice in an academic setting, emphasis on 'thinking like a lawyer' can, it seems, leave students with limited opportunity to develop an embodied and ethical understanding of law as a discipline or a practice.

The move towards a more holistic approach to professional identity formation as an aspect of legal education

In the UK, these international findings are recognised as a matter for concern, and this is reflected in recent literature asserting the need to explore the development of positive professional identities (Strevens & Field, 2020) and arguing for the importance of the role of emotion in legal education (Maharg & Maugham, 2011; Jones, 2018, 2019). In university curricula, there is growing interest in areas for study such as alternative dispute resolution (Waters, 2017) which enable students to take an experiential approach to learning professional skills of negotiation and mediation, areas of practice that require students to demonstrate emotional intelligence, empathy and ethical awareness, as well as cognitive skills of legal analysis. To this end, clinical legal education, through which students engage directly with advising live clients about legal issues, has also been growing steadily. A 2014 survey by the UK clinic support network LawWorks (2014) showed that 70% of law schools offered a pro bono programme or clinic. Yearly reports on level of demand reflect continuing growth in demand for university clinic services (LawWorks, 2018). While the resourcing of clinics is likely to be driven at school and university level by an employability agenda focusing specifically on professional skills and attributes, that does not prevent the potential for clinical education to also promote development of Shulman's "habits of the heart".

The Carnegie apprenticeship model

The Carnegie Foundation report, *Educating Lawyers* (Sullivan et al., 2007), of which Shulman was one of the authors, provided an influential starting point in drawing together a more holistic approach to clinical legal pedagogy. The report identified a need to address the disconnect between the study of law and professional practice in the US. It identified a model of professional development that was structured into a three-stage apprenticeship, comprising cognitive, practical and ethical-social stages. The third stage is categorised as "the apprenticeship of identity and purpose" (2007, p. 132) involving professional identity formation, enabling students to develop "conceptions of the personal meaning that legal work has for practicing attorneys and their sense of responsibility towards the profession" (2007, p. 132). The report proposed an aligned pedagogic approach, suggesting "new possibilities for reconnecting the dimensions of craft and meaning with formal knowledge" (2007, p. 8)

The underlying pedagogic design of the Lawyering in Practice module aims to bring together elements of all three stages of the Carnegie apprenticeship, with a view to enabling students to begin to develop 'ways of being', not just 'ways of knowing', as lawyers. The module approaches this aim by focusing on supporting development of a positive professional identity, drawing on the work of Field et al. (2014).

Professional identity involves a "constellation of attributes, beliefs, values, motives and experiences" (Ibarra, 1999, p. 764) which help individuals to define themselves in their professional lives. It is recognised as a "broad, highly individualised concept" (Field et al., 2014, p. 10). The focus is on developing reflective practice in the context of three key identity elements comprising role and personal and social identities.

Field et al. (drawing on White et al., 2011) suggest that:

- *Personal identity* includes factors such as "personal history, your life experiences, your personality, and your feelings, goals and values".
- *Role identity* refers to "professional functions, activities and responsibilities" which arise in relation to the specific profession.
- *Social identity* refers to "collective commitment within your profession to certain values and goals" (2014, p. 11).

All three elements are regarded as important to the development of a positive professional identity, requiring students to consider their "personal self ... self as a lawyer and the place of lawyering in society" (2014, p. 11). Field et al. suggest that the process is a subtle one, not often explicitly acknowledged by law schools. By establishing a pedagogic structure which incorporates these dimensions, my aim has been to create a deliberate and explicit space for students to engage holistically with this process.

Structuring pedagogy around dimensions of positive professional identity formation to support student development as a reflective practitioner

The Lawyering in Practice module is constructed around these three identity dimensions. Involvement in clinic work advising clients provides the basis for development of role identity and specific professional legal skills. Social identity is supported through workshops which explore issues beyond the immediate clinic setting – for example, the role of ethics in lawyering, ongoing changes in the legal profession, access to justice and the role of pro bono work in society. Practitioners from different legal fields are invited to participate in some workshops to open up access to a range of perspectives. A focus on personal identity pervades all aspects of the module, but is specifically supported through use of coaching, drawing on expertise from another programme within the university, Team Entrepreneurship; this approach is discussed below.

The module uses a structured reflective portfolio as the primary assessment method to draw together the three dimensions. Developing the capacity for reflection sounds an obvious thing for law students and lawyers to do, and it is a growing area of interest for legal educators (Hinett et al., 2002; Casey, 2014; Leering, 2014; Gibbons 2015; The Law Teacher, 2019; Madhloom, 2019). However, unlike in other professions – for example, teaching (e.g. Brookfield, 2017) social work (e.g. Fook & Gardner, 2013) or nursing (e.g. Esterhuizen & Howatson-Jones, 2019) – reflection is not an established part of the pedagogical framework. The position is different within clinical legal education, where its use is much more prevalent, representing "the magic ingredient which converts legal experience into education" (Ledvinka, 2006, pp. 29–30). However, clinic teachers frequently work with students who are encountering the use of reflection for the first time, often at a point in their undergraduate studies when a doctrinal approach to thinking about law is well established, and learning to think reflectively requires a significant epistemological shift. My own experience of using reflective portfolios in other settings has led me to recognise that reflection is not something that can be 'taught' (Ledvinka, 2006), and that its use has significant implications for the demands it makes on both students and teachers. Hall warns that reflection "is not soft, neat, bounded or linear"; instead, it is "exposing, potentially painful, time-consuming", exerting "a considerable cognitive load on the reflector and therefore a concomitant load on those who support, train and assess the reflectors" (Hall, 2019, p. 399).

Schön's work (1983, 1987, 1995) on the artistry involved in the reflective process of reflecting 'in' and 'on' action and the development of the reflective practitioner has been influential in my own teaching. However, ironically, in working out what these concepts look like in a teaching environment, Schön himself appears to focus, uncritically, on the concept of developing students to 'think like a lawyer', ignoring the wider complexities of legal practice (Schön, 1995).

The challenges of creating a reflective practicum

The ability to reflect upon "knowing-in-action" (Schön, 1987) relies upon "considerable experience in the profession" (Wong & Trollop-Kumar, 2014, p. 1). Most law students do not yet have this experience to draw on. The clinic teacher needs to demonstrate professional expertise to enable students to instil knowing-in-action through the learning experiences made available to students (Schön, 1987). Schön proposes that the legal educator address this issue by creating a "reflective practicum" (1995, p. 250) to provide a space that can mimic the professional environment. The practicum brings Schön's concept of the swampy lowlands physically and metaphorically into the 'technical rational' university environment in a controlled way that is intended to scaffold the learning experience and support the move towards a new epistemology of professional practice. Within this space, teacher and student are encouraged to engage in a mentoring relationship in which the teacher demonstrates their professional expertise as they model the role of the professional in the processes of knowing-in-action and reflecting 'in' and 'on' action to the student.

Schön does not provide much detail as to the specific form a reflective practicum should take. What has become clear through the process of piloting the Lawyering in Practice module is that establishing a law clinic space, mingling educational and professional environments, is a complex process. Picking up rather clumsily on Schön's metaphor, if the law clinic is seen as an example of a 'swamp', it is one that is also constrained by metaphorical holding fences which impact on the ways in which clinic teachers are able to apply their teaching expertise.

The educational space, both physical and pedagogical, within which a university law clinic sits is unusual. Students are neither fully immersed in legal practice, as they would be on a placement within a law firm (or, by analogy, on teaching practice or on placements in a medical educational setting), nor are they working in a simulated environment. This puts law clinics into a pedagogical space that occupies a halfway house between the traditional university world of academic study and professional practice. As a practical consideration, the law clinic needs its own dedicated physical space and time within the academic schedule. The experience of being in the law clinic needs to be clearly distinguished from that of being in a traditional classroom in order that both students and clinic teachers (if they also teach elsewhere in the law programme) can recognise and respond to the required epistemological shift as they move from academic learning into the immersive, experiential clinic environment. This is not easy to achieve with students used to a traditional, lecture-focused approach to legal pedagogy. Indeed, it has proved particularly challenging in 2020–21, as Covid-19 has blurred the boundaries between university, professional and home spaces while access to campus remains restricted.

The challenges involved in this complex shift are themselves obscured by the shared experience of being immersed in Schön's swamp alongside the students, while retaining responsibility for their educational experience.

Rethinking professional identity as a clinic teacher

This process has required me to think much more explicitly about my own sense of professional identity as I develop as a clinical legal educator. It is not only our students who need to attend to the holistic aspects of development of positive professional identities. My own experience of engaging in clinic teaching within the curriculum, rather than supporting co-curricular activity, is having a significant affective and transformational impact (Mezirow, 1991) on me, which I can see mirrored in my clinic colleagues. This impact requires our attention if we are to enhance our expertise (and at times maintain our sanity).

The Carnegie report suggests that "effective pedagogy to address the students' formative development must be a highly self-conscious, reflexive one" (Sullivan et al., 2007, p. 32). The concept of reflexivity extends beyond that of reflection, requiring "an other and some self- conscious awareness of the process of self-scrutiny" (Chiseri-Strater, 1996, p. 130) within a social context, maintaining alertness to the shifting interaction between self and environment. Although the literature on developing reflective practice for law students is now evolving, there is much less guidance to be found on how clinic educators themselves develop either reflective or reflexive capacities. Gegerson (2019), in her autoethnographic PhD study examining her own experiences as a clinical educator, comments on the surprising scarcity of literature exploring the experiences of clinical educators (examples include Dunlap & Joy, 2004, and Macfarlane & McKeown, 2008). However, this is perhaps not surprising if we consider that legal education does not address professional formation and the development of reflective and reflexive capacity as a matter of course. It would seem to follow that its practitioners, academic or professional, themselves trained in more traditional, positivist ways of thinking, are unlikely to be oriented towards reflexivity. My own teaching practice has led me to explore the use of reflection with my students, but it is the experience of adopting a new identity as a postgraduate researcher, undertaking a doctorate in education, that has exposed me to the need to engage explicitly with the process of my own reflexivity.

Balancing the professional identity 'wobbleboard'

Deliberate use of a reflexive process during the initial pilot stage of the Lawyering in Practice module has led me to consider how the role identity of a clinic teacher shifts constantly between that of educator and lawyer. The metaphor of switching between hats has been applied to this phenomenon in the clinical legal education literature (Castles & Boothby, 2020). I visualise a more precarious activity, that of balancing on a wobbleboard, constantly adjusting from foot to foot and forever alert to falling (painfully) if that balance is not consistently achieved.

On the lawyer side of the wobbleboard, clinic involves real clients. Whether working in a defined physical clinic space or, during the Covid-19 crisis, at home from a kitchen table or student bedroom, we are working with real people who are experiencing complex, often distressing, situations, which do not come neatly presented as a legal 'problem' question for analysis ('Advise Henry'). In the first instance is the challenge of establishing boundaries within the reflective practicum. Clinical educators need expertise to determine which problems are suitable for the clinic to address through a carefully calibrated triaging system, which students will not necessarily see. Managing such complexity requires significant legal expertise from the clinical educators before legal queries even reach a student, including an ability to be able to identify, and at times turn away, issues that go beyond the clinic's scope.

Compliance with the regulatory requirements that apply to law clinic work also sit on the lawyering side of the board. We require practising certificates as solicitors to be supervisors in the law clinic. Our work must be backed by appropriate professional indemnity insurance in case of complaints and, in a worst-case scenario, legal claims. As part of our client care processes, we have to tell our clients how to complain if they are not happy with our service. The threat of a negligence claim is, we hope, remote, but nevertheless present. This has impact on our ability to be spontaneous and creative in our approach in a way that is possible in fully simulated learning environments.

At the same time, the justification for the existence of clinics within university settings is usually driven in the first instance by educational aims, not those of altruistic service to the communities we serve. This is not to say that providing a service may not be regarded as important as a part of a wider university civic agenda, but it is not likely to be the primary driver for the university in funding the resourcing of clinic activities. As identified earlier, the university's focus is more likely to be on provision of opportunities to enhance students' employability skills and attributes in order to satisfy the metrics and key performance indicators it has to meet (for example, in the UK, impact on National Student Survey responses, Office for Students, 2021, and the Graduate Outcomes Survey data; HESA, n.d.). Those involved in directing clinic activities may also be responsible (as I am in my clinic director role) for negotiating clinic resourcing, promoting clinic in wider university marketing activities and providing reports on clinic performance and the impact of clinic work. These are aspects of clinic which involve a wider set of skills and expertise, beyond either pedagogical or legal experience, for which little training may be available.

Our educator role sits on the other side of the professional identity wobbleboard. It draws on our professional expertise and turns it to educational purposes. Within the clinic practicum, we model professional attributes, ethical behaviours and also our own values as we work together with students and clients. It is a form of teaching where we make ourselves visible and accountable (Shulman, 2005) in our work, demonstrating our expertise as lawyers as well as teachers. We act as supervisors who must constantly tread a fine line in ensuring that work is conducted ethically, to a professional standard, working with students who may need considerable support to develop skills, knowledge and confidence. We need to support students to learn how to work together effectively within a time-pressured environment and (as identified already) manage the significant challenge of facilitating the development of reflective capacity. Ultimately, we are responsible for assessment and for providing opportunities for formative and summative feedback.

Staying upright on the board involves a tricky balancing act. It is a serious business: what the students do in clinic really matters. In a simulated, experiential practicum mistakes can be made, reflected upon and let go. In clinic, clients need to receive appropriate and timely legal advice, in line with the service that the clinic offers. If mistakes or omissions are made in the work identifying and providing that advice, the clinic teacher has to judge how much autonomy students can have, where to support and, at times, where to take over to ensure that students learn, but also that clients are not let down. There is significant push and pull involved between the requirements of students and clients, and potential for a lot of wobbling.

Sharing expertise across disciplines to create a community of practice for students and clinic teachers

This is not an environment in which clinic teachers should work alone. Lave and Wenger's (1991) concept of an apprenticeship model, based on the establishing of a 'community of practice' in which a learning apprenticeship involves moving towards full participation in the socio-cultural practices of a community, is a helpful theoretical approach to adopt as an aspect of the reflective clinic practicum. The most significant innovation in the pedagogy of the Lawyering in Practice module is, therefore, the inclusion of coaching through embedding the teaching expertise that informs a business degree programme, Team Entrepreneurship (TE), to support personal development and community building for both students and clinic teachers. TE is based on a project, Team Academy, initially established in Finland in 1993 and now delivered at a number of universities across Europe (Tosey et al., 2015). The TE programme is based on fully immersive, experiential learning which embraces:

> The concept of a micro-culture [that] can bring together four main attributes of learning environments, namely, social embeddedness, real-worldness, identity formation, and normative.
> (Tosey et al., 2015, p. 175)

Students work from the outset in 'teams' to set up projects, and ultimately businesses. Teaching is delivered via a coaching model, delivered in group training sessions. Tosey et al.'s definition of a micro-culture suggests that there are interesting shared elements between the experiential pedagogy of clinical legal education. Introducing an element of coaching into the Lawyering in Practice module was a way for students to benefit directly from, and for clinic teachers to learn from, the expertise of a colleague from TE.

Managing risk, uncertainty, group dynamics and time within a fluid learning environment is a natural part of the TE coaches' daily pedagogic environment. However, this is less familiar territory for those moving into law clinic teaching and also for law students. Rather than attempting to bend my clinical teaching skills to this approach, I utilised the expertise of a TE colleague, who is able to bring her sense of 'comfort with discomfort' to regular coaching with law students. She is able to use her TE experience to encourage the law students to relax and share reflections about their experiences as a group activity, with a view to opening up their ability to take their reflections further. Coaching sessions are run with groups of twelve students (a 'firm') and explicitly provide a confidential space for student discussion. Clinic teachers do not attend. The content of the discussions is shared with clinic teachers on a basis agreed by the students and coach.

I recognised early on in the module design for Lawyering in Practice that it is not only our students who need to attend to the holistic aspects of development of positive professional identities. I anticipated, and the pilot run of the module is confirming, that the experience of teaching the module has significant affective and transformational (Mezirow, 1991) impact on the clinic teachers. We need regular opportunities to discuss the professional and ethical dilemmas that clinic throws up. We also need space to reflect together on the affective challenges clinical teaching presents us with. An important element in the design of the module is, therefore, the inclusion of dedicated coaching sessions for the clinic teachers with our TE colleague, to provide us with our own confidential and safe space for structured reflection and reflexivity. In the early pilot, this has proved invaluable as a regular touch point to step back from our own affective responses to the intense nature of clinic teaching, which can be difficult to boundary.

Conclusion

My experience of clinical education is that it exposes clinic teachers and raises questions about their professional identities in a way that traditional academic teaching does not. In creating a reflective practicum that mimics the swamp of professional practice for our students, we open ourselves up to the same sense of liminality and discomfort that we are deliberately creating for them. Expertise in clinic teaching needs to draw on our reflexive ability to inhabit our own 'ways of being' to an extent that the 'ways of knowing' demanded by traditional teaching of law does not. Creating a community of practice that acknowledges this and includes dedicated space for both students and teachers to develop reflective and reflexive capacity is a suggested approach to address this challenge. We hope it will prove successful as we continue to develop our approach to expertise in the delivery of legal clinical education in the years to come.

References

Alexander, J. & Boothby, C. (2018) Stakeholder perceptions of clinical legal education within an employability context. *International Journal of Clinical Education*, 25 (3), 53–84. doi:10.19164/ijcle.v25i3.768

Archer, M. (2007) *Making Our Way through the World: Human Reflexivity and Social Mobility*. Cambridge University Press, Cambridge. doi:10.1017/cbo9780511618932

Barnett, R. (2009) Knowing and becoming in the higher education curriculum. *Studies in Higher Education*. 34 (4), 429–440. doi:10.1080/03075070902771978

Baron, P. & Corbin, L. (2012) Thinking like a lawyer/acting like a professional: communities of practice as a means of challenging orthodox legal education. *The Law Teacher*, 46 (2), 100–119. doi:10.1080/03069400.2012.681176

Bauman, Z. (2000) *Liquid Modernity*. Polity, Cambridge.

Belenky, M.F., Clinchy. N., Goldberger, N. & Tarule., J. (1986) *Women's Ways of Knowing: The Development of Self, Voice and Mind*. Basic Books, New York.

Bleasdale, L. & Francis, A. (2020) Great expectations: millennial lawyers and the structures of contemporary legal practice. *Legal Studies*, 40 (3), 376–396. doi:10.1017/lst.2020.6

Brookfield, S. (2017) *Becoming a Critically Reflective Teacher*. Jossey-Bass, San Francisco.

Burridge, R. & Webb, J. (2007) The values of common law legal education: rethinking rules, responsibilities, relationships and roles in the law school. *Legal Ethics*, 10 (1), 72–97. doi:10.1080/1460728x.2007.11423883

Casey, T. (2014) Reflective practice in legal education: the stages of reflection. *Clinical Law Review*, 20 (3), 317–350.

Castles, M. & Boothby, C. (2020) Which hat shall I wear today? Exploring the professional and ethical implications of law clinic supervision. In: Strevens, C., & Field, R. (Eds.), *Educating for Wellbeing in Law, Positive Professional Identities and Practice*. Routledge, Abingdon, 117–131.

Chiseri-Strater, E. (1996). Turning in upon ourselves: Positionality, subjectivity, and reflexivity in case study and ethnographic research. In Mortensen, P. & Kirsch, G.E. (Eds.), *Ethics and Representation in Qualitative Studies of Literacy*. National Council of Teachers of English, Urbana, IL, 115–133.

Colombetti, G. (2014) *The Feeling Body: Affective Science Meets the Enactive Mind*. MIT Press, Cambridge, MA.

Dall'Alba, G. & Barnacle, R. (2007) An ontological turn for higher education. *Studies in Higher Education*, 32 (6), 679–691. doi:10.1080/03075070701685130

Davies, M. (2018) Changes to the training of English and Welsh lawyers: implications for the future of university law schools. *The Law Teacher*, 52 (1), 100–125. doi:10.1080/03069400.2017.1394145

Solicitors Regulation Authority (2020) Developing the SQE. www.sra.org.uk/sra/policy/solicitors-qualifying-examination [accessed 09/01/2021].

Dunlap, J.A. & Joy, P. (2004) Reflection-in-action: designing new clinical teacher training by using lessons learned by new clinicians. *Clinical Law Review*, 11, 49–113.

Esterhuizen, P. & Howatson-Jones, L. (2019) *Reflective Practice in Nursing – Transforming Nursing Practice* (4th edn). Sage, Thousand Oaks, CA.

Field, R., Duffy, J. & Huggins, A. (2014) *Lawyering and Positive Professional Identities*. LexisNexis Butterworths, Australia.

Fook, J. & Gardner, F. (Eds.) (2013) *Critical Reflection in Context*. Routledge, Abingdon. doi:10.4324/9780203094662

Gegerson, E. (2019) The Lived Experience of a University Law Clinic Supervisor: An Autoethnographic Inquiry. PhD Thesis, Northumbria University.

Gibbons, J. (2015) Oh the irony! A reflective report on the assessment of reflective reports on an LLB programme. *The Law Teacher*, 49 (2), 176–188. doi:10.1080/03069400.2014.998855

Giddens, A. (1991) *Modernity and Self-Identity: Self and Society in the Late Modern Age*. Polity, Cambridge.

HESA (n.d.) Graduate Outcomes Survey. www.hesa.ac.uk/innovation/outcomes/students [accessed 09/01/2021].

Guth, J. & Dutton, K. (2018) SQE-ezed out: SRA, status and stasis. *The Law Teacher*, 52 (4), 425–438. doi:10.1080/03069400.2018.1534341

Hall, E. (2019) Narcissus in peril: weighing the risks of unthinking practice and excellent practice against the cognitive and emotional load of reflection. *The Law Teacher*, 53 (4), 399–400. doi:10.1080/03069400.2019.1667079

Hess, G.F. (2002) Heads and hearts: the teaching and learning environment in law school. *Legal Education*, 52, 75–111.

Hinett, K., Varnava, T. & University of Warwick. UK Centre for Legal Education (2002) *Developing Reflective Practice in Legal Education*. UK Centre for Legal Education, University of Warwick, Coventry.

Ibarra, H. (1999) Provisional selves: experimenting with image and identity in professional adaptation. *Administrative Science Quarterly*, 44 (4), 764–791.

Jones, E. (2018). Transforming legal education through emotions. *Legal Studies*, 38 (3), 450–479. doi:10.1017/lst.2017.16

Jones, E. (2019) *Emotions in the Law School: Transforming Legal Education through the Passions*. Routledge, Abingdon.

Kelly, M (1992) *A Short History of Western Legal Theory*. Clarendon Press, Oxford.

Krieger, L.S. (2002) Institutional denial about the dark side of law school, and fresh empirical guidance for constructively breaking the silence. *Journal of Legal Education*, 52, 112–129.

LawWorks (2014) The LawWorks Law School Pro Bono and Clinic Report. www.lawworks.org.uk/sites/default/files/LawWorks-student-pro-bono-report%202014.pdf [accessed 28/12/2020].

LawWorks (2018) LawWorks Clinics Network Report. www.lawworks.org.uk/about-us/news/lawworks-clinics-network-report-year-march-2018 [accessed 28/12/2020].

Lave, J. & Wenger, E. (1991) *Situated Learning: Legitimate Peripheral Participation*. Cambridge University Press, Cambridge.

Law Teacher, The (2019) Special Issue. 53(4).

Ledvinka, G. (2006) Reflection and assessment in clinical legal education: do you see what I see? *International Journal of Clinical Legal Education*, 9, 29–56. doi:10.19164/ijcle.v9i0.86

Leering, M. (2014) Conceptualizing reflective practice for legal professionals. *Journal of Law and Social Policy*, 23, 83–106.

Lyotard, J.F. (1984) *The Postmodern Condition: A Report on Knowledge*. University of Minnesota Press, Minneapolis, MN.

Macfarlane, A. & McKeown, P. (2008) 10 lessons for new clinicians. *International Journal of Clinical Legal Education*, 13, 65–70. doi:10.19164/ijcle.v13i0.69

Madhloom, O. (2019) A normative approach to developing reflective legal practitioners: Kant and clinical legal education. *The Law Teacher*, 53 (4), 416–430. doi:10.1080/03069400.2019.1667082

Maharg, P. and Maugham, C. (2011) *Affect and Legal Education: Emotion in Learning and Teaching the Law*. Ashgate, Farnham.

Mason, L. (2018) SQEezing the jurisprudence out of the SRA's super exam: the SQE's bleak legal realism and the rejection of law's multimodal truth. *The Law Teacher*, 52 (4), 409–424. doi:10.1080/03069400.2018.1532170

Mezirow, J. (1991) *Transformative Dimensions of Adult Learning*. Jossey-Bass, San Francisco.

Mertz, E. (2007) *The Language of Law School: Learning to 'Think Like a Lawyer'*. Oxford University Press, Oxford.

Office for Students (2021) National Student Survey. www.thestudentsurvey.com [accessed 09/01/2021].

Lord Chancellor's Advisory Committee on Legal Education and Conduct (1971) Report of the Committee on Legal Education. Cmnd 4595. HMSO, London.

Sheldon, K.M. & Krieger, L. S. (2007) Understanding the negative effects of legal education on law students: a longitudinal test of self-determination theory. *Personality and Social Psychology Bulletin*, 33 (6), 883–897. doi:10.1177/0146167207301014

Schön, D.A. (1983) *The Reflective Practitioner: How Professionals Think in Action*. Basic Books, New York.

Schön, D.A. (1987) *Educating the Reflective Practitioner: Toward a New Design for Teaching and Learning in the Professions*. Jossey-Bass, San Francisco.

Schön, D.A. (1995) Educating the reflective legal practitioner. *Clinical Law Review*, 2, 231–250.

Shulman, L. (2005) *The Signature Pedagogies of the Professions of Law, Medicine, Engineering, and the Clergy: Potential Lessons for the Education of Teachers*. Carnegie Foundation for the Advancement of Teaching, Math Science Partnerships (MSP) Workshop Teacher Education for Effective Teaching and Learning, 6–8 February 2005, National Research Council's Center for Education, Irvine, CA.

Somerlad, H. (2016) "A pit to put women in": professionalism, work intensification, sexualisation and work–life balance in the legal profession in England and Wales. *International Journal of the Legal Profession*, 23 (1), 61–82. doi:10.1080/09695958.2016.1140945

Strevens, C., & Field, R. (2020) *Educating for Wellbeing in Law, Positive Professional Identities and Practice*. Routledge, Abingdon. doi:10.4324/9781351104401

Sullivan, W.S., Colby, A., Wegner, J.W., Bond, L. & Shulman, L.S. (2007) *Educating Lawyers: Preparation for the Profession of Law*. Jossey-Bass, San Francisco.

Susskind, R.E. (2017) *Tomorrow's Lawyers: An Introduction to Your Future* (2nd edn). Oxford University Press, Oxford.

Thornton, M. (2012) The new knowledge economy and the transformation of the law discipline. *International Journal of the Legal Profession*, 19 (2), 265–281. doi:10.1080/09695958.2013.771126

Tosey, P., Dhaliwal, S. & Hassinen, J. (2015) The Finnish Team Academy model: implications for management education, *Management Learning*, 46 (2), 175–194. doi:10.1177/1350507613498334

O'Brien, M.T., Tang, S. & Hall, K. (2011) Changing our thinking: empirical research on law student wellbeing, thinking styles and the law curriculum. *Legal Education Review*, 21 (2), 149–182. doi:10.53300/001c.6247

Twining, W. (1988) Legal Skills and Legal Education. *The Law Teacher*, 22 (1), 4–13.

Waters, B. (2017) The importance of teaching dispute resolution in a twenty-first-century law school. *The Law Teacher*, 51 (2), 227–246. doi:10.1080/03069400.2016.1162069

Webb, J. (2011) The body in (e)motion: thinking through embodiment in legal education. *Affect and Legal Education: Emotion in Learning and Teaching the Law*. Ashgate, Farnham, UK, 211–234.

White, M., Borges, N.J. & Geiger, S. (2011) Perceptions of factors contributing to professional identity development and specialty choice: a survey of third and fourth year medical students. *Annals of Behavioural Science and Medical Education*, 17 (1), 18–23. doi:10.1007/bf03355144

Wong, A. & Trollope-Kumar, K. (2014) Reflections: an inquiry into medical students' professional identity formation. *Medical Education*, 48 (5), 489–501. doi:10.1111/medu.12382

Chapter 9

Reflective practice as a threshold concept in the development of pedagogical content knowledge

Rebecca Turner and Lucy Spowart

The acquisition of pedagogical content knowledge (PCK) necessarily requires an integration of knowledge about the content one is teaching with an understanding of appropriate underpinning pedagogic theories and good practice. Experienced colleagues in higher education who did not have the benefit of a taught course to develop their teaching practice sometimes only encounter pedagogic literature when they are required to reflect on their practice and take an evidence-informed approach for the purposes of formal professional recognition. Traditionally, many academics have prioritised the development of their subject expertise and engaged in CPD relevant to their discipline over the development of their teaching expertise (Parsons et al., 2012). Therefore, when they are required to engage with pedagogic literature, it can at times prove challenging (Loads, 2013). For teaching practitioners working within higher education, successful engagement in professional development relating to teaching, learning and assessment is a prerequisite of the UK Professional Standards Framework for teaching and supporting learning (UKPSF). The UKPSF is used by HE providers in the UK, and increasingly internationally, to benchmark their CPD offer, signal a commitment to teaching and learning, and recognise individuals' contribution to student learning and teaching (Spowart et al., 2020). It also provides a common language and descriptions of dimensions of good practice for HE teaching and learning (Hibbert & Semler, 2016). The UKPSF is hosted by Advance HE which accredits CPD provision against the standard in the form of either taught courses, such as postgraduate certificates, or institutional schemes that recognise experiential learning. Professional recognition achieved through either of these routes is in the form of an appropriate category of fellowship of the Higher Education Academy.

The expectation for lecturers to engage with professional recognition through the UKPSF is increasingly commonplace (Spowart et al., 2020). However, this has not always been the case. In the UK, like many other countries, the professional development of lecturers as educators was frequently overlooked (Parsons et al., 2012). The UKPSF was introduced in 2006, and the emphasis was, at this time, on supporting the development of new lecturers (Spowart et al., 2016). Following the relaunch of the UKPSF in 2011, an avenue was created for established HE professionals to gain recognition for their sustained and ongoing commitment to

DOI: 10.4324/9781003198772-12

teaching and learning. Most importantly, the Higher Education Academy created the opportunity for institutions to develop their own schemes, accredited against the UKPSF, to recognise experienced staff via the achievement of a fellowship award. This move placed a focus on the development of experienced HE professionals as well as those new to teaching.

The research outlined in this chapter draws on qualitative interviews with university staff members from across five faculties within a single institution. Through the lens of threshold concepts (Meyer & Land, 2003), we will examine how the experienced academics engaged with reflective practice, which underpins this form of CPD. Unlike Berliner's (1988) model of skill development in which an expert teacher reaches a stage of unconscious competence, we propose that the development of expertise in teaching requires the practitioner to question consciously all aspects of their practice in the quest for continual improvement. Reflective practice is widely recognised as underpinning many models of professional learning (Clegg et al., 2002). In framing this chapter, it is worth heeding the words of King (2019), who presents professional development for those recognised as 'expert' higher education practitioners as a "self-determined and purposeful process of evolution of teaching and learning approaches informed by evidence gathered from a range of activities" (p. 4).

Threshold concepts and their application in educational development practice

Threshold concepts represent a crucial stage in the learning journey. As individuals are exposed to new concepts or ways of thinking, their existing preconceived ideas may be challenged. As a result, while learners grapple with threshold concepts, they are enter an unstable liminal space (Perkins, 2006). This reflects the fact that engaging with threshold concepts can run counter to the habits, conviction and experiences individuals hold and, thus, can lead to a new way of seeing the world. Given this, it is not surprising that Meyer and Land (2003) present threshold concepts as transformative but troublesome, as they shift learners' subjectivity.

Threshold concepts have been widely applied in a number of undergraduate disciplines – for example, health care education (Neve et al., 2017) and geography, earth and environmental sciences (King, 2009) – to explore concepts that are challenging for students to learn but are transformative once grasped. Threshold concepts have also been applied to postgraduate research education (Kiley & Wisker, 2009) and in the educational development literature to frame the pedagogic development of new lecturers (Kilgour et al., 2019). In this latter work, the lecturer is framed as a learner engaging in learning that is transformative, leading to the development of new ways of thinking about their practice. We build on this work to explore how experienced academics engage with reflective practice through an accredited CPD scheme, and how it supports their emerging PCK.

Reflective practice and its role in CPD schemes

Reflective practice is integral to the development of all educators, regardless of the sector in which they teach (Clegg et al., 2002), and is widely used to frame professional learning in practice-based disciplines. There are a number of models of reflective practice that have been developed to guide individuals' engagement in reflective practice, with the works of Schön (1983), Kolb (1984), Brookfield (1995) and Gibbs (1988) all used to underpin reflective practice undertaken by HE professionals. Reflective practice is a core aspect of the UKPSF. To gain recognition as an experienced HE professional, individuals are required to reflect on both the effectiveness of their practice *and* the impacts it has on others, drawing on scholarly literature to support the reflective analysis of their practice (Lea & Purcell, 2015). These reflections can be presented in the form of a written application (the most commonly used method) or via professional dialogue (Asghar & Pilkington, 2018). At the study institution, applicants are required to submit four written case studies and undertake a peer review of practice.

The challenges of the use of reflective practice to underpin professional development have been widely acknowledged and are worth considering owing to the potential impacts they could have on the development of PCK. For example, Macfarlane and Gourlay (2009) questioned whether reflective practice is engaged in a meaningful, developmental way when it is tied to an accredited CPD offer where certain criteria have to be demonstrated. They were concerned whether the emphasis is on demonstrating the relevant criteria, rather than stimulating professional development. Similarly, van der Sluis et al. (2017) suggested the retrospective nature of reflection associated with CPD schemes left little room to consider future innovation or development.

Study context

We present data captured through a longitudinal evaluation study instigated following the introduction of a university CPD scheme in 2012 accredited by the then Higher Education Academy to award fellowships in all four categories (associate fellowship, fellowship, senior fellowship and principal fellowship). The study institution is a large, publicly funded teaching-focused university in southern England. It was an early advocate of teaching-related CPD, though traditionally this centred on new lecturers. The relaunch of the UKPSF in 2011 created the opportunity for the institution to focus on the CPD, and recognition, of established lecturers. Though there was no institutional mandate to engage with the scheme, the requirement for institutions to declare to the Higher Education Statistics Agency the number of qualified teaching staff meant that there was a clear university steer to encourage participation and for staff to gain fellowship in one of the four categories.

Data collection

All participants enrolled in the CPD scheme during its first 2 years (2012–14) completed an online survey to capture their initial reflections on their experiences (n = 146). A purposeful sample were invited to participate in an in-depth interview, and 30 staff were interviewed. All participants had been teaching for at least 3 years (a prerequisite for access to the scheme), but did not hold a teaching qualification. Job roles varied from associate lecturers, senior lecturers through to senior managers. Whereas some admitted to only a superficial level of engagement with the process (18), others found that it facilitated professional development in a myriad of ways. Twelve expressed a significant change in the ways they conceived of, and enacted, their teaching roles. The results from this evaluation were published (Spowart et al., 2016) and represented the first empirical study of an institutional CPD scheme accredited by the Higher Education Academy.

The 12 transcripts in which participants expressed significant change were re-scrutinised in 2019 through the lens of threshold concepts to identify the challenging or 'sticky' moments that resulted in participants entering the liminal space that stimulates learning and development.

Findings

Three themes emerged from our analysis, two of which, as we go on to explore, represented major conceptual challenges for academics who do not have an educational background. These themes provide a nuanced picture of reflective practice and the role it plays in the development of effective PCK:

1 Reflection through dialogue
2 Reflection through writing
3 Reflection through pedagogic literature.

Reflection through dialogue

In developing an application, all participants engaged in dialogue around teaching, learning, student support and the impacts of their practice with a number of people from across the university. Although applicants to the CPD scheme submitted written applications, there were a number of formal and informal opportunities to engage in a reflective dialogue. Initially, all participants were invited to a workshop where the process was explained. Here, participants engaged in conversations about teaching and learning with peers. Second, all applicants were required to complete a peer review of their teaching. Finally, following the submission of a draft application, the scheme manager provided verbal feedback via a one-to-one meeting.

These opportunities to engage in a dialogue about teaching were regarded as hugely valuable. One talked of it as providing "cerebral stimulation" (CPD019), and another welcomed the opportunity to "hear other people's ideas" (CPD018). Interestingly, these conversations represented an unanticipated but significant, and potentially transformative, moment within the process. They created reflective spaces for participants to engage in meaningful conversations about teaching and learning with peers. These conversations seemed particularly powerful when they brought people from different schools or disciplines together, exposing teachers to different perspectives or teaching practices:

> [XXXX] did mine and because we've got different subjects it made her come and see my subject and likewise, I've gone to PBL and watched her do hers. It gave her an understanding of [XXXX] teaching and since then they've been a real ally.
>
> (CPD019)

The conversations allowed an interest in teaching to be shared and, potentially, celebrated. Indeed, because of the forum through which they were meeting, there was a sense it legitimised a conversation around teaching and learning practices, rather than on the administration of teaching:

> That process of having to get teaching evaluations and stuff [...] I think it's quite good so the more of a sort of culture of continual reflection [...] linking it up with a bit more of a process of development I think is useful. That's the sort of thing that I would probably like to continue even if it wasn't through any sort of particularly prescribed route, just having a bit more feedback.
>
> (CPD05)

As these extracts demonstrate, this was not a troublesome part of the process, but it was transformative, in that it indicated value in dedicating time to talk about their practice, an activity that had not previously been prioritised.

Similarly, engaging in peer review was highly valued, despite some initial reservations. Some regarded it as a mechanistic part of the process: "a hoop to jump through". However, throughout the interviews, the developmental nature of the activity was highlighted. Several talked of it in emotive terms, experiencing anxiety beforehand but afterward valuing the conversation and the process. For example:

> I'm very positive about it, I actually hated doing it at the time. But the teaching review was really useful because like a colleague of mine came and watched my plenary and to be honest it made me really think about the teaching components, the interactivity, the pacing, the timing, you know I use a bit of video clips in there and so it really helped me focus.
>
> (CPD019)

> It can be quite intimidating, but it was somebody I know very well [...] you almost take for granted that you know what you're going to go and do, but

when you've actually got to focus because you think ooh somebody's going to be watching me do this, then I think that's a good thing.

(CPD008)

It did feel at times that why have I got to do this ... but I was with the colleague I share an office with; we decided to go for it together and that was really helpful. We did our observations together, we could discuss the applications together, we supported each other by giving each other feedback so that worked really well for me.

(CPD009)

Engaging in the CPD scheme opened up spaces to talk critically with colleagues about teaching and learning. These spaces were sometimes formal, such as after the peer review of teaching or during the workshops, or, as the last quotation demonstrated, sometimes informal, with an office mate who was also going through the process. These quotations also illustrate the frequently 'uncomfortable' nature of the process, with participants expressing negative emotions such as intimidation or anxiety. Yet, despite this, participants recognised the value of focusing on individual practice, rather than talking about teaching from an administrative, quality assurance or student perspective, as was frequently the case.

Our research revealed that the space to talk about individual practice was previously overlooked by participants, and the requirement to do this through the CPD scheme prioritised such conversations. The peer review in particular was transformative for some participants who were able to move out of a liminal space where motivation was lacking to a position where they were receptive to feedback from others. This resonates with the work of Senge (1998), who proposed the idea of a "learningful conversation" as signifying a conversation that engages in the process of reflection, which he identified as a prerequisite for professional learning.

Reflection through writing

Examining participants' approach to, engagement with, and experiences of, reflective writing through the lens of threshold concepts demonstrates what a challenging and troublesome process this was. As participants did not hold a prior teaching qualification, they had not engaged with pedagogic literature before, and many, particularly from science subjects, had not engaged in reflective writing. Consequently, it was an unfamiliar way of writing and presenting oneself:

Um I think I found it, it's quite an unusual writing style, it's not something that we normally adopt [...] I found once I got to grips with the idea it's ok to say how you feel, that was fine.

(CPD015)

> Because one of the odd things about doing something like this is the way that you write it, you talk in first person which in science you never do, it's like a complete and utter no-no! So you have to rethink how you're going to put something together.
>
> (CPD008)

The unfamiliarity of writing about teaching has been explored by others (e.g. Lea & Stierer, 2000) who articulate value in the process, in that it helps individuals to codify practice. However, the value of writing about practice for professional recognition is more widely contested (e.g. Leigh, 2016). This partly reflects the need to demonstrate key aspects of a so-called high-order genre of writing that involves invoking specific ways of writing, academic conventions and engagement with a potentially new body of literature in order to achieve recognition (Heron & Corradini, 2020). Botham (2018) also identified a lack of familiarity with reflective writing, and reflective practice, as a barrier to engagement with the CPD scheme she was evaluating.

There was also clear evidence of participants' oscillating between pre-liminal, liminal and post-liminal states, where they experimented and explored reflective practice until they gained mastery:

> I was talking almost quite abstractly about approaches rather than actually saying I did this and this is how it worked and this is what I thought about it [...] Once I got to that stage and identifying these areas of what I thought were my sort of strengths then going back and restructuring it [...] again useful but is very unfamiliar to me.
>
> (CPD005)

However, potentially more concerning was that entering a state of liminality placed participants in an 'unsafe' space. Participants commented on experiencing stress. For some, there was a sense of discomfort and potentially trauma reported, which almost lead to disengagement:

> There were a few moments while I was trying to do the exercise in which I felt no I'm not going to make it, I'm not going to do it because oh golly I need to find the right references etc. Why do I bother?
>
> (CPD012)

> Even thinking about it now, it was stressful because you know, it's like going through an exam basically, and an exam where I hadn't been working in that field.
>
> (CPD008)

These quotations run counter to the developmental objectives of engaging in a CPD scheme, a process designed to reward and recognise expertise. Although learning can be disruptive, troublesome and transformative – indeed, these are the core characteristics of threshold concepts – the impact on experienced academics' future engagement in teaching-related CPD, and the value they place on it, may be undermined by the experience of developing a fellowship application if it is not carefully supported. Related work has raised concerns that engaging in a CPD scheme risks being time-consuming and tokenistic unless appropriately framed (Peat, 2015). Some have reported time spent on a fellowship application as impinging upon limited research time (Spowart et al., 2016). If the process of reflective writing is remembered as traumatic, it could undermine any developmental gains for the individual.

Repeatedly, mastery only came with support from the educational developer facilitating the CPD scheme, and the support from this individual was cited as integral to success:

> I think [scheme manager] managed pretty well in the sense that they were very sympathetic, they understood I think in my case how I felt and how I felt as let's say as a senior academic and used the right language and the right approach towards facilitating this process ... I'm used to writing, I'm ok at writing papers and things like that in my discipline and so on, but I'm not used to dealing with pedagogic writing.
>
> (CPD018)

Heron and Corradini (2020) comment on the private and confidential nature of the reflective writing that individuals engage with through the fellowship process. Yin (2016) highlights the gatekeeping role of the awarding body. Both these factors can serve to mystify the process of reflective writing for the professional recognition of teachers in HE, though this has been identified as being mediated by local support. Heron and Corradini (2020) identified local support as crucial and talked of those providing such support as taking on the role of a "literacy broker", as well as other sources of support (e.g. mentors, writing retreats), in facilitating the development of applications for the CPD scheme that was the focus of their work.

Reflection through the literature

Writing reflectively and engaging with pedagogic literature were not challenging for all participants. However, in analysing their discussion of engagement with literature, some participants evidenced mimicry rather than mastery of reflective writing. Mimicry is associated with learners occupying a liminal space, adopted owing to a sense of loss, exposure or uncertainty (Land & Meyer, 2010). This position was indicated by the functional or mechanistic approach several participants recounted having taken to engaging with pedagogic literature. Rather than using it to stimulate critical reflection, it was used in a limited sense to confirm practice:

> I had some feedback from [scheme manager], asking for the case studies to be put more into the pedagogic context. Once she told me that, for me it's straightforward, that's something I can do very simply. As I often tell students, if you present a piece of what you call research to me and I think I can do that in two hours sitting in front of my PC, to me it's not research, it's just a simple exercise and in fairness this to me is a simple exercise.
>
> (CPD018)

> So why should I read pedagogic literature there? I'm not sure there's an easy or clear-cut answer to that because my experience is, again it sounds totally big-headed but it's useful in confirming that what you're doing is grounded.
>
> (CPD015)

> I expected it to be more of a learning experience and less of a documentation experience. You were supposed to reflect on this and I did but it sort of felt more like ok I'm just writing down evidence here, I'm not trying to learn from this activity.
>
> (CPD007)

Mimicry can also be adopted before learners gain the conceptual understanding associated with ontological and epistemological shifts (Land & Meyer, 2010). The following extract was part of an email communicated to the scheme manager prior to submission of a complete draft. It clearly illustrates the challenges this process of critical reflection, underpinned by the pedagogic literature, presented.

> This thing is proving very demanding and fairly time-consuming as all things which do not 'naturally' come together ... I am now attaching a draft which does not have any literature references yet (and still have few ideas about where to find them). Literature apart, I am not even sure the case studies work and are of any interest. I do not talk the 'pedagogues' talk, and despite being rather convinced that I have done a lot of good teaching, with passion and a good spirit, and can design and carry out effective teaching, I am aware this might not look like even remotely good enough.
>
> (CPD018)

Conclusions and implications for the development of experienced teachers

In this research, we sought to understand whether there were particular concepts academics grappled with, while they were working towards professional recognition of their teaching via an in-house CPD scheme, that meet the characteristics of threshold concepts (Meyer & Land, 2003). This research suggests that examining teaching through reflective writing and the pedagogic literature presents two major conceptual challenges for academics who do not have an educational background. This is particularly the case for academics from STEM subjects for whom reflective writing is 'not how they usually work'.

Highlighting forms of reflective writing as troublesome is not new or unexpected. Clegg et al. (2002) questioned whether reflective writing was diverting attention away from the *act* of reflecting and learning *through* reflection. In such instances, reflecting through literature may seem removed from reflecting *in, on* or *through* practice, as advocated by models of reflective practice such as Schön's (1983). This echoes the challenges some PhD students experience in articulating the relevance or significance of their research (Kiley & Wisker, 2009). In this case, PhD students only overcame these challenges when they began developing connections with extant work and finding their voice. Perhaps the same could be said of experienced teachers who are new to reflective writing and pedagogic literature and have PCK that is bounded by their prior lack of engagement with teaching-related CPD (Vereijken & van der Rijst, 2021). If teachers acquire a more sophisticated understanding of the purpose of such practices, they are more likely to fully 'buy in' to the process and become insightful teachers with well-established PCK.

Interestingly, the third approach to reflection, professional dialogue, emerged as relatively unproblematic and, if undertaken with key individuals (e.g. scheme managers, peers), could provide support. Several educational developers have explored the role of dialogue and discussion in supporting the professional development of new lecturers. Spiller (2002) highlighted conversations as creating safe spaces for new lecturers to explore their role. Brockbank and McGill (1998) engaged in a reflective conversation to support a curriculum redesign, and this facilitated exploration of new approaches. Therefore, it is unsurprising that conversation emerged here as a significant part of the process. However, with more explicit structuring, or foregrounding in the process, dialogue could promote innovative development rather than retrospective confirmation. Educational developers supporting CPD schemes could explore the potential of a variety of methods to structure conversations to stimulate learning such as storytelling or guided conversations (Haigh, 2005).

The participants in this study were required to engage in a range of reflective practices in order to gain fellowship via an in-house CPD scheme. In other words, they were 'forced' to step outside their comfort zones. This placed experienced academics in, at times, challenging or uncomfortable spaces. Having effective support structures in place is, therefore, vital. Effective mentoring to introduce and foster reflective practice is key. Likewise, engaging in reflective practice with colleagues from an individual's home department could extend the value and impact of the reflective process.

For most of the participants, engaging with the CPD scheme represented the first time they considered the scholarship underpinning their pedagogic practice; previously, their focus was upon disciplinary scholarship and associated signature pedagogies. Developing PCK provides lecturers with a foundation on which to build their practice (Shulman, 1986). Having a wider conception of teaching and student learning allows lecturers to respond to the many challenging situations they frequently face. Studies have highlighted that working in the absence of PCK can leave lecturers practice-bound, unable to innovate or to examine their practice critically (Fraser, 2016; Vereijken & van der Rijst, 2021). This study highlights how teaching practices, or ways of thinking, transformed, as they became HE professionals engaged with PCK through the processes associated with reflective practice.

For the developmental potential of reflective practice to be realised, it is important opportunities are created for individuals to engage with approaches that suit their learning needs (e.g. through dialogue, writing and/or literature), to ensure that the practice of reflection does not become a barrier to teacher expertise being realised.

References

Asghar, M. & Pilkington, R. (2018) The relational value of professional dialogue for academics pursuing HEA Fellowship. *International Journal for Academic Development*, 23 (2), 135–146. doi:10.1080/1360144x.2017.1386566

Berliner, D.C. (1988) *The development of expertise in pedagogy*. American Association of Colleges for Teacher Education, Washington, DC.

Botham, K.A. (2018) The perceived impact on HE teachers' teaching practice of engaging with a higher education institution's CPD scheme. *Innovations in Education and Teaching International*, 55 (2), 164–175. doi:10.1080/14703297.2017.1371056

Brockbank, A. & McGill, I. (1998) *Facilitating reflective learning in higher education*. Society for Research into Higher Education and Open University Press, Milton Keynes.

Brookfield, S. (1995) *Becoming a critically reflective teacher*. Jossey-Bass, San Francisco.

Clegg, S., Tan, J. & Saeidi, S. (2002) Reflecting or acting? Reflective practice and continuing professional development in higher education, *Reflective Practice*, 3 (1), 131–146. doi:10.1080/14623940220129924

Fraser, S.P. (2016) Pedagogical content knowledge (PCK): exploring its usefulness for science lectures in higher education. *Research in Science Education*, 46, 141–161. doi:10.1007/s11165-014-9459-1

Gibbs, G. (1988) *Learning by doing: A guide to teaching and learning methods*. Further Education Unit. Oxford Polytechnic, Oxford.

Haigh, N. (2005) Everyday conversations as a context for professional learning and development. *International Journal for Academic Development*, 10 (1), 3–16. doi:10.1080/13601440500099969

Heron, M. & Corradini, E. (2020) Writing for professional recognition in higher education: understanding genre and expertise. *Higher Education Research & Development*, 39 (5), 968–981. doi:10.1080/07294360.2019.1705256

Hibbert, P. & Semler, M. (2016) Faculty development in teaching and learning: the UK framework and current debates. *Innovations in Education and Teaching International*, 53 (6), 581–591. doi:10.1080/14703297.2015.1022201

Kiley, M. & Wisker, G. (2009) Threshold concepts in research education and evidence of threshold crossing. *Higher Education Research & Development*, 28 (4), 431–441. doi:10.1080/07294360903067930

Kilgour, P., Reynaud, D., Northcote, M., McLoughlin, C. & Gosselin, K.P. (2019) Threshold concepts about online pedagogues for novice online teachers in Higher Education. *Higher Education Research & Development* 38 (7), 1417–1431. doi:10.1080/07294360.2018.1450360

King, H. (2009) Exploring practices, improving student learning: Threshold Concepts Conference 2008. *Planet*, 22 (1), 80–84. doi:10.11120/plan.2009.00220080

King, H. (2019) Continuing professional development: what do award-winning academics do? *Educational Developments*, 20 (2), 1–5.

Kolb, D.A. (1984) *Experiential learning: experience as the source of learning and development*. Prentice Hall, Englewood Cliffs, NJ.

Land, R. & Meyer, J.H.F. (2010) Threshold concepts and troublesome knowledge (4): issues of variation and variability. In: Land, R., Smith, J. & Ballie, C. (Eds.), *Threshold concepts and transformative learning*. Sense, Rotterdam, 59–74. doi:10.1163/9789460911477_006

Lea, M. & Stierer, B. (2000) Student writing and staff feedback in higher education: an academic literacy approach. In: Lea, M. & Stierer, B. (Eds.), *Students' writing in higher education: new contexts*. Open University Press, Buckingham, 32–46.

Lea, J. & Purcell, N. (2015) Introduction: the scholarship of teaching & learning, the Higher Education Academy, & the UK Professional Standards Framework. In: Lea, J. (Ed.), *Enhancing learning & teaching in higher education: Engaging with the dimensions of practice*. Open University Press, Maidenhead, 1–16.

Leigh, J. (2016) An embodied perspective on judgements of written reflective practice for professional development in higher education. *Reflective Practice*, 17 (1), 72–85. doi:10.1080/14623943.2015.1123688

Loads, D. (2013) Collaborative close reading of teaching texts: one way of helping academics to make sense of their practice. *International Journal for Academic Development*, 18 (8), 950–957. doi:10.1080/13562517.2013.810844

Macfarlane, B. & Gourlay, L. (2009) The reflection game: enacting the penitent self. *Teaching in Higher Education*, 14 (4), 455–459. doi:10.1080/13562510903050244

Meyer, J.H.F. & Land, R. (2003) Threshold concepts and troublesome knowledge: linkages to ways of thinking and practicing. In Rust, C. (Ed.). *Improving student learning – theory and practice ten years on*. Oxford Centre for Staff and Learning Development, Oxford, 412–424.

Neve, H., Lloyd, H. & Collett, T. (2017) Understanding students' experiences of professionalism learning: a 'threshold' approach. *Teaching in Higher Education*, 22 (1), 92–108. doi:10.1080/13562517.2016.1221810

Parsons, D., Hill, I., Holland, J. & Willis, D. (2012) *The impact of teaching development programmes in higher education*. Higher Education Academy, York.

Peat, J. (2015) Getting down to the nitty-gritty: the trials and tribulations of an institutional professional recognition scheme. *Perspectives: Policy and Practice in Higher Education*, 19 (3), 92–95. doi:10.1080/13603108.2015.1029999

Perkins, D. (2006) Constructivism and troublesome knowledge. In Meyer, J.H.F. & Land, R. (Eds.), *Overcoming barriers to student understanding: Threshold concepts and troublesome knowledge*. Routledge, Abingdon, 57–71. doi:10.4324/9780203966273-11

Schön, D. (1983) *The reflective practitioner: How professionals think in action*. Basic Books, New York.

Senge, P. (1998) *The fifth discipline fieldbook: strategies and tools for building a learning organization*. Nicholas Brealey, London.

Shulman, L.S. (1986) Those who understand: knowledge growth in teaching. *Educational Researcher*, 15 (2). 4–14. doi:10.3102/0013189x015002004

Spiller, D. (2002) *Conversations for change: Mentoring conversations for induction into an academic career.* Staff and Educational Development Association and All Ireland Society for Higher Education, Dublin.

Spowart, L., Turner, R., Dismore, H., Beckmann, E., Carkett, R. & Khamis, T. (2020) *Assessing the impact of accreditation on institutions.* Advance HE, York.

Spowart, L., Turner, R., Shenton, D. & Kneale, P. (2016) "But I've been teaching for 20 years ...": encouraging teaching accreditation for experienced staff working in higher education. *International Journal for Academic Development*, 21 (3), 206–218. doi:10.1080/1360144x.2015.1081595

van der Sluis, H., Burden, P. & Huet, I. (2017) Retrospection and reflection: the emerging influence of an institutional professional recognition scheme on professional development and academic practice in a UK university. *Innovations in Education and Teaching International*, 54 (2), 126–134. doi:10.1080/14703297.2016.1273790

Vereijken, M.W.C. & van der Rijst, R.M. (2021) Subject matter pedagogy in university teaching: how lecturer use relations between theory and practice. *Teaching in Higher Education*, 1–14. doi:10.1080/13562517.2020.1863352

Yin, B. (2016) An exploratory genre analysis of three graduate degree research proposals in applied linguistics. *Functional Linguistics*, 3 (1), 7. doi:10.1186/s40554-016-0032-2

Chapter 10

Developing pedagogical content knowledge through the integration of education research and practice in higher education

Erika Corradini

Introduction and rationale

In UK higher education institutions, evidence-informed teaching is demonstrated through engagement with the UK Professional Standards Framework for Teaching and Learning (UKPSF); elsewhere, the scholarship of teaching and learning is considered an aspect of practice crucial to the development of teaching expertise (e.g. Kenny et al., 2017; Gannaway, Chapter 4, this volume; McFadden & Williams, 2020). Although engagement with evidence-based education is encouraged and supported, at least in some institutions, the adoption of evidence-based methods is, however, still underdeveloped. The take-up of evidence-based approaches to inform teaching practice has not been studied or applied thoroughly, and certainly not systematically. While some scholars invoke models underpinned by the ideal of the teacher as "educational researcher" (D'Andrea & Gosling, 2001) as a necessary condition for excellent practice (Macfarlane & Hughes, 2009, pp. 9–10), the extent to which higher education educators in the disciplines engage with education research and/or scholarly approaches to teaching remains to be fully determined.

Evaluating and researching teaching are central for developing educators' expertise. For instance, Shulman (1986) argues that teachers need content knowledge as well as pedagogical knowledge in order to achieve good students' outcomes. This view is further advocated in Hattie's work (Hattie, 2015; Hattie & Zierer, 2017) on visible learning, to which the role of the teacher as evaluator is central. According to this view, a combination of knowledge of the subject matter and of pedagogy brings together expertise and experience of teaching, and this combination is something educators can develop through interrogating their teaching on an ongoing basis. In exploring self-regulatory knowledge (the knowledge that controls the application of other knowledge), Bereiter and Scardamalia (1993, p. 59) note that the development of increasingly sophisticated knowledge and skills is central to the process through which expertise is acquired. Furthermore, expertise itself should be understood as a continuous process as opposed to performing consolidated teaching routines. Applying pedagogical knowledge and evaluating practice seem, therefore, to be processes enabling

DOI: 10.4324/9781003198772-13

teachers to approach educational problems at a higher level of complexity, thus enabling them to develop more sophisticated approaches to their teaching practice and to tailor teaching to the changing needs of students. The development of expertise—seen as the ability to continue to develop competence as opposed to plateauing on established routines of practice—is grounded in the integration of theory and practice not only in the realm of education, but also in other professions, as shown in *The Nature of Expertise*, a seminal work on the topic (Chi et al., 1988). Moving on from this, the question is: is it possible to develop expertise without engaging with the scholarship?

This chapter outlines a study that explores lecturers' attitudes to adopting scholarly approaches and to embedding them into academic practice. Through shedding light on the potential that researching teaching practice has for evaluating the quality of teaching and for improving it (Guskey, 1999; Coldwell & Simkins, 2011), this study makes the case for a wider adoption of these practices across disciplines (McKinney, 2007), with a view to normalising scholarly practice, integrating it into curriculum design and ultimately institutionalising it. The final remit of this work is to devise strategies for developing a culture in which academics are supported in adopting sustainable scholarly practices in the mid to long term. The following discussion seeks to make a case for affording teaching academics the time, spaces and tools to nurture their teaching and to invest in their professional learning, with potential advantages for the individual, the students, the co-workers and the academic communities. Two compelling questions thus arise: how can research into teaching enhance the quality of teaching practice? Why should highly pressured academics spend time on it?

A methodology based on applied education research underpins the study. Centred on the principles of action research (Norton, 2009), this study strives to examine how teaching practitioners engage with scholarship and explores effective ways in which the outcomes of such engagement are transferred into their teaching practice. Far from proposing a one-size-fits-all solution, this study maintains that an inquisitive approach to teaching provides a valuable means of measuring and improving the quality of students' outcomes. In reiterating the message that investigating teaching practice is strategic as well as good academic practice, the complex interaction of education research and teaching practice is problematised, and suggestions for sustaining their integration effectively in the long term are presented.

A scholarly approach to teaching involves accounting for a complex and uncertain process that requires support at individual and institutional levels. The uncertain ground on which educators and teaching practitioners operate when researching education practice is articulated in the words of Paseka et al. (2019, p. 318): "uncertainties arise because our knowledge is not sufficient enough. But even if we accumulate more knowledge, in the dynamics of the process of carrying out a research project situations occur that cannot be known in advance". Navigating uncertain ground is the difficult task scholarly educators are faced with, especially in institutions where research and teaching exist in rather separate compartments, causing academics to identify with either one or the other (Evans & Tress, 2009, pp. 4–6). This distinction has increasingly caused academics to compartmentalise their activities instead of searching for commonalities which would bridge the gap (Macfarlane & Hughes, 2009, pp. 10–12). In order to be able to identify and solve the challenges of their education remit, educators are, thus, required to learn and deploy skills which, without being new, nevertheless require development. This is especially in evidence when transferring research abilities from content research to doing research in discipline-specific education. A potential risk for academic units and institutions is that, in a fragmented HE environment, academic staff become resistant to improving teaching practices, thus becoming dominated by the structures they work in instead of becoming an active part of them. The potential normalisation (institutionalisation) of an integrated approach to education research thus brings about the challenge of negotiating the dynamics between the institution, academic communities and individual academics. The uneven distribution of resources and the diversity of situations in which academics operate affect how educators develop their skills and practice. For this reason, a collaborative model might be worth considering that catalyses expertise, knowledge and experience and, in so doing, fosters a culture where a scholarly approach to teaching is as beneficial for the individual academic as it is for the teaching and learning community.

Aims and methodology

This study adopts a methodology based on the collection and analysis of qualitative evaluations and is underpinned by the importance of reflective practice. Norton (2009, pp. 22–24) argues that reflective practice is inextricably linked to action research and stipulates that these two practices—reflection and action research—go hand in hand in a systematic way. Looking at engagement with education research through the practice of reflection has the potential to help us to determine whether or not teachers engage with scholarly approaches. Further, Zimmerman (1998) defines 'self-reflection' as the processes that occur after the learning efforts have happened. These processes influence a learner's reaction to experience. More generally, reflective practice and writing are regarded as means teachers utilise for making sense of teaching in their respective contexts. For this reason, reflective texts are examined in this study with the aim to surface participants' behaviours in relation to the adoption of scholarly approaches. This approach aims to uncover how educators make sense of their experience of teaching through developing as scholarly practitioners.

Did the adoption of scholarly approaches to teaching practice support teachers in making sense of their own experience? Evidence underpinning the following discussion was extracted from reflective texts produced by educators. These reflections are structured around the development of education interventions carried out by the participants in the study with their students. The education interventions were carried out as part of a continuing professional development programme extending across a large research-intensive university in the UK. Participation in this initiative was optional and open to academics with teaching responsibilities. Individuals working in disciplines in the following broader areas—social sciences, medicine, STEM and humanities—conducted education interventions with students during which they implemented evaluation processes in one or more areas of the teaching and learning process. This study centres on the reflection phase, with reflections being recorded in the form of text briefed to a set of generic outcomes. These outcomes are used in this study as a list of topics/variables providing a brief to the participants' reflections. (Kreber et al., 2005, p. 91). The reflective activity was linked to a particular educational development activity—that is, an education enhancement intervention for which participants set a learning goal; reflections are based on how participants worked towards reaching their goal (Kreber et al., 2005, p. 93).

Data collection

The study relied on collecting evidence from texts produced by a small group of 14 participants undertaking development activity (for a study of similar size, see McLean & Price, 2017). In this case, participants were individually approached and recruited through email after ethical approval had been obtained from the institutional ethics committee (ERGOII–53025). Albeit this is a relatively small sample, the data sets collected allow for a preliminary analysis. It is rare to obtain data of this kind for the very reason which instigated this study, that the level of engagement with scholarly practices in university education is elusive and fragmented. This study aims, therefore, to collect and start to analyse a pool of data which, however limited, will support a preliminary understanding of the potential impact that utilising scholarly methods to improve teaching practice may have on teachers and students alike (Tracy, 2010). This group of texts contains reflections created by participants in development interventions in the period 2018–2020. The reflection was guided by the following brief, with intended outcomes formulated as follows:

- Apply knowledge of generic and subject-specific educational theory and/or evidence in the design of a learning enhancement activity within your subject area
- Informed by the analysis of evaluation data, develop strategies for enhancing the student experience
- Apply education design and delivery skills in different contexts.

The choice of the above pointers aligns with two dimensions of scholarship, identified by Kember (1997) and Prosser et al. (1994). Here, the authors conceptualise scholarship of teaching and learning (SOTL) along four different dimensions: (1) the sources of information individuals draw upon, (2) the focus of their reflection, (3) the extent and nature of their communication of insights and

(4) their conceptions of teaching and learning. Likewise, Kreber (2001, 2002, p. 7), in a survey using the Delphi method, identified similar conceptualisations of the scholarship of teaching on which academics could reach consensus. The briefing points above were chosen to align with points 1 and 2 in order to bring the reflections into focus. Following on from these premises, the analysis of the data set looked for evidence that teachers consult pedagogical literature and that they inform their practice with evaluation of the teaching and the learning experience.

Data analysis

The reflective texts collectively build up a corpus of approximately 12,000 words.

Raw data were extracted from individual submissions and organised in three macro groups, one for each of the points in the brief. Through this procedure, all texts were later analysed and searched for elements relating to the following variables, recognised as key levels of engagement in scholarly approaches (Kreber et al., 2005):

1 Reading and referencing pedagogical articles
2 Consulting pedagogical articles in discipline-specific journals
3 Collaborating with colleagues in teaching
4 Actively working in collaboration with students
5 Experimenting with different teaching approaches
6 Reading theoretical articles on teaching
7 Doing evaluation on teaching.

A close line-by-line analysis of the corpus was adopted. This choice is justified by the relatively short nature of the reflective texts and the limited sample. No texts were analysed before completion of the individual project; hence, this study includes reflective texts written over a period of time spanning the years 2017–2020.

Data presentation

Texts were anonymised, randomised and grouped under the relevant outcome. All reflective texts were searched for evidence of engagement with any of the areas indicated above, with sentences singled out in which an active behaviour was in evidence. The combination of these two elements—relevance to one of the variables above and active engagement (expressed through use of active verbs in the reflections)—shows a participant's commitment to evidencing the intended outcome, something which is often associated with comments revealing (perceived) improvements to the students' learning experience (Biggs & Tang, 2011, pp. 51–53, 283–285). Participants in the study often comment on the fact that their project resulted in a measurable improvement in the student learning, for example, even though it was not a requirement of the reflection to present the measurements. This approach thus involved forming a more nuanced and refined picture than we currently have of the ways evaluation data are collected and used to provide a snapshot of how lecturers make sense of their own experience of teaching, of their students' progress and of the teaching process.

Table 10.1 reports key data analysed during the first stage of the study. Original reflections were broken up into sentences and parsed for active verbs to highlight the behaviours activated by the outcomes expressed in the general brief. Each of the sentences singled out and analysed was then looked at and matched to the variables. A few examples from the corpus analysed are provided in the table, juxtaposed to the variables discussed above.

Analysis of the active language is based on the principle that expressions using 'active verbs' demonstrate engagement by taking action. The reflective aspects surfaced reflections (usually positive) about participants' engagement with scholarship in their teaching practice. As evidenced in some of the reflective sentences presented above, these are often in parallel with students having a positive learning experience. This first step of the analysis evidences active engagement with elements of SOTL and shows participants' active development in that the process

Table 10.1 Key data analysed during the first stage of the study

	Variables	Examples from the corpus
1.	Reading and referencing pedagogical articles	Designing relevant engaging materials has bolstered my understanding of education theory and practice
2.	Consulting pedagogical articles in discipline-specific journals	When designing my enhancements, I looked at the literature behind good practice in online learning and assessed how this could be applied to existing and new resources
3.	Collaborating with colleagues in teaching	Participatory strategies have played a significant role and their application has helped to strengthen engagement
4.	Actively working in collaboration with students	As facilitator [...] I abandoned my typical mode of delivery to engage students in a conversation after their own self-assessment. Points of improvement and realistic challenges were provided
5.	Experimenting with different teaching approaches	I reflected on how education design in university may adapt to the workplace where students learn on placement
6.	Reading theoretical articles on teaching	Learning more from the relevant literature on teaching innovation allowed me to attempt to introduce innovative changes to the modules I redesigned
7.	Doing evaluation on teaching	Drawing on the numerical and written feedback I collected and analysed, I have developed a clearer vision of how to support my students' learning and enhance their experience by building on the aspects of my teaching that have effectively worked

guided them to make sense of their experience through the means of reflection. However, there is another pressing question which this analysis begins to explore: is there an indication that educators changed their teaching practice?

The aim of this second part of the study is to gauge whether or not there is an indication that educators made changes in their practice as a result of researching their teaching, as emerging in the reflections. Although the sample examined is a small one, (approximately) 74% of the sentences extracted for analysis show a relation evidencing that application of education research and/or the adoption of evidence-informed approaches had a positive impact on practice. A further 53% of this portion show direct connection between evidence-based enquiry and enhancement of teaching practices, specifically implying that a transfer from research/evaluation/engagement with the SOTL to practice has occurred, often with an indication that analysis of evaluation data justified a change in the design of the teaching.

Have educators translated research into practice? The statements extracted from the reflections and analysed provide an impression of the participants' engagement with education research/literature and of them using evaluation data to understand their students' learning needs. The majority of the actions participants took had a positive impact on their teaching practice and instigated change in teaching design which—some participants reflect—entailed improvements either in the structure of the course, in the relationships with students and colleagues or in decision-making processes. Thus, this study corroborates further that knowledge in matters related to teaching and learning is constructed through active experimentation in teaching guided by reflection on experience (Kreber, 2002, pp. 7–8).

Reflexivity

Acknowledgement of the fact that the author of this article coordinates the education interventions to which the reflective texts studied in this case relate deserves attention and discussion. This point was raised and addressed during the process for obtaining ethical clearance, which was granted by the faculty ethical committee. As a consequence, participants were informed that their participation in the study and withdrawal from the study would in no way impact on the completion of the projects. In recruiting participants, a deliberate choice was made to approach individuals who had already completed such projects. The author's position is potentially a limitation of the study owing to preconception in data analysis (Tracy, 2010, p. 842). However, an informative and transparent approach was adopted during the recruitment phase, supported by documentation approved by the ethics committee. Admittedly, the author of this study was in a privileged position for receiving the information pertaining to this study, and, similarly, the author's involvement in supporting participants in the module could potentially pose a challenge to the study. Thus, a transparent approach to data collection was adopted as well as a collegial attitude in sharing drafts of the resulting paper with expert colleagues who commented on the processes, decisions made and research activities. Data sets were anonymised, disaggregated from their original contexts, randomised and rid of any explicit reference to specific details through which participants in this study might be identified, such as module titles, practices or terminology specific to a certain discipline.

Discussion

Interpretation of the data suggests that, along the learning journey, participants in the study were enabled to apply a developmental spin to their practice through engagement with education research and evidence-informed methods. The briefed reflection supported participants in processing their experience. The reflective approach led participants to integrate educational theories into their teaching and to generate data and use these in their practice. This analysis has surfaced that active engagement with research-informed, scholarly approaches to teaching resulted in participants being proactive about their teaching practice and led them to make informed choices when implementing changes in the design and practice of teaching. Buttressing practice with theory and transferring the outcomes of evaluation into practice resulted in participants gaining the confidence to make changes and to experiment in an informed manner.

Is a scholarly approach to teaching sustainable in the long term? This study has shown that lecturers' engagement in SOTL as well as the development of expertise require support structures and a supportive academic infrastructure. With provision of supporting structures such as time, evaluation support and professional development, participants were enabled to be inquisitive about their practice and to interpret it in light of their findings. However, this study covers a relatively short time span, with participants engaging in a project lasting approximately one academic year. Through this focused approach, participants were encouraged to monitor their teaching, or one area of it, by introducing evaluation mechanisms which allowed them to adjust their practice to the students' needs and thus to devise strategies for producing better student outcomes. To determine whether or not these approaches became established in the longer term is desirable but beyond the scope of this enquiry. What this study has started to show is that, when participants engaged with reflection based on an education intervention and were briefed on a scholarly approach to teaching, they were guided to understand how and why their practice works, or indeed does not, and to make informed decisions about solving challenges. Such scholarly approaches, if more widely adopted and studied, could potentially have an impact on the quality of teaching and learning design—for example, at module and programme levels—by furnishing educators with the tools and supporting structures for ensuring that teaching is monitored and developed on an ongoing and evidence-informed basis. How this knowledge, however preliminary and limited, can encourage further studies into what can bring about change in the culture in which educators teach remains a challenge, however.

In this study, it was possible to discern the impact upon participants of scholarly approaches to teaching practices. For example, university educators are often burdened with heavy teaching loads and, for this reason, they often lament lack of time, support, instruments and flexibility to justify their lack of engagement in new design and teaching innovation, falling back on to routine teaching behaviours. A preliminary analysis of the data collected for this study showed that engagement with pedagogical theory and evidence-informed methods provided participants new intellectual spaces and methodological tools for enquiring into their teaching. In a similar way, this study surfaced that the application of research-based and evidence-based processes enabled participants to think about teaching design inquisitively rather than as a routine activity. Albeit the study focuses on a small data pool, one significant benefit of engaging with scholarly teaching practices as a method for making sense of experience is that it can be replicated across disciplines and a larger number of adopters reached. This approach, however, requires support structures underpinning and stimulating engagement and a culture promoting coaching and mentoring support along the journey, similar to that offered to participants during this study. Conversely, the nature of this study, restricted by a time limit of one academic year and by a small number of participants, raises concerns about the sustainability of such approaches and their dissemination at school level and beyond. Furthermore, findings reveal that such approaches to teaching practice depend on arbitrary variables such as individual beliefs, school/department/faculty culture and time management, and for all these reasons their adoption may vary rather radically across the same institution. This is, therefore, an important consideration for academic and education developers who support HE teachers in curriculum design and more broadly in teaching and learning design.

Conclusion

In this study, I focus on the role HE teachers play in adopting research- and evidence-based methods to teaching and learning for accruing expertise and potentially accessing excellence. Among the benefits of this study, four stand out which, if carefully studied, could potentially have an impact on the quality of teaching, on the implementation of support systems and ultimately on professional learning in HEIs. The benefits for academics that emerge from the findings of this study are:

1   An ability to transfer education research results to the practice of teaching productively
2   An ability to use data in making sense of teaching and students' needs
3   A raised awareness of scholarly practices in teaching and their effects on learning
4   The potential for the institutionalisation of support systems.

The outcome of this study provides ground for exploring new approaches to the development of educators. Similarly, the implementation of support structures can influence the teaching behaviours and values of individual lecturers (Healy et al., 2019, pp. 32–34). This can lead to increased uptake of practices which would encourage academic staff to measure and monitor the quality of their teaching accurately, responsively and responsibly.

Engaging lecturers with education research regularly proves to be a demanding task. This is especially true for early career academics who find themselves under the pressures of research and are often unsupported in their long-term development but for attending teachers' development programmes. Finding the time and space to develop teaching practices is often overlooked or simply a low priority. While the reflections analysed broadly indicate that a positive attitude and a sense of confidence derive from questioning and making sense of teaching practice (Webster-Wright, 2009), they also reveal a reticence to take risks in areas such as evaluation of teaching, which are not part of the disciplinary identity of most academics. For this reason, and given the strategic importance of in-depth evaluation of education provision in HEIs, support should be encouraged.

How do we develop the ability and capacity to integrate evaluation into the design of teaching and ultimately into practice? The support models developed in Evans (2017) and Paseka et al. (2019) provide a preliminary impression of the areas where support is needed for teachers and education researchers. The starting point is the model Evans (2017, p. 544) developed to enhance school teachers' research literacy. Evans's model places particular emphasis on the self in context as one of the areas which educators find difficult to navigate. In developing this dimension of the model, Evans highlights the following areas as being critical for supporting school teachers in creating knowledge originating from a research-informed, scholarly approach to their teaching. These are:

1   Finding the time and space to effect change
2   Identifying opportunities to use ideas in their own contexts
3   Securing support from mentors and senior management
4   Having access to a range of support networks (Evans, 2017, p. 544, Figure 1, area no 3).

In addition to this, it might be helpful to point out that, compared with schools, HEIs, especially research-intensive universities, have a research remit. In these institutions, academics research in their own discipline; can they transfer the same curiosity to their teaching? Similarly, there is an expectation that academics teach students in research-rich environments to encourage the development of research skills and inquisitiveness; educators should do the same by modelling a scholarly approach to teaching, which they often have an opportunity to develop in academic development programmes such as postgraduate certificates.

A different model but similarly focused on education research is articulated in Paseka et al. (2019). This model centres on the role of the emerging education researcher by defining the levels of decision making and dimensions of uncertainty the researcher faces when trying to find their identity and roles in education research. Particularly, the model shows that the institutional background and cultures influence the process in which education researchers develop and where they have to make decisions about their educational research. The model is an aspirational one in that it advocates that researchers become able to influence the levels of the model, as opposed to being dominated by them, and have an impact on the culture of the institution (Paseka et al., 2019, pp. 318–319, Figure 15.1). Although the two models discussed above describe the dynamics of engaging with education research in two rather different arenas—the school sector and the field of education research per se—they provide useful structures when trying to understand where the challenges may be for HE educators trying to approach their teaching in a scholarly manner. These models highlight areas of overlap with the findings of this case study. Some of these areas key to further support for academics with teaching responsibilities are:

- Evaluation methods
- Ethics approval
- Theories of learning
- Support networks/dynamics between institution and individual
- Embedding sustained evaluation practices into curriculum design.

If acquiring pedagogical content knowledge is important for the development of expertise for teachers in higher education, then scholarly educators will need to interface with the above dimensions in order to engage with and sustain research-integrated, evidence-based practices in their teaching. An ability to navigate institutional dynamics and access institutional support networks seems, therefore, worth reflecting on. Creating support networks, protecting spaces for experimenting with new methods and encouraging academics to think outside their comfort zones and practise outside established routines would support a culture in which knowledge and expertise are developed and sustained. This study shows that educators need to be supported to acquire PCK and to integrate SOTL into their practice long term, as, owing to time and other priorities, this cannot happen naturally. As this study shows, when spaces are created for doing so and time is protected, there are numerous benefits to the quality of teaching and of student learning.

References

Bereiter, C., & Scardamalia, M. (1993) *Surpassing ourselves: An inquiry into the nature and implications of expertise*. Open Court, Chicago, IL.

Biggs, J. & Tang, C. (2011) *Teaching for quality learning at university*. McGraw-Hill, New York.

Chi, M.T.H., Glaser, R. & Farr, M.J. (Eds.) (1988) *The nature of expertise*. Lawrence Erlbaum, Hillsdale, NJ.

Coldwell, M. & Simkins, T. (2011) Level models of continuing professional development evaluation: a grounded review and critique. *Professional Development in Education*, 37 (1), 143–157. doi:10.1080/19415257.2010.495497

D'Andrea, V. & Gosling, D. (2001) Joining the dots: reconceptualizing educational development. *Active Learning in Higher Education*, 2 (1), 64–80. doi:10.1177/1469787401002001006

Evans, C. (2017) Early career teachers research literacy: what does it look like and what elements support its development in practice? *Research Papers in Education*, 32 (4), 540–551. doi:10.1080/02671522.2017.1324013

Evans, L. & Tress, M. (2009) What drives research-focused university academics to want to teach effectively? Examining achievement, self-efficacy and self-esteem. *International Journal for the Scholarship of Teaching and Learning*, 3(2), 1–17. doi:10.20429/ijsotl.2009.030212

Guskey, T. (1999) *Evaluating professional development*. Corwin Press, Thousand Oaks, CA.

Hattie, J. (2015) The applicability of visible learning to higher education. *Scholarship of Teaching and Learning in Psychology*, 1 (1), 79–91. doi:10.1037/stl0000021

Hattie, J. & Zierer, K. (2017) *10 Mindframes for Visible Learning Teaching for Success*. Routledge, Abingdon. doi:10.4324/9781315206387

Healy, M., Matthews, K.E. & Cook-Sather, A. (2019) Writing scholarship for teaching and learning articles for peer-reviewed journals. *Teaching and Learning Inquiry*, 7 (2), 28–50. doi:10.20343/teachlearninqu.7.2.3

Kember, D. (1997) A reconceptualization of the research into university academics' conceptions of teaching. *Learning and Instruction*, 7, 255–272. doi:10.1016/s0959-4752(96)00028-x

Kenny, N., Berenson, C., Chick, N., Johnson, C., Keegan, D., Read, E. & Reid, L. (2017) *A developmental framework for teaching expertise in postsecondary education*. International Society for the Scholarship of Teaching and Learning (ISSOTL) Conference, Calgary, Canada.

Kreber, C. (2001) Conceptualizing the scholarship of teaching and identifying unresolved issues: the framework for this volume. *New Directions for Teaching and Learning*, 86, 1–18. doi:10.1002/tl.12

Kreber, C. (2002) Teaching excellence, teaching expertise, and the scholarship of teaching. *Innovative Higher Education*, 27 (1), 5–23.

Kreber, C., Castleden, H., Erfani, N. & Wright, T. (2005) Self-regulated learning about university teaching: an exploratory study. *Teaching in Higher Education*, 10 (1), 75–97. doi:10.1080/1356251052000305543

Macfarlane, B. & Hughes, G. (2009) Turning teachers into academics? The role of educational development in fostering synergy between teaching and research. *Innovations in Education and Teaching International*, 46 (1), 5–14. doi:10.1080/14703290802646214

McFadden, A. & Williams K.E. (2020) Teachers as evaluators: results from a systematic literature review. *Studies in Educational Evaluation*, 64. doi:10.1016/j.stueduc.2019.100830

McKinney, K. (2007) *Enhancing learning through the scholarship of teaching and learning. The challenges and joys of juggling*. Anker, Bolton MA.

McLean, N. & Price, L. (2017) Identity formation among novice academic teachers—a longitudinal study. *Studies in Higher Education*, 44 (6), 990–1003.

Norton, L.S. (2009) *Action research in teaching and learning*. Routledge, Abingdon. doi:10.4324/9781315147581

Paseka, S., Marques da Silva, C.L. & Honerod Hoveid, M. (2019) Educational research—a space of risk and uncertainty. In: Paseka, S., Ciolan, L., Honerod Hoveid, M. &

Marques da Silva, C.L. (Eds.) *Doing educational research. Overcoming challenges in practice*. Sage, London.

Prosser, M., Trigwell, K. & Taylor, P. (1994) A phenomenographic study of academics' conceptions of science learning and teaching. *Learning and Instruction*, 4, 217–231. doi:10.1016/0959-4752(94)90024-8

Shulman, L.S. (1986) Those who understand: knowledge growth in teaching. *Educational Research*, 15 (2), 4–14. doi:10.3102/0013189x015002004

Tracy, S.J. (2010) Qualitative quality: eight "big-tent" criteria for excellent qualitative research. *Qualitative Inquiry*, 16 (10), 837–851. doi:10.1177/1077800410383121

Webster-Wright, A. (2009) Reframing professional development through understanding authentic professional learning. *Review of Educational Research*, 79 (2), 702–739. doi:10.3102/0034654308330970

Zimmerman, B.J. (1998) Developing self-fulfilling cycles of academic regulation: an analysis of exemplary models. In: Schunk, D.H. & Zimmerman, B.J. (Eds.), *Self-regulated learning: from teaching to self-reflective practice*. Guilford Press, London.

Part III

Professional learning for higher education teaching

Chapter 11

Professional learning for higher education teaching

An expertise perspective

Helen King

Professional learning and development in higher education

This chapter extends and deepens the discussion in Chapter 1 on intentional learning and development to consider what an expertise perspective might bring to the concept of professional learning and development in higher education, and what practical wisdom this might offer for teachers, educational developers and institutions. A new definition of professional learning is offered for teaching in higher education which places the teacher at the centre, developing their expertise through autonomous, self-determined and evidence-informed progressive problem-solving.

Although there is no common definition for professional development in higher education, usually in the literature it refers to processes and activities "that, through strengthening and extending the knowledge, skills and conceptions of academics, lead to an improvement in their teaching and consequently to an enhanced learning experience for students" (Inamorato et al., 2019, p. 4). These might include attending workshops or conferences, reading relevant literature, conversations with colleagues, peer observations and so on (e.g. Ferman, 2002; King, 2004). The ultimate goal of these activities is to improve student learning; however, there is evidence to suggest that engaging in professional development also has a positive impact on other elements such as career progression and institutional culture. Despite this evidence for the benefits of professional development, the engagement of teachers in higher education with these processes is generally variable and unsystematic. Obstacles to engagement include resistance to change, lack of formal requirements or incentives, and lack of or perceived lack of time (Inamorato et al., 2019).

In contrast to the above conceptualisation of professional development as external processes with an extrinsic motivator and goal, models of professional learning and expertise development focus more on the intrinsic actions and goals of the practitioner themselves. Indeed it is this intrinsic motivation that is more likely to engender expertise development (Ericsson et al., 1993) and engagement with good teaching practices (Stupnisky et al., 2018). As the expert practitioner progresses in their career, their professional learning activities become more

DOI: 10.4324/9781003198772-15

autonomous and self-determined (e.g. Schön, 1982; Dreyfus & Dreyfus, 1982; Eraut, 1994), and it is the intentional learning and development that distinguish the expert from the experienced non-expert (Bereiter & Scardamalia, 1993).

As well as there being no clear definition for professional development in higher education, there are also multiple terms used for the same processes of improving teaching and learning, including faculty development, educational development and academic development. It has been suggested that such terms might take away aspects of agency from the teacher themselves as they convey the sense of something being done 'to' them. The term 'professional learning' has been advocated as being more appropriate for this context (e.g. van Schalkwyk et al., 2015; Trowler & Knight, 1999).

Teaching is often just one of multiple roles and professional identities encompassed by individuals working in higher education. Research, professional practice, management and leadership, and administrative tasks are also key components. Stress can arise owing to conflicts and tensions of culture and values, priorities and monitoring/reward mechanisms between these roles (Richards & Levesque-Bristol, 2016). In addition, for many individuals, teaching in higher education is a secondary profession into which they have been introduced after gaining subject-based knowledge and experience through research or professional practice. Some individuals may not conceptualise themselves as teachers at all, rather focusing their identity on their primary profession. Indeed, the word 'teacher' is not often used in a higher education setting where terms such as 'professor', 'lecturer' or 'academic' are far more common and usually equated far more with research (though, ironically, all these words derive from concepts related to teaching). Morantes-Africano (Chapter 2 this volume) proposes the term 'educator' as being more appropriate. Furthermore, the values, norms and approaches of professional learning in their 'home' profession may not be immediately translatable for developing their teaching. Unsurprising, therefore, that many teachers in higher education with complex roles find (or create) barriers for engaging with professional learning.

Where academics strongly identify with their role as teacher, their values are likely to include care for students and care for providing them with a high-quality learning experience (McCune, 2021), which, in turn, may provide more intrinsic motivation to engage with professional learning. If staff don't feel motivated in their teaching in the first place, then they are likely to prefer to invest their time and cognitive energy in other activities. Research with school and, to a much lesser extent, higher education teachers indicates that, when their basic psychological needs of autonomy, competence and relatedness are met, they are more likely to be motivated to support their students' learning effectively (self-determination theory: see Deci & Ryan, 1985; Stupnisky et al., 2018). Stupnisky et al. (2018, p. 16) suggest that

> Teaching could satisfy the needs for competence (when professors have a meaningful impact on their students, such as "ah-ha moments"), autonomy

(professors have freedom to teach lesson content in their own way), and relatedness (opportunities for professors to relate to colleagues and students). However, faculty are also paid, evaluated, required to meet deadlines and follow particular curriculum, and may work with difficult colleagues – all factors that can lead to extrinsic motivation and negative consequences.

Professional learning for the development of expertise

Dreyfus and Dreyfus (1982) suggest a five-stage model for the acquisition of expertise whereby the learner gradually becomes more autonomous and their professional practice evolves from rule-based processes to more intuitively driven actions as they develop their 'artistry' (King, Chapter 1, this volume). Facilitation of this professional learning also changes from a structured pedagogical approach, often located outside day-to-day practice, to a more mentor/coach-supported heutagogical approach whereby the expert professional has agency and self-determination in their learning integrated within their workplace context (Hase & Kenyon, 2000). In higher education, programmes for new lecturers are often carefully designed and structured and, in the UK, are often delivered as credit-bearing postgraduate certificates and/or accredited by a professional organisation (such as Advance HE or the Staff & Educational Development Association) against established standards. Following Dreyfus and Dreyfus's model, professional learning for more experienced teachers should be much more embedded within the workplace and designed to support the ongoing enhancement of teaching as part of the everyday role and in alignment with their department's goals and priorities, with the experienced lecturer being the main agent for their own learning (Stoten, 2021; Kreber, 2000; Stigler & Miller, 2018). This approach to educational development was also advocated by Knight (1998), who suggested that integrating learning opportunities into the day-to-day activities of academic departments, such as programme design and review, would help to combat the stagnation of practice and professional 'obsolescence'.

This five-stage model provides a useful framework for educational development and the design of provision of support for professional learning. However, this still does not address the need for the intrinsic motivation that enables teachers to make use of their agency and become autonomous and self-determined in the ongoing development of their teaching practice. Professional learning is still often presented by educational developers and conceptualised by higher education teachers as the engagement with external activities, traditionally formal training or events, and seen as an add-on to everyday practice. This conceptualisation itself creates a barrier and provides an excuse for not having time to engage. A new conceptualisation is required that recognises expertise and embodies professional learning as an integrated part of teaching and wider academic practice.

The expertise literature includes two dominant models which describe the processes by which the expert practitioner engages in this self-determined learning: "Deliberate Practice" (Ericsson et al., 1993) and "progressive problem solving"

(Bereiter & Scardamalia, 1993). These processes have been explored empirically in a number of professions (van de Wiel et al., 2004). It has been suggested that, if they can be articulated for a particular field, then professional learning activities which align to them are likely to lead to improvements in performance (Ericsson, 2017; Saroyan & Trigwell, 2015).

Deliberate practice

Deliberate practice (Ericsson et al., 1993) is activity which is designed with the specific goal of improving performance. It is most easily described in the context of domains such as music or sport, where repetitious rehearsal takes place in advance of a formal performance. However, simply repeatedly playing a piece of music or throwing a javelin, for example, will not necessarily lead to improvements. Practice doesn't make perfect so much as it makes 'permanent'. From a neuroscience perspective, the repetition of an action will fix it in the brain so that one becomes good at doing that thing in that particular way. It then becomes very difficult to 'unlearn' should it be wrong or if a different approach is needed. Practice, therefore, needs to be 'deliberate', carefully considered and focused on specific areas of weakness. Rather than practising a whole piece of music over and again, one selects the phrases that are particularly tricky and plays these slowly and carefully before gradually getting up to full speed as the correct technique is achieved. This approach to practice is time-consuming and, at times, boring but it achieves results if persisted at for a long period of time. Motivation is critical, therefore, to maintain engagement and develop expertise.

Another key element of deliberate practice is feedback. Simply repeating an exercise, however carefully and deliberately, will not yield improvements unless there is analysis and critique of the output. Were the notes played correctly, in the right order? Did it sound good? If not, what needs to be changed? Feedback can be in the form of self-reflection (in this musical example, listening and self-critiquing) or can come from someone else such as a teacher or coach. As well as within practice sessions, feedback can also come from the audience of the formal performance. Heeding and responding to the feedback then help to hone the deliberate practice and improve performance.

Deliberate practice in higher education teaching

For teaching in higher education, the concept of deliberate practice reminds us that "developing one's teaching practice takes time; it evolves through small or large adjustments over many years of experience, and development needs to be prioritised as an integral part of one's role" (King, 2019, p. 3). Feedback is also important for continual improvement; this might come from self-reflection, students, peer observations or conversations with colleagues. What is critical for the development of expertise is that one doesn't simply repeat the same approach again and again without thought or care.

Research with UK National Teaching Fellows (NTFs) – winners of a competitive award for teaching excellence in higher education – provides some insights into the nature of deliberate practice in this context. Achievement of the award was used as a proxy for expertise, and semi-structured interviews were held with nine self-selected NTFs to explore how they learned to teach and developed their teaching practice (King, 2019).

In teaching, the notion of practice as rehearsal doesn't quite fit. It is unusual for there to be a prolonged, private period of practice followed by a performance. One might talk through a formal presentation, but, particularly with an interactive and student-centred approach, the classroom environment is rarely routine and predictable. Teaching is less like playing in a note-perfect string quartet in a quiet concert hall and more like playing with an experienced jazz band in a late-night bar. The key elements of the performance are there (e.g. a structured session plan), but how it actually works will depend on how the students react and interact with the teacher, with the learning materials and with each other. One NTF noted that, when they were new to teaching, they did rehearse entire lectures, but this was soon abandoned as it was so time-consuming. Others noted that they would sometimes rehearse, in their heads, segments of lectures or go over the stories they wanted to tell. As Stigler and Miller (2018) suggested in their work with secondary school teachers, the NTFs felt that practising teaching takes place while they are actually doing it. This aligns to Schön's conception of the professional practitioner as "a specialist who encounters certain types of situation again and again" (Schön, 1982, p. 60) – hence, the dual meaning of the noun 'practice'.

Unlike sport, for example, it is unusual for an experienced lecturer to have a coach or mentor to provide regular feedback and guidance. Their practice, instead, is informed by feedback or evidence from a variety of sources such as self-reflection, students, occasional peer observations, reading the literature, conversations with colleagues, workshops and events. Sometimes, this cycle of feedback and practice is almost instantaneous as the lecturer reacts to student behaviour, questions or feedback. This improvisatory approach is akin to Schön's reflection-in-action and his recognition of "the artistic, intuitive processes which some practitioners do bring to situations of uncertainty, instability, uniqueness and value conflict" (1982, p. 49). In other cases, the repetitive practice occurs at the next opportunity to teach the same students or the same session, which may not be until the next academic year. Here, the keeping of notes on slides, module handbooks, session plans and so on is essential to ensure the feedback is remembered and applied.

The NTFs interviewed in the research all articulated a strong purpose and motivation for wanting to develop and improve their teaching. Initially, when they were newer to teaching, the goal was to feel more confident and not look foolish. Later, as they became more experienced, this changed to a focus on wanting to improve student learning and to not stagnate or become bored. Their focus for the deliberate practice was on a number of areas such as where a teaching activity didn't produce the desired outcome or where students were less engaged. This was seen as a low-risk–high-reward development opportunity: if something wasn't working anyway, then changing it was likely to be positive in terms of the student experience. Other foci for attention included refining a specific aspect of teaching such as PowerPoint slides or the stories they told in lectures, teaching something new or in a new context, introducing technology into their teaching, or changing an aspect of their teaching they were bored with and wanted to reinvigorate.

The NTFs agreed that time was a key factor in developing expertise in teaching, both in terms of length of time and experience of teaching, and in deliberately setting aside time to improve their teaching. The latter was in short supply. Whereas other professions advocate a structured approach to deliberate practice – particularly within sport and music, for example – there was little evidence of formal structure in the deliberate practice of teaching, although two interviewees, with a background in healthcare, discussed how they applied a structured approach to reflection on teaching that they had derived from their profession.

Progressive problem-solving

The concept of progressive problem-solving for the development and maintenance of expertise aligns to Dreyfus and Dreyfus's (1982) model and particularly focuses on improvements after a basic competence has been achieved. Bereiter and Scardamalia (1993) suggest that, rather than the professional themselves being seen as an 'expert', it is their approach to their career and professional learning that indicates their expertise.

> What makes it an expert career is that it is pursued [through] addressing and re-addressing, with cumulative skills and wisdom, the constructive problems of the job, rather than reducing the dimensions of the job to what one is already accustomed to doing.
>
> (p. 18)

As one becomes more experienced in one's profession there will be many aspects which become routine and automated. This frees up cognitive space and time to do other things. For example, learning to drive a car takes a lot of cognitive energy as we learn how to tackle the gears, be aware of other road users and follow the rules of the road; however, with experience, we find we can do these processes without much conscious effort and can continue to drive safely and effectively while also holding a conversation or listening to music. Within a profession, this additional cognitive space and time might be used for other activities or it might be reinvested in finding ways to continue to improve.

Within the progressive problem-solving model of expertise development, the opposite of expertise is 'problem reduction'. Rather than exploring new approaches, the experienced non-expert will continue to apply their accustomed processes whether or not they continue to have positive outcomes: "most professionals reach a stable, average level of performance, and then they maintain this modest level for the rest of their careers. In contrast, some continue to improve and eventually reach the highest level of professional mastery" (Ericsson, 2018, p. 745). This plateauing of performance and stagnation of processes is fine if it works for the teacher and their students. However, it can be particularly problematic when it comes to situations which necessitate change – for example, during the 2020 Covid-19 pandemic when teaching had to be moved online. Colleagues for whom progressive problem-solving was part of their everyday practice had the flexibility to adapt; those who had always taught in exactly the same way found this change much harder to achieve.

Progressive problem-solving in higher education teaching

Tiberius et al. (1998) build on Bereiter and Scardamalia's (1993) characterisation of progressive problem-solving to consider how it is manifest in teachers in higher education. They expanded the generic characteristics of the approach to include progression in how teachers engage with the classroom and students:

> New teachers focus mainly on content. With more experience they begin to focus on delivery, that is, teaching performance. Eventually, when both the content and the delivery become second nature, they begin to notice the social and personal aspects of their students. They become more interactive and responsive ... expertise is not a static feature, to be achieved once and then abandoned, but a continual process over time. Expertise in teaching is an approach toward one's career.
>
> (p. 131)

This progression was seen in the research with the NTFs. All nine expressed a sense of change and progression throughout their career. The space and time required to progress their teaching came not so much from having automated some practices but through being more comfortable and confident in the classroom. This confidence came from building on their experience and increasing their 'practical wisdom', intuitive knowledge that comes from having encountered similar situations many times before. And the confidence also came in the form of self-belief, rooted in experience and evidence, to do what their students need rather than what they want.

Higher-level problem-solving was clearly evident in the NTFs' accounts as progression or evolution of their teaching: small tweaks or larger-scale changes implemented over time and based strongly on evidence of what works and what doesn't work. Such evidence came from a range of sources such as self-reflection, student feedback, peer observations, the pedagogic literature and conversations with colleagues. This evolution was particularly focused on redefining the classroom and moving from didactic to student-centred approaches. For example, as described in the extract below, one NTF discussed how they made small changes to their physics lectures over many years to eventually shift from didactic lecturing from notes to engaging students in different active problem-solving activities to develop conceptual understanding. Two interviewees also discussed significant changes to their pedagogies, moving to problem-based learning and the flipped classroom, which were implemented in a relatively short period of time.

These pedagogical changes were instigated by a recognition that students can bring something to the classroom and contribute new ideas and perspectives. For five of the NTFs, this understanding was enhanced by their own recent experiences as learners, which strongly informed and influenced their teaching. This learning about students also extended to an appreciation of their social and personal situations. All nine NTFs expressed acknowledgement that students as a cohort change over time, that they are different from each other and from oneself as a teacher, that individual students were people in whom they were interested and whom they wanted to help learn, and that teaching is about a two-way relationship, not a one-way monologue.

Extract from a mini case study of teaching development

The following is from a physics lecturer with 31 years' experience (paraphrased from the interview transcript; direct quotes are in italics):

> The development of my teaching has been a slow evolution. *"As far as lectures are concerned I suddenly got to the point where I found working from notes very restrictive, so I developed my own style of being quite free with what I did."* Though, *"it takes me about 3 or 4 years between starting a subject and being confident enough to teach it, so I always base my sessions on notes if it's fairly new to me."* I evolved a system of trying to describe the physics to students. I was reluctant to give them notes because I didn't want them just to learn information by rote, but they weren't very good at taking their own notes so I gradually evolved my processes. Around 2004, I started getting interested in physics education research after attending a talk, organised by the HEA Subject Centre for Physical Sciences, by Lillian McDermott, a noted physics education researcher. It didn't have an immediate influence on me but over time it led me to literature and thinking that had a significant impact.
>
> I started looking at the literature on cognitive processes and came across Biggs' SOLO taxonomy, which I thought was fantastic. I put together student surveys to find out what they were taking away from the lectures. In one survey, *"I just asked students what's the one thing you can remember from this lecture, can you remember anything else and can you relate that to anything that you already know?"* The responses to the last question were mostly 'no' and *"I realised then that the students did not have the time within a lecture to start making connections with things, so I stopped trying to do that, I realised I was asking them to do too much"*. Another survey was really interesting: in the lecture I said, *"if there's one thing that you take away from this lecture I want it to be this"*. And I repeated this five or six times. When the survey responses

were returned, "*not one person had put that down as the one thing they could remember and I found that remarkable*". I found then that the only way people would remember was if I approached the topic from different angles, and so my lecturing has slowly evolved. I now include aspects of modelling to help students build a conceptual understanding. I'm keen on having a theoretical basis for what I do, and so my modelling protocol is based on the cognitive psychology of problem-solving.

(Mini case studies from all nine NTF interviews are available on the author's personal website at https://drhelenking.wordpress.com/expertise-workshop-resources/)

In this extract, it can be seen how a progressive problem-solving approach was informed and motivated, in part, by engagement with other colleagues and ideas. Bereiter and Scardamalia (1983, p. 105) note that "expertise seldom exists in isolation", but that people are connected through associations, networks or simply collective traditions. An 'expert subculture' exists within many, if not all, fields and professions. Being part of

> a scientific subculture, for instance, requires more than mastering a body of scientific knowledge and skills. One is expected to make some advance on an unsolved problem between this year's convention and the next. ... In non-expert environments, the process of expertise is deviant. Within an expert subculture, however, progressive problem solving and continued building of competence are not deviant but are central to one's participation in the life of the expert community.
>
> (p. 105)

In higher education, despite the fact that many people are involved with teaching and the majority of institutions will have excellence in education as part of their overall mission, there is rarely an organisational-level culture of expertise. Rather, it exists as an expert subculture confined to smaller numbers of keen individuals within institutions, or specific national and international networks. Academics are likely to be more motivated to participate in the subculture related to their personal research or professional practice and to channel their energies towards developing their expertise in that field. Without an institutional culture for expertise in teaching, it can be difficult for some people to be motivated to engage in professional learning.

Developing expertise for teaching in higher education

A key feature of both these models is that they recognise that experience alone is insufficient for the development of expertise. As Ericsson (2017, p. 3) notes,

> In many domains of expertise, longer periods of experience do not by themselves lead to higher levels of performance. Simply doing the same thing again

and again does not increase the quality of performance; it merely makes it less effortful and more automatic.

In this respect, Bereiter and Scardamalia (1993, p. 11) assert the difference between experts and experienced non-experts as being that "the expert addresses problems whereas the experienced non-expert carries out practiced routines". The teacher in higher education who has delivered the same lectures in the same way for the last 20 years might be highly experienced, but they are unlikely to be considered as having expertise. Such lack of expertise might be exposed when student cohorts change or the subject matter becomes out of date, and feedback starts becoming negative and critical. A teacher with expertise would address this, seek to identify and solve the problem, and continue to improve. A non-expert teacher might be more likely to blame the students and not take any action to change their approach. Kreber (2002) suggests that this distinction between expert and experienced non-expert might also offer a comparison of 'excellence' versus 'expertise' in higher education. Teachers who have well-established, routine approaches may well be effective or even excellent in terms of student outcomes at a particular point in time. But it is "by identifying, analyzing, and solving problems that experts, over time, develop problem solving strategies that are even more effective. This desire to be even more effective underlies the motivation of experts" (p. 13).

One critique of these models is that they emphasise the importance of learning from experience and have little to offer about the role of theory or evidence (Eraut, 1994), albeit deliberate practice does include the importance of feedback to inform development. Given the continually changing nature of the higher education environment, the students themselves and external factors such as technology, employability and sustainability, developing one's teaching practice solely based on experience is not sufficient. All of the NTFs' interviews in the author's research identified a range of evidence which informed the development of their teaching. As argued by Corradini (Chapter 10, this volume) and Baume (see Box 11.1), the scholarship of teaching and learning is a crucial contributory factor to the enhancement of teaching practice and the development of expertise.

Box 11.1 Expertise in teaching considered as effective, values-informed, scholarly competence

Competence sounds a dull quality. But I'll take genuine, properly certified, criterion-referenced, authentically assessed competence over an ill-defined, perhaps spuriously claimed, excellence, any day.

Doctors and airline pilots have life and death jobs. Their education and training start with an account of competence. So does, in the UK at least, the training and certification of those who teach in higher education. A teacher can do as much damage as a doctor or pilot, although usually rather more slowly.

Competence is not enough. We must add authentically assessed effectiveness.

"what would I have wanted at university if I had given in this piece of work... what, would that have helped me?"

Scaffolding and support

Respect

Students

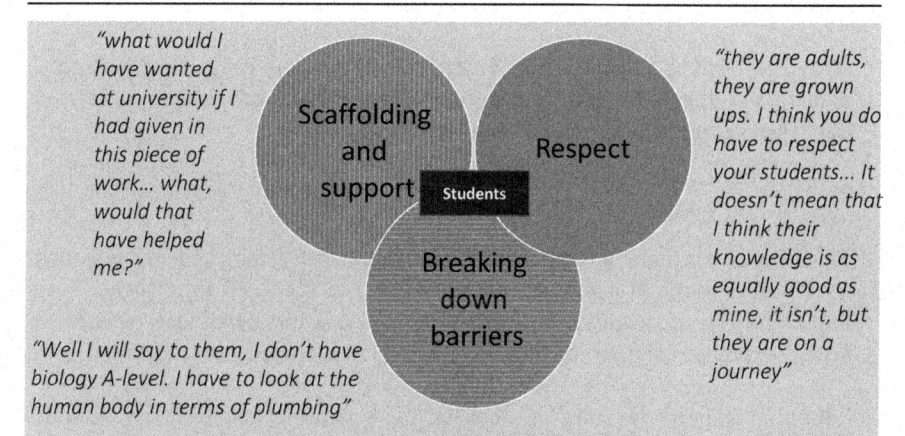

Breaking down barriers

"they are adults, they are grown ups. I think you do have to respect your students... It doesn't mean that I think their knowledge is as equally good as mine, it isn't, but they are on a journey"

"Well I will say to them, I don't have biology A-level. I have to look at the human body in terms of plumbing"

Figure 11.1 Overview of key themes from thematic analysis with selected quotes from participants
Source: (Suzanne Fergus)

Expertise needs more. Teaching is a professional activity. Values, or principles, must underpin our practice. (Values aren't just what we believe – they are what we do.) Competence, effectiveness and values bring us closer to a useful account of expertise in teaching in higher education. We're not there yet. Competence is often, mistakenly, taken to be a static quality. In truth, the world changes – sometimes with startling speed. The nature, the meaning, of competence therefore also has to change. What to do?

We could constantly fiddle with the standards. Or we could use a more powerful engine for change.

That powerful engine for change, and a further essential component of expertise, is scholarship, being scholarly. Here is a three-step account of being scholarly (Baume, 2016; Popovic & Baume, 2016):

Taking an enquiring, critical, approach to our own practice; asking hard questions, about what we do, and why, and whether it works, and how we know, and how we could do it better.
Using what is already known about, in our case, learning and teaching.
Undertaking publishable research.

This ladder of scholarship gives us a dynamic account of expertise as a further necessary quality for those who teach in higher education. For me, expertise includes a commitment to continual, informed, scholarly improvement. Without that movement, competent becomes steadily less competent, if we do not change, as the world changes around us. We may or not wish to get to the suggested third rung of scholarship – research and publication – although our enquiring, critical and literature-informed investigations and development work may, as Ashwin and Trigwell (2004) suggest, help us towards that third rung.

> But we all need to be comfortable on each of the first two rungs: continuing to enquire and using what is already known. We should be scholarly to increase our effectiveness, and so our evolving teaching expertise.
>
> (David Baume)

This idea of continual analysis and improvement of teaching practice is evident in other conceptions of expertise which do bring in the need for evidence – for example, the idea of 'adaptive' or 'innovative' expertise compared with 'routine' or 'efficient' expertise (Hatano & Inagaki, 1986; Hammerness et al., 2005):

> Routine experts become efficient at implementing relatively set routines without necessarily understanding why they work ... Adaptive experts deal with constantly changing problems and need to develop both an understanding of why things work as they do and an ability to alter their approach as circumstances change.
>
> (Stigler & Miller, 2018, p. 436)

With a similar conclusion to Hattie's (2008) review of higher education teaching, Stigler and Miller find that secondary school teacher expertise cannot be equated with specific best practices but is related to the learning opportunities they create for their students. In Box 11.2, Fergus summarises research with students that corroborates this further. In order to create these learning opportunities, expert teachers need to have appropriate knowledge, skill and, crucially, judgement – they must analyse and evaluate their practice. As Hattie (2008, p. 181) notes,

> It is the attention to the purpose of innovations, the willingness to seek negative evidence (i.e. seeking evidence on where students are not doing well) to improve the teaching innovation, the keenness to see the effects on all students, and the openness to new experiences that make the difference.

Such analysis and evaluation of evidence to improve teaching might also be considered as reflection-on- and in-action (Schön, 1982). To relate these ideas of evidence-informed practice back to deliberate practice, Dunn and Shriner (1998, p. 647) suggest that "teachers do not practice teaching in order to improve but instead engage in [mindful] patterns of planning, evaluation and revision so that students improve".

Box 11.2 Lecturers with top student feedback and ratings: what are they doing?

To explore the key behavioural attributes of teacher expertise, an exploratory study with 9 lecturers (from the disciplines of Chemistry, Geoscience, Microbiology,

Pharmacy, Pharmacology, Physics, Psychology, Sports Therapy) from the University of Hertfordshire was employed. Senior managers in the School of Life and Medical Sciences nominated lecturers that received high feedback ratings from undergraduate students they teach, and these lecturers were invited to participate in a 1-hour semi-structured interview. The Teacher Behaviour Checklist (TBC), developed in the United States (Kirby et al., 2018), was used to provide a structured focus and facilitate further contextual discussions on teaching expertise during the research interviews.

It was evident from the results that participants always or frequently exhibited the TBC attributes. Discussions helped to further elaborate and justify the scoring on items, for example, the category 'encourages and cares for students' included the attribute 'knows students' names', which was identified as a challenge with larger first year cohorts. Another category 'establishes daily and academic term goals' was questioned in relation to supporting independent adult learners and encouraging students' self-regulation with goals.

The themes identified from thematic analysis are shown in Figure 11.1 with selected quotes from participants. The three themes were: scaffolding and support, respect, and breaking down barriers with students placed at the centre. The findings align with research from Hattie (2015) whereby teacher effectiveness is independent of the pedagogy or method used and a greater importance is placed on clear success criteria and the quality of the interactions among students and between students and the teacher.

Conclusion

Given the complexity of professional identities discussed above and in Chapter 8 (Wood's "identity wobbleboard"), it is not surprising that academics are likely to persist within the field of experience and comfort – that is, the research and/or professional practice which formed the foundations of their career. Although they may have to engage in teaching, only a few will also participate in the teaching expert subculture within their institution and wider networks. Without an institutional-level culture for expertise in teaching, this will continue to remain niche and, despite expertise potentially being achievable by all, will still only be pursued by the few. Kreber (2002) asks whether "the present reward structure in higher education support[s] the development of expertise in teaching?" – a question that is still relevant two decades on. In the UK, the National Teaching Fellowship Scheme – a competitive excellence award – and the UK Professional Standards Framework, which underpins the professional recognition of fellowship of the Higher Education Academy, both highlight continuing professional development as a key criterion. However, reward and recognition schemes within institutions still tend to focus solely on the quality of teaching outcomes rather than on the professional learning process that enabled them.

As learning organisations, higher education institutions should be fostering a culture of professional learning for teaching. Changing how we conceptualise professional learning may be a helpful step towards changing this institutional culture. Rather than being add-on activities 'delivered' by others, it is an ethos and way of working that is integrated into everyday practice and aligned to individual and departmental goals. In addition, motivation for professional learning might also be aligned to a key driver for research: curiosity. "You teach and you are curious in that room" (Jenny Stephens, artistic director, Bristol Old Vic Theatre School, personal communication). What is going on and why? How can I make it more effective?

This discussion and research on professional learning from an expertise perspective marry with the extensive and generally convergent literature on professional development in higher education. The recommendations arising from the research with the nine NTFs (King, 2019) support Saroyan and Trigwell's (2015, p. 94) summary that

> The literature alerts us about (a) the value of reflection in improving teaching, especially when it is based on feedback from multiple sources, including student course ratings, peers, and experts ... (b) the benefits of engaging in the scholarship of teaching and learning ... (c) the role of communities of practice, networking, and peer interaction in supporting professional learning ... (d) the importance of situated learning in facilitating transfer ... and (e) the necessity and significance of developing a professional identity.

Implications for educational development and higher education institutions

The use of the term 'professional development' tends to lead to a solely training-based conception which ignores much of what the research and literature tell us about professional learning in higher education. In alignment with models of expertise development, structured learning opportunities can be beneficial for the novice entering the profession or someone taking on a new role or addressing a new theme within teaching. For the more experienced teacher, support should be in the form of resources, facilitation of communities of practice and coaching related to their specific context and goals.

The way educational development is traditionally presented in higher education points to a more 'training'-focused view of development through qualifications and workshops. Anecdotally, experience shows that academics tend to focus on this formal training when they are asked to describe what professional development they have done or to plan professional development activities for the future. There seems to be a disconnect between how the literature claims professionals learn, how expert teachers learn and what teachers actually think about when asked to formally describe their professional development.

Rather than persisting with the term 'professional development' in higher education and expecting colleagues to conceptualise it beyond being a list of training activities and events, the term 'professional learning' might be used for encouraging, enabling and supporting the development of expertise such that it becomes a narrative for one's career. Professional learning in higher education is the improvement and transformation of one's teaching over time. Bringing together the ideas discussed in this chapter – the development of expertise, problem-solving and evaluation of practice, the importance of evidence and scholarship, and motivation through curiosity, expert subcultures and care for students' learning – a definition of professional learning is proposed as *an evidence-informed evolution of teaching practice motivated by curiosity, community and care.*

Even with a self-directed, heutagogical conception of professional learning, there continues to be an important role for faculty/educational development, and this should be aligned to models of the development of expertise. Activities should include support for networking and learning communities, enabling individuals to proactively engage in deliberate practice or progressive problem-solving, and providing feedback and coaching. To encourage more intrinsic motivation, educational development should support teachers' competence (and not be perceived as remedial to challenge it) and give them autonomy to develop their own teaching approaches and relatedness through community activities.

For example, at the University of the West of England, the Academic Practice Directorate (APD; a centrally based educational development department) provides structured learning opportunities for colleagues new to teaching at the university in the form of personalised routes through a postgraduate certificate in Academic Professional Practice and facilitates workshops for those new to their roles as module or programme leaders or addressing particular themes for the first time. For more experienced teachers, support is offered through resources and guidance, facilitating the design or review of academic programmes, enabling opportunities for conversation and sharing through communities of practice and networks, promoting scholarship by funding and advising research and development projects, enabling professional recognition for teaching through the Higher Education Academy Fellowship scheme, and contributing to the development of institutional strategy and policy. Throughout its activities, the APD highlights and encourages an evidence-informed evolution of teaching so as to support teachers to better conceptualise, plan and integrate professional learning within their practice so that it is meaningful to them and their context.

If higher education institutions truly wish to pursue excellence, then the value of professional learning must be an explicit part of their culture and environment, structures, policies and processes, including reward and recognition. Professional learning and development should be considered an integrated part of all roles, including teaching, not an 'add-on' to be considered in one's spare time. Expertise in teaching should not be left as a subculture but encouraged and enabled as an expectation for all.

References

Ashwin, P. & Trigwell, K. (2004) Investigating educational development. In: Baume, D. & Kahn, P. (Eds), *Enhancing academic development*, Kogan Page, London, 117–131. doi:10.4324/9780203416228_chapter_7

Baume, D. (2016) Scholarship in action. *Innovations in Education and Teaching International*, 54 (2), 111–116. doi:10.1080/14703297.2016.1257950

Bereiter, C. & M. Scardamalia (1993) *Surpassing ourselves: an enquiry into the nature and implications of expertise*. Open Court, Chicago, IL.

Deci, E.L., & Ryan, R.M. (1985) *Intrinsic motivation and self-determination in human behaviour*. Plenum, New York. doi:10.1007/978-1-4899-2271-7

Dreyfus, H. & S. Dreyfus (1982) *Mind over machine*. Free Press, New York.

Dunn, T.G. & Shriner, C. (1998) Deliberate practice in teaching: what teachers do for self-improvement. *Teaching and Teacher Education* 15, 631–651. doi:10.1016/s0742-051x(98)00068-7

Eraut, M. (1994) *Developing professional knowledge and competence*. Falmer Press, Basingstoke. doi:10.4324/9780203486016

Ericsson, K.A. (2017) Expertise and individual differences: the search for the structure and acquisition of experts' superior performance. *WIREs Cogn Sci*, 8 (1–2). doi:10.1002/wcs.1382

Ericsson, K.A. (2018) The differential influence of experience, practice, and deliberate practice on the development of superior individual performance of experts. In: Ericsson, K.A., Hoffman, R.R., Kozbelt, A. & Williams, A.M. (Eds), *The Cambridge handbook of expertise and expert performance* (2nd edn). Cambridge University Press, Cambridge. doi:10.1017/9781316480748.038

Ericsson, K.A., Krampe, R.T. & Tesch-Römer, C. (1993) The role of deliberate practice in the acquisition of expert performance. *Psychological Review*, 100 (3), 363–406. doi:10.1037/0033-295x.100.3.363

Ferman, T. (2002) Academic professional development practice: what lecturers find valuable. *International Journal for Academic Development*, 7 (2), 146–158. doi:10.1080/1360144032000071305

Hammerness, K., Darling-Hammond, L., Bransford, J., Berliner, D.C., Cochran-Smith, M., McDonald, M. & Zeichner, K. (2005) How teachers learn and develop. In Darling-Hammond, L., Bransford, J., LePage, P., Hammerness, K. & Duffy, H. (Eds.), *Preparing teachers for a changing world: What teachers should learn and be able to do*. Jossey-Bass, San Francisco, CA, 358–389.

Hase, S. & Kenyon, C. (2000) From andragogy to heutagogy. In ultiBASE In-Site, RMIT, Melbourne.

Hatano, G. & Inagaki, K. (1986) Two courses of expertise. In: Stevenson, H., Azuma, H. & Hakuta, K. (Eds.), *Child development and education in Japan*. W.H. Freeman, New York, 262–272.

Hattie, J. (2008) *Visible learning: A synthesis of meta-analyses relating to achievement*, Routledge, London. doi:10.4324/9780203887332

Hattie, J. (2015) The applicability of visible learning to higher education. *Scholarship of Teaching and Learning in Psychology*, 1, 79–91. doi:10.1037/stl0000021

Inamorato, A., Gaušas, S., Mackevičiūtė, R., Jotautytė, A. & Martinaitis, Z. (2019) *Innovating professional development in higher education: An analysis of practices*. EUR 29676 EN, Publications Office of the European Union, Luxembourg.

Kirby, L.A., Busler, J.N., Keeley, J.W. & Buskit, W. (2018) A brief history of the teacher behavior checklist. *New Directions for Teaching and Learning*, 156, 21–29. doi:10.1002/tl.20313

King, H. (2004) Continuing professional development in higher education: what do academics do? *Educational Developments*, 5 (4), 1–5.

King, H. (2019) Continuing professional development: what do award-winning academics do? *Educational Developments*, 20 (2), 1–5.

Knight, P. (1998) Professional obsolescence and continuing professional development in higher education. *Innovations in Education and Training International*, 35 (3), 248–256. doi:10.1080/1355800980350309

Kreber, C. (2000) Becoming an expert university teacher. In: Long, H.B. & Associates (Eds.) *Practice & Theory in Self-Directed Learning*, Motorola University Press, Schaumberg, IL.

Kreber, C. (2002) Teaching excellence, teaching expertise, and the scholarship of teaching, *Innovative Higher Education*, 27 (1), 5–23.

McCune, V. (2021) Academic identities in contemporary higher education: sustaining identities that value teaching, *Teaching in Higher Education*, 26 (1), 20–35. doi:10.1080/13562517.2019.1632826

Popovic, C. & Baume, D. (2016) Introduction: some issues in academic development. In: Baume, D. & Popovic, C. (Eds) *Advancing practice in academic development*, Routledge, Abingdon, 1–16.

Richards, K.A.R & Levesque-Bristol, C. (2016) Assisting in the Management of Faculty Role Stress: Recommendations for Faculty Developers. *Journal of Faculty Development*, 30 (1), 7–14.

Saroyan, A. & Trigwell, K. (2015) Higher education teachers' professional learning: process and outcome. *Studies in Educational Evaluation*, 46, 92–101. doi:10.1016/j.stueduc.2015.03.008

Schön, D. (1982) *The reflective practitioner: how professionals think in action*. Routledge, Abingdon.

Stigler, J.W. & Miller, K.F. (2018) Expertise and expert performance in teaching. In: Ericsson, K.A., Hoffman, R.R., Kozbelt, A. & Williams, A.M. (Eds.) *The Cambridge handbook of expertise and expert performance* (2nd edn). Cambridge University Press, Cambridge. doi:10.1017/9781316480748.024

Stoten, D.W. (2021) Building adaptive management capability: the contribution of heutagogy to management development in turbulent times. *Journal of Management Development*, 40 (2), 121–137. doi:10.1108/jmd-10-2019-0448

Stupnisky, R.H., BrckaLorenz, A., Yuhasb, B. & Guay, F. (2018) Faculty members' motivation for teaching and best practices: testing a model based on self-determination theory across institution types. *Contemporary Educational Psychology*, 53, 15–26. doi:10.1016/j.cedpsych.2018.01.004

Tiberius, R.G., Smith, R.A. & Waisman, Z. (1998) Implications of the nature of "expertise" for teaching and faculty development. *To Improve the Academy*, 17, 123–138. doi:10.3998/tia.17063888.0017.011

Trowler, P. & Knight, P. (1999) Organizational socialization and induction in universities: Reconceptualizing theory and practice. *Higher Education*, 37, 177–195.

van de Wiel, M., Szegedi, K.H.P. & Weggeman, M.C.D.P. (2004) Professional learning: deliberate attempts at developing expertise. In: Boshuizen, H.P.A., Bromme, R. &

Gruber, H. (Eds.) *Professional learning: gaps and transitions on the way from novice to expert.* Kluwer Academic, Amsterdam, 181–206. doi:10.1007/1-4020-2094-5_10

van Schalkwyk, S., Herman, N., Leibowitz, B. & Farmer, J. (2015). Reflections on professional learning: choices, context and culture. *Studies in Educational Evaluation,* 46, 4–10. doi:10.1016/j.stueduc.2015.03.002

Chapter 12

Educative case-making

A learner-centred approach to supporting the development of pedagogical expertise in higher education

Alexandra Morgan and Emmajane Milton

Introduction

This chapter outlines an approach to working with educators and students in higher education called educative case-making. It builds directly upon the way in which Shulman (1996) used complex cases to support teachers' professional learning and asserted that the development of confidence and competence in teaching (what might be called expertise) demands a deep understanding of several knowledge categories. These include content knowledge, general knowledge about teaching and learning, curriculum knowledge, pedagogical content knowledge, knowledge of learners and their individual characteristics, knowledge of educational contexts and knowledge of educational outcomes. We outline how this case-making approach might be used to provide both educators and students in HE with the opportunity to develop and enhance their understanding of some or all of these categories in a way that is contextually specific and personally educative.

Why use educative case-making?

Typically, in universities worldwide, academics are appointed because they have established expertise in their subject. Usually this is in relation to research and publications that clearly demonstrate their contribution to a specific area of study and a high level of content knowledge in a relatively narrow disciplinary domain and/or extensive experience of professional practice. Although strong subject knowledge is likely to be an important requirement for high-quality teaching and learning experiences in higher education, this alone is not enough to prepare individuals for the exceptional performance demands made of educators in this sector. Failure to acknowledge this neglects to recognise and understand the range of multifaceted aspects that underpin the development of educators' expertise over time (Shulman & Shulman, 2004; Eraut, 1994). To imagine that the passive absorption of subject knowledge is all that is necessary for high-quality educational experiences has been described as a medieval but still commonly held understanding of what is required (Lawlor, 1990). Educators need to be able to

DOI: 10.4324/9781003198772-16

communicate their high level of content knowledge in ways that respond to the abilities and experiences of their learners and in a form that meets learners *where they are* in order to provide accessible, engaging and powerful learning experiences. Put simply, they need to develop good professional judgement (expertise) about the optimum approaches to use in supporting the learning of others.

Central to educative case-making is critical reflection on practice, acknowledged as being an essential feature of the development of practitioner professional judgement (Korthagen, 2017). Perhaps less well acknowledged or understood is, first, that the process of engaging in critical reflection can be an uncomfortable one. Second, that critical reflection on practice, as a solitary activity, is challenging and particularly difficult for those who have not attempted thinking in this way before. Third, that knowing exactly what you could or should focus on in an episode and reflect about is not always apparent (Shulman, 1996). In essence, higher education educators who are inexperienced in using critical reflection to consider their practice can face a number of barriers in doing so. These could prevent them from embracing external or alternative viewpoints and, therefore, engaging in deep and critical thought about particular episodes related to teaching and learning. This way of working is vital to support educators in refining their practice and improving the quality of teaching and learning experience. This approach can also be hugely valuable and supportive for students, helping them to examine their own approaches to learning, motivation and engagement and giving them ways of working that support their ongoing study.

Without this type of reflective experience, the learning of HE educators from a traditional academic career pathway and their students can become focused only on knowledge as defined by empirical research. It is perhaps easy to see why some academics who teach in universities might be particularly susceptible to doing this, as they are in the business of placing high value on published empirical findings! This (mis)application of research-based theory directly to practice with limited regard to the complexity of the learning situation was labelled by Schön (1987) as technical rationality. He asserted there was an over-emphasis on the use of scientifically derived approaches and theoretical ideas in what were fundamentally complex problems of practice (Schön, 1987). The idea that knowledge generated through critical reflection is of the same value (perhaps more value) to educators and students than established and published academic knowledge (Schön, 1987) does not suggest research-based professional knowledge should be disregarded; rather, it questions its direct practical significance and acknowledges the importance of practitioner experience and expertise. Rolfe (2002) suggests this approach is a move beyond polarised thinking in terms of understanding the development of professional expertise.

The understanding that critical reflection on practice is challenging but of great benefit to teachers is the basis for Shulman's advocating the use of teacher-written cases as valuable tools for professional learning (Shulman, 1996). Educative case-making also aligns with Dewey's (1916) ideas of thinking about practice as an active process, in which hypothesising how you might do it differently next time plays an important role. Seeing reflection as thinking deeply about the experience of past episodes of teaching and learning, as a means of exploring how things could be done differently and what might be tried out next, positions reflection as a type of active experimentation. Similarly, Schön (1983) talked about educators in the process of teaching being involved in a continual reflective dialogue with the situation they found themselves in. In this way, the educative case-making process, which privileges discussion and dialogue, creates a space to *pause for thought*, to enable deeper contextual understandings.

Dewey (1916) articulated knowledge as a verb, something we do, as a relationship, a way of acting on the world. He saw little difference between thinking, reflecting and researching. By emphasising the research process rather than the outcome, he asserted that research was the activity of all thinkers rather than a particular domain of scientists and academics. We argue that all HE educators (regardless of discipline and career pathway) and students need to undertake research as understood by Dewey (1916) and Schön (1987) and gain the skills to do so, because even the best evidence- and research-based theory is unlikely to adequately equip them for the numerous complex issues that will inevitably arise during their pedagogical practice. This is because, in meeting the needs of their learners, educators are likely to encounter problems which do not have obvious solutions and to which findings from empirical research cannot directly be applied. These unique, complex and multifaceted problems, which Rittel and Webber (1973) termed wicked problems, may not even have a *right* or *best* solution for all involved and cannot be solved by the direct application of evidence-based ideas or the application of theory in practice.

What is educative case-making?

Educative case-making is situated in day-to-day pedagogical practice. It allows for the consideration of this practice in a way that is not driven by overarching, empirically derived theoretical ideas or general principles. Cases, focused firmly on a bounded episode of teaching or learning experience, in a particular context, are identified by participants (students or educators) themselves. It is not that theoretical ideas and general principles about teaching and learning are not of value – simply that professional discourse about teaching and learning needs to be grounded in relevant experience(s) in a way that acknowledges the complexity of the endeavour. The focus is always on real events rather than principles or theory; although, once the cases have taken form, they may draw on theoretical understandings at a later stage, they *never begin* with this (Shulman, 1996).

Cases created as part of this process are original accounts of learning episodes which developed over time and, with support, become complex and detailed narratives. Rooted in specific events, these cases are stories of teaching and learning experiences. Utilising the power of 'narrative ways of knowing' (Bruner, 1996, in Shulman, 1996, p. 464), cases are valuable tools for professional learning because their richness illuminates the uncertainty and messiness of teaching and learning and the complexity of what needs to be considered. They are often focused on experiences that have already provoked thought (although this may not have been a deep and critical consideration up until this point!). This way of working gives participants the opportunity to reflect more deeply on their experiences, scrutinising these with others. They work through a structured process of collaborative critical reflection which supports their thinking and deepens understanding of their case.

The term educative describes the emphasis placed on two features of the precise methodology adopted. First, the questioning approaches adopted during the group discussion sessions align with an educative mentoring stance (Daly & Milton, 2017) and, second, detailed and research-informed responses (glosses) are provided by facilitators with substantial experience in educational practice. These glosses support participants in developing and extending their thinking about their practice and experiences further. The case-making process is also educative because it goes beyond recalling the event(s); rather, participants are supported to articulate and rearticulate their experiences and understandings collaboratively over time. This process of collaborative critical reflection brings into focus deep, conceptual understandings of what was really going on, which may not have been clear to the author when the events took place. These new insights have capacity to inform and shape their and others' practice going forward.

How can educative case-making be used in practice? Who is educative case-making for?

We have used this way of working both within and outside our own institution, and, whoever the participants were, educative case-making gave rise to valuable contextualised professional learning experiences for all involved. The process is always carefully tailored to the specific contexts of the participants with whom it is being undertaken. Anyone wishing to adopt this approach should be mindful of the time required to ensure that all have appropriate, shared understandings of what is to be achieved, including the leadership in the setting where it is being undertaken and the participants themselves.

In undertaking educative case-making, it is possible to have a specific focus or to take a broader and more open approach, depending on the purpose and overall aim. Examples include:

- Exploring something fairly general such as experiences of teaching and learning on a particular programme or at a specific institution, or
- Exploring more specific issues such as challenges of moderating work for a particular module or providing insights to student experiences of feedback.

This process also provides an opportunity to reflect on teaching and learning from the perspective of the student as well as the educator. It is potentially empowering for students on an individual level to be supported to think metacognitively and consider their educational experiences. Improved metacognition has been linked with promoting students' overall academic success (Ohtani & Hisasaka, 2018). In addition, this way of working with students moves beyond the superficial compliance that can often be the reality of engaging with student voice (Rudduck & Fielding, 2006). The process privileges the elicitation of genuine student voice and engagement – there is a big difference between the commonly articulated practice of *listening to students* and genuinely empowering them to explore issues and recommend solutions. The process of engaging with their lived experience in narrative ways moves away from approaches that are rushed and tokenistic. It is about empowering students as *change agents* and active collaborators. It enables students and HE educators to work in partnership, exploring their experiences through different lenses and engaging together in possibility thinking about how things might be done differently, while also considering the complexities and parameters with regard to what might be practicable.

Educative case-making allows participants to become active researchers of their own experiences of education. It provides them with strategies and experiences to support their ongoing reflection-in-action in order to better equip them with the professional judgement to deal, in real time, with the complex teaching and learning situations that occur on a day-to-day basis. Therefore, it is a process of professional learning that allows for the development of professional judgement and expertise through critical reflection on a specific aspect of practice. The insights developed and documented can have benefits both for the individuals who participate and also, more widely, in better understanding of a predetermined module, programme or institutional focus. The artefacts produced – the detailed written cases and posters – can also be hugely valuable materials. These have the ongoing potential to support rich, contextualised professional learning dialogues which are crucial to supporting the improvement of teaching, learning and student experience.

What is the process for undertaking educative case-making?

The process is always tailored to the focus, participants and context. It follows the structure outlined below:

- *A planning meeting* between the process facilitators and senior leaders in the setting to discuss the overarching aims and who will be participating. It is vital at this stage to establish a genuine commitment from all involved to *work with* participants as *change agents*.
- *A participant briefing session* providing a clear idea of the aims, expectations and ways of working. It should outline the focus and attendance requirements, address ethical issues including consent and make clear expected outputs and the time frame for delivery.
- *Three sessions* – each around 3 hours in length – allowing necessary time for each participant to engage in dialogue with others. This is crucial to support

the critical consideration of each case from which the written cases are then developed. These written cases are ultimately distilled into posters which synthesise the ideas and learning from each case. We have found these sessions, together with the briefing session, work well when spread evenly over a 4-week period. The timings might be adjusted, but it should be noted that a generous allocation of time is needed to achieve the depth required through the collaborative oral rehearsal of ideas, drafting of a detailed case based on these, provision of and consideration of external comments on the detailed case and distillation of thinking into a final poster presentation.

The examples below exemplify the process, key considerations and outcomes in different contexts.

Example 1: understanding the experiences of third-year students in pharmacy

The MPharm is a 4-year programme at a large research-intensive university in the UK and is currently ranked highly in terms of research excellence and student satisfaction with teaching. It is designed to equip students with the knowledge, skills and experiences needed to become practicing pharmacists.

Planning meeting

We initially met with the programme lead to explain educative case-making, including the rationale for the approach, discussing if this way of working might be something they would be willing to trial and commit to. We then agreed on the specific focus to be addressed, identified as understanding student experiences of the third year of the programme. We also discussed ethical issues, logistics regarding recruiting and communicating with participating students, timings and content of sessions, the booking of suitable rooms (computers were required for Sessions 2 and 3) and refreshments.

Participant briefing session

Participation in the process was voluntary. Students were fully aware that doing so would confer no advantage beyond what they learned from the process itself. They were informed that a single payment would be made to them by the university. This would be received on completion of the whole experience, which would acknowledge their time commitment in attending all sessions and in completing the detailed written case and poster in the way outlined in the brief.

Before committing to participation, students were made aware of the ways of working that would be adopted and expected during the project. It was explained that the Chatham House Rule (International Affairs Think Tank; Chatham House, 2021) would apply throughout all sessions. This meant that participants and the facilitators would be free to share the information received but should not reveal the identity of who said it. Adopting this rule helped to build trust and create a safe environment in which to discuss ideas and solve complex problems. This was crucial, as we wanted the students to discuss their experiences in a full and frank way. The approach to confidentiality was discussed at the earliest stage of the process and was negotiated and student-led. It was important that these ways of working were clear from the outset so that participants were able to establish a space where they could openly share experiences that had been *challenging* or *provoked deep thinking* and discuss key features of their student experience. Ethical consent was obtained to share the findings of this work more widely.

The programme lead who had co-planned the event was present and made clear that students should feel free to speak honestly about all their experiences; this worked to reassure the students and legitimised the honest contributions, *warts and all*. It was made clear that this process was about finding out more about their individual student experiences, with the aim of improving the programme. The sessions were co-led by higher education educators from the School of Pharmacy and others with expertise in educational practice. Those facilitators from outside the School of Pharmacy predominantly led the sessions, but the Pharmacy staff (who had in-depth understandings of the ways of working) were crucial in helping to elicit and explain programme-specific information and develop shared understandings. Students were told at the briefing session that, for the first session, they should choose and be ready to discuss

> an aspect of your student experience from the third year of study in the school which has been challenging or provoked deep thinking. It is important that the issues involved have taken effort to resolve or remain unresolved. Your experience will include particular events or episodes which stand out vividly.

They were also asked to bring one artefact that helped to illustrate the event(s) or episode(s). Fifteen participants were recruited from this year group, approximately two-thirds of the way through the academic year.

Session 1

The students spent time working in triads, taking turns to discuss and listen carefully to each other's cases and offer reflections on what they had heard. Three 'acts' (Shulman, 1996) were used as a structure to support and encourage the students to consider their identified episode iteratively in more depth each time.

Act 1 provided a brief context requiring each student to provide a provisional title for their case. Each student, in turn, presented their identified issue or episode (s) for 5 minutes and discussed this with peers for another 5 minutes.

In Act 2, students presented the artefact they had brought, telling the story of what happened in detail. This included the episode(s), event(s) and things that were said, remembered or written down. They were asked to present a full story but, at this stage, to try not to offer an interpretation of what was really going on. Students were required to present this for 10 minutes without interruption. Peers could make notes about the issues that they felt had emerged and any tensions and challenges as they saw them. At the end of each individual account, these notes were shared and discussed with each other.

Act 3 focused on what the case was *really about*, and here a deep exploration of the issues that emerged from the case occurred. Challenges were identified, and the deeper insights that had been extracted were documented. The students began to speculate on how the issues could be resolved by specific actions or through a deeper understanding of what was going on. Each participant prepared an individual handwritten poster of their case, including the provisional title and also their revised title (if it had changed).

The session concluded with sharing the posters though a gallery activity – putting them up around the room, with students and staff taking time to view and comment on aspects of them using post-it notes. A whole-group discussion identified common themes and interesting insights.

Session 2

The students continued to work in triads in a computer suite with their posters and post-it notes from Session 1. They then developed their written case, again using the three-act structure outlined in Session 1. They again discussed their individual cases in the same triads. They were supported in their writing by the higher education educators from Pharmacy who had programme-level understanding (so that specific questions could be answered) and by the external higher education educators with expertise in educational practice. At the end of this session, students shared developed written cases electronically with the facilitators.

Glosses. At this stage, each of the developing cases was read by all the facilitators – internal and external to the programme. Together, they provided a written response identifying where further consideration or clarification might develop the ideas or thinking.

Session 3

In a computer suite, students continued to develop their written case responding to the written response (gloss). This gave rise to further discussion and dialogue in their triads. Once the written case was complete, the students then carefully selected the key information, conclusions and insights developed from their case for inclusion on their final poster (see Figure 12.1). These anonymised posters provided an optimal way of sharing students' experiences, for wider consideration, with different groups such as teaching teams and staff–student committees.

Example 2: understanding experiences of educators in higher education

Using this approach with HE educators (engaged on a professional learning programme focused on considering pedagogical practice in their own academic field), a similar process of considering the focus and recruitment of participants with a senior

Educative case-making 183

THE CASE OF PROBLEMATIC COURSEWORK IN PH3202
Using case-making to share and document third year experience in Pharmacy

Expectations of third year:
My expectations for third year were that it would be the most mentally challenging but the most important year of study, consisting of applying and adapting prior knowledge from our previous years to new concepts whilst preparing us for fourth year projects and pre-registration.

PH3202 aims to make sure we had the skills in order to be able to critically analyse and discuss papers, which was found to be challenging in a few different aspects.

The Problem:
PH3202 is Research Methodology and consists partly of a paper appraisal which was originally placed in the second semester of third year but had been moved to the first semester to help spread the workload across the year more evenly.

Timescale of events:
- Monday 8th October was an introductory workshop to the coursework, then two further workshops on scientific/clinical papers.
- The deadline for submission was originally set for 13th November.
- Allocations were not given until the 17th October; students felt the allocation was unfair due to differences in difficulties of papers.
- Many were told understanding of the paper wasn't necessary to do a critical appraisal which wasted time on researching.
- The deadline for submission was changed firstly to 9th November, then to the 21st and ultimately 30th

On the 26th of October, a serious personal circumstance occurred which was beyond my control, effecting my mental and physical health, meaning I had to return home.

Finding solutions:
- The Paper Appraisal coursework could be made formative; produce a good quality analyses with help from academic professionals for a set deadline.
- Split PH3202 through the semesters; SWOT analysis in the first term and the Paper Appraisal in second semester, with a deadline around mid/late February.
- Implement an allocation system based on personal interests; students would be asked to fill in a form online and choose keywords related to the titles of papers and their interests. Allocate papers based on chosen keywords.

If I were faced with a similar situation again, I would look at the positives and think of the coursework as a way to explore an area of research I wouldn't normally be interested in.

MY EXPERIENCE IN THE CASE MAKING PROCESS
I found this process particularly difficult to reflect back on because of the personal nature of the case, however it has helped me make sense of the order of events, where the difficulties within the module actually arose from and how I react to a challenging situation. Being able to discuss my difficulties with my peers has reassured me that I was not alone in my struggles and feelings toward the module and their opinions on how the module could be adapted were insightful. I would not have had any other opportunity to discuss my problems otherwise.

Figure 12.1 Example of a final poster

leader was undertaken. Again, this example consisted of a planning meeting, participant briefing session and the first session where the chosen episode(s) or issue was discussed in three acts, concluding with the handwritten poster *gallery* activity. The second session similarly involved a detailed reflection on and write-up of cases, after which the *glosses* were written by the facilitators. This was followed by Session 3, where the written cases were discussed and refined before a summary poster was produced.

The HE educator participants also engaged with pertinent higher education pedagogical practice literature. This was identified and provided by the facilitators before Session 3 as part of the glosses. This allowed participants to consider their case from an alternative or established perspective and to develop deeper understandings of the identified and/or emerging issues. This supported them to articulate what implications their case had for their current educational practice and adjusting this moving forward.

These two examples were undertaken independently; however, it is quite plausible that an institution might chose to work in this way with both HE educators and students, simultaneously or sequentially.

What is important to consider when doing educative case-making?

There needs to be a clearly articulated focus and rationale for participating in this work from senior leaders, as it would be inappropriate for this to be something *done to* staff or students in an institution, department or programme. The approach is predicated on ideas of *working with*: it is necessary for all involved to embark on this process with real commitment to working with students/staff as change agents; not to do this would be unethical and disingenuous. A genuine commitment to the spirit of this process should be the first thing to establish prior to proceeding further. Similarly, participation in the process should be voluntary at all levels. It is demanding in terms of both time and, more importantly, fully committing to the aims of the process. This is because it is about *working with* colleagues and students in an open, authentic and principled way – which for some may be a significant paradigm shift. Indeed, rich cases of practice that no one ever really acknowledges or takes any further are of little use and may in fact make staff's and students' experience and relations worse.

The process requires dedicated time and space in which to work collaboratively in small groups. We have generally worked with groups of between 15 and 30, but there is the potential to work in larger groups with the appropriate space, resources and support. Consideration also needs to be given to how to compensate students for their time – the students in this example were paid a one-off fee equivalent to the living wage. We felt this was appropriate compensation for students taking time out of their study schedule and part-time jobs.

Facilitation of the educative case-making process requires staff who understand the process and have insight into educational literature and high-quality pedagogical practice, in particular:

- Overseeing, planning and structuring the whole process for all involved;
- Ensuring ethical ways of working (BERA, 2018);
- Creating an environment which values everyone and their views – encouraging honesty, openness and a questioning stance is central;
- Pacing the sessions sensitively to ensure learning opportunities are maximised and supported but also ensuring full coverage of the session aims; and
- Encouraging dialogue and the development of the written narratives without influencing or directing them.

Other important considerations in relation to facilitators include needing staff who:

- Provide externality to the setting;
- Have experience of this process or way of working and the underpinning rationale;
- Have expertise in the area of study that is being focused upon; and
- Have a strong understanding of educational and pedagogical practice.

The expectations on the facilitators to provide carefully structured and informed support should not be underestimated. For the process to be of value for all concerned, they need to ensure that the written cases remain focused on the event, contain sufficient detail to enable robust understanding of the teaching and learning context and present deep rather than superficial insights into the event(s) experienced.

What are the benefits of educative case-making?

Educative case-making can directly address the barriers staff and students encounter in relation to critically reflecting on their practice by providing:

- Support (an emotional safety net) that acknowledges the discomfort and sometimes painful nature of scrutinising your own practice and subjecting this to external and alternative viewpoints;
- Structure and scaffolding for oral, collaborative critical reflection and the development of a written reflective case – particularly helpful for those not already immersed in this way of thinking and learning;
- Guidance and reassurance, through working with others, that the episode(s) or event(s) being focused upon is a *valuable* thing to think deeply about. This means the conclusions drawn and insights arrived at are more robust than those that could have been drawn by staff or students working alone, and they are documented and shared.

Engaging in retelling, revisiting and reflecting on direct experiences allows participants the opportunity to actively consider experiences and to support others to consider theirs. The stories, episodes, recollected words and interactions offer rich material and support participants to *make sense* of events and to work collaboratively to deepen their understandings through problematising shared experiences. Actively engaging in this by presenting their case, adding detail to it, asking and responding to questions, sharing case materials, identifying tensions, challenges and commonalities, engaging in careful listening and offering ideas together supports the participants in understanding themselves as learners – providing the opportunity for 'going meta' about their experiences (Hutchings & Shulman, 1999, p. 13).

The insights illuminated through students documenting their lived experiences in this way are something quite different from the insights gained from a questionnaire or questions raised at a staff–student committee. While walking around the gallery of handwritten posters, a programme lead exclaimed 'this is just gold dust!' – commenting specifically on the richness of the insights that were emerging. In this way, the process offers dual learning for both participants and facilitators, and the outputs at each stage offer further opportunities for ongoing professional learning beyond the immediate group involved.

A range of opportunities can be presented by the insights generated by the participants – for example:

- Quick wins – things that students or educators may wish to change immediately and which is in their gift to make happen;

- Medium-term improvements – changes that cannot be implemented without resources or support from colleagues or senior leaders;
- Longer-term, institution-wide benefits and learning – related to policy or wider institutional practice.

From experience, the educative case-making process has been positively received by participants in all contexts to date, indicating that this way of working is potentially scalable and transferable to other education contexts.

What are the challenges/limitations of educative case-making?

Educative case-making is not a quick-fix: it is rich, contextualised professional learning. It demands time and a commitment by all involved to responsive action, particularly from senior leaders. Without this, it is potentially a waste of participants' time and could be construed as disingenuous and unethical. It requires careful facilitation and expertise in:

- The area of focus;
- Broader understandings of pedagogical approaches in HE; and
- The theoretical ideas on which these approaches are based.

Throughout, the ethical considerations of this process need careful and sensitive management, because participants can understandably feel vulnerable when considering and sharing individual learning experiences and actions. The facilitators need to plan how exactly they will provide appropriate levels of confidentiality and anonymity.

Conclusion

Educative case-making provides both educators and students in HE with the opportunity to:

- Develop professional expertise in a way that is contextually specific and research-informed;
- Engage in rich professional learning based on the premise of research into practice;
- Support participants to critically reflect on their practice;
- Move beyond superficial compliance in terms of student voice;
- Develop better shared understandings of underpinning rationales for approaches to teaching and learning within a teaching team;
- *Work with* participants as change agents to research teaching practice from respective perspectives.

All who work and study in HE can benefit from the opportunity to utilise understandings developed from their critical reflection on cases situated in their own experiences and/or the experiences of others. This approach to professional learning can then support the development of shared understandings (even where participants agree to disagree) through reasoned debate and discussion.

References

British Educational Research Association [BERA]. (2018) *Ethical Guidelines for Educational Research* (4th edn), www.bera.ac.uk/researchers-resources/publications/ethicalguidelines-for-educational-research-2018 [accessed 01/02/2021].

Chathamhouse. (2021) International Affairs Think Tank, Chatham House. www.chathamhouse.org/ [accessed 27/04/2021].

Daly, C. & Milton, E. (2017) External mentoring for new teachers: mentor learning for a change agenda. *International Journal of Mentoring and Coaching in Education*, 6 (3), 178–195. doi:10.1108/ijmce-03-2017-0021

Dewey, J. (1916) *Democracy and Education* (Public domain, numerous editions).

Eraut, M. (1994) *Developing Professional Knowledge and Competence.* Falmer Press, London. doi:10.4324/9780203486016

Hutchings, P. & Shulman L. (1999) The scholarship of teaching: new elaborations, new developments. *Change*, 31 (5), 11–15. doi:10.1080/00091389909604218

Korthagen, F. (2017) Inconvenient truths about teacher learning: towards professional development 3.0. *Teachers and Teaching*, 23 (4), 387–405. doi:10.1080/13540602.2016.1211523

Lawlor, S. (1990) *Teachers Mistaught: Training in Theories or Education in Subjects.* Centre for Policy Studies, London.

Ohtani, K. & Hisasaka, T. (2018) Beyond intelligence: a meta-analytic review of the relationship among metacognition, intelligence, and academic performance. *Metacognition Learning*, 13 (2), 179–212. doi:10.1007/s11409-018-9183-8

Rittel, H. & Webber, M. (1973) Dilemmas in a general theory of planning. *Policy Sciences*, 4, 155–169. doi:10.1007/bf01405730

Rolfe, G. (2002) Reflective practice: where now? *Nurse Education in Practice*, 2, 21–29. doi:10.1054/nepr.2002.0047

Rudduck, J. & Fielding, M. (2006) Student voice and the perils of popularity. *Educational Review*, 58 (2), 219–223. doi:10.1080/00131910600584207

Schön, D. (1983) *The Reflective Practitioner.* Temple Smith, London.

Schön, D. (1987) *Educating the Reflective Practitioner: Toward a New Design for Teaching and Learning in the Professions.* Jossey-Bass, San Francisco.

Shulman, L. (1996) Just in case: reflections on learning from experience. In: Colbert, K., Trimble, K. & Desberg, P. (Eds.) *The Case for Education: Contemporary Approaches for Using Case Methods.* Allyn & Bacon, Boston, MA, 463–482.

Shulman, S. & Shulman, J. (2004) How and what teachers learn: a shifting perspective. *Journal of Curriculum Studies*, 36 (2), 257–271.

Chapter 13

Collaboration and mentoring to enhance professional learning in higher education

Warren Code, Ashley Welsh, Dawn Reilly, Liz Warren, Laura Heels, Lindsay Marshall, Isabelle Barrette-Ng, John Dawson and Eliana El Khoury

Professional learning is a key feature of the acquisition and maintenance of expertise. Although this might be pursued as a solo activity, Bloom's ground-breaking study of the development of talent (1985), Eraut's exploration of professional knowledge and competence (1994), Ericsson et al.'s deliberate practice (1993) and other models of professional learning often emphasise the importance and value of other people's input as guides, mentors or coaches at all stages of professional development. Furthermore, dialogue around learning and teaching is "viewed as important for the construction of meaning and identity within 'learning communities' (Wenger, 1998), and is widely and effectively used to support critical reflection on practice (Brookfield, 1995; Brockbank & McGill, 2007)" (Pilkington, 2011 p. 13).

This chapter offers a composite of four short pieces that describe different approaches to supporting professional learning in higher education through collaboration and mentoring. As well as providing practical examples, the approaches also reveal the two-way nature of such learning support and highlight the benefits to mentees and their mentors of this dialogic way of working.

Discipline-based education specialists: an embedded model for supporting the development of teaching expertise in undergraduate science education.

The Carl Wieman Science Education Initiative (CWSEI) at the University of British Columbia (UBC) in Vancouver, Canada, was a 10-year initiative that transformed curriculum and pedagogy in mathematics and science, with nearly 200 UBC faculty members adopting research-informed practices in their teaching (Wieman, 2017). UBC is a large, research-intensive university with about 9,000 undergraduate students in science and mathematics programs within nine departments in the Faculty of Science. As with the Science Education Initiative at the University of Colorado Boulder, the main mechanism for change was the hiring and training of *discipline-based education specialists* (DBESs) at the postdoctoral or

DOI: 10.4324/9781003198772-17

contract faculty level to partner with faculty members in bringing the principles of *scientific teaching* (Handelsman et al., 2007) into courses. These specialists brought their existing disciplinary knowledge and teaching experience to the role and through the position engaged with – and eventually contributed to – education research.

A growing number of initiatives are implementing similar models, including Imperial College London and Cornell University (Chasteen & Code, 2018, Appendix 1). Such specialist positions offer early career academics opportunities to enrich their own teaching practices and to partner with faculty members in the development, implementation, and evaluation of instructional choices (assessment, course design, etc.) and scholarship; in other words, we see growth in multiple facets of teaching expertise for all involved.

In reflecting on this 10-year initiative, we found it useful to connect and situate our lessons learned for faculty development to the broader scholarship and practices emerging in academic development. In particular, we mapped our CWSEI work to Kenny et al.'s (2017) Developmental Framework for Teaching Expertise in Post-secondary Education (discussed in more detail in Chapter 4), which offers a developmental continuum of exploration, engagement, and expansion (Table 13.1) within five facets of teaching expertise:

1. Teaching and supporting learning;
2. Professional learning and development;
3. Mentorship;
4. Research, scholarship, and inquiry; and
5. Educational leadership.

Table 13.1 Relationships between the development of teaching expertise within the CWSEI and the facets of teaching expertise

2007 Explore	1.	Teaching & supporting learning: learner-centred pedagogies, course reform, conceptual understanding, assessment redesign
	2.	Professional learning & development: training and development of DBESs
2011 Explore & engage	1	Teaching & supporting learning: ongoing focus throughout the initiative.
	2	Professional learning & development: continued training for DBESs and increased training for faculty.
	3	Mentorship: senior DBESs mentoring new/junior DBESs
	4	Research, scholarship, & inquiry: building momentum
2014 Explore, engage, & expand	1	Teaching & supporting learning: ongoing focus throughout the initiative
	2	Professional learning & development: shift to the creation and facilitation of graduate courses in STEM education.
	3	Mentorship: introduction of paired teaching model (faculty–faculty mentorship with DBES facilitation)
	4	Research, scholarship, & inquiry: over 100 publications
	5	Educational leadership: increased connections with teaching faculty; dispersion of CWSEI alumni to other institutions

The continuum starts with the *exploration* of oneself in self-awareness, moves to actively *engaging* with practices to enrich teaching expertise, and then *expands* to the growth of others and the broader educational community. We find this framework particularly useful given its grounding in growth and development of people and systems over time. Table 13.1 is a summary of how the CWSEI fostered teaching expertise in people and expanded its reach to the broader community along three main timelines.

The CWSEI launched in 2007 as a place of exploration for those involved. Work largely centred on transforming science and math courses to be learner-centred, engaging students more actively with their learning. There was considerable focus on the development of clear learning goals, conceptual understanding, and assessment design to enrich student learning in particular courses or subjects. In terms of professional learning and development, the initiative was committed to training DBESs in their new role, providing opportunities to learn more about educational research, and supporting their role in working with faculty members.

Come 2011, more faculty members were implementing new pedagogical strategies in their courses, and both DBESs and faculty members were seeking out new opportunities for innovation (Wieman et al., 2010). Professional learning and development became more community-focused, with DBESs providing facilitated training for faculty members. The more senior DBESs began to mentor new DBESs in the roles, skills, and responsibilities of the position; the regularity of weekly DBES meetings was a great way to facilitate such conversations and learning. Finally, momentum was building within the facet of research, scholarship, and inquiry, and work was being shared at conferences and in peer-reviewed publications.

A snapshot of 2014 reveals how the CWSEI moved along a continuum of expansion. The work in teaching and learning was ongoing, with professional development being expanded to graduate students via the creation and facilitation of graduate courses in teaching and learning in STEM. Mentorship was further enriched by the development of a "paired teaching" model supported by the DBESs (Strubbe et al., 2019). Members of the CWSEI collectively published over 100 peer-reviewed articles, influencing STEM education practices internationally. Finally, within the realm of educational leadership, CWSEI collaborations built capacity within the tenure-track teaching stream, and many CWSEI alumni contributed to teaching expertise as faculty or staff in teaching and learning at other institutions.

As the initiative began to wrap up, with the departments having established a high level of expertise among faculty, interest in the embedded model and what it afforded remained, including consideration of programme-level and equity issues now that teaching methods had shifted to a significant degree. This led to an expansion of the existing Science Centre for Learning and Teaching (https://sky

light.science.ubc.ca/) to create a new set of ongoing, department-based staff positions: *science education specialists*. The specialists have been integral to these curriculum-focused student experience projects while also supporting various other teaching endeavours in departments, and they were a critical part of the emergency shift to online teaching in 2020. These embedded roles expand what is possible in our departments and lead to continued growth and development of teaching expertise.

Developing teaching expertise through peer support

This case study is set in the Business School of a UK university which has a teaching focus and is research informed. We discuss two ways in which colleagues are supported by their peers to develop teaching expertise. Both initiatives potentially include all colleagues who teach in the Business School.

First, in 2019–20, the university introduced a new version of our *Peer-Supported Development* (PSD) scheme for the peer observation of teaching. Previously, we ran a traditional scheme where colleagues selected their own pairing. Under the old scheme, colleagues almost always selected a peer observer from their discipline. This gave the benefit of both technical and teaching content being reviewed in the observations. However, this approach missed the opportunity to consider alternative methods of teaching as demonstrated by colleagues from other disciplines. In contrast, under the new 2019–20 PSD scheme, we randomly matched people across Business School departments. We then checked the pairings with the relevant heads of department to ensure we observed any relevant sensitivities.

There is a PSD lead for the Business School who informs colleagues about their pairing and sends out information about the scheme. Everyone chooses which session they want to have observed. Pre-observation documentation has been minimised to respect the many demands on colleagues' time (Carbone et al., 2019). The documentation provides the opportunity to give the context for the observation and raise any issues the observee wants feedback on from their observer. After the observations, each pair meet to discuss the teaching sessions. The observations and feedback are confidential, and colleagues are only asked to confirm to the PSD lead the dates that the observations took place and that they have met to discuss feedback. The PSD scheme includes all colleagues who teach, and, because paired colleagues observe each other, there is no hierarchy involved. For example, in the summer of 2019, the Business School commenced a major initiative to replace its sessional contracts with permanent (mainly part-time) teaching-only posts (Leathwood and Read, 2020). These colleagues are included in our PSD, which means they not only receive feedback on their teaching from a colleague to improve their practice, but also give feedback to the same colleague in a two-way exchange (Bell & Mladenovic, 2015). This reinforces their position as valued members of the academic community.

The new PSD scheme was supported by workshops framed as 'maximising the potential of PSD'. These provided interesting perspectives about staff perceptions of the rationale behind the scheme, showing that, despite the information circulated at the start of the year and presented by the PSD lead, there appeared to be staff uncertain of the goals. The workshops proved invaluable in reassuring those colleagues and, indeed, enthusing them. Feedback from the workshops included:

> The session was very useful; it gave context to PSD and I am now positive about it.
> Gave me confidence in my own observation feedback.
> Opened my mind and decreased anxiety!.

It is hoped this message will be further disseminated going forward as the total attendance at the workshops was only around 30 colleagues. When it was rolled out, the scheme was very well received. Colleagues liked working with people outside their department and using the experience to think 'outside the box' to improve teaching. It also enhanced the notion that this was about sharing practice rather than it being an assessment of a teaching session. However, for anyone wanting to proceed with this type of developmental initiative, we would recommend using a similar approach to our information workshop to address any initial concerns from colleagues.

Second, the university runs its own *internal teaching fellowship scheme*, which is accredited by Advance HE against the UK Professional Standards Framework for teaching and supporting learning in higher education (Advance HE, 2011). We provide mentors who support colleagues to work towards a Fellowship of the Higher Education Academy (FHEA). The scheme recognises colleagues in the associate fellow, fellow and senior fellow categories, so the benefits of this type of mentee–mentor relationship have a positive impact on colleagues at all stages of their teaching career. For example, many of our new part-time teaching-only colleagues have professional qualifications and current industry experience in the sectors which our students want to join after graduation. However, they can lack a formal teaching qualification. Here, the appropriate category of fellowship is often associate fellow. Bell and Mladenovic (2013) note how important it is for new teachers to reflect on their practice. Discussing an application, including a teaching observation, with a mentor facilitates reflection to develop teaching expertise.

The UKPSF points fellowship applicants to scholarship in teaching and learning. For a new part-time lecturer, scholarship can be a hitherto unexplored area. However, Shulman (1986) argues that this type of engagement is necessary in the development of teaching expertise. Reflecting on the UKPSF under a mentor's guidance helps colleagues to engage with scholarship:

> I had not engaged to a great extent with scholarship in Teaching and Learning prior to my appointment ... scholarship provided additional techniques that I intend to use in my teaching in the future. The process has opened my eyes to the relevance and importance of continuing my professional development using scholarship.

We encourage associate fellows to work toward submitting a fellowship application in the next few years, where appropriate. This provides the opportunity to extend the mentoring relationship and promote increasing engagement with scholarship in teaching and learning, including as future authors. We also provide mentors to work with colleagues who are completing fellowship and senior fellowship applications. The mentoring process encourages dialogue about teaching, review of scholarship together and, in the case of senior fellowship, how the applicant is supporting others in their development as teaching experts.

Both the PSD scheme and mentoring toward an HEA fellowship are structured ways through which colleagues can develop expertise in teaching through peer support. However, the benefits are ongoing because, when the peer observations are complete or fellowship achieved, we have built new relationships with colleagues who can offer advice and support as we develop our teaching practice.

Two heads are better than one

Teaching is rarely a solitary activity, though it may look like that to our students. Many people need to work together to deliver coherent courses and to support the breadth of knowledge covered in most subjects. At an individual module level, there is division of labour, whether it be preparing material, marking or delivery of specific strands of content. It is common for two (or more) teachers to share a module, but this usually involves delivering topics individually or separating teaching from coursework. From the point of view of educator development, observation by, and feedback from, others is essential, underlining the importance of peer dialogue, but these observers are not teaching and only affect the student experience in the longer term.

It is much less common to find people practising pair teaching – that is, where two people work together in the same classroom *at the same time*, supporting each other's delivery of the module content. Andersson and Bendix (2006) relate their practice of it in computer science to the idea of pair programming popularised by exponents of XP (extreme programming), where two programmers work side by side to develop software. However, the general principle is much older than this, and some teachers have worked together in this way quite regularly. Essentially, the approach is mutualistic – both working together to the same end with both benefitting. It should not be competitive, nor should it be a commensalism where nobody suffers, but only one party really benefits. There are multiple stakeholders involved with pair teaching: the students who are taught, the staff taking part in the paired teaching and those who organise the teaching timetable and staff allocation.

Students

For students, the interplay between the two teachers can make a session livelier and more interesting, and, more importantly, their different strengths and backgrounds often lead to better, easier to understand explanations, fuller discussion of topics and a window to a wider range of experiences and opinions than is offered by a single lecturer. Students, particularly those who are a minority on a course owing to their background or demographics, need role models to develop a sense of belonging (Lockwood, 2006; Bryson & Hand, 2007). Being taught in a class by two different teachers gives more opportunity for a student to relate to and develop role models. Students also stand to learn better as they can respond to the varied teaching styles of the different teaching staff (Vaughn & Baker, 2008).

Staff

For staff, pairs make working with large classes easier: if one is talking, the other can be alert for questions or for signs of lack of understanding which are easy to miss when teaching solo. Anything where there needs to be supervision or organization, such as handing out notes or group work, is easier with two, and the flow of the class will not be disrupted as much. More important, however, is the benefit gained from working closely with another. With a pair, you always gain from watching and listening to the partner, whether they are just starting out or have years of experience to pass on, and, equally, if things go wrong, there is someone there to support and help you get back on track. Before and after a teaching session, there can be discussions and active reflection on the teaching and learning, helping with planning and motivation (some things are simply hard to teach) but also allowing for feedback and acting as critical friends (Raines & Shadiow, 1995). From the point of view of wellbeing, pair teaching can also allow for continuity if one of the staff members is ill, alleviating any concerns about cancelling classes that the sick teacher may have.

Administration matters

Having a module taught by two has useful organisational benefits: for example, as mentioned above, if a staff member is ill, there is no cost in terms of sick cover as the other member of the pair knows the class and the material and can teach solo for a while. If someone moves to another job and needs to be replaced, the new member has someone there who can fill them in and get them up to speed much more quickly. The principal disadvantage is that those in senior management roles tend to see pair teaching as "inefficient" and a poor use of "resources" and so simply do not allow it, although, of course, there is nothing to stop someone "sitting in" on a set of lectures. Simple lack of staff and punishing workloads may also make it impossible to provide pair teaching, even if staff would like to work together in this way.

Conclusion

Pairs can also help in different learning environments such as online, where, for example, effectively managing chat and questions while teaching is extremely demanding on a single person's attention. This could be an ideal way of introducing graduate teaching assistants to teaching in pairs and interacting with students more academically, rather than just handling practical work, as is more usual for them.

Pairs can be diverse in age, experience, culture, and background (but they do not have to be); this again supports the role models argument proposed earlier. Clearly, the participants need to be able to work together – enemies do not make a good pairing – but neither necessarily do close friends. They can often unintentionally fall into patterns of behaviour that exclude others, with in-jokes and references. Sometimes, seemingly unlikely pairings work especially well, even if there is no obvious rapport between the participants.

Anecdotal evidence from personal experience and gathered from talking to others across varying subject areas supports our contention that, overall, pair teaching is a benefit for all involved. It works well for the students to see different individuals discuss the subject and experience different teaching approaches and supports them in finding role models. It is especially good as a vehicle for sharing expertise. You will always learn from watching and listening to someone practising their craft, no matter who they are.

Program SAGES: promoting collaborative teaching development through graduate student/faculty partnerships

Each year in North America, graduate students shoulder many hours of instructional time with undergraduate students, and some have more contact hours with students than academic staff in large, introductory undergraduate courses (Sundberg et al., 2005). However, many graduate students are given minimal opportunities for teaching development, and there is a great need to help them develop a scholarly and reflective teaching practice (Kenny et al., 2014). As a result, formal teaching development programs in graduate education are becoming increasingly valued as institutions and academics face the challenge of meeting the changing and increasingly diverse expectations of new generations of students (Chick & Brame, 2015).

The positive effects of formal teaching development programs for graduate students in STEM have already been described by a number of different studies. Most importantly, it has been shown that exposure to formal training in education results in increases in self-efficacy and changes in pedagogical beliefs (DeChenne et al., 2012; Chapman & McConnell, 2018; Connolly et al., 2018). Instructors' changes in pedagogical beliefs have in turn been shown to make major impacts on how they design and teach courses, and whether they choose to adopt evidence-based, student-centered teaching strategies (Freeman et al., 2014; Woodbury & Gess-Newsome, 2002; Chapman & McConnell, 2018). Altogether, the literature on formal teaching development programs shows that enhancing the teaching skills of graduate students at a critical stage of their development leads to long-lasting effects on their beliefs and future teaching practices, without leading to increases in time to completion (Shortlidge & Eddy, 2018).

The SAGES program

To support STEM graduate students in the development of an evidence-based teaching practice, the SAGES (SoTL Advancing Graduate Education in STEM) program was designed and implemented at three different research-focused post-secondary institutions in Canada. The design of SAGES rests on providing graduate students with four critical and complementary components that align with previously reported best practices (Sublett et al., 2010; Kenny et al., 2014; Chick & Brame, 2015). First, students are provided with a formal single-semester course on the scholarship of teaching and learning (SoTL) within the context of STEM. This course is focused on collaborative learning and discussion among peers, and it is led by experts in a variety of key topics related to pedagogy. Second, each student works closely with an academic staff mentor to develop ideas for implementing principles from evidence-based teaching practices to redesign a unit in a course normally taught by the mentor. This mentorship component leads to the third critical component, which is a practicum teaching opportunity for the student to teach and assess the redesigned course module developed in collaboration with the faculty mentor. The final component of SAGES consists of the development of a peer network. The peer network is built around two basic principles: (1) completion of the program as a cohort and (2) introduction of peer observation and feedback opportunities throughout the program.

SAGES as a vehicle to promote collaborative teaching development

Three major outcomes from the first 3 years of the SAGES program are particularly encouraging. First, as reported previously by other educational development programs, students who completed the program made significant gains in teaching self-efficacy and in adopting student-centered teaching approaches. These changes were assessed using a mixed-methods approach that included pre-test and post-test surveys (DeChenne et al., 2012; Trigwell & Prosser, 2004), as well as semi-structured interviews administered to 57 graduate students across three cohorts in the SAGES program. Thematic analyses of the interviews revealed: (1) how graduate students perceived changes in their teaching practice because of their experiences in the program, (2) the forms of support they felt were most useful, and (3) their experience working with both faculty mentors and undergraduate students.

The other two major outcomes of SAGES were unexpected and have not previously been reported in the literature. Originally, we expected that the practicum component of SAGES would allow students to learn from the expertise of their faculty mentors as they put into practice what they had learned from the formal course on SoTL. While this was observed, however, we discovered that the students inspired most of the faculty mentors to also engage in growing their teaching practice by learning about the SoTL from their student mentees as they worked collaboratively to redesign a portion of their courses. Somewhat surprisingly, this collaborative framework fostered a "stealth" approach to teaching development in the faculty mentors, many of whom admitted to being poorly informed about the SoTL and approaches to scholarly teaching prior to their experience with SAGES. The effects of the collaborative teaching development on faculty were revealed through semi-structured interviews conducted with 23 of the faculty mentors across three cohorts of the program. Thematic analyses of these interviews revealed that: (1) mentees became mentors by creating safe environments for faculty development, (2) mentors learned and adopted new teaching strategies, (3) mentors became more reflective teachers, and (4) mentors began to shift their teaching identities. Many faculty mentors commented on how the students' enthusiasm and ideas helped to inspire transformative changes in courses that had stagnated owing to the lack of time and ideas for further development. Many also commented that changes in their attitudes and acceptance of educational development were just as important as the specific changes and improvements to their courses.

The second unexpected, and perhaps even more rewarding, outcome of the SAGES program was how the fully collaborative relationships fostered by the student–faculty partnerships created the space for new, significant conversations about educational development. These relationships have in turn created new, broad and dynamic networks of engagement between graduate students and faculty members, where both mentees and mentors can collaboratively enhance their teaching practice through significant conversations on teaching (Roxå & Mårtensson, 2009, 2015). Establishing these partnerships through the teaching practicum component of SAGES has provided the spark to initiate new networks of practice that can foster future innovation and teaching development.

In conclusion, the combination of a formal course on SoTL in the context of STEM and a collaborative student–faculty teaching development project provides a unique and impactful platform for educational development. Based on the encouraging initial results from the SAGES program, we expect that the networks of practice arising from the student–faculty partnerships will become a particularly powerful and transformative force for driving the further adoption of evidence-based teaching practices and student-centered learning.

References

Advance HE (2011) UK Professional Standards Framework for Teaching and Supporting Learning in Higher Education. www.advance-he.ac.uk/knowledge-hub/uk-professional-standards-framework-ukpsf [accessed 07/03/2021].

Andersson, R. & Bendix, L. (2006) *Pair Teaching – an eXtreme Teaching Practice*. Pedagogiska inspirationskonferensen-Genombrottet, Lunds University, Sweden. https://journals.lub.lu.se/pige/article/view/20911

Bell, A. & Mladenovic, R. (2013) How tutors understand and engage with reflective practices, *Reflective Practice*, 14 (1), 1–11. doi:10.1080/14623943.2012.732949

Bell, A. & Mladenovic, R. (2015) Situated learning, reflective practice and conceptual expansion: effective peer observation for tutor development, *Teaching in Higher Education*, 20 (1), 24–36. doi:10.1080/13562517.2014.945163

Bloom, B.S. (1985) *Developing Talent in Young People*. Ballantine Books, New York.

Brockbank, A. & McGill, I. (2007) *Facilitating Reflective Learning in HE* (2nd edn). SRHE/Open University Press, Maidenhead.

Brookfield, S. (1995) *Becoming a Critically Reflective Teacher*. Jossey-Bass, New York.

Bryson, C. & Hand, L. (2007) The role of engagement in inspiring teaching and learning. *Innovations in Education and Teaching International*, 44 (4), 349–362. doi:10.1080/14703290701602748

Carbone, A., Drew, S., Ross, B., Ye, J., Phelan, L., Lindsay, K. & Cottman, C. (2019) A collegial quality development process for identifying and addressing barriers to improving teaching. *Higher Education Research & Development*, 38 (7), 1356–1370. doi:10.1080/07294360.2019.1645644

Chapman, L.Y. & McConnell, D.A. (2018) Characterizing the pedagogical beliefs of future geoscience faculty members: a mixed methods study. *Innovations in Higher Education*, 43, 185–200. doi:10.1007/s10755-017-9416-9

Chasteen, S.V. & Code, W.J. (2018) *The Science Education Initiative Handbook*. BCCampus Pressbooks. https://pressbooks.bccampus.ca/seihandbook/

Chick, N.L. & Brame, C. (2015) An investigation of the products and impact of graduate student SoTL programs: observations and recommendations from a single institution. *International Journal for the Scholarship of Teaching and Learning*, 9 (1). Article 3. doi:10.20429/ijsotl.2015.090103

Connolly, M.R., Lee, Y.G. & Savoy, J.N. (2018) The effects of doctoral teaching development on early-career STEM scholars' college teaching self-efficacy. *CBE – Life Sciences Education*, 17 (1). doi:10.1187/cbe.17-02-0039

DeChenne, S.E., Enochs, L.G. & Needham, M. (2012) Science, technology, engineering, and mathematics graduate teaching assistants teaching self-efficacy. *Journal of the Scholarship of Teaching and Learning*, 12 (4), 102–123.

Eraut, M. (1994) *Developing Professional Knowledge and Competence*. RoutledgeFalmer, Abingdon. doi:10.4324/9780203486016

Ericsson, K.A., Krampe, R.T. & Tesch-Römer, C. (1993) The role of deliberate practice in the acquisition of expert performance. *Psychological Review*, 100 (3), 363–406. doi:10.1037/0033-295x.100.3.363

Freeman, S., Eddy, S., McDonough, M., Smith, M.K., Okoroafor, N., Jordt, H. & Wenderoth, M.P. (2014) Active Learning increases student performance in science, engineering, and mathematics. *Proceedings of the National Academy of Sciences*, 111 (23), 8410–8415. doi:10.1073/pnas.1319030111

Handelsman, J., Miller, S. & Pfund, C. (2007) *Scientific Teaching*. W.H. Freeman, New York.

Kenny, N., Berenson, C., Chick, N., Johnson, C., Keegan, D., Read, E. & Reid, L. (2017) *A Developmental Framework for Teaching Expertise in Postsecondary Education*. International Society for the Scholarship of Teaching and Learning Conference, Calgary, Canada.

Kenny, N., Wason, G.P.L. & Watton, C. (2014) Exploring the context of Canadian graduate student teaching certificates in university teaching. *Canadian Journal of Higher Education*, 44 (3), 1–19. doi:10.47678/cjhe.v44i3.186035

Leathwood, C. & Read, B. (2020), Short-term, short-changed? A temporal perspective on the implications of academic casualisation for teaching in higher education. *Teaching in Higher Education*, 1–16. doi:10.1080/13562517.2020.1742681

Lockwood, P. (2006) "Someone like me can be successful": do college students need same-gender role models?. *Psychology of Women Quarterly*, 30 (1), 36–46. doi:10.1111/j.1471-6402.2006.00260.x

Pilkington, R. (2011) What about dialogue? An alternative assessment mechanism for professional learning. *Educational Developments*, 12 (2), 13–16.

Raines, P. & Shadiow, L. (1995) Reflection and teaching: the challenge of thinking beyond the doing. *The Clearing House*, 68 (5), 271–274. doi:10.1080/00098655.1995.9957248

Roxå, T. & Mårtensson, K. (2009) Significant conversations and significant networks – exploring the backstage of the teaching arena. *Studies in Higher Education*, 34 (5), 547–559. doi:10.1080/03075070802597200

Roxå, T. & Mårtensson, K. (2015) Microcultures and informal learning: a heuristic guiding analysis of conditions for informal learning in local higher education workplaces. *International Journal for Academic Development*, 20 (2), 193–205. doi:10.1080/1360144x.2015.1029929

Shortlidge, E.E. & Eddy, S.L. (2018) The trade-off between graduate student research and teaching: a myth? *PLOS One*, 13 (6). doi:10.1371/journal.pone.0199576

Shulman, L. (1986) Those who understand: knowledge growth in teaching, *Educational Researcher*, 15 (2), 4–14. doi:10.3102/0013189x015002004

Strubbe, L.E., Stang, J., Holland, T., Sherman, S.B. & Code, W.J. (2019) Faculty adoption of active learning strategies via paired teaching: conclusions from two science departments. *Journal of College Science Teaching* 49 (1), 31–39. doi:10.2505/4/jcst19_049_01_31

Sublett, M.D., Walsh, J.A., McKinney, K. & Faigao, D. (2010) Student voices through researching and promoting learner autonomy. In Werder, C. & Otis, M.M. (Eds.), *Engaging Student Voices in the Study of Teaching and Learning*. Stylus, Sterling, VA, 146–161.

Sundberg, M.D., Armstrong, J.E. & Wischusen, E.W. (2005) A reappraisal of the status of introductory biology laboratory education in U.S. colleges and universities. *The American Biology Teacher*, 67 (9), 525–529. doi:10.2307/4451904

Trigwell, K. & Prosser, M. (2004) Development and use of the approaches to teaching inventory. *Educational Psychology Review*, 16 (4), 409–424. doi:10.1007/s10648-004-0007-9

Vaughn, L.M. & Baker, R.C. (2008) Do different pairings of teaching styles and learning styles make a difference? Preceptor and resident perceptions. *Teaching and Learning in Medicine*, 20 (3), 239–247. doi:10.1080/10401330802199559

Wenger, E. (1998) *Communities of Practice: Learning Meaning and Identity*. Cambridge University Press, Cambridge.

Wieman, C.E. (2017) *Improving How Universities Teach Science: Lessons from the Science Education Initiative*. Harvard University Press, Boston, MA.

Wieman, C., Perkins, K. & Gilbert, S. (2010) Transforming science education at large research institutions: a case study in progress. *Change*, 42 (2), 6–14. doi:10.1080/00091380903563035

Woodbury, S. & Gess-Newsome, J. (2002) Overcoming the paradox of change without difference: A model of change in the arena of fundamental school reform. *Educational Policy*, 16, 763–782. doi:10.1177/089590402237312

Part IV

The artistry of teaching

Chapter 14

Developing adaptive expertise
What can we learn from improvisation and the performing arts?

Richard Bale

Introduction

Teachers in higher education usually belong to a particular academic discipline, or they fulfil another important role in the institution's work, such as librarian, learning technologist or graduate teaching assistant (GTA), for example. This means we all have a range and different levels of expertise, some of which may relate to our primary role or discipline, and others to teaching and learning. Many universities now provide training, workshops and postgraduate qualifications covering a range of teaching, learning and assessment issues. Such training, along with teaching practice, may lead to the development of routine expertise (Bransford et al., 2000), where the teacher has the procedural and pedagogic knowledge, as well as a bank of previous experiences, to draw upon in order to plan for and react to predictable situations that arise in the classroom. However, not all situations can be predicted, and so it is perhaps more appropriate to consider expertise from an adaptive perspective (Hatano & Inagaki, 1986), in which the teacher is able to think intuitively and solve novel problems as they arise (Siklander & Impiö, 2019). This unpredictability requires dynamism and creativity in a process of artistic negotiation between all parties involved in the practice. This artistic dimension of practice, according to Schön (1991), is something that can be learned:

> If it is true that there is an irreducible element of art in professional practice, it is also true that gifted engineers, teachers, scientists, architects, and managers sometimes display artistry in their day-to-day practice. If the art is not invariant, known, and teachable, it appears nonetheless, at least for some individuals, to be learnable.
>
> (Schön, 1991, p. 18)

I start from this premise that the artistry of teaching, as one characteristic of expertise in higher education teaching (King, 2019), can be learned. A particularly interesting group of teachers in higher education are GTAs – doctoral researchers who teach and support learning. They are becoming experts in their field of research but are usually relatively new to teaching. Routine teaching expertise can

DOI: 10.4324/9781003198772-19

be developed by attending workshops, gaining teaching experience and observing others. However, GTAs often express concerns about their teaching which relate to non-routine aspects of their performance in the teacher role, such as their ability to communicate with and engage students, their levels of confidence and identities as teachers, and their (lack of) preparation and rehearsal time (Bale, 2020). Particularly common is the last aspect, preparation, where GTAs often report feeling anxious about dealing with unexpected situations and not knowing the answers to students' questions. This relates to improvisation as an adaptive activity, which emphasises the skill of acting in the moment and reacting to the unexpected.

In this chapter, I outline a workshop for GTAs focusing on performative aspects of teaching, exploring how skills and techniques used by actors, singers, dancers, stand-up comedians and other performing artists can be applied in the teaching context to help increase GTAs' confidence and performance in the teacher role. I begin by exploring the distinction between routine and adaptive expertise and discuss how these concepts relate to improvisation, a form of theatre in which the action on stage is unplanned, unscripted and created spontaneously by the performers in collaboration with the audience. I then briefly describe the workshop on performance, focusing in particular on examples of improvisation exercises used in the session to develop participants' skills of observation, collaboration and adaptation. The idea of teaching as a performance or entertainment might not sit well with all; in Box 14.1, Derounian sets out why it is indeed an important feature of education.

> **Box 14.1 Entertainment, jouissance and the artistry of teaching**
>
> Whether classes are synchronous, asynchronous, online or face-to-face, student absenteeism is a significant problem, regardless of location, discipline or study level. Sawon et al. (2012, p. 583) concluded
>
> > the low attender does not like attending lectures, finds them boring ... and explains any absence as due to a belief that it was not worth attending or they could not be bothered attending. The high attender, in comparison, likes attending lectures, finds them interesting but also easy to understand.
>
> Surely, even at a common-sense level, whether it's leisure or a student session, entertainment is a purposeful means by which to attract and engage an audience both during and even after a session. As Gibbs (2010) pointed out, the amount of contact matters less than the quality of learning generated. In 1964, US marketeer McLuhan coined the term the 'medium is the message'. That is, the way we do things, such as teach, is as important as content. Entertainment, including 'fun', is a key component of teaching and learning (Derounian, 2018).

> I argue for purposeful and constructive disruption as a pedagogic strategy. For example, Race and Pickford (2007) commend disruption of a student's equilibrium to trigger learning and movement towards new understandings. Phil Race commends 'unfinished business' as an enticement to learning: such a cliffhanger at a session's end can intrigue students to attend next time.
>
> Cohen and Jurkovic (1997) commended deployment of surprise packages, such as asking students from one discipline (arts) to look at issues such as 'staging plays' through an environmental lens to engender new insights. Or town planning undergraduates paired – one in a wheelchair, one pushing – as fieldwork to learn the realities of disability and dealing with potholes. Other means include shaking things up: just as Greek hero Theseus, after killing the monstrous Minotaur, followed a line of string back to the entrance, begin at the end of an idea and work back to the start, or provide answers that require students to determine the questions (that lead to them).
>
> Or why not break the rhythm in class by using an energiser or ice-breaker? An example would be discussing how to present a group assignment in public. For this, I role-played a 1-minute presentation of 'howlers': exiting the class or online space, then re-entering looking a shambles, dropping notes, crossing arms defensively, mumbling and facing away from the audience. Students, in pairs, then identified my mistakes. Such activities may foster *jouissance* – that is, pleasure from a 'light bulb moment' when a complex issue is solved or understood. This can trigger deep learning, which should surely be the aim of teaching practices. There is also the possibility of reflected pleasure as a lecturer sees students have understood.
>
> (James Derounian)

From routine to adaptive expertise

Viewing teaching as a creative, improvisatory activity has implications for how we define and develop teaching expertise. This brings us to the distinction between routine and adaptive expertise. Hatano and Inagaki (1986) used the term routine expertise to refer to a high degree of efficiency and competence in carrying out particular actions. For a routine expert, the level of efficiency will remain high as long as the demands of the task at hand are similar to what has been experienced previously. Perhaps more fundamentally, Bransford et al. (2000) note that there are differences between how experts and novices experience the same situation: "experts have acquired extensive knowledge that affects what they *notice* and how they organize, represent, and interpret information in their environment. This, in turn, affects their abilities to remember, reason, and solve problems" (Bransford et al., 2000, p. 31; emphasis added). As we will see later in this chapter, observing and *noticing* are key when developing skills of improvisation. This is also briefly discussed in Chapter 15 by Nick Sorensen (in this volume).

Where routine experts are adept at applying their knowledge and skills in predictable, largely expected situations, adaptive experts are able to respond in different ways to less predictable situations. In Japan, Hatano and Inagaki (1986) used the example of abacus masters to illustrate routine expertise as a starting point, where the user becomes highly efficient at carrying out a relatively narrow procedure (performing calculations) using a highly specific tool (an abacus). From this, Hatano and Inagaki were interested in how to move beyond the routine to the adaptive – "those who not only perform procedural skills efficiently but also understand the meaning of the skills and nature of their object" (Hatano & Inagaki, 1986, p. 262). This understanding of skills, and considering how, why and when to apply them, is the essence of adaptability in Hatano and Inagaki's concept. As Siklander and Impiö (2019) explain, adaptive expertise is not fixed, inherent or something that an expert possesses; instead, it is a set of strategies that can be called upon and brought to bear when confronted with new situations and problems.

At the heart of adaptability is variation, change and the opportunity to experience different situations and problems (Lin et al., 2007). Without such variation, the learner, or in our case the teacher or GTA, will be unable to apply their skills to novel situations (Siklander & Impiö, 2019). In their original work on adaptive expertise, Hatano and Inagaki (1986) considered three important issues surrounding variation: randomness in the situation, playfulness and risk taking, and promotion of understanding. If we apply these to the context of GTA training, the first of these concerns whether there are different paths that can be taken, or whether the whole learning encounter, from the planned activities to the examples used, is predetermined by the instructor. This is linked to the second issue of playfulness and risk taking: if teaching is seen solely as a serious, high-stakes activity, those engaged in pedagogic training are unlikely to feel empowered to take risks or to approach their training in a playful way. And this links to the third issue of developing understanding: if pedagogic training programmes are underpinned by a performative culture – that is, learn these skills sufficiently and then go and teach adequately – participants are likely to take a superficial, tick-box approach, rather than seeking to understand, pedagogically, how and why we teach in the ways that we do. This focus on how and why encourages reflection-in-action (Schön, 1991) and an ability to respond intuitively to what is happening in the room – what we might call improvisation. Focusing on the how and the why of our practice also has the potential to encourage experimentation and a deeper understanding of the teacher's role in facilitating learning. We might link this to how our students learn, borrowing the terms surface and deep learning from Marton and Säljö (1976).

So, as teachers, we want to be competent at helping our students to learn; we want to develop our expertise in this domain. However, if we return to the beginning of this brief discussion of routine and adaptive expertise, we are reminded that teaching – and learning – is far from a routine experience. Teaching and learning first and foremost involve complex interactions between people –

people engaged in the messy and perhaps frustrating and challenging business of learning something new. This complexity and this focus on human interaction mean that there is inherent unpredictability, which is likely to require a more adaptive rather than a more routine mindset. This is where the concept of improvisation meets adaptive expertise.

Improvisation and teacher expertise

Improvisation generally refers to actions which are unplanned and unforeseen. In the performing arts context, improvisation is a type of live theatrical performance which is curated on the spot by the performers, often involving collaboration with and input from the audience. The term is often shortened to impro or improv, with the former more prevalent in the British context and the latter used more in North America. Over time, however, the North American abbreviation has come to be used more and more, regardless of location.

The notion of making something up on the spot might seem unprofessional, unthoughtful or ill-considered in other professional contexts. This is understandable if we focus on the improviser and what they are doing at the moment in question. However, if we shift our perspective and focus instead on the skills which enable the improviser to (re)act spontaneously, it becomes clear that improvisation is not merely about making something up at a given moment; instead, it is about drawing on years of experience and expertise in order to notice what is happening and then to respond and adapt to an unfolding situation. As Kneebone (2020, p. 221) puts it: "In addition to practising, learning to listen, getting things wrong and putting them right, improvisers have to have made the transition 'from you to them'". The ability to improvise is underpinned by a depth of expertise which enables the improviser to shift their attention from themselves to the other 'actors'. This, I would argue, is the essence of what makes improvisation so attractive in the context of teaching and learning: a teacher who is an adept improviser focuses on 'them', in Kneebone's terms, and is inherently student-centred in their teaching practice.

The idea that improvisation is about more than thinking and reacting in the moment is echoed in the context of teaching by Sawyer (2011), who uses the term *disciplined improvisation*, explaining that "[g]reat teaching involves many structuring elements, and at the same time requires improvisational brilliance. Balancing structure and improvisation is the essence of the art of teaching" (Sawyer, 2011, p. 2). This conception of improvisation means that teachers use their extensive skills and knowledge – of content, but more importantly of pedagogy – to provide structure, but to view this structure as a guide rather than a rigid, restrictive plan of action (Sorensen & Coombs, 2009). The improvisational brilliance referred to by Sawyer (2011) lies in the teacher's ability to notice what is happening in the complex learning and teaching space and then to adapt their plan and to respond accordingly.

For teachers, then, improvisation can have a liberating effect, giving us permission to adapt our plans, to take risks, to be creative, to be more dynamic and to be more collaborative. In the context of teacher education, Toivanen et al. (2011) highlight the usefulness of drama and performance, including improvisation, in helping teachers to be more creative practitioners. In a previous publication (Bale, 2020), I drew on the work of Toivanen et al. (2011) to summarise the potential benefits of developing improvisation skills for teachers. These include:

- To increase self-awareness;
- To increase awareness of others;
- To increase empathy, ability to *notice*;
- To increase skills of interaction, ability to engage others in *dialogue* (see Sorensen, Chapter 15, in this volume);
- To improve clarity of verbal and nonverbal communication;
- To encourage creativity in methods of teaching.

A teacher who possesses some or all of these attributes is also likely to be more confident, present and able to adapt to situations and scenarios as they unfold. It seems difficult to argue that any expert teacher, or any aspiring expert teacher, should not display these improvisatory qualities. Here, I return to Roger Kneebone, who summarises succinctly why it is not only beneficial, but necessary, for experts in any field to develop adaptive expertise and to be able to improvise: "Improvising is what experts do – it's what makes experts expert. And that's across the board: in every field of activity, experts have to improvise" (Kneebone, 2020, pp. 219–220).

Case study: workshop on performative aspects of teaching

With this perspective that improvisation, as well as wider performing arts skills, can help in the development of teacher expertise, I designed a workshop called Performative Aspects of Teaching. The workshop was planned as part of a programme for GTAs who, in our institutional context, are doctoral researchers who are paid to teach undergraduates. The programme includes core sessions on aspects of teaching which aim to develop participants' routine expertise around topics such as session planning, assessment and feedback, and departmental policies and procedures. What was missing, however, was the more creative, artistic dimension of teaching and discussions about how GTAs might experiment with their practice and learn from each other across different disciplines. In workshops and in conversations with GTAs, it became apparent that there were recurring anxieties about teaching, many of which related to aspects of performance and a perceived lack of ability to adapt, in the moment, to developing situations, as shown in Table 14.1.

The issues around identity and confidence seem fundamental, as there is a lack of awareness of self or of what it means for a GTA to perform the role of a teacher. We all have different facets of our identities, but, depending on our role in the university, we may be less secure in particular aspects of ourselves. For the

Table 14.1 Common teaching anxieties of GTAs (adapted from Bale, 2020, p. 23)

Preparation & rehearsal	*Communication*	*Confidence & identity*
Extensive time required to prepare teaching sessions	Competence in English expression	Fear of public speaking
Not knowing answers to students' questions	Accent in English	Lack of teacher identity; more pronounced researcher/discipline identity
Balancing time spent on teaching and research	Ability to communicate clearly; dealing with disruptive behaviour	Assertiveness and ability to hold students' attention

GTAs I have worked with, the discipline or researcher identity tended to be more pronounced, and the teacher identity less so. This was perhaps unsurprising, as GTAs are first and foremost enrolled as doctoral researchers, most of whom have little or no teaching experience. Furthermore, there is evidence that research tends to enjoy a higher status than teaching in higher education institutions (cf. Dugas et al., 2020; Bolander Laksov et al., 2008). It therefore seemed important, linking back to the benefits of improvisation for teachers (Toivanen et al., 2011), to provide opportunities for GTAs to develop their sense of self as teachers, and I considered that improvisation offered one way of doing this. Similarly, the other categories in Table 14.1 might be addressed by looking at aspects of performance. From what we have discussed so far, skilled improvisers are likely to be able to find ways to express themselves clearly, regardless of regional or national accent, and be able to use skills of observation to notice what is happening in the classroom. Finally, I considered that improvisation would liberate GTAs from the largely self-imposed stress of over-preparation and the erroneous belief that they, as teachers, must always have all the answers to students' questions.

This was the rationale for designing the workshop on performative aspects of teaching; it was a 3-hour session exploring: the idea of teaching as performance, discussions about participants' anxieties about teaching, experiences of 'stage fright' and public speaking, effective and safe use of the voice, use of the body and improvisation. In the next section, I present some of the improvisation exercises used in the workshop.

Examples of improvisation exercises

The improvisation section of the workshop was designed to introduce participants to the idea of spontaneity in their teaching practice. In other courses and discussions during the programme, teaching is presented as a planned, structured activity, so this was potentially a point of conflict in our messaging. However, as explained above, learning to improvise is not about discarding plans and structure. Instead, it is about being in the present and recognising that mistakes – such as things going off script or not going according to plan – are not to be feared (Grayson & Napthine-Hodgkinson, 2020), but rather embraced as learning opportunities, both for the teacher and their students. There are many improvisation exercises, or games, which can be used in various contexts. The American actress and educator Viola Spolin devised over 200 improv games (Spolin, 1986, 1999), many of which can be adapted to help teachers develop their practice, but also to help students learn. In this section, I outline three examples of the exercises used in the workshop.

Yes, and ...

One of the key principles of improvisation is 'yes, and...'. This is a way of creating a positive, open and collaborative environment in which ideas and discussions can flow. It is about accepting, without judgement, the ideas of others and then building on these ideas. In previous work (Bale, 2020), I gave an example of grammar revision in a German class, combining a game of speech tag (Spolin, 1999) with the 'yes, and ...' principle.

TEACHER: So what can you say about the German case system? Let's generate some ideas and revise what we have already learned. Build on each other's ideas starting with 'yes, and'. I'll start. Someone tag me when you want to add something. So, there are four cases in German ...

(Student A tags the teacher.)

STUDENT A: Yes, and these four cases are called the nominative, the accusative, the dative and the genitive. These can be difficult for English speakers to learn because there's no case system in English ...(Student B tags Student A.)
STUDENT B: Yes, and the cases mean that word order in German can be more flexible than in English because you can easily identify the subject, the direct and the indirect object of a sentence because of the case endings ...(Student C tags Student B.)
STUDENT C: Yes, and the endings are also determined by the gender of nouns. There are three genders in German: masculine, feminine and neuter, and these genders have specific endings in different cases ...

(Student D tags Student C.)

STUDENT D: Yes, and an example of this is ...(Adapted from Bale, 2020, p. 116)

In this exercise, the teacher and students collaborate to draw together their knowledge of the subject at hand. If anyone makes a mistake, or gives incorrect information, this is not emphasised at this point, as to do so would interrupt the flow of ideas and interrupt the spontaneous energy of the group. After the exercise, any incorrect information can be identified and corrected in a debrief discussion. In the GTA workshop, a similar exercise is used early on to create this open and energetic environment, where participants are asked to share one thing that they like about teaching. For example:

PARTICIPANT A: I see teaching as a way of giving something back after my own education.
PARTICIPANT B: Yes, and I feel a real sense of achievement when I'm able to help a student to understand something.
PARTICIPANT C: Yes, and, for me, teaching makes my day more varied and gives me a break from my research.
PARTICIPANT D: Yes, and …

This exercise demonstrates to participants how it feels to adopt an open, collaborative and spontaneous mindset. The exercise is presented both as a way for GTAs to develop this more spontaneous, present mindset and as a learning and teaching activity that can be used to foster an open and collaborative environment with their students, much like the first example above about revising German grammar. We then build on this idea of presence and spontaneity by emphasising the skill of observation and noticing, drawing on an exercise from the world of acting, the Meisner technique.

The Meisner technique

Once participants have become used to building on others' ideas in an improvised, non-judgemental and collaborative way, the next exercise highlights the importance of observing and then responding to these observations. The actor and teacher Sanford Meisner devised a repetition exercise to help actors to develop their listening and observation skills. He wanted his acting students to react instinctively to what they had seen or heard, rather than working with a script (Meisner & Longwell, 1987). In the workshop, participants are asked to work in pairs. They face each other and focus only on each other, observing and noticing everything about that person. Then, one person in the pair begins to verbalise what they notice, and the other person repeats this observation in the first person, as follows:

PARTICIPANT A: You're wearing a blue shirt.
PARTICIPANT B: I'm wearing a blue shirt.
PARTICIPANT A: You're wearing a blue shirt.
PARTICIPANT B: I'm wearing a blue shirt.
PARTICIPANT A: You're starting to laugh.
PARTICIPANT B: I'm starting to laugh.
PARTICIPANT A: You touched your left ear.
PARTICIPANT B: I touched my left ear

In this example, Participant A starts by noticing the colour of Participant B's shirt. When there is a noticeable change in Participant B's behaviour, Participant A reacts to this by verbalising: "You're starting to laugh". Perhaps Participant B starts to feel awkward or simply has an itch, and they raise a hand to touch their left ear. Participant A notices this and comments accordingly. This exercise builds on the spontaneity introduced in the 'yes, and …' exercise by adding an observational element. Participants learn to trust their instincts and to respond to the behaviours and actions of others as they happen. Transferring this to the teaching context, the aim is to heighten participants' awareness of their students' behaviours, body language and so on. If we return to our discussion of routine and adaptive expertise, this means the teacher is better equipped to notice what is happening at that moment and to respond accordingly (Bransford et al., 2000). This exercise also focuses on active listening skills, as the person in the role of Participant B has to listen carefully and repeat Participant A's observations. Enhanced listening skills are essential for the improvising teacher, as they need to make use of all possible senses to notice, and then respond to, action as it unfolds in the classroom.

Playing with status

After developing a sense of spontaneity and heightening skills of observation, we combine the essence of the previous exercises by introducing the concept of status. The renowned pioneer of improvisational theatre Keith Johnstone used status to help actors to focus on characters' actions and behaviours rather than the inherent social status attached to a particular character. Johnstone illustrates this with an example of characters playing their status higher or lower than might be expected (Johnstone, 2019, p. 29):

TRAMP: 'Ere! Where are you going?
DUCHESS: I'm sorry, I didn't quite catch …
TRAMP: Are you deaf as well as blind?

For Johnstone, awareness of status is important in the development of observation and improvisation skills. In the workshop, we explore this concept, and then participants reflect on the status they tend to exhibit when they are teaching. The discussions tend to result in some participants identifying themselves as generally high status, exhibiting rather strict, authoritarian behaviours, while others play with lower status, perhaps being quite friendly and informal with students. We then play a game called 'guess the status', which once again focuses on the participants' skills of observation. Using a scale from 1 to 10, we agree as a group what kind of status we would expect at each level on the scale, with 1 representing the lowest status and 10 the highest. Then, one at a time, each participant decides on a status level that they wish to exhibit and they walk in front of the group displaying this status using their movement, body language and, if they wish, some improvised spoken language. The rest of the group tries to guess the status on the agreed scale from 1 to 10. After each participant has revealed which level of status they were playing, the rest of the group provide their observations and share where they had placed each person on the scale. Importantly, each person is asked to explain their reasoning. For example, if a participant guessed that another participant was displaying a status level of 8, they would then be asked to explain what they had observed that brought them to this conclusion. They might say that the participant walked slowly and smoothly, with upright posture, making eye contact with the others and projecting an air of confidence, which gave the impression of high status, for example.

For teachers, the discussion about status is useful for two reasons: first, it raises our awareness of how we tend to portray ourselves when we are teaching, and how our students perceive us; second, it enables us to react to our observations of others' status by 'mirroring' what we see. We can raise or lower our status spontaneously in response to what is happening in the room. If we want to get our students' attention and emphasise an important point, we might play with high status, speaking slowly and calmly and with a still body. If we want to build a rapport with a student who is perhaps disengaged or looking bored, we might mirror this by lowering our status as a sign of empathy and a means to entering into a conversation. As with the previous exercises, the key skills are observation and then intuitive, spontaneous reactions based on those observations.

Participant feedback and reflections

When I was designing this workshop, it was not clear whether participants would opt to attend. I knew that there were common anxieties among GTAs about their teaching roles (see Table 14.1 above), but I was unsure whether there would be an appetite to view teaching through a performance lens, especially as I was working in an institution focused mainly on STEMM subjects (science, technology, engineering, mathematics and medicine) where, I was concerned, an artistic and performative view of teaching might be unpopular. However, this concern proved unfounded. The workshop participants were very open-minded and willing to explore their teaching roles from a performance perspective. They were also keen to engage in a variety of activities which were unfamiliar and, to some, perhaps even uncomfortable. One participant commented that it was "quite a refreshing and unique experience".

Participants also commented that the workshop helped them to identify links between teaching and performance, foregrounding student-centred learning while also recognising that they, as teachers, can feel more confident and facilitate learning more effectively by increasing their awareness of performance aspects of their practice. An important part of this was having the time and space to get to know themselves as teachers, to find their own teacher persona. Returning to the concept of adaptive expertise, I would argue that this process of self-discovery is fundamental if a teacher is to learn, as we discussed earlier, how, why and when to apply particular strategies in their teaching practice, and to learn how to adapt their responses and (re)actions in different situations. In short, we need to focus on ourselves before we can focus on others. The improvisation exercises in the workshop, as well as the wider discussion about teaching as a performance activity, enabled participants to focus on themselves, as teachers, and to review their 'performance', before looking outwards and learning to observe, notice and respond to others.

Improvisation, as shown through just the small number of examples and exercises above, is also inherently playful, where participants are invited and encouraged to take risks, to make mistakes and to play. The opportunity to take risks and to play is one of the key factors in Hatano and Inagaki's (1986) concept of adaptive expertise. Improvisation is also inherently reflective, as an adept improviser is constantly reflecting on, and reacting to, situations as they unfold which, as mentioned earlier, aligns with Schön's (1991) notion of reflection-in-action. In this way, I would argue that ongoing, comprehensive training in improvisation can help to create more reflective, more present, more student-centred and more responsive teachers.

Next steps

In the workshop and in the discussion in this chapter, I have presented teaching as a creative endeavour and drawn on the skills and mindset demonstrated in the theatrical context of improvisation. Although teaching involves planning and structure, it is clear that plans and structures can, do and should change as complex learning and teaching encounters unfold. We therefore explored how improvisation can help teachers – in our case graduate teaching assistants – to become more confident in responding to unpredictable situations in their teaching practice: that is to say, how they can develop adaptive expertise.

The context of the workshop so far was that participants attended a standalone session on one occasion. From the participant feedback, and from my own observations, it seems there were benefits to participants in viewing teaching through a creative, performance lens and in using improvisation exercises to raise participants' self-awareness and observation and noticing skills. However, I view this session as a starting point, but also as a part of the provision that needs to be expanded further. Workshop participants commented that they would like more, and longer, workshops on specific aspects of performance, such as longer sessions focusing solely on improvisation or the voice, for example. Some participants also commented that they would like to explore performance aspects when teaching online, such as questions around being on camera and 'teaching to a screen', and how to engage and 'read' students when access to visual cues and body language might be impaired (see Jeddere-Fisher's advice regarding voice and online teaching in Box 14.2).

It seems, then, that there is an appetite for further research on the artistic, performance and creative aspects of teaching, and specifically on how viewing teaching through this lens can aid in the development of teacher expertise. I have started here by designing a one-off session, but the techniques and the overall mindset displayed by adept improvisers are not one-off or discrete: this mindset and these skills become integral to how the person behaves, observes, responds and reacts. As such, I would argue that such a mindset ought to be nurtured in educators by taking inspiration from improvisation and embedding the key principles of observation, collaboration and adaptation throughout the educational development provision offered to teachers.

> ### Box 14.2 Developing your online voice for teaching
>
> The voice can be an important tool for building positive lecturer–student relationships, particularly in online teaching.
>
> *The pre-recorded, edited voice*
>
> This voice is for short recordings, ensuring clarity and accuracy in communicating a learning objective. It is also the voice less heard by ourselves, as we are not naturally accustomed to hearing our own recorded voice.
>
> *Tackling voice confrontation*: This is physiological, but then, in turn, psychological, as we hear our primary emotions exposed by our voices (Rousey & Holzman, 1967). The lecturer can address this by listening back to recordings regularly, aiding neural reassignment, and then develop this by using the emotional engagement to foster positive lecturer–student relationships (Sagayadevan & Senthu, 2012).
>
> *The live voice*
>
> This voice is exciting and gripping for the listener as it is raw and can be unpredictable, even when listened to asynchronously.
>
> *The radio voice*: A radio host curates the live airways second by second while making you feel part of a spontaneous conversation. This appears one-way, but has the essence of a dialogue that brings the listener closer to the speaker's personality, identity and self. Provided that the lecturer voice does not dominate the session or isolate particular groups of students, then, applied to a virtual classroom environment, this voice can help build a classroom cohort identity.
>
> *The aural breath*: There is a critical difference between a radio show and an online lecture. Instead of music to break up the host's dialogue, the lecturer needs to curate additional time for the students to process the learning content. I call this the 'aural breath', as it is a break from the aural sensory input – for example, stating "That was a lot of information in the last few slides. I'm going stay silent for the next two minutes, and allow you time to consider any questions". This gives a clear boundary for the silence, while allowing time for students to think. A lecturer, in effect, hosts a virtual space, welcoming students to listen to their curated piece and setting clear boundaries for interaction.

> **Ongoing voice development**
>
> *Vocal resilience*: Use short, regular exercises to keep the vocal muscles supple, from breathing exercises to tongue twisters.
>
> *Peer-support groups*: Set up a small peer group to explore these concepts and share experiences, supporting each other with vocal development. The group should be small enough for the members to feel comfortable to expose their vulnerabilities and include an element of shadowing or one-to-one feedback.
>
> (Fabia Jeddere-Fisher)

References

Bale, R. (2020) *Teaching with confidence in higher education: Applying strategies from the performing arts*. Routledge, London. doi:10.4324/9780429201929

Bolander Laksov, K., Mann, S. & Owe Dahlgren, L. (2008) Developing a community of practice around teaching: a case study. *Higher Education Research and Development*, 27 (2), 121–132. doi:10.1080/07294360701805259

Bransford, J.D., Brown, A.L. & Cocking, R.R. (2000) *How people learn: brain, mind, experience, and school* (expanded edn). National Academy Press, Washington, DC. doi:10.17226/9853

Cohen, S. & Jurkovic, J. (1997) Learning from a masterpiece. *Training & Development*, 51 (11), 66–70.

Derounian, J.G. (2018) The thrill of the unexpected in HE teaching and learning. In: Broughan, C., Steventon, G. & Clouder, L. (Eds.), *Global perspectives on teaching excellence: A new era for higher education*. Routledge, London, 168–179. doi:10.4324/9781315211251-13

Dugas, D., Stich, A.E., Harris, L.N. & Summers, K.H. (2020) "I'm being pulled in too many different directions": academic identity tensions at regional public universities in challenging economic times. *Studies in Higher Education*, 45 (2), 312–326. doi:10.1080/03075079.2018.1522625

Gibbs, G. (2010) *Dimensions of quality*. Higher Education Academy, York.

Grayson, N. & Napthine-Hodgkinson, J. (2020) How improvisation techniques can support researchers with the development of public speaking skills. *Journal of Learning Development in Higher Education*. doi:10.47408/jldhe.vi19.611

Hatano, G. & Inagaki, K. (1986) Two courses of expertise. In Stevenson, H., Azuma, H. & Hakuta, K. (Eds.), *Child development and education in Japan*. Freeman, New York, 262–272.

Johnstone, K. (2019) *Impro: Improvisation and the theatre* (revelations edn). Bloomsbury, London.

King, H. (2019) Continuing professional development: what do award-winning lecturers do? *Educational Developments*, 20 (2), 1–4.

Kneebone, R. (2020) *Expert: Understanding the path to mastery*. Viking Penguin, London.

Lin, X., Schwartz, D.L. & Bransford, J.D. (2007) Intercultural adaptive expertise: explicit and implicit lessons from Dr Hatano. *Human Development*, 50, 65–72. doi:10.1159/000097686

Marton, F. & Säljö, R. (1976) On qualitative differences on learning: I – outcome and process. *British Journal of Educational Psychology*, 46, 4–11. doi:10.1111/j.2044-8279.1976.tb02980.x

Meisner, S. & Longwell, D. (1987) *Sanford Meisner on acting*. Vintage, New York.

Race, P. & Pickford, R. (2007) *Making teaching work: Teaching smarter in post-compulsory education*. Sage, London. doi:10.4135/9781446214886

Rousey, C. & Holzman, P. S. (1967) Recognition of one's own voice. *Journal of Personality and Social Psychology*, 6 (4, Pt. 1), 464–466. doi:10.1037/h0024837

Sagayadevan, V. & Senthu, J. (2012) The role of emotional engagement in lecturer–student interaction and the impact on academic outcomes of student achievement and learning. *Journal of the Scholarship of Teaching and Learning*, 12 (3), 1–30.

Sawon, K., Pembroke, M. & Wille, P. (2012) An analysis of student characteristics and behaviour in relation to absence from lectures. *Journal of Higher Education Policy and Management*, 34 (6), 575–586. doi:10.1080/1360080x.2012.716004

Sawyer, R.K. (2011) What makes good teachers great? The artful balance of structure and improvisation. In Sawyer, R.K. (Ed.), *Structure and improvisation in creative teaching*. CUP, Cambridge, 1–24. doi:10.1017/cbo9780511997105.002

Schön, D. (1991) *The reflective practitioner: How professionals think in action*. Routledge, London.

Siklander, P. & Impiö, N. (2019) Common features of expertise in working life: implications for higher education. *Journal of Further and Higher Education*, 43 (9), 1239–1254. doi:10.1080/0309877x.2018.1471126

Sorensen, N. & Coombs, S. (2009) *Creating a culture of professional learning: the role of metaphor, teacher narrative and improvisation in school-based CPD*. British Educational Research Association International Conference, University of Manchester, Manchester.

Spolin, V. (1986) *Theatre games for the classroom: A teacher's handbook*. Northwestern University Press, Evanston.

Spolin, V. (1999) *Improvisation for the theatre: A handbook of teaching and directing techniques* (3rd edn). Northwestern University Press, Evanston.

Toivanen, T., Komulainen, K. & Ruismäki, H. (2011) Drama education and improvisation as a source of teacher student's creativity. *Procedia Social and Behavioral Sciences*, 12, 60–69. doi:10.1016/j.sbspro.2011.02.010

Chapter 15

Developing the improvising teacher

Implications for professionalism and the development of expertise

Nick Sorensen

Introduction

As a teacher, academic and musician, I have developed a particular interest in pedagogy, specifically the process by which good teachers become great. The insights I have gained on advanced professional practice have been derived from my work in schools and universities combined with my practice and experience as a jazz musician. I see teaching as a fundamentally improvisatory practice that is relational and dialogic in nature, and that an important and desirable aim for the professional development of teachers should be to encourage the ability to improvise, a vital aspect of advanced professional practice and a mode of expertise. This chapter outlines how a professional development programme designed to encourage teacher improvisation in higher education could be structured and offers a theoretical framework to promote expertise in teacher improvisation. The theory underpinning this framework is derived from the findings of an empirical research project, a comparative study of seven outstanding secondary school teachers (Sorensen, 2014).

A framework for the professional development of the 'improvising teacher' cannot be looked at in isolation, and there are two particular issues that require consideration. First, there is the need to establish that professional development in improvisation is a viable and desirable professional goal. Second, there needs to be an acknowledgement that our understanding of professional development is necessarily dependent on our understanding of professionalism and what it means to be a professional. The concept of 'the improvising teacher' requires a reconceptualisation of teacher professionalism. These two factors provide the foundations for establishing a theoretical framework for developing improvising teachers.

This chapter addresses each of these issues in turn by asking three questions:

- Is 'the improvising teacher' a viable and desirable professional goal?
- How does improvisation inform the way we understand professionalism?
- How do we go about the professional development of 'the improvising teacher'?

DOI: 10.4324/9781003198772-20

The improvising teacher: a viable and desirable professional goal?

Improvisation is a contested term owing to its carrying a number of different, and often conflicting, meanings. Improvisation has been defined within artistic contexts, yet it is also a feature of everyday life. For some people, it is an important and significant mode of expression; for others, it is just about 'making do', an inferior response due to the fact that it appears to have no forethought or consideration. These contradictory meanings contribute to the confusions that arise concerning the importance of improvisation.

Definitions and understandings of improvisation range from Aristotle's *Poetics* (Dorsch, 1965) and Kandinsky's *Concerning the Spiritual in Art* (1977) to poststructuralist perspectives and systems theorists (Stacey et al., 2000). Analysing and coding a range of definitions and meanings allow the identification of the characteristics of improvisational activity. This analysis is given below, with the defining characteristics shown in bold text.

Improvisation is an **intentional** activity that occurs in a **context** – there is a need to have something to improvise on or with. As such, it is a **creative** activity that occurs in **'real time'**. The final outcome of an improvisation will be **unpredictable**, and consequently every improvisation will be **unique**. What happens in an improvisation is determined by **intuition** and **interaction**. Interaction might occur with other improvisers, with the material environment or with an audience (if there is one). The context of an improvisation will define the boundaries within which improvisation occurs. There are two kinds of structure: those that are fixed and non-negotiable (these are called design structures) and those that permit adaptability and generative action (these are called emergent structures). Improvisation emerges from the dynamic interplay between the fixed and non-negotiable (design structures) and the adaptable (emergent structures) in real time. Given the pervasive nature of improvisation, present in all aspects of life, the conditions of improvisation are dependent on the **permission** that the improviser gives themselves and/or is given by others to act in this way.

This synthesis of the key concepts and practices associated with improvisation provides a working definition that informs my research and subsequent work with improvisation (Sorensen, 2016).

About the research: methodology and data sources

The research I initiated was a small-scale empirical study that took place between November 2011 and January 2014. I used a case study approach to compare findings from seven experienced teachers working in secondary schools in South West England. As improvisation is an 'enacted' experience that comes into being through doing and where knowledge in improvisation is expressed through action, I chose a qualitative methodology in order to explore the participants' understanding and practice of improvisation.

The seven teachers that formed the case studies were acknowledged to be expert within their school setting and were identified during an interview with the headteacher (the principal) of each school. Having obtained their consent to participate in the research, each teacher was interviewed at the outset of the research and then observed teaching, with each lesson followed by a post-observation interview to elicit their understanding of what had been observed. Constant comparative methods of analysis were used to draw out themes from the data, and these contributed to the grounded theory model below. This model is relevant and applicable to all phases of education, including higher education, given its concerns with the fundamental interactions between teacher and learner. The age of the learner, the professional identity of the teacher and the nature of the curriculum have no relevance with regard to the issues and concepts that it outlines.

The research findings: a grounded theory model of teacher expertise

The research was driven by two main research questions. The first was "in what ways is the expert practice of secondary school teachers improvisatory?", and the second was "what does the improvisatory practice of teachers look like in the classroom?" Data from the interviews and lesson observations were analysed using a constant comparative methodology in order to draw out significant themes that were used to construct a theoretical framework of teacher expertise (see Figure 15.1).

This theoretical model acknowledges that teacher expertise is culturally situated. Given that all cultures are concerned with, and defined by, the relationship

Figure 15.1 Theoretical framework showing the dimensions of teacher expertise
Source: Sorensen, 2014.

between fixed and emergent structures, they are therefore improvisatory in their social nature and their constructed being. The relationship between improvisation and expertise is seen in Dreyfus and Dreyfus's (1986) model of skills acquisition, a fluency model that outlines five stages of development, from novice to expert. Level 5 (expert) sees that practitioners no longer rely on rules, guidelines or maxims. They have an intuitive grasp of situations based on deep tacit understanding, and analytic approaches are used only in novel situations or when problems occur. This suggests a strong relationship between expertise and improvisation, where intuition and tacit knowledge inform spontaneous decision-making. In other words, expert practice is improvisatory in nature, and we can see improvisation as a mode or facet of expertise.

Figure 15.1 reflects a prototype model of expertise described by Sternberg and Horvath (1995) who consider that, although there are no well-defined standards that all experts meet, they recognise that experts have family resemblances. Although my model identifies the different aspects of teacher expertise, the teachers I observed did not demonstrate all of the characteristics to the same extent. There were variations in the way each teacher displayed these "dimensions of teacher expertise" (shown in Figure 15.1).

Teacher expertise and improvisation

The theoretical framework (Figure 15.1) shows us that teacher expertise is fundamentally improvisatory and socially constructed (Burr, 2003) and is grounded in dialogic teaching (Alexander, 2008); it identifies the key dimensions of teacher expertise and shows how they are interrelated to each other. Most importantly, it outlines the fundamental way in which expert practice is improvisational. We can see this by relating these dimensions to the defining characteristics of my working definition of improvisation.

When we consider expertise as a journey, we recognise it as an emergent process, one in which the outcome will be **unpredictable** and **unique** for every individual. Expertise is formed through **interaction** and dialogue and corresponds to what has been described as a transformative teleology (Stacey et al., 2000). Teleology is the word we give to an end state or goal, and a transformative teleology is a movement towards a future that is under perpetual construction. There is no mature or final state, but just the perpetual engagement with identity and difference, continuity and transformation that happens in **real time**. This is at the heart of improvisational activity.

Dialogic teaching is an **intentional** activity that is by definition improvisatory, requiring decisions to be made in **real time** in response to the **interactions** with pupils and the environment. This is dependent on building relationships and the process of personalisation, which contributes to the unique nature of improvisational activity. The commitment to the 'nuts and bolts' of teaching provides the resources with which teachers are able to improvise, the **context** within which they can creatively adapt their approaches.

These teachers give themselves permission to improvise because they know that this is the way in which learning becomes a dynamic activity that engages the pupils. Furthermore, within the culture of the school, they are given permission to 'be themselves', and this is seen to be an important expression of the aims and values of the school.

These approaches and characteristics inform what I am calling 'the improvising teacher', a concept that significantly challenges our understanding of advanced professional practice. This view of teaching recognises that learning to improvise is not an 'add-on', an additional skill to be learned. Instead, teaching is viewed as being fundamentally improvisational, and we therefore need to reflect on and explicitly develop existing practices. The study of expertise is now being recognised as being able to offer important insights into advanced professional practice and marks a shift away from attending to concepts such as 'excellence', 'effectiveness' or 'good practice'. This shift admits the importance of agency in teaching and recognises that the development of expertise is not 'one thing' – expertise takes on different forms, and experts have family resemblances.

My argument is that 'the improvising teacher' is not only viable (being an extension of the fundamental reality of teaching) but also desirable (given that improvisation is a characteristic of expert performance). In the next section of this chapter, I shall explore how the concept of 'the improvising teacher' informs the way we understand professionalism.

How does improvisation inform the way we understand professionalism?

Professionalism is a complex concept, being both dynamic and contested. It is dynamic in the sense that what it means to be a professional has shifted over time, and contested given that notions of professionalism are formed from the interplay of conflicting interests: the historical, the political (as evidenced in changes to policy) and the empirical (the evidence of professional practice; Hargreaves & Fullan, 2000; Whitty, 2008). However,

> more recent sociological perspectives on professionalism have rejected normative notions of what it means to be a professional. Instead they see professionalism as a shifting phenomenon – a profession, they suggest is whatever people think it is at any particular time [...] Rather than asking whether the profession lives up to some supposed ideal, such an approach encourages us to explore the characteristics of teaching as an occupation in the present.
>
> (Whitty, 2008, p. 32)

The argument of this chapter is that professionalism has to be grounded in reality, "something that people – professionals – actually 'do', not simply something that the government or any other agency wants them to do, or mistakenly imagines they are doing" (Evans, 2008, p. 27). To start with, it is important to take account of the particular characteristics of teaching in the context of higher education.

Much of the discussion about teaching as a profession is focused on the statutory phases of education. Teachers have been viewed as 'quasi' or 'semi-professionals' (Etzioni, 1969) owing to the fact that they do not have the same levels of formal entry processes, regulatory bodies with powers to admit and discipline members or autonomy over their affairs compared with medicine or the law. The professionalisation of teaching in HE, however, has been a relatively recent development. This shift, driven by the need for greater accountability and 'value for money', has seen an increased political involvement in the shaping of HE by successive UK governments. The professionalisation of teaching in higher education has emerged from complex and demanding accountability frameworks: the Research Assessment Exercise (RAE; now the Research Excellence Framework, REF), the Teaching Excellence and Student Outcomes Framework (TEF), the National Student Survey (NSS) and the Knowledge Exchange Framework (KEF). Universities now face multiple challenges to metricise their worth within an increasingly competitive environment.

There are, however, significant differences in teaching between higher education and the statutory phases of education. As has been already noted, the first difference is that teaching in higher education has only comparatively recently received the attention or scrutiny that has been afforded to that in other phases of education. It could be argued that academics have never been viewed as 'professionals' but rather as individuals with high levels of expertise within very specific domains. Furthermore, academics work within a significantly different epistemological framework compared with other teachers. Teachers in schools, for example, are engaged in the transmission of previously established bodies of knowledge bounded by curricula and syllabuses. One of the defining features of the modern university is that it is concerned with advancing knowledge, with going beyond what is already known. An additional distinctive characteristic that sets universities apart from other institutions is concerned with the selecting and shaping of future staff:

> the forming of future scholars and scientists is not just an instrumental necessity for universities, but intrinsic to their character. Educating someone to pursue the open-ended search for deeper understanding has to be a kind of preparation for autonomy.
>
> (Collini, 2012, p. 8)

The intrinsic nature of the university has a range of implications: in the past, academics have been perceived as being principally engaged in research, the creation of new knowledge, and consequently teaching has been viewed as a less important priority. However, as we have seen, this has changed significantly with moves to professionalise teaching in higher education as a credible and valuable practice, rather than something you have to do when not researching. We are seeing a restoration of teaching in higher education as a valid and accountable practice of equal value to research.

What factors and assumptions should inform this process if it is to be meaningful? Evans (2008) makes a pertinent point when she asks, "what purpose is served by the renovation or redesign of professionalism, and how successful a process is it likely to be?" (p. 20), arguing that the consideration of possible alternatives needs to be grounded in what *is* rather than what *ought* to be (p. 22). The attention given to teaching in higher education is clearly guided by issues of quality, but who is to decide what is to be deemed to be professional practice?

The key assumption of this chapter is that teaching is an improvisational practice, given that it is relational and grounded in dialogism. This is the reality of teaching and, as such, needs to inform our understanding of professionalism. The jazz band has often been cited as a "root metaphor" (Hatch, 1997) for viewing improvisation within social contexts. The value of this metaphor is in the way it sees individual creativity as being realised in, and dependent upon, a group context. The individual and the collective are symbiotically linked in the social construction of an improvised jazz performance.

This suggests that we need to see professionalism as a social construction (collectively shaped and informed by individual contributions), grounded in the reality of the teaching, situated within specific contexts and acknowledging that "teachers are potentially key players in that construction, accepting or resisting external control and asserting or denying their autonomy" (Helsby, 1995, p. 320). The relationship between individual and collective enterprise can be distinguished by making a distinction between *professionality* and *professionalism*. *Professionality* is seen as "an ideologically, attitudinally, intellectually and epistemologically-based stance on the part of an individual, in relation to the practice of a profession to which s/he belongs, and which influences her/his professional practice" (Evans, 2008, p. 26). *Professionalism*, on the other hand is "the 'plural' of individuals' professionality orientation: the amalgam of multiple 'professionalities' – professionality writ large" (Evans, 2008, p. 26).

Professionalism in higher education needs to be reconceptualised as a relationship between *professionality* and *professionalism*, both an individual and a collective/collegiate process, informed by the view that improvisation "is at its heart a democratic, humane and emancipatory practice" (Fischlin et al., 2013 p. xi). The relationship between the individual and the collective can be seen in the generation of professional self-narratives (Gergen & Gergen, 1988). These are "culturally provided stories about selves and their passage through lives that provide resources drawn upon by individuals in their interactions with one another and with themselves". This reflexive act provides the opportunity to surface tacit assumptions and provide "a glue for collective professional identity" (Sachs, 2001, p. 158). These stories also need to be made public, not necessarily in a written form, so that they can be shared, debated and contested by others. At a collective level, arising out of democratic discourse is the development of communities of practice (Wenger, 1998) which facilitate values of respect, reciprocity and collaboration.

This view of a democratic professionalism informed by professional self-narratives and communities of practice informs a theoretical model of advanced professional practice as 'the authorised teacher', shown in Figure 15.2.

The notion of the authorised teacher is grounded in three powerful and related concepts: authenticity, authorisation and authoring.

The concept and professional assumption of **authenticity** are directly related to the way we understand improvisatory practice in that it acknowledges someone who acts or belongs to her or himself and furthermore whose opinion is entitled to acceptance. The acknowledgement of individual opinions and views is informed by notions of equality and a democratic view of teachers as professionals. The authenticity of the teacher is reflected in the personalisation of their practice.

The concept of **authorisation** is concerned with power, being able to influence action, opinion and belief, and having an opinion of testimony that is accepted. This is a confirmed professional identity that is not self-imposed but is derived from a shared community of practice, as described by Wenger (1998) within a situated learning community. Authorisation acknowledges and recognises the potential of the professional knowledge each teacher has about their educational setting, as well as the self-knowledge teachers have gained from their own unique career pathway.

Authoring, the origination or writing of a statement or account, is concerned with the articulating processes by which teachers 'write' or create their own professional identity within a critical framework. Such situated and personal knowledge, viewed through research and theoretical perspectives, engages them as critical professional learners who can claim authority for their own effective pedagogical practice. Within the context of an ethically led community of practice, there is the potential to share that knowledge with peers.

The authorised teacher offers a concept of advanced professional practice that is jointly constructed as part of an ongoing process that acknowledges the creative

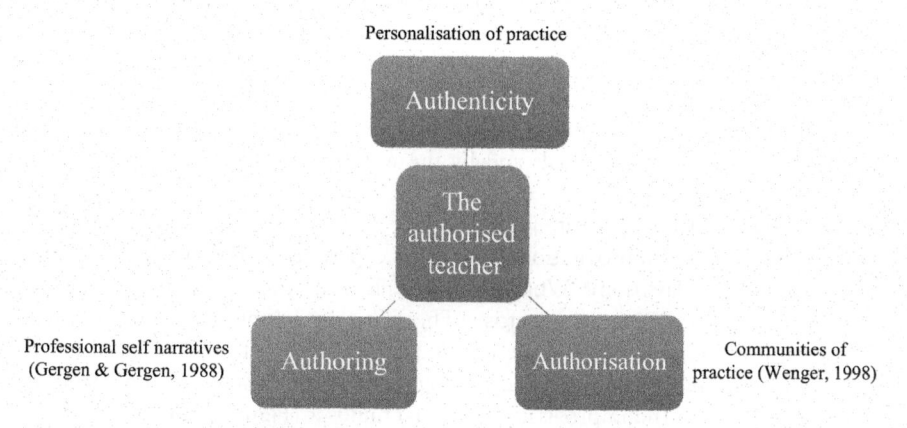

Figure 15.2 The authorised teacher
Source: Sorensen & Coombs, 2010.

and spontaneous reality that is the sum total of a teacher's experience. Given that 'greatness' cannot be mandated, and that expertise is context-bound, the concept of the authorised teacher as developed within communities of practice offers an opportunity to maximise and build on the professional expertise of teachers.

How do we go about the professional development of improvising teachers?

The theoretical framework (Figure 15.1) provides us with a *conceptual* map, showing how the dimensions of teacher expertise are fundamentally improvisatory and that there is a direct correlation between expertise and improvisation. The framework illuminates what the improvisational practice of expert teachers looks like in the classroom. In this section, we use this knowledge to address the issue of how we approach the professional development of 'improvising teachers'.

The research shows that two dimensions inform the improvisational practice of expert teachers. The first dimension is concerned with attitudinal development, the way that they think about their teaching (I call this having an improvisational mindset), and the second is concerned with functional development, the development of specific improvisational skills. The professional development of improvising teachers is based around encouraging and supporting the development of these two dimensions.

The improvisational mindset is characterised by three aspects. The first is that improvising teachers give themselves **permission** (and are given permission) to develop an improvisational approach to teaching. Second, and as a consequence of the first behaviour, they are continually **adapting** their practice. Adaptation takes two forms. One aspect of adaptation was seen in the way that the lesson plan was changed, or even abandoned, in response to a change in the direction of learning; this could be described as adaptation *in* action. Another form of adaptation was the adaptation of a subsequent activity or lesson that took place at a later point in time, which could be described as adaptation *on* action. The third behaviour is concerned with **personalisation**. These teachers personalised their approach to teaching and, where possible, the environment they were teaching in, in the same way that a jazz musician aims to develop a personal sound. This was seen in a personalisation of the teacher–pupil relationships in class, achieved by getting to know the students as individuals and by the way in which the teacher presented themself as an individual.

A willingness to engage in improvisation, adaptation and personalisation is characteristic of the improvisation mindset of expert teachers. So what does this look like in the classroom? What are the skills that teachers need in order to develop their improvisational expertise? The research and my experience as a teacher educator tell me that there are four important skills that improvising teachers have and these are: noticing, creating dialogue, making connections and adapting. They are central to the improvisation (impro) mindset (Figure 15.3).

When the Roman rhetorician Quintilian (circa AD 35–100) states that "the crown of all our study and the highest reward of our long labours is the power of

```
           ┌─────────────────┐
           │  Permission to  │
           │    improvise    │
           └─────────────────┘
                   │
           ┌─────────────────┐
           │    Noticing     │
           │    Dialogue     │
           │   Connecting    │
           │    Adapting     │
           └─────────────────┘
              /           \
  ┌──────────────────┐  ┌──────────────────┐
  │ Adaptation IN and│  │  Personalisation │
  │    ON action     │  │                  │
  └──────────────────┘  └──────────────────┘
```

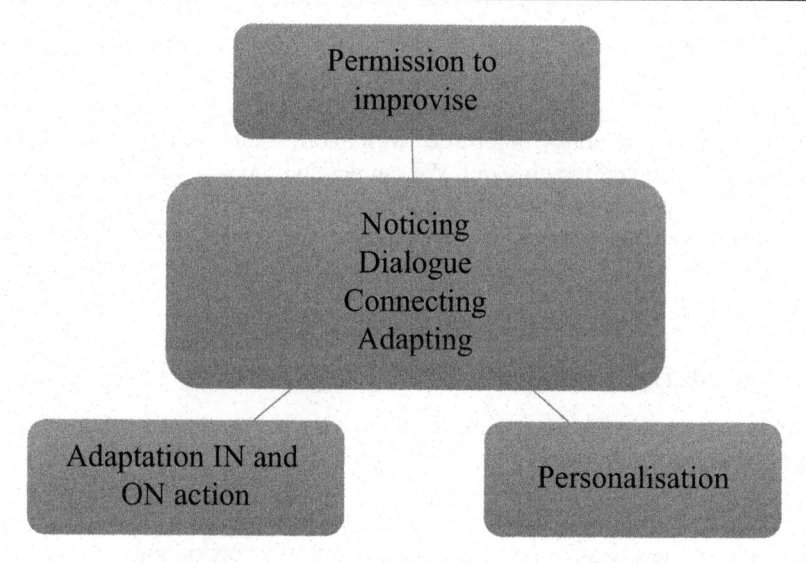

Figure 15.3 The dimensions of improvisational teaching (mindset and skills)

improvisation" (1922, Book 10. 7, p. 133), distinguishes between two different kinds of improvisation: the *artless* and the *artful*. This is a useful distinction to make in this context. Whereas *artless* improvisers rely solely on their ingenuity and natural talent, the *artful* improviser will not only be skilled in their subject, but also be knowledgeable in the repertoire of skills they can draw on. One of the key arguments of this chapter is that improvisation is a defining characteristic of expert teaching. However, explicitly focusing on developing an improvisational mindset and skills helps us to developing expertise in improvisational teaching through becoming artful improvisers.

Let us now look at how we can develop these skills. At the outset, we need to ask what comes first: the skills or the improvisational mindset? The answer is that there is a symbiotic relationship between skills and mindset. Having an improvisational mindset allows you to understand and develop the skills while, on the other hand, working on these skills leads to developing the impro mindset. Expert teaching is based on acknowledging this relationship between disposition (mindset) and action (skills). The good thing to note is that these skills are the things that we do anyway, and, by consciously giving attention to each one, we can all expand our improvisational ability.

Noticing

One of the most important skills that improvisers have is the ability to notice, seeing everything as an offer. The more you notice, the more you have to react and respond to. This is particularly true for the teacher in the classroom, and pupils love the experience of a teacher incorporating their ideas and suggestions.

Poynton (2013) points out that the reason we often don't notice very much is because we are continuously bombarded with information; our way of coping is to screen much of the information out. We can develop the skill of noticing by being selective about what we pay attention to. Poynton suggests focusing on four levels: the wider world, the immediate environment, other people and ourselves. This approach makes the act of noticing more manageable, as it is very difficult to take in all levels at once

Developing dialogic practice

Every time we have a conversation, we are entering into an improvisation because, when we engage in dialogue, we can never know where it is going; we have to wait for a response before we can decide what we are going to say next. Dialogue in the classroom is certainly improvisatory; you never know in advance what is going to be said next. Teachers with an impro mindset embrace this opportunity as they know that building conversation and dialogue around learning is an important way of involving the pupils. Teachers engaging with pupils and incorporating their ideas are what Freire (1972) describes as *actors in intercommunication.*

Dialogic teaching is derived from the theories of Bakhtin, whose view of dialogism implies that there are (at least) two voices and that there is an underlying assumption of difference. Dialogic teaching can create a more equal relationship between teacher and pupils, where there is the possibility for the teacher to learn from their pupils. In bell hooks's view, the dialogic classroom offers the possibility of an engaged pedagogy where the teacher "must genuinely *value* everyone's presence. There must be an ongoing recognition that everyone influences the classroom dynamic, that everyone contributes. These contributions are resources" (hooks, 1994, p. 8). One of the headteachers I interviewed described this practice as *"working with rather than on pupils"*.

Making connections

The classroom is a complex environment. You, the teacher, have a lesson that you have prepared. You begin by opening up a dialogue, and that creates a plethora of questions. Some questions may be 'on target', some seem irrelevant, and some offer ideas that you had never thought of. What do you do? The improvising teacher is able to think on their feet, pick up ideas from the class and incorporate them into their lesson. They are also adept at making the lesson relevant, connecting the content to the real world and the lives of their pupils.

Adaptation

Adapting a lesson plan 'in the moment' is the practice that most teachers think of when they talk about improvisational teaching. This can come about for a number of reasons: responding to or building on the ideas given by pupils, reacting to time constraints, dealing with unexpected interruptions, incorporating current topical issues or news events, accepting that the class 'just don't get' what you are teaching; the list is endless. The ability to be adaptable in order to engage with your pupils or to be able to clarify misunderstandings in a new way is a fundamental skill.

Conclusion

The findings of the research into the expert practice of secondary school teachers illuminates the fundamentally improvisatory nature of teaching, and this knowledge provides us with guidelines for identifying expert improvisational practice in the classroom. The insights into the improvisation mindset and the skills that inform improvisatory practice provide a clear framework and guidelines for the professional development of teacher expertise in higher education.

Finally, I want to emphasise the importance of a climate and culture that are sympathetic to and encouraging of improvisatory teaching. The teachers in my research valued collaboration and collegiality, and these approaches are crucial to creating a climate that fosters an applied impro mindset. Their efficacy allowed them the autonomy to be creative. I called them 'sanctioned mavericks'. Recognising, valuing and developing improvisatory teaching can only happen in a culture that encourages the authorisation of teachers.

Allowing greater autonomy places a high value on relationships (between students, between students and teachers, between teachers and senior management). The kind of climate that I am talking about has been described by Sawyer as "[a] culture of collaborative organisation ... based on flexibility, connection and conversation" (2007, p. 156). The challenge of developing improvising teachers in higher education is that it is as much a collective enterprise as an individual goal.

References

Alexander, R.J. (2008) *Towards Dialogic Teaching: Rethinking classroom talk* (4th edn). Dialogos, London.
Burr, V. (2003) *Social Constructionism*. Routledge, London. doi:10.4324/9780203694992
Collini, S, (2012) *What Are Universities For?* Penguin, London.
Dorsch, T.S. (1965) *Aristotle, Horace, Longinus: Classical literary criticism*. Penguin, Harmondsworth.
Dreyfus, S.L. & Dreyfus, H.L. (1986) *Mind Over Machine: The power of human intuition and expertise in the age of the computer*. Simon & Schuster, New York.
Etzioni, A. (Ed.) (1969) *The Semi-Professions and their Organization*. Free Press, New York.
Evans, L. (2008) Professionalism, professionality and the development of education professionals, *British Journal of Educational Studies*, 56 (1), 20–38. doi:10.1111/j.1467-8527.2007.00392.x
Fischlin, D., Heble, A. & Lipsitz, G. (2013) *The Fierce Urgency of Now*. Duke University Press, London. doi:10.1215/9780822378358

Freire, P. (1972) *Pedagogy of the Oppressed*. Penguin, Harmondsworth.

Gergen, K. & Gergen, M. (1988) Narrative and the self in relationship. *Advances in Experimental Social Psychology*, 21, 17–56.

Hargreaves, A. & Fullan, M. (2000) Mentoring in the new millennium, *Theory Into Practice*, 39 (1), 56–60. doi:10.1207/s15430421tip3901_8

Hatch, M.J. (1997) Jazzing up the theory of organizational improvisation. *Advances in Strategic Management*, 14, 181–191.

Helsby, G. (1995) Teachers' construction of professionalism in England in the 1990s. *Journal of Education for Teaching*, 21 (3), 317–332. doi:10.1080/02607479550038536

hooks, b. (1994) *Teaching to Transgress: Education as the practice of freedom*. Routledge, New York. doi:10.4324/9780203700280

Kandinsky, W. (1977) *Concerning the Spiritual in Art*. Translated from the Russian by Sadler, M.T.H.Dover, New York.

Poynton, R. (2013) *Do/Improvise*. Do Book Company, London.

Quintilian (1922) *The Institutio Oratoria of Quintilian*. Translated from the Latin by Butler, H.E.Heinemann, London.

Sachs, J. (2001) Teacher professional identity: competing discourses, competing outcomes. *Journal of Education Policy*, 16 (2), 149–161. doi:10.1080/02680930116819

Sawyer, R.K. (2007) *Group Genius: The creative power of collaboration*. Basic Books, New York.

Sorensen, N. (2014) Improvisation and Teacher Expertise: A comparative case study. PhD Thesis, Bath Spa University.

Sorensen, N (2016) Improvisation and teacher expertise: implications for the professional development of outstanding teachers. *Professional Development in Education*, 43 (1), 6–22. doi:10.1080/19415257.2015.1127854

Sorensen, N. & Coombs, S. (2010) Authorised to teach? *CPD Update*, 126, 8–9.

Stacey, R.D., Griffin, D. & Shaw, P. (2000) *Complexity and Management: Fad or radical challenge to systems thinking?*Routledge, London.

Sternberg, R.A. & Horvath, J.A. (1995) A prototype view of expert teaching. *Educational Researcher*, 24 (6), 9–17. doi:10.3102/0013189x024006009

Wenger, R. (1998) *Communities of Practice: Learning, meaning and identity*. Cambridge University Press, Cambridge.

Whitty, G. (2008) Changing modes of teacher professionalism. In Cunningham, B. (Ed.), *Exploring Professionalism*. Institute of Education, London, 28–49.

Chapter 16

Emotion work and the artistry of teaching

Peter Fossey

Introduction

The rise of emotion work in UK higher education has not gone unnoticed (e.g. Constanti & Gibbs, 2004, p. 243; Ogbonna & Harris, 2004; Rietti, 2009, p. 57; Hagenauer et al., 2016). The conceptual framework of emotional labour has been used to shed light on the well-being and job satisfaction of academics and facilitate understanding of trends in the type of work that academics are doing. Roughly speaking, the focus has been on how much time and energy staff spend on emotional labour, why, and how it affects them. As yet, less attention has been paid to the use of these concepts and resources to understand and support academic practice. The pedagogical role of emotions is explored in specific contexts: notably in connection with the study of political emotions and social justice education, drawing on the work of Nussbaum and Arendt, among others; see for example, Leibowitz et al. (2010), Zembylas (2002, 2020), and Boler (1999). Emotional labour as an aspect of the artistry of teaching practice is still under-investigated.

The primary aim of this chapter is to spark some interest and debate about the use of Hochschild's (1979, 1983) framework in order to shed light on teaching practice and classroom interactions. The second aim is to argue in favour of one conclusion we can draw from considering teaching practice in light of the emotion work framework: that the emotional rules governing students in the classroom should be as permissive as possible. That is to say, teachers should regard students' emotional reactions to the content and process of learning as an integral part of learning, not an extra factor to be "managed away".

The next section introduces Hochschild's work and the idea of framing, feeling and display rules. The third and fourth sections are concerned with what emotional rules teachers should promote in the classroom, in broad terms. It is argued that the most obvious considerations – socio-political reasons, pedagogical reasons, moral reasons relating to emotions, and concern for teachers' well-being – point in favour of permissive emotional rules. In the conclusion, some ideas are raised about the limits of permissiveness.

DOI: 10.4324/9781003198772-21

Emotion work

The 1970s and 1980s in the USA saw a rapid rise in the number of people employed by the service industries, as well as in the economic significance of the service sector (Ott, 1987; Plunkert, 1990). The migration of jobs out of the agriculture and manufacturing sectors and into the service sector had started in the post-war years, accelerated through the middle decades of the 20th century, and continues today, albeit more slowly (for the UK context, see Chiripanhura & Wolf, 2019). The growth of the service sector was fuelled by the creation of new kinds of jobs – such as call centre operative, air stewardess, tech support, and so on – and by the rising proportion of women going into employment (Urquhart, 1984). So, in the US (and UK) of the 1970s and 1980s, an increasingly large proportion of people, especially women, were employed in areas that had not existed even a handful of years previously.

The high rate of turnover and burnout associated with the new service sector was of growing concern. Perlman and Hartmann (1982), for example, note that the term "burnout" first appeared in academic literature in 1974, and they associate the term closely with the demands and conditions of "professions with a high degree of people contact" (ibid., p. 283). Much of Hochschild's research in the late 1970s and early 1980s was intended to shed light on the character and conditions of these new types of labour. She attributed the burnout to the strenuous and alienating nature of the labour in the service sector; she found that service sector jobs tended to involve workers in the process of managing their emotional responses and expressions in order to meet the demands of the role and provide the client with the intended kind of experience, whether the client liked it or not (Hochschild, 1983, pp. 96–97)!

In ordinary adult social life, our emotional engagement with situations is surprisingly predictable. It would be strange if we saw people who were very sombre at a wedding or happy and laughing at a funeral, for example. That kind of emotional behaviour would be out of the ordinary and would be recognised as such by the other participants.

Hochschild theorised that there are three interlocking sets of "conventions of feeling" (1979, p. 552) that govern our emotional response to a situation:

- First, there are framing rules. These are the rules that determine how we perceive or conceptualise a certain situation or stimulus. Framing rules are about how we think about stimuli, in terms that are emotionally salient;
- Second, there are feeling rules, which govern the appropriate kind of felt emotional reaction to the situation as we perceive it. Feeling rules are about the emotional responses (that is, felt emotions, not expressions of emotion) that are appropriate to those stimuli;
- Finally, there are display rules, which govern how we should express ourselves emotionally in a given situation.

These three sets of rules can influence each other, come apart, or come into conflict, in various ways. This is particularly likely in contexts where one is playing a social or professional role which has its own set of rules, which might differ from those which would otherwise be in place. Hochschild's original and best-known examples were airline cabin crew and debt collectors. Higher education contexts provide a ready supply of examples.

Consider, for instance, a spirited argument between colleagues who know each other well, about some aspect of their shared research. This description, as written, could apply to a disagreement between friends, a difference of opinion between experts, or a flat-out squabble. The underlying events, separated as far as possible from the judgements we make about them, might not lend themselves to one description decisively over the others. Whether it is an argument, disagreement, or quarrel depends to a large extent on what we think about it, and how it is appropriate to feel about it depends on how we frame it. As a bystander, it makes sense to feel sympathy for friends who have fallen out, but not so much for researchers who have reached opposite conclusions. Colleagues having an altercation, rather than an argument, should perhaps be reminded of their professional values; friends who are quarrelling need not be. The way that we frame a situation goes a long way to determining how it is appropriate to feel about it and, therefore, what appeals to emotion are available, what expressions of emotion are likely to be expected or unexpected, and so on. As the example suggests, we are sometimes able to choose how to frame a situation, and this can be a strategic choice as well as an evaluative one.

The way that we frame a given stimulus is part and parcel of the way we understand and respond to the social situation of which it is an element. Some ways of framing a situation can present themselves more forcefully than others; some framed stimuli are associated by feeling rules with emotions that are easier to evoke, harder to suppress, and more influential over our actions. Once one begins to see some action as an insult, for example, the argument gains inertia, and it can be difficult to change course. Even so, any stimulus will be susceptible to more than one possible framing. By playing with these multiple possible framings, we can evoke and acknowledge emotions that are inappropriate or non-standard, but nevertheless part of our experience, and create a space in which to express them. For example, we can imagine two otherwise kind and professional lecturers expressing their frustration about a novice mistake in an advanced student's work through caustic humour and sarcasm. The student's performance can be framed as a silly mistake and a disappointing failure, even though, in an educational context, it is desirable to frame it first and foremost as the work of a learner. Both of these framings are available, and it may be that, despite best intentions, it is sometimes hard not to see poor student performances in a light that gives rise to negative feelings. Acknowledging that alternative framing through a private joke with a colleague creates a space in which negative emotions can be expressed that would otherwise have to be managed in some other way.

This leads us to the third category of rules: display rules. These connect expressions of emotion to social contexts. The kinds of emotional expression that are appropriate to a particular stimulus depend more on the way that it is framed than on the way we are liable to feel about it. Display rules take their cue from framing rules, not feeling rules. Expressions of emotion and social norms are both public in a way that felt emotions are not. The emotional expressions a lecturer, doctor, retail assistant, or member of cabin crew should direct towards their learner, patient, or client are not determined by the way they actually feel in any given instance, but by their social role. As such, there may be a discrepancy between the subject's felt emotional response and the emotion they should express.

This can be handled in one of two ways: either by conforming the expression to the display rule and letting the felt emotions come as they may ("surface acting"), or by conforming the felt emotional response to the emotions implied by the display rules and allowing the expression to follow spontaneously ("deep acting"). The surface actor manages the outward appearance of emotion, but not their inner life; this requires considerable effort and leaves it open that the subject is emotionally disengaged from or at odds with their work. Surface acting is effortful and alienating and is part of the explanation of the high level of burnout in service sector jobs. Research indicates that the relationship between surface acting and burnout holds true in the education sector (e.g. Zhang & Zhu, 2008, pp. 114–5).

The deep actor works on internalising the framing rules so that their spontaneous emotional responses are in line with the emotional expressions required by the professional context. Deep acting is less effortful in the moment, and less alienating, as, if successful, the deep actor becomes emotionally engaged with their work. We might, however, wonder whether deep acting could be alienating or depersonalising in some deeper sense; Diefendorff et al. (2005) distinguish between deep acting and "the expression of naturally felt emotions" (p. 340).

Norms and emotions

Applying the emotion work framework to the classroom reveals the ways in which the emotional climate of the classroom is constructed and regulated, and what the classroom context permits and demands, from both learners and teachers. By making explicit the framing, feeling, and display rules in operation in the classroom, and in wider contexts of education such as university subcultures, the emotion work framework shows us what education is supposed to feel like. It shows us how we are supposed to feel about education and the regulatory mechanisms that are in place to make sure that we feel that way. Employing the emotion work framework enables us to expose these rules to evaluation and make deliberate, targeted efforts to improve them.

So, how should we feel about learning? How should we feel about the kind of learning that brings to light past mistakes or unethical behaviour? Furthermore, what is the force of the "should" in the preceding questions? Hochschild convincingly argues that there are rules about emotional feelings and expressions, but are they descriptive or prescriptive rules? There are rules which describe a typical pattern of response, but awareness of those rules also shapes both the individual's emotional vocabulary and what they can expect with regard to the emotional responses of others. When these expectations are not met, there is a sense of deviation which can lead to awkwardness (e.g. Kotsko 2010, esp. ch. 1) or provoke a different kind of emotional response. But there is a difference between what is expected in the sense of being predicted and what is expected in the sense of being justified, or pragmatic, or "right" in an ethical or moral sense. It might help to distinguish between expectations in the sense of predictions, which do not carry normative force, and expectations that relate to entitlements and obligations, which are normative. I expect/predict that the sun will rise; I expect/oblige students to do their best. I can expect/predict that students will do their best, but I cannot expect/oblige the sun to rise. So, if we are to ask how one ought to feel about learning in general and specifically about becoming aware of one's past mistakes or poor performances, then it is important to know that we are talking about the same kind of justification.

Hochschild's rules play a descriptive role when used by the sociologist and a normative role when encountered by the individual. Here, we are discussing how these rules might be useful in thinking about teaching practice. Given that teachers are typically in a position of power and authority over students and have some ability to use learning design and teaching presence to shape the rules in the classroom, we can regard the emotional rules from the teacher's perspective as having a normative role.

One might think that these questions are in some way wrong-headed: there cannot be normative rules about emotions. One might hold this view on the grounds that emotions essentially belong to the private, inner life of the mind and are not subject to ethical or social appraisal. Or because feeling an emotion is in some respects non-voluntary and, therefore, not the sort of thing for which a person can be praised or blamed. Or, again, one might think that emotional states themselves are not constituted by actions, judgements, or evaluations, and so there is nothing there which might be governed by a norm. One might hold that being angry, for example, does not include or imply taking any particular view of the person with whom one is angry; then, it would make no more sense to think about the rightness of being angry than it would the rightness of being tall. Readers who find these lines of objection somewhat convincing may want to focus instead on the question, "what framing rules ought educators to endorse?"

Feeling about learning

How ought learners to feel about learning? Our answer to this question should guide our teaching practice. The framing and display rules we endorse and enforce in the classroom shape the way that learners think about, feel about, and express themselves with regard to the content and process of learning. In this section, I will try to give some more sense to the question and put forward some reasons in favour of the claim that the framing, feeling, and display rules in play in the classroom should be very permissive.

On what basis can we answer the question, how ought learners to feel about learning? I will consider four possibilities and, in each instance, make an argument in favour of permissive rules.

First, there is the broader socio-political context in which learning occurs and the relationship between education, learner, and society. Restrictive rules about how one ought to think and feel about learning result in a diminished range of permissible emotional responses and expressions. Emotional expression is not amoral or apolitical. The way we feel about ourselves and each other, wealth and poverty, sickness and health, justice and injustice, education and ignorance, and so on, goes a long way to determining the shape of political discourse (Saul, 2017). Crude dualisms about cognition and emotion tend to be involved here. Thought is rational, measured, and productive and, therefore, to be preferred, whereas feeling is irrational, wanton, and counterproductive and, therefore, to be suppressed. But thought is also regarded as masculine, sophisticated, and white, whereas emotion is feminine (Shields, 2013, p. 425), unsophisticated (Squire, 2001, p. 8), and black (Corbin et al., 2018).

Permissive emotional rules are preferable in that they validate a broader range of responses and are in that regard progressive. If part of the purpose of education is to enable the learner to imagine new social roles and possibilities for themselves, then learners will need to be able to feel positively about choices that conservative tendencies in society would see in a negative light. For example, despite changes in society and higher education, there is still a strong underlying sense that maths-based subjects are "masculine". Classroom framing rules ought to guide female learners to conceptualise their motivation towards and abilities in maths-based subjects in positive terms, and display rules should legitimise female learners' expressions of pride and satisfaction with their achievements.

Second, there is the question of what kind of emotional climate is most conducive to learning. There is considerable research on emotional responses to criticism which shows that at least certain classes of negative emotional response tend to impede the learning process. Learners who feel anxious, angry, or threatened by critical feedback are at a disadvantage compared with their more accepting peers. For example, Ackerman and Gross (2010, pp. 178–9) found that learners were more likely to respond positively to critical feedback if they could identify a clear opportunity to act on it and thereby repair the damage to their self-esteem. Learners without such an opportunity might resort to less constructive tactics.

Plausibly, it would be better for learners if they did not experience this kind of negative emotional response to learning; and, when they do, it will be better for them if they are able to use a range of strategies in order to cope with it. As such, there is a strong face-value reason to prefer emotional rules that do not require students to engage in surface acting. Surface acting, as we have seen, is effortful. It saps energy and motivation which could otherwise be directed towards learning.

We can extend this line of thought to learners who find new ideas threatening, potentially because they experience them as a threat to their self-image, or because they are uncomfortable with the tacit admission of past errors. Or, students might experience negative emotions relating to feeling vulnerable or self-conscious when discussing issues of identity and society. Research literature on teaching on issues of race, gender, and sustainability addresses cases like these. Widerberg (1998) writes: "Gender conceived as equality was obviously no fun at all, it only made [learners] feel bad or wrong" (p. 195). In the context of continuing professional development, Walker (2007) discusses course participants who, when faced with the truth about their company's green credentials, experience "grief, sadness, fear, impotent anger", or go into denial (p. 30).

There are, nevertheless, reasons to believe that negative emotions, particularly relating to past behaviour that is revealed to be unethical, have a role to play in learning (see, for example, work on the pedagogy of discomfort by, in particular, Zembylas, 2002, 2020; Leibowitz et al., 2010; Boler, 1999)). Framing and feeling rules which conceptualise learning as inherently positive or which delegitimise negative feelings in the classroom risk inhibiting and marginalising this kind of learning. This may seem to be at odds with the above point regarding anxiety, but the two ideas can be reconciled. In the discomfort cases, students are encouraged to be aware, be responsible for, and explore their negative emotions as part of the learning process. Experiencing and expressing those emotions is legitimised by the learning process, which also functions as a way to work through those feelings. To return to the cases above, Widerberg worked with participants' negative responses in order to provoke action for change, and Walker used students' discomfort as a catalyst for more honest and meaningful discussion. In the anxiety cases, however, the negative emotions are not utilised within learning and, indeed, tend to stifle it. Having those emotions is not explicitly recognised as an understandable, familiar, or even intended response to the situation, and the learning experience might not provide the learner with any clear way to discharge them.

Third, there are moral considerations relating to the emotions themselves and the emotional dimensions of classroom interactions. Negative emotions are described as such because they are generally unpleasant or undesirable to experience (though there are interesting exceptions, such as the paradox of horror; Carroll, 1990). It seems to follow that there is at least a prima facie ethical duty for educators to exercise emotional care towards their learners. A rough sketch of such a duty might be to take reasonable steps to avoid creating situations in which the learners are likely to experience strong negative emotions in the context of their learning. The existence of this kind of ethical prohibition on negative emotions in learning is the root of important objections to the pedagogy of discomfort (e.g. Zembylas, 2015).

If learning either constitutes or promotes positive social change, then there might be an ethical reason to frame learning in a way that gives rise to positive and pro-social emotions. The point could be argued on utilitarian grounds, if it is more effective to encourage learners to feel positively about learning. There is a more general point here about harmony between emotional experiences and ethical values. It seems plausible that educators should lead their learners to think and feel positively about learning, if learning is a social and ethical good.

Fourth, and finally, we can consider the impact of the emotional rules on teachers. The conclusion of Hochschild's research (1983) was that the strain of engaging in too much surface acting was a significant factor in explaining the phenomenon of burnout in the service industries. Higher education is a different context, but the type of work involved bears some similarities. In both cases, the worker or teacher expends effort to create and maintain a particular kind of experience for their "client". In both cases, there is an expectation that the worker behave in a professional manner, and there are strong, socially mandated expectations about the emotions it is appropriate for the worker to express. Teachers and lecturers perhaps have more freedom than, say, cabin crew; but there are still extensive rules. The education context contains many situations in which the emotional dimension of the learning experience, including the emotions the teacher expresses with and towards the student, can make a significant difference to student learning.

As we use the emotion work framework to examine teaching practice and begin to think about the emotional rules that we would want in place in our own classrooms, it seem important that we pay attention to the level of surface acting required of the teacher. Less energy spent on surface acting implies a lower risk of burnout and, perhaps, leaves the teacher better positioned to engage in activities that would enhance the quality of their teaching, or devote time to research, or support their colleagues.

The demand for surface acting is determined by the relationship between the framing rules; the display rules; the teacher's individual emotional dispositions, meaning to what extent they have internalised the framing rules already; and the particulars of the situation that gives rise to emotional responses. In a classroom where the framing and display rules are very restrictive, a teacher who has not yet internalised the framing rules might need to engage in some acting. They may choose between conforming their expressions to the display rules – that is, surface acting – or conforming their spontaneous emotional responses to the framing rules – that is, deep acting. Suppose, instead, we were to slacken the framing and display rules, making it permissible for the teacher to conceptualise the situation in a greater variety of different ways and display a broader range of emotions. The need for acting is thereby reduced.

I will conclude this section with a brief illustration of these ideas in practice.

Imagine a situation in which students are learning that some of their preferred behaviours are environmentally damaging and unsustainable, and that unsustainable practices are ethically wrong because we have ethical obligations both to future generations and to those who are already suffering the ill-effects of climate change. The students are, therefore, being encouraged to see their own actions and preference as ethically wrong and as actively harming others. Successful learning here could also lead to a transformation of their perspective. If they are able to see themselves as part of an interconnected environment and as having ethical responsibilities to distant others, then they will be better able to bring about positive change in their own actions and those of others. But failure to deal with the negative emotions evoked, failure to make the transformation, will leave the students "caught in [their] own history and ... reliving it" (Mezirow, 1978, p. 101).

What framing rules are preferable in this situation? What actions on the part of the lecturer might communicate and enforce those rules? What display rules are desirable for the lecturer and the students?

Experiencing a certain amount of guilt about engaging in unsustainable consumption might well be appropriate, but too much negative affect could trigger a defensive response. It seems plausible that students will be better able to internalise the new ideas if they are able to freely express their negative emotions, rather than having to work to repress them. This has implications for the appropriate display rules.

It might be advisable for the lecturer to give the students increased agency within the classroom and opportunity to discuss their feelings with their peers, in order to be better able to process them. When students create and lead learning activities, determining what goes on in the classroom, then they also have a chance to create new rules about how it is permissible to feel and what feelings may be expressed. When students can speak with their own authority, not overshadowed by the lecturer, what they say and how they say it become part of the network of implicit emotional rules in the classroom. If a student talks about the way that the course content has made them feel about their consumer behaviour and is met with tacit approval by the room, then those kinds of feelings pass into the canon of what is permissible – the framing, feeling, and display rules.

So, too, it might be better if students are encouraged to focus on the future and to think of their past behaviour not as a damning indictment of their character, but as a period of ignorance, from which they now have an opportunity and a responsibility to move on. We might compare this to a more common case in which a student receives a disappointing grade and negative feedback: the important thing is, as always, to grow.

Conclusion

All other things being equal, I take it that a situation in which teachers and students have to engage in less acting, and particularly less surface acting, is better than one in which they have to engage in more acting. I have argued that permissive emotional rules are preferable on the grounds that they are progressive, conducive to learning, ethically preferable, and less burdensome, particularly for teachers.

While I take these arguments to provide adequate support for the general principle that it is better to aim for permissive rules than restrictive ones, I have not considered what the limits of this permissiveness might be. Presumably, there will have to be prohibitions on at least certain kinds of other-directed emotions, particularly negative ones. Indeed, self-directed negative emotions should be handled with care too, although there is, as we have seen, a place for negative emotions in learning.

Clearly, this is an area for further work. For now, let me say that the permissiveness principle contains its own limitations. The general rule in play here is that coping with emotional responses to learning, whether positive or negative, is part of the learning process. No emotional response on the part of the student should be marginalised or delegitimised by the emotion rules; that is to say, no emotional response on the part of the students should in advance be ruled out of the scope of what can be expressed, scrutinised, and discussed in the learning process. Pedagogues of discomfort make the student's emotional response the basis for learning when dealing with contentious topics. Even where the content of learning seems less likely to provoke an emotional reaction, students will still be personally invested in their learning and in the social experience of learning. The emotions evoked in these contexts are just as legitimate responses, and just as much a part of learning, as the grief, shame, and indignation that are the province of the pedagogy of discomfort. To make an emotional response part of the learning process, one must pay attention to it, examine its causes and its objects, and ask whether it espouses an evaluation that we want to endorse. The recommendation here to work with permissive emotional rules is not a declaration that "anything goes" with regard to behaviour in the classroom. Rather, it is a recommendation to let students and teachers acknowledge and share their emotional responses without passing judgement. It is a recommendation to subvert and do away with the feeling that feelings have no place in most classrooms.

Education is about the way a person relates to the wider context in which they find themselves, and in particular how they see their role or place in that context: what opportunities are open to them, what actions they can take, how they can relate to others, and so on (Mezirow, 1978). In Box 16.1 Akenson et al. discuss the 'WOKE' approach to supporting mindful discussions with students. The higher education classroom is a place in which those relationships and contexts are developed, worked, and reconfigured for adult life. Applying the emotion work framework gives us a way to develop a systematic understanding of the flows and causes of emotional responses within that place. The emotion work framework throws open a hidden structure of power relations and emotional meanings which are in play in the classroom and offers us an opportunity to shape it for the benefit of the learners.

Box 16.1 Wide open knowledge environments (WOKEs) in higher education

Wide open knowledge environments (WOKEs) were created by infusing transformative learning practices (Hoggan, 2016; Mezirow, 1997, 2003, 2008) with mindfulness to address challenging issues at the intersection of equity and education at a predominantly White, 4-year doctoral institution serving a largely rural community.

Recognizing those who contribute *woke* practices and theories (e.g., Babulski, 2020; Bunyasi & Watts Smith, 2019; Doyle, 2018; Harvor, 2019, Roy, 2018; Williams, 2020), we respectfully adopt and adapt the term to denote (1) the use of reflexivity and mindfulness, (2) the acknowledgement of the failure to call in intersectionality and equity for those who have been marginalized, and (3) the courage and integrity creating and sustaining these WOKEs require.

WOKEs offer educational spaces conducive to curiosity-driven, equity-focused, critical conversations. These spaces:

- **W**iden understandings of self, cultures, contexts, identities, intersectionality, and relationships;
- **O**pen equity-focused inquiry and cultivate willingness to engage in active listening, reflexive practices, compassionate curiosity, and mindful awareness;
- Examine intrapersonal, interpersonal, institutional, and structural/systemic **k**nowledge and processes; and
- Create safe, respectful educational **e**nvironments that encourage mindful, critical, civil discussion around challenging concepts.

Embodiment is crucial to cultivating WOKEs. Before debuting practices, instructor/facilitators should model them, offering a point of connection and comprehension of the courage and sense of safety required. To enhance this practice, familiarity with trauma-sensitive mindfulness (Treleaven, 2018) is strongly encouraged. Reflexive practices might be as simple as guided journal prompts concerning explorations of, reactions to, and ideas about challenging concepts. In a well-established WOKE, opportunities for mindful discussion of prompts or journal entries may be possible. Mindfulness practices – such as RAIN (Brach, 2012, 2017), STOP (Wolf & Serpa, 2015), Just Like Me (Chödrön, 2009), awareness of breath – may provide ways to check in with the self, acknowledge immediate experience, and recognize connection to others when engaging with ideas and perspectives counter to one's own. Active listening and nonviolent communication practices (Rosenberg, 2015) further contribute to WOKE.

Cultivating curiosity, compassion, and respect when encountering discomfort and challenging content offers the possibility for awareness, examination, and transformation. Using WOKEs, we (students and educators) are able to begin to be present with discomfort and encourage respectful curiosity about our experiences and those of others, becoming less reactive and more responsive. This, we hope, leads to speaking *with* others and deep listening – where critical, mindful transformation through education thrives.

(Ashley B. Akenson, Andrea Arce-Trigatti, & James E. Akenson)

References

Ackerman, D.S., & Gross, B.L. (2010) Instructor feedback: how much do students really want? *Journal of Marketing Education*, 32 (2), 172–181. doi:10.1177/0273475309360159

Babulski, T. (2020) Being and becoming woke in teacher education. *Phenomenology & Practice*, 14(1), 73–88. doi:10.29173/pandpr29399

Boler, M. (1999) *Feeling Power: Emotions and education*. Routledge, Abingdon.

Brach, T. (2012) *True Refuge: Finding peace and freedom in your own awakened heart*. Random House, New York.

Brach, T. (2017) The RAIN of self-compassion. www.tarabrach.com/selfcompassion1/ [accessed 28/08/2021].

Bunyasi, T.L, & Watts Smith, C. (2019) *Stay Woke: A people's guide to making all Black Lives Matter*. New York University Press, New York.

Carroll, N. (1990) *The Philosophy of Horror: Or, paradoxes of the heart*. Routledge, Abingdon. doi:10.4324/9780203361894

Chiripanhura, B., & Wolf, N. (2019) Long-term trends in UK employment: 1861 to 2018. Office for National Statistics, London.

Chödrön, P. (2009) *Taking the Leap: Freeing ourselves from old habits and fears*. Shambhala, Boulder, CO.

Constanti, P., & Gibbs, P. (2004) Higher education teachers and emotional labour. *International Journal of Educational Management*, 18 (4), 243–249. doi:10.1108/09513540410538822

Corbin, N.A., Smith, W.A., & Garcia, J.R. (2018) Trapped between justified anger and being the strong Black woman: Black college women coping with racial battle fatigue at historically and predominantly White institutions. *International Journal of Qualitative Studies in Education*, 31 (7), 626–643. doi:10.1080/09518398.2018.1468045

Diefendorff, J.M., Croyle, M.H., & Gosserand, R.H. (2005) The dimensionality and antecedents of emotional labor strategies. *Journal of Vocational Behavior*, 66 (2), 339–357. doi:10.1016/j.jvb.2004.02.001

Doyle, J.L. (2018) Becoming a sailor: A (critical) analytic autoethnographic account of navigating tensions as a 'woke' white woman working for racial justice [Doctoral dissertation]. doi:10.13140/RG.2.2.33062.06727

Hagenauer, G., Gläser-Zikudab, M., & Volet, S.E. (2016) University teachers' perceptions of appropriate emotion display and high-quality teacher-student relationship: similarities and differences across cultural-educational contexts. *Frontline Learning Research*, 4 (3), 44–74. doi:10.14786/flr.v4i3.236

Harvor, F. (2019) Woke, "theory woke", geo-woke: on the difficult evolution of progressive thought as evidenced by intellectual trends. *International Journal of Foreign Studies*, 12 (2), 61–83. doi:10.18327/ijfs.2019.12.12.61

Hochschild, A.R. (1979) Emotion work, feeling rules, and social structure. *American Journal of Sociology*, 85 (3), 551–575. doi:10.1086/227049

Hochschild, A.R. (1983) *The Managed Heart: The commercialisation of human feeling*. University of California Press, Oakland, CA.

Hoggan, C.D. (2016) Transformative learning as metatheory: definition, criteria, and typology. *Adult Education Quarterly*, 66 (1), 57–75. doi:10.1177/0741713615611216

Kotsko, A. (2010) *Awkwardness*. Zero Books, Ropley.

Leibowitz, B., Bozalek, V., Rohleder, P., Carolissen, R., & Swartz, L. (2010) "Ah, but the whiteys love to talk about themselves": discomfort as a pedagogy for change. *Race, Ethnicity and Education*, 13 (1), 83–100. doi:10.1080/13613320903364523

Mezirow, J. (1978) Perspective transformation. *Adult Education*, 28 (2), 100–110. doi:10.1177/074171367802800202

Mezirow, J. (1997) Transformative learning: theory to practice. *New Directions for Adult and Continuing Education*, 74, 5–12. doi:10.1002/ace.7401

Mezirow, J. (2003) Transformative learning as discourse. *Journal of Transformative Education*, 1 (1), 58–63. doi:10.1177/1541344603252172

Mezirow, J. (2008) An overview on transformative learning. In Sutherland, P. & Crowther, J. (Eds.), *Lifelong learning: Concepts and contexts*, 24–38. Routledge, Abingdon.

Ogbonna, E., & Harris, L.C. (2004) Work intensification and emotional labour among UK university lecturers: an exploratory study. *Organization Studies*, 25 (7), 1185–1203. doi:10.1177/0170840604046315

Ott, M. (1987) The growing share of services in the U.S. economy – degeneration or evolution? *Federal Bank of St Louis Review Journal*, 69 (6), 5–22. doi:10.20955/r.69.5-22.bzk

Perlman, B., & Hartmann, E.A. (1982) Burnout: summary and future research. *Human Relations*, 35 (4), 283–305. doi:10.1177/001872678203500402

Plunkert, L.M. (1990) The 1980s: a decade of job growth and industry shifts. *Monthly Labour Review*, 113 (9), 3–16.

Rietti, S. (2009) Emotion-work and the philosophy of emotion. *Journal of Social Philosophy*, 40 (1), 55–74. doi:10.1111/j.1467-9833.2009.01438.x

Rosenberg, M.B. (2015) *Nonviolent Communication: A language of life* (3rd edn). Puddledancer Press, Encinitas, CA.

Roy, L.A. (2018) *Teaching While White: Addressing the intersections of race and immigration in the classroom*. Rowman & Littlefield, Washington, DC.

Saul, J. (2017) Racial figleaves, the shifting boundaries of the permissible, and the rise of Donald Trump. *Philosophical Topics*, 45 (2), 97–116. doi:10.5840/philtopics201745215

Shields, S.A. (2013) Gender and emotion: what we think we know, what we need to know, and why it matters. *Psychology of Women Quarterly*, 37 (4), 423–435. doi:10.1177/0361684313502312

Squire, C. (2001) The public life of emotions. *International Journal of Critical Psychology*, 1, 27–38.

Treleaven, D.A. (2018) *Trauma-Sensitive Mindfulness*. Norton, New York.

Urquhart, M. (1984) The employment shift to services: where did it come from? *Monthly Labour Review*, 107 (4), 15–22.

Walker, P. (2007) Different planets: belief, denial and courage: the role of emotion on turning learning into action. In: Galea, C. (Ed.) *Teaching Business Sustainability*. Routledge, Abingdon. doi:10.4324/9781351281201

Widerberg, K. (1998) Teaching gender through writing 'experience stories'. *Women's Studies International Forum*, 21 (2), 193–198. doi:10.1016/s0277-5395(98)00002-8

Williams, J.M. (2020) *Stay Woke: A meditation guide for the rest of us*. Sounds True, Louisville, CO.

Wolf, C., & Serpa, J.G. (2015) *A Clinician's Guide to Teaching Mindfulness: The comprehensive session-by-session program for mental health professionals and healthcare providers*. New Harbinger, Oakland, CA.

Zhang, Q., & Zhu, W. (2008) Exploring emotion in teaching: emotional labor, burnout, and satisfaction. *Chinese Higher Education, Communication Education*, 57 (1), 105–122. doi:10.1080/03634520701586310

Zembylas, M. (2002) Structures of feeling in curriculum and teaching: theorizing the emotional rules. *Educational Theory*, 52 (2), 187–208. doi:10.1111/j.1741-5446.2002.00187.x

Zembylas, M. (2015) "Pedagogy of discomfort" and its ethical implications: the tensions of ethical violence in social justice education. *Ethics and Education*, 10, 1–12. doi:10.1080/17449642.2015.1039274

Zembylas, M. (2020) Hannah Arendt's political thinking on emotions and education: implications for democratic education, *Discourse: Studies in the Cultural Politics of Education*, 41 (4), 501–515. doi:10.1080/01596306.2018.1508423

Index

Page numbers in italics refer to figures. Page numbers in bold refer to tables.

ableism: academic 75–77, 81; definition of 75–76
academic knowledge 32, 101
academic tasks of higher education teachers 21
Ackerman, D.S. 236
action research 143, 144
adaptation by improvising teachers 226, 228–229
adaptive expertise 7–8, 17, 167–168, 203, 206, 213–214; improvisation 207–208; Performative Aspects of Teaching workshop 208–214; variation in situations/problems 206; *see also* improvisation
agency, teacher 8, 38, 158, 159, 222
Akenson, Ashley B. 8
Akenson, James E. 8
alternative dispute resolution 117
Andersson, R. 193
anti-oppressive education 78, 79
Arce-Trigatti, Andrea 8
Arendt, H. 231
artistry of teaching 7–8, 9, 20–22, 24, 94, 203, 215; *see also* emotions; improvisation
Ashwin, P. 167
authenticity 225
authoring 225
authorisation 225
authorised teacher 8, 225–226, *225*

Babin, J.J. 86
Baglieri, S. 76
Bakhtin, M. 228
Bale, Richard 7–8, 22
Barnacle, R. 32, 115

Barnett, R. 114
Barrett, N. 51
Barrette-Ng, Isabelle 7
Barton, L. 70
Basow, S.A. 92
Baume, David 6, 166
Bell, A. 192
Bendix, L. 193
Benner, P. 49
Benschop, Y. 94
Bereiter, C. 46, 142, 162, 163, 165, 166
Berliner, D. 48, 49, 50, 51, 130
Biggs, John B. 165
black letter approach to law 116
Bloom, B.S. 17, 188
Boler, M. 231
Bolt, D. 72
Bostock, John 6
Botham, K.A. 135
Bransford, J.D. 205
Brockbank, A. 138
Brookfield, S. 131
burnout 8, 232, 233, 238
Butcher Ding allegory (*Zhuangzi, The*) 44, 45–46, 47–48, 49–50, 51–53

Campbell, F.K. 75
career satisfaction 47
care (for students' learning) 8, 9, 22, 158, 160, 168, 171, 237
Carless, D. 36
Carl Wieman Science Education Initiative (CWSEI) 188–190, **189**
Carnegie Foundation 118
Carr, W. 40
Carter, D. 34

Casals, Pablo 18
Chai, D. 49–50
Chase, W.G. 16
Chatham House Rule 180–181
Chaucer, Geoffrey 15
Chiu, W.W. 52
Clarke, D. 49
Clegg, S. 138
clinical legal education 6, 114; Carnegie apprenticeship model 118–119; challenges of creating a reflective practicum 120–121; holistic approach to professional identity formation 117–118; knowing-in-action 120; Lawyering in Practice module 114, 118, 119, 120, 121, 123–124; ontological turn 115; pedagogy of formation 115–116; professional identity of educators 121–123; reflective practice 118, 119–120; sharing expertise across disciplines 123–124; shift from knowing to being 114–116; structuring of pedagogy 119–120; swampy lowlands 117, 120; Team Entrepreneurship programme 119, 123–124; thinking like a lawyer 116–117, 120
Clow, R. 108
coaching 7, 119, 123–124, 150, 159; *see also* mentoring/mentors
Code, Warren 7
Cohen, S. 215
collaboration 23, 39, 69, 109, 144, 188, 228; discipline-based education specialists 188–191; pair teaching 193–195; peer support 191–193; SAGES program 196–197; 'yes, and … ' principle 210–211; *see also* people with disabilities, expertise of
communities of practice 101, 107, 123–124, 170, 224–225, 226
competence 46, 166–167; and gender 86, 90, 91, 94; practical skills 33; proactive 6, 8, 22, 44
content knowledge 31–32, 102, 109, 175
continuing professional development (CPD) 102, 103, 108, 110, 129, 169–170, 237; anti-oppressive pedagogy 79; contextual values associated with 109; mentoring aspects of 104; reflection through literature 136–137, 138; reflective dialogue 132–134, 138; reflective practice 131; reflective writing 134–136, 137–138

Coolwell, Casey 58
Corradini, Erika 6, 136, 166
Cotton, D.R.E. 74
course reps 79–80
critical disability studies 69, 71–72, 73, 74
critical feedback, emotional responses to 236
critical reflection 5, 29, *37*, 101, 106, 110; dialogic feedback 36–38; educative case-making 176–177, 178, 179; loop input approach 35–36; normative dimension of 38–40; pedagogical content knowledge 31–35; professional learning 35–38; purpose of 29
Csíkszentmihályi, M. 51
Cuban, L. 41
culture: expert subculture 18, 165, 169; micro-culture 123; organisational-level culture of expertise 165, 169–170; and stories 57; and teacher expertise 220–221

Dall'Alba, G. 32, 115
Dawson, John 7
deep acting 234, 238
deep learning 216
de Groot, A.D. 16
deliberate practice 48, 160; and expertise 17–18; feedback 160, 161, 166; in higher education teaching 22, 160–162
Delphi method 146
Derounian, James 8, 204
Dewey, J. 30, 176
dialogue 31, 101, 106, 107, 110, 111–112, 188; dialogic feedback 36–38; educative case-making 177, 179; and expertise 221; and improvisation 228; reflective 132–134, 138, 177
Diefendorff, J.M. 234
dilemmas 31, 34, 38, 39, 41, 124
disability studies 71, 72
discipline-based education specialists (DBESs) 188–191
disciplined improvisation 207
discipline-specific pedagogies 104, 112
display rules (emotional response) 232, 233–234, 235, 238
Dolmage, J.T. 76, 77
Dreyfus, H. 159, 162, 221
Dreyfus, S. 159, 162, 221
dual professionalism 6, 30, 101, 103–104, 107–108, 110

Dunn, T.G. 22, 168
Dweck, C.S. 17

educational research and practice, integration of 6, 142–144; active engagement with scholarship 147–148, 149, 150; data analysis 146; data collection 145–146, 148; data presentation 146–148; implementation of changes in teaching practice 148, 149; provision of support structures 149, 150, 151, 152; replication of scholarly teaching practices across disciplines 150; support models 151–152; uncertainties 143–144, 151
Education & Training Foundation (ETF) 30
educative case-making 7, 175, 177–178; area of focus 178; artefacts 179, 181; benefits of 185–186; challenges/limitations of 186; commitment of participants 184; critical reflection 176–177, 178, 179; dialogue 177, 179; ethics 181, 186; experiences of educators in higher education 182–183; facilitators 184–185, 186; glosses 178, 182; participant briefing session 179, 180–181; participants of 178–179; planning meeting 179, 180; posters 180, 182, *183*, 185; process for undertaking 179–183; questioning approaches 178; rationale of 183–184; reasons for using 175–177; sessions 179–180, 181–183; student voice and engagement 179; time and space factors 184
Edwards, R. 38
Ehrich, L.C. 39
Eisner, E.W. 9, 34
El Khoury, Eliana 7
emotions 8, 231, 232–234; deep acting 234, 238; display rules 232, 233–234, 235, 238; emotional climate conducive to learning 236–237; emotional labour 231; and ethical duty for educators 237; feeling about learning 235–239; feeling rules 232, 233, 235; framing rules 232, 233, 235, 238; impact of emotional rules on teachers 238; limits of permissiveness 239–240; negative 134, 233, 236–237, 239–240; and norms 234–235; role in legal education 117; and student perceptions of teaching excellence 90, 92; surface acting 234, 236, 238

emptiness, and expertise 49–50, 51, 54
epistemic invalidation 76
Eraut, M. 188
Ericsson, K.A. 17, 47, 48, 52, 73, 74, 165, 188
ethical decision-making 5, 31, 38, 39, 40, 41
evaluators, teachers as 9, 22, 142
Evans, C. 151
Evans, L. 224
evidence-based education 9, 142, 148, 150, 166, 167, 168, 171; *see also* educational research and practice, integration of
excellence in teaching in higher education 1, 2–3, 10, 23; characteristics of 85; excellence *vs.* expertise 59, 80–81, 166; *see also* gendered differences in student perceptions of teaching excellence
experiential learning 6, 31, 35–36, *35*, 123
expertise 1, 3–4, 8, 15, 94, 142–143; accessibility of 73; adaptive 7–8, 17, 167–168, 203, 206, 213–214; characteristics of 221; definition of 59, 73; domain-specific nature of 17; dynamic conceptualisation of 4; *vs.* excellence 59, 80–81, 166; experienced non-experts 17, 158, 162–163, 166; grounded theory model of teacher expertise 220–221; growth of 48–49; guiding action of 32; high performance based on knowledge and skills 15; intentional learning and development 17–18, 22; mental representations of experts 48, 52; pedagogical 74; phenomenology of 46–48; routine 167, 203–204, 205, 206, 208; and state of flow 51; of students 79–80; subject 73–74, 129; teacher, and improvisation 207–208, 221–222; teacher, dimensions of *220*; ways of thinking and practising 16–17; and wisdom 25; *wu wei* 45, 51, 53; *see also* critical reflection
expertise for teaching in higher education 4–5, 9, 53–54; artistry of teaching 20–22; characteristics of 19–23, 44; context of higher education 21; developmental continuum of exploration, engagement, and expansion 189–190, *189*; development of 165–169; effective, values-informed, scholarly competence 166–167; experts *vs.* experienced non-

experts 158, 162–163, 166; features of performance 23; implications for institutions and educational development 23–25; learning opportunities for students 168; lecturers with top student feedback and ratings 168–169; model for 20; organisational-level culture of expertise 165, 169–170; pedagogical content knowledge 19; professional learning 22–24, 159–165; undergraduate education 188–191; University of Queensland 64–65, 65; see also collaboration
expert subculture 18, 165, 169

feedback: critical feedback, emotional responses to 236; and deliberate practice 160, 161, 166; dialogic 36–38; pair teaching 194; participant, Performative Aspects of Teaching workshop 213–214; peer support 191, 192; student 168–169
feeling rules (emotional response) 232, 233, 235
Fergus, Suzanne 6, 168
Field, R. 118
flipped classroom 164
flow, state of 51
Fossey, Peter 8
framing rules (emotional response) 232, 233, 235, 238
free and easy wandering 47, 49, 50
Freire, P. 228
Furlong, J. 31, 33

Gannaway, Deanne 5
Gegerson, E. 121
gendered differences in student perceptions of teaching excellence 5, 85–86; cognitive aspects 90, 91; emotional aspects 90, 91, 92; female student nominations 88, 89, 90; female-type competencies 91; gender distribution of nominations 87–88; male student nominations 89–90; perceived attractiveness of female teachers 86; preservation of personal status 92–93; shifting standards theory 92; study limitations 93; themes 88–90, **89**
generic teacher education programmes 33
Gibbs, G. 37, 131, 215
Gillberg, C. 76, 80
Goodley, D. 72

Goodson, I. 102
Gourlay, L. 131
Graal, N. 103
graduate students: formal teaching development programs for 195; partnerships with faculty 195–197
graduate teaching assistants (GTAs) 203–204, 206; and pair teaching 195; Performative Aspects of Teaching workshop 208–214; teaching anxieties of **209**
Greenstein, A. 72, 77
Gross, B.L. 236
grounded theory model of teacher expertise 220–221
Grundmann, R. 32
'guess the status' (game) 212–213
Guidance Through Time, A 58, 66

Hall, E. 119
Hansen, C. 44
Hargreaves, A. 102
Hartmann, E.A. 232
Hatano, G. 205, 206, 214
Hattie, J. 22, 142, 168, 169
Hatton, N. 30
HEA@UQ programme, University of Queensland 66–67
Heels, Laura 7
Heron, M. 136
Hochschild, A.R. 231, 232, 233, 234, 235, 237
Hodkinson, P. 102
Hollingsworth, H. 49
hooks, bell 228
Hordern, J. 33
Horvath, J.A. 221
Huberman, M. 47

Impiö, N. 206
improvisation 7–8, 9, 204, 206, 218, 219; adaptation 228–229; artful 227; artless 227; characteristics of 219; climate/culture encouraging 229; definition of 207, 219; dialogic practice 228; disciplined 207; exercises 209–213; 'guess the status' (game) 212–213; improvisational mindset 226, 227, *227*, 229; improvising teacher 8, 218, 219–222; jazz band metaphor 224; making connections 228; Meisner technique 211–212; noticing 227–228; Performative Aspects of Teaching workshop

208–214; professional development of improvising teachers 226–229; and professionalism 222–226; skills 207, 208, 226, 227–229, *227*; skills, benefits of developing 208; and teacher expertise 207–208, 221–222; 'yes, and ... ' principle 210–211
Inagaki, K. 205, 206, 214
inclusive arts 77–79
innovation, teaching 58, 168
intellectualisation 30
intentional learning and development 17–18, 22–23, 24, 94, 157, 158; *see also* professional learning
intersectionality, and professional identity 111–112
in vivo coding 106–107
Issit, M. 102

Jeddere-Fisher, Fabia 8
Jenkins, A. 105
Johnstone, Keith 212
Jurkovic, J. 215

Kapp, S. 75
Kember, D. 145
Kemmis, S. 29, 33, 39
Kennedy, A. 103
Kenny, N. 189
King, A. 53
King, Helen 4, 6–7, 44, 59, 94, 102, 130
Kinsella, E. 39–40
knack passages 44
Kneebone, Roger 50, 207, 208
Knight, P. 159
knowing-in-action 34, 120
knowledge 142; academic 32, 101; automation of 47; categories 175; content 31–32, 102, 109, 175; environments, wide open 8, 240–241; of experts 15, 16, 17; generated through critical reflection 176; pedagogical 32–34, 104, 108; practical 32, 33, 40; professional 102; as a verb 177; *see also* pedagogical content knowledge
Kolb, D.A. 35, 131
Kreber, C. 146, 166, 169
Kumashiro, K.K. 78
Kvale, S. 106
Kwek, D. 52
Kwok, Kathryna 5

Laes, T. 77
Lalvani, P. 76
Lampert, M. 74
Land, R. 130
language 39, 66
Lave, J. 123
Lawyering in Practice module 114, 118, 119, 120, 121, 123–124
learning 206–207; as an aesthetic experience 34; deep 216; emotional climate conducive to 236–237; emotional responses to critical feedback 236; experiential 6, 31, 35–36, *35*, 123; feeling about 235–239; intentional, and development 17–18, 22–23, 24, 94, 157, 158; lifelong 35; opportunities, for students 168; problem-based 164; scholarship of teaching and 145–146, 147, 149, 166, 167, 196–197; socio-political context of 236; visible 142; work-based 33, 74; *see also* professional learning
learningful conversation 134
Leibowitz, B. 231
Lenze, L.F. 109
Lindblad, S. 102
liquid modernity 114
listening skills 211, 212
Listen with Mother (radio show) 57
loop input approach 35–36
Lubet, A. 69, 78

Macfarlane, A. 131
Mancktelow, Kyra 58
Marshall, Lindsay 7
Marton, F. 206
Mazur, E. 50
McDermott, Lillian 165
McGill, I. 138
McLaughlin, T.H. 30
Meisner, Sanford 211
Meisner technique 211–212
mental models 48, 52, 54
mental representations of experts 48, 52
mentoring/mentors 7, 104, 150, 159, 188; discipline-based education specialists 188–191; peer support 192–193; SAGES program 196–197; in teacher education programmes 33
metacognition 34, 38, 178–179
Meyer, J.H.F. 130
micro-culture 123
Miller, K.F. 74, 161, 168

Milton, Emmajane 7
mindfulness 240–241
Mitchell, D. 72, 77, 81
Mladenovic, R. 192
Moeller, H. 44, 51, 52–53
Morantes-Africano, Leonardo 5, 158
Morgan, Alexandra 7
motivation for professional learning 62, 157, 158, 159, 160, 170, 171
Murtonen, M. 74

narrative ways of knowing 177
National Teaching Fellowship (NTF) 161, 169
natural talent 17
neurotypical university 76, 78
Norton, L.S. 144
noticing skills of improvising teachers 227–228
Nussbaum, M. 231

observation skills 209, 211–212
online voice for teaching 204–205

pair teaching 7, 190, 193–195
Paseka, S. 143, 151
Pathways to Expertise in Teaching and Learning (PETL) 67
pedagogical content knowledge (PCK) 6, 19, 31, 34–35, 101–102, 104, 129; as artistry 34; connections between different disciplines 109; content knowledge 31–32, 102, 109; of contractually employed staff 108; core concepts of teaching 109–110; definition of 31; and gender bias 94; ideas for staff understanding of 111; pedagogical knowledge 32–34, 104, 108; professional identities 112–113; professionalism/teacher professionalism 102–104; subject pedagogies 104–105, 108, 109, 110; teacher identity 108–109; *see also* reflective practice
pedagogical experience 34, 36
pedagogical expertise 74; *see also* educative case-making
pedagogical knowledge 32–34, 104, 108
pedagogic literature, reflection through 136–137, 138
pedagogy of discomfort 237, 240
pedagogy of formation 115–116
peer network 196

peer review 66, 131, 133–134
peer support 7, 191; internal teaching fellowship scheme 192–193; Peer-Supported Development (PSD) scheme 191–192; vocal development 205
Penketh, C. 72, 75
people with disabilities, expertise of 5, 69, 73; ableism in academia 75–77; critical disability studies 71–72; inclusive arts project 77–79
Performative Aspects of Teaching workshop 208–209; improvisation exercises 209–213; participant feedback and reflections 213–214
performative student 114
Perlman, B. 232
permission for improvisation 226
personal identity, and clinical legal education 118, 119
personalisation of teaching approach 226
phenomenology of expertise 46–48
phronesis 40
Pickard, Beth 5
Pickford, R. 215
Pink, D.H. 62, 64
Pitman, A. 39–40
Pool, R. 48, 52
Potter, Jackie 5
Poynton, R. 228
practical knowledge 32, 33, 40
practical wisdom 163
practicums 33
praxis 40
Priestley, M. 76
problem(s) 30–31; -based learning 164; setting 31, 37; reduction 162; wicked 177
problem-solving 31; expert approach to 16, 39; progressive 18, 22, 46, 47, 49–50, 52, 53, 162–165
professional development 21, 22, 47, 49, 102–103, 129, 218; definition of 157; and dual professionalism 103–104; in higher education 157–159, 170–171; of improvising teachers 226–229; of law students 118; structured learning opportunities 170, 171; University of Queensland 60–61; *see also* improvisation
professional identity 8, 106, 108, 118, 225; of clinical legal educators 121–123, 124; dual 110; elements of 118; and

intersectionality 111–112; of law students 117–118, 119–120; *see also* clinical legal education
professional indemnity insurance 122
professionalism 8, 102, 218, 224; authorised teacher, the 8, 225–226, *225*; democratic 224–225; dual 6, 30, 101, 103–104, 107–108, 110; dynamic and contested nature of 222; and improvisation 218, 222–226; modern universities 223; professionalisation 39–40, 223
professionality 224
professional learning 6–7, 10, 22–23, 131, 171, 188; barriers for 158; critical reflection 35–38; culture of 23–24; definition of 157, 171; deliberate practice 160–162; dialogic feedback 36–38; for expertise development 159–165; external activities 157, 159; heutagogical approach to 159, 171; in higher education 157–159; intrinsic motivation for 157, 158, 159, 171; loop input approach 35–36; organisational-level culture of expertise 165, 169–170; progressive problem-solving 162–165; *see also* educative case-making; expertise for teaching in higher education
professional learning, University of Queensland: career journey maps 63; Developing Expertise in Teaching (DET) 65, 66; development of expertise continuum 64–65, *65*; motivation 62, 64; roadmap 61–62, *63*, 65; target audience 63
progressive problem-solving 18, 22, 46, 47, 49–50, 52, 53, 162–163; case study of teaching development 164–165; in higher education teaching 163–164
Prosser, M. 145
purposeful/constructive disruption 215

Quintilian 226–227

Race, P. 215
radio voice 205
reflection-in-action 9, 119, 120, 161, 168, 179, 206, 214
reflection-on-action 119, 120, 168
reflection on practice 47, 54, 176, 188
reflective portfolios 119
reflective practice 9, 18, 24, 30, 130, 131, 144; and continuing professional development 131; development of experienced teachers 138; and professional identity 118, 119–120; reflection through literature 136–137, 138; reflective dialogue 132–134, 138, 177; reflective writing 134–136, 137–138, 144; *see also* critical reflection; educational research and practice, integration of
reflective practicum, clinical legal education 120–121, 122, 123
reflexivity of clinical legal educators 121
Reilly, Dawn 7
Reis, Charlie 5, 25
research literacy of teachers 151
rewards 169–170
Rittel, H. 177
Robson, J. 108
Rodgers, C. 30, 36
role identity, and clinical legal education 118, 119, 121
role models, and pair teaching 194, 195
Rolfe, G. 176
routine expertise 167, 203–204, 205, 206, 208

SAGES (SoTL Advancing Graduate Education in STEM) program 196–197
Säljö, R. 206
Saroyan, A. 170
Sawon, K. 215
Sawyer, R.K. 207, 229
Scardamalia, M. 46, 142, 162, 163, 165, 166
scholarship of teaching and learning (SOTL) 145–146, 147, 149, 166, 167, 192–193, 196–197
Schön, D.A. 9, 20, 46, 54, 119–120, 131, 138, 177; on artistic dimension of professional practice 203; on problems 30; reflection-in-action 161, 214; swampy lowlands 39, 114, 116–117, 120, 121; technical rationality 41, 116, 176
self-reflection 144
Senge, P. 134
service sector 232, 233, 238
shifting standards theory 92
Shriner, C. 22, 168
Shulman, L.S. 41, 118, 142, 175, 176, 192; on pedagogical content knowledge 19, 31, 104; on pedagogical knowledge 32, 34; pedagogy of formation 115
signature pedagogies 24, 115

Siklander, P. 206
Simon, H.A. 16
skills 142; acquisition, Dreyfus model of 221; automation of 18, 47; of experts 15, 17, 18; improvisation 207, 208, 226, 227–229, 227; intellectual, of law students 116–117; listening 212; noticing 227–228; observation 209, 211–212; practical 33; progressive levels of 48–49; research 151; *wu wei* 45, 51, 53
Skovholt, T.M. 73, 74
Slingerland, E. 51
Smith, D. 30
Smith, J. 47
Smith, T. 33, 39
social confluence 69, 78
social identity, and clinical legal education 118, 119
social model of disability 71–72
socio-political context of learning 236
Solicitors Qualifying Examination (SQE) 115
SOLO taxonomy (Biggs) 165
Sorensen, Nick 8, 22
Spiller, D. 138
Spolin, Viola 210
Spowart, Lucy 6
Standards for Teachers and Trainers in Education and Training 30
standpoint epistemology 69–70, 71, 75, 77, 79
status, and improvisation 212–213
Sterckx, R. 46, 52
Sternberg, R.A. 221
Stigler, J.W. 74, 161, 168
Stone, E. 76
stories 57, 65
student absenteeism 215
student academic representation (SAR) 79–80
Stupnisky, R.H. 158
subject expertise 73–74, 129
subject pedagogies 104–105, 108, 109, 110
surface acting 234, 236, 238

Taubman, D. 103
Teacher Behaviour Checklist (TBC) 168
teacher education 30, 33, 38–39, 208; dialogic feedback 36–38; generic 33; loop input approach 35–36

teacher professionalism 101, 102–103, 106, 107; conceptualisation of **107**; and context 109; dual professionalism 101, 103–104, 107–108, 110; *see also* professionalism
Teaching Excellence and Student Outcomes Framework (TEF) 2, 85
Team Entrepreneurship programme 119, 123–124
technical rationality 41, 116, 176
testimonial injustice 76
threshold concepts 24, 130; *see also* reflective practice
Tiberius, R.G. 163
Toivanen, T. 208
Toole, B. 75
Tosey, P. 123
transformative teleology 221
Trigwell, K. 167, 170
Turner, Becky 5, 6
Twining, William 116

UK Professional Standards Framework (UKPSF) 30, 64, 66, 101, 105, 129–130, 131, 142, 169, 192
unconscious action, and expertise 45, 53, 54
University of British Columbia (UBC) 188
University of Calgary 64
University of Queensland (UQ) 5, 57, 58–60; development of expertise continuum 64–65, *65*; *Guidance Through Time, A* 58, 66; HEA@UQ programme 66–67; professional learning roadmap 61–62, *63*; research-focused academics 61; rewarding of teaching excellence 58; staff development 60–61, 62; student experience at 59; target audience 63; teaching innovations 58; UQ Student Strategy 60
University of the West of England 171
Usher, R. 38

values, and teaching expertise 38–40, 167
van den Brink, M. 94
van der Sluis, H. 131
van Dijk, Esther 5, 19, 20–21, 23
visible learning 142
vocal resilience 205
voice for teaching 204; aural breath 205; development 205; live voice 204–205; pre-recorded/edited voice 204; radio

voice 205; voice confrontation, tackling 204

Warren, Liz 7
Watson, B. 46, 47, 52
ways of thinking/practising 16–17, 20, 24, 50
Webber, M. 177
Welsh, Ashley 7
Wenger, E. 123, 225
West, K. 76
Westerlund, H. 77
Whitty, G. 31, 33
whole-university approach *see* University of Queensland (UQ)
wicked problems 177

wide open knowledge environments (WOKEs) 8, 240–241
Widerberg, K. 237
Wood, Rachel 6
work-based learning 33, 74
writing, reflective 134–136, 137–138, 144
wu wei 45, 51, 53

'yes, and ... ' principle 210–211
Yin, B. 136

Zembylas, M. 231
Zhuangzi 5, 44, 47, 48, 49, 51, 52, 53
Zimmerman, B.J. 144
Ziporyn, B. 45, 47, 51